THE WORKS OF

H. G. WELLS

THE WORKS OF

H. G. WELLS
1887-1925

A BIBLIOGRAPHY

DICTIONARY

AND SUBJECT-INDEX

BY

GEOFFREY H. WELLS

THE H. W. WILSON COMPANY

958-972 University Avenue

New York

PRINTED IN GREAT BRITAIN BY THE DEVONSHIRE PRESS, TORQUAY

PREFACE

THIS volume would never have been compiled—by myself, that is— had it not been for my quite definite belief that its subject is, beyond all doubt and by any standard, a very great writer indeed, and certainly one of the two greatest living English novelists, and consequently that some compact record such as this of all his writings, of whatever length or nature, must possess not only interest, but a certain material value for all students, critics and collectors of his works. My belief, I know, is not universally held ; it is fourteen years since Arnold Bennett commented in The New Age upon the lack of spontaneity, the " mean reluctance " which he found, invariably, in the welcome granted to even the best books of H. G. Wells, yet there is now, as then, a tendency to patronise, a habit of approval . . . with damning reservations, a detailing of faults rather than of excellences. The " growing perception " which Bennett discerned then dawns very slowly ; it is still possible for Sunday journalists, with the agreement and approval of their readers, to bludgeon his meaning and mutilate the corpse, to set down the author of *A Modern Utopia* and *Tono-Bungay* and *The History of Mr. Polly* and *The Dream* as an " unprofitable pro- pheteer " and a " megalomaniacal scribbler "—to quote a Mr. James Douglas from a weekly column entitled, with surprising honesty, " Babble About Books."* There is, necessarily, little if any expression of personal opinion in the body of this compilation, but the latter itself will, I think, make obvious the wide sweep of Wells's mind, the breadth of his interests, his " marvellously true perspective," and, above all, his utter lack of egotism. It should reveal, too, what has so often been disputed, the essential oneness, the logical coherence of all that he has written, and establish behind it all, its common source, the unity of a developing, but always constant and consistent mind.

* Babble : Idle, foolish talk ; senseless prattle. *Dictionary.*

Wells has written much—at times, perhaps, too much—and some writings have been less good than others, but in everything, even the worst, his pen has been too strongly impelled by the fresh enquiring vigour of his brain for him to be ever merely dull or repetitive.   There have been few subjects which have not, sooner or later, pre-occupied him ; to all he has brought an unfailing interest, an innate scepticism, a " colossal interrogation " which has renewed and enlivened and illuminated them.   It would be entirely untrue, unfortunately, to say that he has been in any way an interpreter of his times, but he has seen them with a keener eye and pictured them with a surer hand than has any other living writer.   His work is, indeed, so essentially contemporary that it seems necessary when treating of it in any way as a whole to begin by placing him more or less definitely in time and space ; the Introduction, which gives as concisely as possible the main biographical facts, is no more than an integral part of this compilation.

The Bibliography which follows is in three parts, the first and longest providing, in the order of publication and with relevant notes, collations of the first issues of all the volumes, pamphlets and leaflets by H. G. Wells.   The notes include comments on first serial publication, dramatisation, remainder issues, and so on, but full particulars are given of editions later than the first only when they include some new material or some essential revision of the old.   At the end will be found a collation of the first volume of *The Atlantic Edition of the Works of H. G. Wells*, followed by detailed particulars of the contents of the remaining twenty-seven volumes ;   it should be noted here that throughout this book no mention whatsoever is made of *The Atlantic Edition* except in this one place.   Part Two contains brief notes on various books and pamphlets to which Wells has contributed a portion only, or for which he is not altogether responsible, while Part Three gives a list of the books by other writers for which he has written introductions or prefaces.

It may be mentioned here, in passing, that the various notes to the collations were all written before the publication of any of the special prefaces to the volumes of *The Atlantic Editon ;* it has seemed best to leave my notes entirely unaltered.

The Appendix mentions one or two minor matters of some interest which seemed to find no place in either the Bibliography or the Dictionary—notably a chronological list of unreprinted writings, a selected list of letters to the press, and a list of criticisms of his work by various writers.

The Dictionary gives in one alphabetical list all the volume, story and essay titles, and the names of the chief characters in the novels and tales. Each title is prefixed by a number and followed by details of publication of the particular story or essay, and by a brief summary of the item; the number is used for reference in the Subject-Index which is printed directly after the Dictionary. (It must be noted that where the same item has been printed under more than one title, each is noted, but only the final one is numbered, etc.; cross references are provided in every case. Where, too, there has been simultaneous publication in various papers—as with the Washington Conference articles or with those reprinted in *A Year of Prophesying*—it has been deemed sufficient to mention particulars of London publication only, though in some cases the notes to the Bibliography will supply further information.) The character-names are in each case followed by full notes, and the title of the story or stories in which the character appears. Throughout the Dictionary, for the sake of space, contractions of certain titles have been used; these contractions are, however, so immediately recognisable that it has seemed unnecessary to provide a key.

In the Subject-Index will be found, also in alphabetical order, a list of practically every subject upon which Wells has ever written at any length, including the names of actual people. Each name is followed by numbers which refer to those prefixed to titles in the Dictionary. A system of indexing which has to take (say) *Tono-Bungay* as one unit has, obviously, its faults, but it will, I hope, used together with the summaries, prove sufficiently exact for most purposes. No attempt, I would add, has been made to index either *The Outline of History* or *A Short History of the World* with any completeness; reference has, however, been made to them in a number of cases where they mention subjects already dealt with elsewhere.

It is unavoidable that there should be some omissions in this compilation—though the Bibliography, at least, I believe to be complete—but it is hoped that nothing of the least material importance has been overlooked.

For assistance in carrying my task to its present degree of completeness I have to render thanks, in the first place, to Mr. H. G. Wells himself, not only for so generously allowing me the fullest access to his own library at Easton Glebe, but also for lending me his old notebooks which recorded his literary beginnings, and for submitting so patiently to my questions and researches. Mrs. H. G. Wells too has been, from the beginning, unfailingly kind and patient in settling dates, suggesting fruitful sources of information, and in reading through and checking my material, both in typescript and in proof; I can only feebly express my appreciation of all that she has done by stating that without her constant help the present volume would have been an impossibility. I wish also to thank for varied services—Mr. Ralph Straus, Mr. Eric R. Thomas, Mr. Edward R. Pease, Mr. K. W. Cotton (of the British Library of Political Science, London School of Economics), Mr. E. Griffiths (of The Daily Mail Library), Mr. B. Drinkwater (editor of The Phœnix, the still surviving descendant of The Science Schools Journal), Mdlle. Monnier (of La Maison des Amis des Livres, Paris), M. Vallette (of Le Mercure de France, Paris), Mr. H. C. Green, Mr. Leonard Selden, and the Editors (too numerous, I fear, to mention one by one) of many of the various periodicals to which Mr. Wells has contributed at one time and another. And finally, for all the help given me during the latter stages of the preparation of this material, and for relieving me of much of the tedious task of re-reading my work both in typescript and proof, word by word and line by line, I have to express my thanks to my friend Mr. Jack C. Turner.

In conclusion, I would repeat that this compilation is not, and in no sense attempts to be, critical; it offers, rather, a comprehensive and annotated guide to the would-be critic.

G. H. W.

January, 1926.

CONTENTS

A BIBLIOGRAPHY OF THE WORKS OF H. G. WELLS

PART ONE: BOOKS AND PAMPHLETS

CONTENTS

PAGE

72. THE SALVAGING OF CIVILISATION 53
73. THE NEW TEACHING OF HISTORY 53
74. WASHINGTON AND THE HOPE OF PEACE 54
75. THE MIND IN THE MAKING 55
76. THE SECRET PLACES OF THE HEART 55
77. A SHORT HISTORY OF THE WORLD 56
78. UNIVERSITY OF LONDON ELECTION, 1922 56
79. THE WORLD, ITS DEBTS, AND THE RICH MEN . . . 57
80. MEN LIKE GODS 57
81. SOCIALISM AND THE SCIENTIFIC MOTIVE 58
82. UNIVERSITY OF LONDON ELECTION, 1923 58
83. UNIVERSITY OF LONDON ELECTION, 1923 58
84. THE LABOUR IDEAL OF EDUCATION 58
85. THE STORY OF A GREAT SCHOOLMASTER 59
86. THE DREAM 59
87. THE P. R. PARLIAMENT 60
88. A YEAR OF PROPHESYING 60

89. THE ATLANTIC EDITION OF THE WORKS OF H. G.
WELLS 61

PART TWO : BOOKS AND PAMPHLETS CONTAINING MIS-
CELLANEOUS CONTRIBUTIONS 66

PART THREE : BOOKS BY OTHER WRITERS WITH
PREFACES 71

APPENDIX i. CHRONOLOGICAL LIST OF UNREPRINTED WRITINGS . 73
ii. LETTERS TO THE PRESS 80
iii. TRANSLATION INTO FOREIGN LANGUAGES . . 82
iv. PARODIES BY VARIOUS WRITERS . . . 83
v. CRITICAL STUDIES OF H. G. WELLS . . 84

A DICTIONARY OF THE WORKS OF H. G. WELLS. AN ALPHA-
BETICAL LIST OF THE TITLES OF STORIES AND ESSAYS, AND
THE NAMES OF THE CHIEF CHARACTERS, WITH FULL NOTES
AND COMMENTS 89

A SUBJECT-INDEX TO THE WORKS OF H. G. WELLS . 255

INTRODUCTION

THE origins of both the parents of H. G. Wells were, as he himself is, so essentially English that it is difficult to realise that it was only the coincidence of a temporary illness and a business opportunity which prevented him from being, in all probability, born an American citizen. Very much more was saved for England than a first class cricket professional when Mr. Joseph Wells decided to put the " stout oak box," made specially for his intended emigration, to some less adventurous use. His one achievement—the taking, for the first time in county cricket, of four wickets with consecutive balls in a match between Kent and Sussex at Brighton on June 26th, 1862—might have been (in fact, *was*) soon equalled, or even dispensed with, but one feels that H. G. Wells would have been, on the whole, a more serious loss. Happily he became, instead of an emigrant, proprietor of a small general store, and when his fourth child, Herbert George, was born some years later, on September 21st, 1866, it was behind the little shop at No. 47, High Street, Bromley, then on the extreme south-eastern outskirts of London.

" I am not," H. G. Wells has said, " a bit aristocratic ; I do not know any of my ancestors beyond my grandparents, and about them I do not know very much, because I am the youngest son of my father and mother and their parents were all dead before I was born." Joseph Wells was originally a gardener, as befitted the son of a head-gardener (also a Joseph Wells) of Lord de Lisle at Penshurst Castle in Kent. His wife was a daughter of George Neal, a Midhurst innkeeper " who supplied post-horses to the coaches before the railways came "; she was, before her marriage, maid to Miss Featherstonehaugh of Up Park, Petersfield.

The Bromley shop was never a success ; it struggled on for a dozen years after 1866, but the family lived in a state of constant poverty. There was not, at times, sufficient food, but there were compensations ; the household was not, seemingly, an unhappy one. Joseph Wells " had a taste for reading and would go to sales to pick up a cheap lot of books whenever opportunity offered " ; this was a taste which, before the age of thirteen, H. G. Wells, too, had acquired to a marked degree.

Bromley was fortunate enough to possess a literary institute with a lending library, and the boy, not content with the irregular supply at home, had read, before he left school, a large proportion of its available books, among them volumes of exploration and adventure and natural and other histories which filled him with curiosity, a desire to see and know and understand. He was educated altogether locally; at first, apparently, at a small school for children run by an elderly lady, and later at Mr. Thomas Morley's more impressively named Bromley Academy, which he left in June, 1879.

Joseph Wells had had, some months before, a serious fall which incapacitated him for, at any rate, a lengthy period; soon after this the shop had to be closed. He took refuge in an inexpensive cottage, while Mrs. Wells returned, now as housekeeper, to her former mistress. H. G. Wells was taken from school to be apprenticed to a firm of Windsor drapers, Messrs. Rogers & Denyer. Happily, perhaps, he was rejected by the drapery as " unsuitable for that high trade," and went at once as pupil-teacher to a cousin who was a master at the National School in Wookey, Somerset. This time the fault lay more with his cousin's qualifications than with his own, there was some trouble and he returned to his mother in time to spend the Christmas of that year— still 1879—with her at Up Park. After a brief holiday he was sent on trial as apprentice to a chemist in Midhurst; he himself refused to remain there, fearing that the total cost of his training would put too much of a strain upon his mother's extremely limited resources. For a few weeks he was a boarder with Mr. Horace Byatt, M.A., then head-master of the Midhurst Grammar School, who was impressed by his quickness in learning Latin and elementary science. In May, 1880, he was apprenticed again, this time at Hyde's Drapery Stores, 9, King's Road, Southsea. " I stuck that hell of a life for two years to August, 1882. Then I declared that I would kill myself if I could not have my indentures cancelled." " I ran away one Sunday morning to my mother, and told her that I would die rather than go on being a draper. That seventeen mile tramp, without breakfast, to deliver that ulti-matum is still very vivid in my memory. I felt then most desperately wicked, and now I know that it was nearly the best thing I ever did in my life." His father and Mr. Byatt were persuaded to the boy's side, the latter promised him temporary employment, and instead of returning to Southsea he became general utility master at the Midhurst Grammar School, a post which he held until the September of the following year, when he was awarded a studentship of a guinea a week at the Normal School of Science in South Kensington. There, for three years, he studied physics, chemistry, geology, astronomy, biology and physiography, his biological professor being T. H. Huxley. Then he became an assistant master in a school at Holt, near Wrexham, in North Wales ; there he had a bad football accident from the effects of which he did not wholly recover for the next twelve or fifteen years. Its immediate result was the greater part of a year of invalidism spent partly at Up Park, and partly with an old fellow-student in the Five Towns. In 1887 he reurned to London, found temporary work drawing diagrams for a teacher of biology, and then joined the staff of Henley House School, Kilburn, under a Mr. J. V. Milne. Here he remained for two years, during which he took his B.Sc. degree at London University, with first-class honours. For two more years he was biological tutor for the University Correspondence College, where he first met his future wife, Miss Amy Catherine Robbins, she being one of his pupils. In the summer of 1893 a blood-vessel burst in one of his lungs, and the consequent severe illness necessitated a long holiday at Eastbourne and the adoption of some entirely sedentary occupation. There had always been " some little kink in my mind " which " made the writing of prose very interesting to me," and during his convalesence he devoted all his time to writing and produced the series of humorous essays which gave him his first success in journalism and made his continuance as an author a practicable possibility.

He had been already, for some years now, actively interested in the art of literature, beginning at an early age with a love of reading and making his first entry into amateur journalism as the founder and editor of, and contributor to, The Science Schools Journal (an organ of the students at the Normal School of Science, started in 1886). His nine contributions to the Journal are his earliest printed writings. A few years later, while teaching at Henley House School, he became editor of a school publication, The Henley House Magazine, which owed its origin to a boy who became, later in life, Lord Northcliffe. To this Wells contributed less than half-a-dozen brief items in 1889 and 1891. About this time he commenced to write for the educational journals, but without, in the beginning, much success. His first essay, *The Subtle Examinee*, appeared in The University Correspondent in April, 1891, and three months later, more encouragingly, The Fortnightly Review printed *The Rediscovery of the Unique*. A few more articles, mainly dealing with education, were printed during 1892, and in 1893 text-books of biology and physiography (the latter written in collaboration) were published. It was about this time that he began to give all his energies to writing, and 1893, 1894 and 1895 were years of active

B

journalism. Encouraged by the interest of men such as Lewis Hind, C. B. Marriott Watson, and W. E. Henley he was soon contributing short stories, essays and reviews to The Pall Mall Gazette, Pall Mall Budget, St. James's Gazette, Black and White, Ludgate Magazine, Nature, National Observer, New Review and other papers. From 1894 till 1896 he was one of the most active literary critics on the staff of The Saturday Review, and during 1895 he was for a while dramatic critic for The Pall Mall Gazette. In this same year he published two volumes of short stories and sketches, reprinted from various sources, and two novels, the earlier of which, *The Time Machine*, established him at once as a writer of unusual imaginative and literary power.

Shortly after this first success he married Miss Robbins and went to live on the South Coast, between Folkestone and Sandgate.

The next few years brought a steady output of short stories, essays, articles, a novel or two, and a series of scientific romances which made him world-famous. About 1897 or 1898 he went abroad for the first time, spending two months in Italy and returning to be attacked, once more, by severe illness. (Liability to illness, Wells says, " has played a much larger share in my life than you would suppose, it has inter-fered with travel and kept me out of public life.") With *Anticipations* (1901), the first of a trilogy of volumes dealing directly with social and political questions, he broke fresh ground again. The next ten years saw a steady increase of interest in these questions, a gradual cessation of the romances, and their replacement by a series of novels dealing with modern life, which was continued without a break till 1915, and which contains some of the very finest of his artistic achievements. In the early months of 1906 he made his first trans-Atlantic trip, visiting New York, Boston, Niagara, Chicago and Washington. In 1903 he had joined the Fabian Society and the Independent Labour Party; he was a member of both these organisations for several years, and published Socialist pamphlets in 1906 and 1907, and *New Worlds for Old*, a " plain account of modern Socialism," in 1908. About the end of 1908 he resigned from the Fabian Society, being dissatisfied with its general political basis. In March, 1912, a stage adaptation of *Kipps* was produced in London, and early in 1914 a contract was signed with a film company for the production of his novels and romances. The war prevented any development of these plans and it was not until 1919 that the first film, *The First Men in the Moon*, was completed. In January, 1914, Mr. Wells made his first visit to Russia, spending two weeks in Petersburg and Moscow.

Upon the outbreak of war in August, 1914, being " greatly alarmed

at the prospect of a Pacifist stampede among the Liberals over here,"
he contributed articles to a number of papers supporting this as a
" war to end war." He visited the war-zones in Italy and France in
August and September, 1916. At the beginning of 1918 he accepted
Lord Northcliffe's invitation to become a member of the Enemy
Propaganda Committee, and in May was made the first Director of the
German Section. While holding this position he prepared a *Memorandum on Propaganda Policy Against Germany* which was used as a
basis for the British propaganda campaign during the last months of the
war. He resigned his directorship in July, though still retaining his
place as a member of the committee. About this time he assisted in
the formation of the League of Free Nations' Association, holding
positions on the Council and on the Executive and Research Committees. In all his books written towards the end of the war he had
been insisting upon the supreme importance of, and the place of history
in, education, and in 1919 and 1920, after some two years of preparation,
was published *The Outline of History*. He went again to Russia, this
time with his elder son, in September, 1920, at the invitation of the
Russian Trade Delegation in London ; the account of his fifteen days'
visit was published in December. In that month he was to have
proceeded to the United States on a lecturing tour, but severe illness
made this impossible, and, instead, he went to Italy to recuperate. In
February, 1921, an adaptation of *The Wonderful Visit*, by H. G. Wells
and St. John G. Ervine, was produced in London. Early in November
he proceeded to America, not however to fulfil his cancelled lecture
engagements, but as the special correspondent of The New York World
at the Washington Conference ; he did not remain for the full
duration of the Conference, his last paper being dated December
18th. *A Short History of the World* appeared in 1922, " a much more
generalised history " than *The Outline*, " planned and written afresh."
It was announced during the summer that he would contest London
University as a Labour candidate in the next Parliamentary election.
This occurred in the following November, when he was defeated ; he
stood again at the next election (1923) with a similar result. In his
two latest novels, *Men Like Gods* and *The Dream*. there is more direct
story-telling than in anything he had written for many years ; both
are, partially at any rate, pictures of " the Utopia of a world state." In
1924 he published his only " biographical effort," a life of the late
F. W. Sanderson, headmaster of Oundle School. In the autumn
appeared the first volumes of *The Atlantic Edition of the Works of H.
G. Wells*, the only uniform edition, in twenty-eight volumes, each of

which contains a valuable and illuminating preface written specially by the author.

During the past few years Mr. Wells has been troubled even more by ill-health, and has had to spend the worst of the winter months in the warmer climates of Southern Europe. But his home has always been in the south-east corner of England. "There I was born," he says, "and except for a little travel and a few years in London, there I have lived all my days."

H. G. Wells was, from childhood, a natural sceptic, unable to accept things, to take them for granted; he had, even in early youth, that constant questioning desire to know and understand. Before he left Bromley he was reading, at home and at the library, books which were forcing him to a criticism of accepted points of view. While staying, later, at Up Park he borrowed, surreptitiously, books from the enlightened regions "above stairs"—Tom Paine, Swift, Voltaire, Plato, Lucretius, Plutarch, Beckford; he even found a Gregorian telescope in an attic and attempted some tentative astronomy. He began to acquire points of view with which his mother, at least, one feels, would not have agreed. At Southsea, in the drapery, he was speculating upon such problems as "What is matter?" and "What is space?" and he was only fifteen when "certain theological and speculative curiosities" brought him to the study of elementary science. "His or her place in space and in time and in the adventure of life," he declares, "is what everyone should learn at school," but it is just this, very largely, that he himself has been learning and testing and defining during the whole course of his literary career. It has necessarily led him, as has been pointed out by Van Wyck Brooks (in the only critical study of Wells really worth reading), through a "gradual process of slowing down" to the contemplation of an immediate here and now. The early romances attempt, broadly speaking, to settle Man's place in space and time; they regard him not as some finished product of the ages, but as a being upon whose past and still more upon whose future his whole present depends. Another series of novels written about the same time make no attempt to see him in this vast perspective; the author's questioning is directed less to Man's position in the universe, and more to the immediate problem of what he is doing with himself, and of what he is doing with the world of to-day to make it a worthy heritage for the future. Wells's criticisms begin amid the jealousies and petty interests of country villages, but widen their scope until at last, in *Tono-Bungay*, one book becomes "the arraignment of a whole epoch." Still later his interests seem to turn

from the question of the behaviour of society as a whole to that of the
personal conduct of the individual as a member of society ; throughout
several novels the protagonists are preoccupied with this problem, in
each case without definite or satisfying result.   At this point the war
intervened, with all its overwhelming demands and anxieties ; his
writings during the next five years, however accurate and interesting
as a record of the period, are not among his best and most enduring
work.   Yet it would seem that the war (together with the subsequent,
and almost as intolerable, peace) had, very largely, settled his main
problem for him.   " The gist of it," he has written of his work as a
whole, " is an extraordinarily sustained and elaborated adverse
criticism of the world as it is, a persistent refusal to believe that this is
the best or even the most interesting of all possible worlds.   There is a
developing attempt, culminating in *The Outline of History*, to show
that the world of men is only temporarily what it is and might be
altered to an enormous extent.   There is a search through every sort of
revolutionary project and effort for the material of effective alteration."
After the war this alteration of the world, and the establishment of a
world st,ate of peace and plenty and happiness became an urgent
necessity the only alternative, possibly, to the destruction of civilisation.   This last quotation was written in 1924, but as long ago as 1904
he was declaring that " indeed Will is stronger than Fact, it can mould
and overcome Fact.   But this world has still to discover its will, it is
a world that slumbers inertly, and all this roar and pulsation of life is
no more than its heavy breathing. . . . My mind runs on to the
thought of an awakening."   It is that awakening which it is now his
desire, his aim to bring about, and to serve that desire, that aim, he
has turned again to the creation of a Utopia which is, he insists, attainable, a Utopia of a world at peace in the possibility of which he believes
so firmly " that I must needs go about this present world of disorder
and darkness like an exile doing such feeble things as I can towards
the world of my desire, now hopefully, now bitterly, as the moods may
happen, until I die."

Each time I read *The Food of the Gods* I seem to discern a certain
resemblance between Wells and Redwood and there is more than a
family likeness.   Wells too is in revolt against the world of " little
people " ;   he too, entrenched behind the barriers of his intellectual
integrity, fires out his ammunition, book by book, pamphlet by
pamphlet, upon an—as yet, alas !—only very slightly disturbed world.
There are no more powerful guns in action to-day, no more devastating
bombs ; the world must be very sound asleep ! But the Food is being

sown ; it is, however slowly, taking effect. Those earliest detached
criticisms, the more constructive suggestions of the later books, the
inquiry into personal conduct—these, surely, were enlivening enough :
yet after all, his most effective and stimulating contribution to modern
thought—his Herakleophorbia IV., so to speak—may prove to be his
belief in the pressing nearness of this finer, sweeter world, his conviction
that it is indeed attainable, a thing to be worked for with hope and
happiness ; it may prove to be this nostalgia which he has made us
share with Mr. Barnstaple, with the Owner of the Voice, a nostalgia
which must give all our lives a certain undercurrent of dreariness and
discontent until at last that Utopia, that fairer world state, becomes
a visible and material possibility.

It has been his works of fiction, his works as an artist, that have
given Wells his world-wide fame and popularity ; it is as an artist, I
suppose, that he will be remembered in the future. But one is tempted
to believe, at times, that it is rather his thought, and his power of
making his ideas vital and moving, that give him his present significance ; certainly, one feels, it is by his ideas that he would prefer
to be judged. For it has seemed a fact almost incidental to his main
purpose that he has produced in the course of his work some of the
most brilliantly imaginative and original, some of the most vivid and
tremendous, and some of the most humorous and truly English novels
and shorter tales of the last half-century. As a whole his achievement stands, to-day, unrivalled. Like all great men he has his de-
tractors, but a great man, nevertheless, he remains and will remain,
no more to be forgotten or disregarded than Fielding, Dickens, or
Hardy.

GEOFFREY H. WELLS.

ADDENDA

THE BIBLIOGRAPHY

Part I

(20)

THE DISCOVERY OF THE FUTURE

In 1925 a "new and revised edition" ot this lecture was issued by Jonathan Cape, Ltd., London.

(70)

THE OUTLINE OF HISTORY

On Oct. 1st, 1925, Messrs. Cassell & Co., Ltd., London, commenced the publication in twenty-four fortnightly parts of a completely new edition of *The Outline of History*. For this edition both revisions and additions were made in the text, particularly with regard to the development of the arts; the footnotes were omitted, their matter being incorporated as far as possible in the text itself. "It has, the writer hopes, lost its last traces of the student's notebook and has become plainly and simply an *Outline of History*." "The chief purpose of the present revision has been to make the *Outline* simpler and easier to read." The parts are printed throughout in photogravure, with entirely new illustrations (though retaining J. F. Horrabin's diagrams). "Every one of these illustrations has been carefully selected by the author himself."

(90)

CHRISTINA ALBERTA'S FATHER : 1925

Christina Alberta's Father / *by* / H. G. Wells / (*publisher's device*) / Jonathan Cape Ltd / Thirty Bedford Square London

Crown 8vo.; pp. 410, consisting of a blank leaf not reckoned in the pagination; a leaf blank on recto (verso, list of books *Mr. Wells has also written*), pp. (1, 2); Half-title, *Christina Alberta's Father* (verso blank), pp. (3, 4); Title-page, as above (verso, at head, *First Published In MCMXXV* / *Made & Printed In Great Britain* / *By Butler & Tanner Ltd* / *Frome And* / *London*), pp. (5, 6); List of *Contents*, pp. 7, 8; Divisional Fly-title, *Book the First* / *The Coming of Sargon, King* / *Of Kings* (verso blank), pp. (9, 10); Text, pp. 11-410.

Issued in dark red cloth, lettered and lined in gilt across back, with blind border line on front cover and publisher's blind device on back cover. Back: (three lines) / *Christina* / *Alberta's* / *Father* / *H. G. Wells* / *Jonathan Cape* / (three lines). Top-edges stained to match covers ; other edges trimmed. White end-papers.

This story was first printed serially under the title, *Sargon King of Kings*, in Collier's Weekly (Feb. 21st—May, 1925), and under its present title in The Daily Telegraph (July 30th—Sept. 8th, 1925).

PART II

1925

George Whale (1849-1925). Edited by Edward Clodd, C. K. Shorter, and Winifred Stephens Whale (Jonathan Cape, Ltd., London. 1925.). (Contains a " tribute " from H. G. Wells).

The World's Great Books in Outline : Entirely new revision by J. A. Hammerton (Amalgamated Press, Ltd., London. Part 1 issued Nov. 3rd, 1925 ; remaining parts, about forty in all, to appear one every fortnight until completion).
(This publication contains " epitomes " of four books by H. G. Wells— *The Time Machine*, *The War of the Worlds*, *A Modern Utopia*, and *Tono-Bungay*. They were written by Mr. Wells himself for the first issue of this compilation, published about 1910, and are here reprinted apparently without alteration).

APPENDIX

V

(b) Essays in Books

Looking At Life, by Floyd Dell (Duckworth, London. 1924). XXXVIII. *Wells the Destroyer*, pp. 275-288.

Lectures to Living Authors, by " Lacon," with caricatures by " Quiz " (Bles, London. 1925). *H. G. Wells*.

THE DICTIONARY

78a. Christina Alberta's Father. See above. Mr. Albert Edward Preemby, a house-agent's clerk, is on a holiday at Sheringham in 1899, when he meets and is practically forced into marriage by Chrissie Hossett, who on the death of her father becomes owner of the Limpid Stream Laundry, near Woodford Wells. She has one child, Christina Alberta, born a few months after the marriage. Until Mrs. Preemby's death in

1920, Mr. Preemby assists her in the management of the laundry, though his interest lies rather in books, and particularly in the lost continent of Atlantis, than in such practical affairs. When he is left a widower he immediately sells the business to a relative, and after a day or two in London he and Christina go to a boarding-house in Tunbridge Wells. She returns to London, leaving him there. One evening a Cambridge undergraduate pretends to be a medium and convinces Mr. Preemby that he (Preemby) is a reincarnation of Sargon, King of Sumeria, sent back to earth to heal the world's disorders. He comes back to London, and while Christina, alarmed, is consulting her friend, Paul Lambone, a novelist, he goes out to survey his "kingdom." He finds a room in a Bloomsbury house, where a journalist, Bobby Roothing, is also staying. Next day he gathers together a mixed company of disciples, and after creating a disturbance in a restaurant by attempting to deliver his " message," he is arrested ; he is kept for three days in the Gifford Street Observation Ward and then sent to the Cummerdown Hill Asylum, having been certified insane. When Christina learns what has happened to him, Lambone takes her to see Wilfred Devizes, a mental specialist, thinking that he may be able to procure her supposed father's release. She dis- covers that Devizes is her real father. Bobby Roothing, in the meantime, having also learnt where Preemby is, succeeds in rescuing him and hiding him away in a cottage at Dymchurch. He gets into communication with Christina, and she and Devizes join them there. But Preemby has caught a bad cold which develops into congestion of the lungs, and eventually he dies in Lambone's country house at Udimore, after realising that he is not the only Sargon, and that " the real thing was to be just a kingly person and work with all the other kingly persons in the world." Six months later there is a gathering of the chief characters at Udimore. Roothing is in love with Christina, and she has promised to marry him, but now she breaks their engagement and says that she will never marry anyone. One evening Lambone and Devizes and the rest discuss their belief that " our race has reached, and is now receding from, a maximum of individuation. That it turns now towards synthesis and co-operation." Christina revolts against this, but Devizes tells her that her feeling repre- sents " only a phase in your development."

THE BIBLIOGRAPHY

PART I

(1)

TEXT-BOOK OF BIOLOGY : 1893

Univ. Corr. Coll. Tutorial Series. / *(line)* / Text-Book Of Biology. / By /
H. G. Wells, B.Sc.Lond., F.Z.S., / Lecturer In Biology At University
Tutorial College. / With An Introduction / By / G. B. Howes, F.L.S.,
F.Z.S., / Assistant Professor Of Zoology, Royal College of Science, London. /
Part I.—Vertebrata (Part II.—Invertebrates And Plants.) / *(device)* /
London : W. B. Clive & Co., / University Correspondence College Press. /
Warehouse : 13 Booksellers' Row, W.C.

2 Vols., Crown 8vo.

Vol. I, pp. x + 150, consisting of Half-title, *Text-Book of Biology /
Part I.—Vertebrata.* (verso blank) and Title-page, as above (verso
blank), neither reckoned in pagination ; List of *Contents*, pp. (i, ii) ;
Introduction, pp. (iii)-v ; p. (vi) blank ; *Preface*, pp. (vii)-x ; Text,
pp. (1)-149 ; p. (150) blank.   There are 24 sheets with plates, and at
the end a 36-page catalogue of the publishers' books, dated 19/9/92.
Vol. II, pp. viii + 158, consisting of Half-title, *Text-Book Of Biology. /
Part II.—Invertebrata And Plants* (verso blank), pp. (i, ii) ; Title-page,
as above (verso blank), pp. (iii, iv) ; *Preface*, pp. (v)-viii ; Text,
pp. 1-157 ; p. (158) blank.   There follows one leaf giving the College
terms.   There are 23 sheets with plates and at the end a 32-page
catalogue of publishers' books, dated 21/8/93.
Issued in dark green cloth, lettered with lines across the back in gilt as
follows :   (2 lines) / *Text-Book / Of / Biology /* (short line) / *H. G.
Wells /* (short line) / *Part I. (Part II.) / Vertebrates (Invertebrates /
And Plants) /* (device) / *Univ. / Corr. Coll. /* (2 lines) Blind double
line borders on front and back covers.   Brown end-papers.   All
edges cut.
Later issues of the first edition are in brown cloth, lettered as above
but with the addition of the blind stamp *Biology* in centre of the front
cover.

In the original edition the plates in both parts were drawn by H. G.
Wells.   In 1894 a revised edition of Part I was issued, and in this the
plates were specially redrawn by Miss A. C. Robbins (now Mrs. H. G.

1

Wells), who had been a pupil of Mr. Wells during his two years (1890-2) as lecturer at the University Correspondence College, where biology was his chief subject.

In June 1898 the two parts, revised and rewritten by A. M. Davies, B.Sc.Lond., and with diagrams again specially redrawn, this time by Mrs. Davies, were published in one volume in the same series and by the same publisher with the title *Text-Book of Zoology*. This edition is so much rewritten that only Chapter XIV preserves anything like its original form, " so that while the credit for the general plan of the work belongs to Mr. H. G. Wells, no responsibility attaches to him for any of the present book " (*Introduction*). The 6th edition of the *Text-Book of Zoology* was revised in 1913 by J. T. Cunningham.

It was during his period as lecturer in biology at the University Correspondence College that the *Text-Book of Biology* was written by Mr. Wells, its general plan being settled by his experiences as a correspondence tutor.

(2)

HONOURS PHYSIOGRAPHY : 1893

Honours / Physiography. / By / R. A. Gregory, / Oxford University Extension Lecturer ; Honours Medallist in Physiography ; / Formerly Computer to Solar Physics Committee, the Royal College of Science, / South Kensington ; Fellow of the Royal Astronomical Society ; Foreign / Correspondent of the ' Revue Générale des Sciences ; ' / And / H. G. Wells, B.Sc.,Lond., / Lecturer in Geology at the University Tutorial College ; Third in Honours in / Geology and Physical Geography at B.Sc. ; Fellow of the Zoological Society ; / Fellow (in Honours) and Doreck Scholar of the College of Preceptors. / London : / Joseph Hughes & Co., / Froebel House, St. Andrew's Hill, / Doctors' Commons, E.C. / (*short line*) / 1893. / (All rights reserved.)

Crown 8vo ; pp. viii + 188, consisting of Half-title, *Honours Physiography.* (verso blank), pp. (i, ii) ; Title-page, as above (verso, printers' imprint, *Printed By / W. P. Griffith & Sons, Limited, / Prujean Square, Old Bailey, / London, E.C.*), pp. (iii, iv) ; Preface, pp. (v, vi) ; List of *Contents* (verso blank), pp. (vii, viii) ; Text, pp. (1)-181 ; p. (182) blank ; *Index*, pp. (183-186) ; *List of Authors Mentioned*, pp. (187, 188). There follow 4 pages of publishers' advertisements.

Issued in yellowish-brown cloth, lettering and designs in dark brown as follows. Back, across : (design) / *Honours / Physio- / Graphy /* (design) / *Gregory / & / Wells /* (design) / *Hughes / & Co.* / (double lines) Front cover, across : (double lines) / *Honours : Physiography /* (design) / *By · R · A · Gregory ·* (design) / *And · H · G · Wells /* (design) / *London / Joseph Hughes & Co. / Price Four Shillings & Sixpence /* (double lines) Back cover has publishers' design. All edges cut. White end-papers.

(3)

SELECT CONVERSATIONS WITH AN UNCLE: 1895

Select / Conversations / With / An Uncle / (Now Extinct) / and two other / reminiscences by / ·H·G·Wells· / (decoration) / London : / John Lane / — / New York — / The Merriam / Company (decoration) / 1895. . . (all within a black-edged panel upon a drawing signed F.H.T. which is bordered by two black lines.)

> Foolscap 8vo ; pp. x + 118, consisting of a blank leaf not reckoned in pagination ; Half-title, The Mayfair Set / III / Conversations / With An / Uncle (verso blank), pp. (i, ii) ; Title-page, as above (verso, in centre, Copyrighted in the United States. / All rights reserved.), pp. (iii, iv) ; Dedication, To / My Dearest / And Best Friend, / R. A. C. (verso blank), pp. (v, vi) ; Prefatory, pp. (vii, viii) ; List of Contents, pp. (ix, x) ; Text, pp. (1)-117 ; Printers' imprint at foot of p. 117 as follows : Turnbull And Spears, Printers, Edinburgh ; p. (118) blank. Blank leaf follows. At end of volume is a 16-page List of Books / in / Belle Lettres dated 1895
>
> Issued in silver-green watered silk, lettered across the back in gilt as follows : Select / Conversations / with an / Uncle / H. G. Wells / The / Bodley Head / And / New York. Covers blank. Top edges gilt, other uncut. White end-papers.

This volume contains twelve Conversations, and at the end two very slight stories, A Misunderstood Artist and The Man with a Nose. They were all printed in The Pall Mall Gazette in 1893 and 1894, the staff of which H. G. Wells joined about the end of the latter year as dramatic critic.

Select Conversations with an Uncle was published the day before The Time Machine.

(4)

THE TIME MACHINE: 1895

The / Time Machine / An Invention / By / H. G. Wells / London / William Heinemann / MDCCCXCV

> Crown 8vo ; pp. viii + 152, consisting of Half-title, The/Time Machine (verso, list of volumes in The Pioneer Series), pp. (i, ii) ; Title-page, as above (verso, in centre, Note concerning original publication, and at foot, All rights reserved), pp. (iii, iv) ; Dedication, To/William Ernest Henley (verso blank), pp. (v, vi) ; List of Contents (verso blank), pp. (vii, viii) ; Text, pp. 1-152. Printers' imprint at foot of p. 152 under a line as follows : Richard Clay & Sons, Limited, London & Bungay. There follow 16 pages of publisher's advertisements.

Issued in whitish-grey cloth, lettered across the back in blue and across the front cover in purple. Back : *The | Time | Machine |* (short line) */ Wells | Heinemann* Front cover : *The Time Machine |* (design of a sphinx in purple) */ H. G. Wells* The back cover has the publisher's device in purple. Top and fore edges uncut, lower edges untrimmed. White end-papers.

A later issue of this first edition has covers as above but lettered in brown, and with all edges cut. This issue also omits the publisher's advertisements at the end.

Also issued, simultaneously with the first cloth issue, in light blue paper wrappers, lettered in darker blue along the back and across the front cover. Back : *The Time Machine H. G. Wells* Front cover : *H. G. Wells |* (short line) */ The | Time Machine |* (design of sphinx) */ London | William Heinemann |* (short line) */ Price One Shilling and Sixpence | This volume may be had bound in cloth, price 2s. 6d.* Pp. (ii, iii, iv) of covers bear publisher's advertisements. The collation is the same, but without the publisher's advertisements at the end. All edges cut.

The details of the serial publication of this story are of some interest. In 1886 H. G. Wells, then a third year student at the Normal School of Science, South Kensington, founded a college magazine, The Science Schools Journal. Between 1887 and 1890 he contributed several items to this magazine, chief among which was a serial published in the numbers for April, May and June, 1888, entitled *The Chronic Argonauts*, the main idea of which is that of time-travelling. The close resemblance between the explanation of the Doctor in the earlier story and of the Time Traveller in the later make it no undue exaggeration to call this the first version of *The Time Machine*. Copies of the Journal containing these contributions are now very rare, for about twenty years ago Mr. Wells purchased " all the back numbers then in stock with the current editor, so far as they concerned me, and destroyed them." Six years later the story was entirely rewritten in everything but the essential idea : some parts of it appeared as a series of articles in The National Observer (in 1894), but *The Time Traveller's Story* " appeared, almost as it stands " in The New Review (in 1894-5). This serial version contains at least one episode which is not reprinted in the book. In this the Time Traveller, pausing between the age of the Eloi and Morlocks and that of the giant crabs, finds the dying world inhabited by the last descendants of Man, " puny greyish things, like half-grown kangaroos " and by great centipedes which prey upon them. One of the latter is described : " It stood about three feet high, and had a long segmented body perhaps thirty feet long, with curiously over-lapping greenish-black plates. It seemed to crawl upon a multitude of feet, looping its body as it advanced. It had a blunt round head, with a polygonal arrangement of black eye-spots."

It may be mentioned that the American first edition (Holt & Co., New York. 1895) gave the author's name as H. S. Wells (initials H.S.W.) throughout the book.

(5)

THE WONDERFUL VISIT : 1895

The / Wonderful Visit (*in red*) / By / H. G. Wells / Author of " The Time Machine " / (*device*) / London / J. M. Dent & Co., Aldine House (*in red*) / New York : Macmillan & Co. / 1895

Crown 8vo ; pp. viii + 252, consisting of Half-title, *The Wonderful Visit* (verso, in centre, *All Rights Reserved.*), pp. (i, ii) ; Title-page, as above (verso blank), pp. (iii, iv) ; Dedication, *To The / Memory of my dear Friend, / Walter Low.* (verso blank), pp. (v, vi) ; List of *Contents*, pp. (vii, viii) ; Text, pp. 1-251 ; p. (252) blank. Printers' imprint on p. 251 as follows : *Turnbull And Spears, Printers, Edinburgh*

Issued in red buckram, gilt ornament and lettering across back as follows : (ornament) / *The / Wonderful / Vis t.* / (ornament) / *H. G. Wells.* / *J·M·Dent·&·Co.* Front and back covers blank. Top edges gilt, others uncut. White end-papers.

A few, possibly advance, copies of the first edition bear title and design of figure of the Angel, both in gilt, on the front cover. The third edition adopted this cover for all copies.

The statement has been repeated more than once that this novel was dramatised by Mr. Wells himself in 1896 and produced at The Gaiety Theatre, Hastings, on April 8th of that year. This is incorrect : the performance, such as it was, was no more than a formal reading over of the dialogue for copyright purposes, and in this Mr. Wells had no part. The only dramatisation is that prepared by H. G. Wells and St. John Ervine in collaboration, and produced by Basil Dean and the Reandean Company at The St. Martin's Theatre, London, on February 10th, 1921. The story of the play differs somewhat from the original : it is modernised, the action taking place in the year 1920. The incident of the Angel's visit is presented as a dream of the vicar (whose name is changed from Hilyer to Benham). Sir John Gotch is a war-profiteer and a K.B.E., and the Angel's attack upon him is provoked by his attempt to seduce Delia. Delia is the unmarried mother of a child whose father was killed during the war. At the end of the play, when the vicar's house is burnt down, Delia rushes into the flames to save her child, not the Angel's violin as in the novel. The Angel follows her and all three perish, but the Angel appears to the vicar once more before he wakes. The chief parts were taken as follows :

Delia	Moyna Macgill
Rev. Richard Benham	J. H. Roberts
A Visitor (the Angel)	Harold French
Rev. George Mendham	Lawrence Hanray
Mrs. Mendham	Ethel Griffies
Henry Crump	Fewlass Llewellyn
Lady Hammergallow	Miss Compton
Sir John Gotch	A. G. Poulton

There are four other characters in the play, Grummet, Peter Jekyll, Nicky and Mrs. Hinijer. The play was severely criticised at the time of its production, largely on account of certain scenic affects. Mr. St. John Ervine stated that " Mr. Wells not only has no responsibility for them, but, so far as I know, is actually unaware that they exist." The production only ran for a month or five weeks.

(6)

THE STOLEN BACILLUS : 1895

The Stolen Bacillus / And Other Incidents / By / H. G. Wells / Author of " The Time Machine " / Methuen & Co. / 36 Essex Street, Strand / London / 1895

> Crown 8vo ; pp. x + 276, consisting of a blank leaf not reckoned in the pagination ; Half-title, *The Stolen Bacillus* (verso blank), pp, (i, ii) ; Title-page, as above (verso blank), pp. (iii, iv) ; Dedication. *To / H. B. Marriott Watson* (verso blank), pp. (v, vi) ; Note of acknowledgments (verso blank), pp. (vii, viii) ; List of *Contents* (verso blank), pp. (ix, x) ; Text, pp. (1)-275 ; p. (276) has Printers' imprint, *Printed By / Turnbull And Spears, / Edinburgh* There follows a 32-page *List Of New Books*, dated *September*, 1895.

> Issued in dark blue cloth, lettered in gilt across back and front cover, with gilt design on front cover. Back : *The / Stolen / Bacillus / . . . / H·G·Wells /* (design) / *Methuen* Front cover : *The Stolen Bacillus /* (design) / *H·G·Wells* Edges uncut. White end-papers.

This volume contains fifteen short stories, *The Stolen Bacillus, The Flowering of the Strange Orchid, In the Avu Observatory, The Triumphs of a Taxidermist, A Deal in Ostriches, Through a Window, The Temptation of Harringay, The Flying Man, The Diamond Maker, Æpyornis Island, The Remarkable Case of Davidson's Eyes, The Lord of the Dynamos, The Hammerpond Park Burglary, A Moth—Genus Novo, The Treasure in the Forest.*

In 1894 H. G. Wells was writing short stories and articles for The Pall Mall Gazette, when C. Lewis Hind asked him to do a series of " Single Sitting Stories " for The Pall Mall Budget, which printed them weekly. Most of the tales in this book appeared under that general heading : one or two were first printed in The Pall Mall Gazette, and one each in Black and White and The St. James's Gazette. They were all written and printed 1893-5.

(7)

THE ISLAND OF DR. MOREAU: 1896

The Island of / Doctor Moreau / By / H. G. Wells / Author of ' The Time Machine,' / ' The Wonderful Visit,' and / ' The Stolen Bacillus ' / London / William Heinemann / MDCCCXCVI

Crown 8vo ; pp. x + 222, consisting of a blank leaf not reckoned in the pagination ; Half-title, *The Island of / Doctor Moreau* (verso, publisher's advertisement), pp. (i, ii) ; Frontispiece, not reckoned in the pagination ; Title-page, as above (verso, in centre, *Copyright, March* 1896 / *Entered at the Library of Congress / Washington, U.S.A.*), pp. (iii, iv) ; *Introduction,* signed *Charles Edward Prendick,* pp. (v)-vii ; p. (viii) blank ; List of *Contents,* pp. (ix),x ; Text, pp. (1)-219 ; p. (220) blank ; *Note* by the author (verso, Printers' imprint, *Printed by T. and A. Constable, Printers to Her Majesty / at the Edinburgh University Press*), pp. (221, 222). There follow one page bearing an advertisement of " The Time Machine " (verso blank), and 32 pages of the publisher's announcements.

Issued in brown cloth, lettered across the back in black, and across the front cover, with a design, in black and red. Back : *The / Island / Of / Doctor / Moreau / H. G. / Wells / Heinemann* Front cover : (design of the island) / *The Island / of / Dr Moreau / H·G·Wells* Back cover has publisher's blind device. Top and fore edges uncut. White end-papers.

Only one portion of this book was previously printed, the substance of Chapter XIV, *Dr. Moreau Explains* : under the title of *The Limits of Individual Plasticity* it appeared as an unsigned middle article in The Saturday Review (Jan. 19th, 1895).

Though everyone recognised the imaginative power of the story, a considerable outcry was raised by critics who thought that the book should never have been written. " We feel bound to expostulate against a certain departure which may lead we know not whither, and to give a word of warning to the unsuspecting who would shrink from the loathsome and repulsive. . . . The book should be kept out of the way of young people and avoided by all who have good taste, good feeling, or feeble nerves. It is simply sacrilege to steep fair nature in the blood and antiseptic of the vivisecting anatomical theatre." (The Times, June 17th, 1896) ! Others, more intelligently, drew parallels with the work of Dean Swift, and that there was at least a satirical intention is proved by the fact that H. G. Wells considered calling it variously *A Satire* and *A Satirical Grotesque.* Some American editions are entitled *The Island of Dr. Moreau : A Possibility.*

Mr. St. John G. Ervine, in his chapter on H. G. Wells in *Some Impressions of My Elders* (Allen & Unwin, London. 1923), writes : " I have heard that Mr. H. G. Wells thought of the plot of that clever, devilish story of his, *The Island of Dr. Moreau,* in the Tottenham Court Road on a Bank Holiday when he was in a mood of discontent." (p. 253).

(8)

THE RED ROOM : 1896

The Red Room.   By H. G. Wells.

Issued by Stone & Kimball, Chicago, in 1896.

Twelve copies only of this one short story, printed from the type used for publication in The Chapbook, were issued in pamphlet form for American copyright purposes, not to be sold.

(9)

THE WHEELS OF CHANCE : 1896

The / Wheels of Chance (*all red*) / A Holiday Adventure / By / H. G. Wells / Author of / " The Wonderful Visit," " The Time Machine," etc./ With 40 illustrations by / J. Ayton Symington / (*device*) / London / J. M. Dent and Co. (*red*) / New York : The Macmillan Co. / 1896

> Crown 8vo ; pp. xiv + 312, consisting of Half-title, *The Wheels of Chance* (verso, advertisement of " The Wonderful Visit "), pp. (i, ii) ; Frontispiece, pp. (iii, iv) ; Title-page, as above (verso : (*All rights reserved*) / *Printed by Ballantyne, Hanson & Co. / At the Ballantyne Press*), pp. (v, vi) ; Dedication, *To / My Dear Mother* (verso blank), pp. (vii, viii) ; List of *Contents*, pp. ix, x ; *List Of Illustrations*, pp. xi-xiii ; p. (xiv) blank ; Text, pp. 3-313 ; p. (314) has printers' imprint as follows : *Printed by Ballantyne, Hanson & Co. / Edinburgh and London*   There follows a 10-page list of the publishers' books, dated *October* 1896.

> Issued in red buckram, lettered in gilt, with gilt designs, across back and front cover.   Back : (decoration) / *The / Wheels Of / Chance* / (decoration) / *H. G. Wells. / J. M. Dent · & · Co.*   Front cover : *The Wheels Of Chance* / (drawing of Mr. Hoopdriver as on p. 59)   Top edges gilt, others uncut.   White end-papers.

> Later issues of the first edition are blank on p. (314) and have no list of publishers' books.   Owing to an error in the pagination, there are no pp. 1, 2 in any copies of the first and some later editions.

This story was first printed serially in Today (in 1896).   The title of the American edition is *The Wheels of Chance : A Bicycling Idyll*.

A film version of *The Wheels of Chance* was produced in 1921 by Harold Shaw for The Stoll Film Company.   The part of Hoopdriver was taken by George K. Arthur, that of Jessica Milton by Olwen Roose.   The story was followed closely, and many of the incidents were filmed in the actual spots referred to in the book.

(10)

THE PLATTNER STORY : 1897

The / Plattner Story / And Others / By / H. G. Wells / Methuen & Co. / 36 Essex Street, W.C. / London / 1897

Crown 8vo ; pp. viii + 302, consisting of Half-title, *The / Plattner Story / And Others* (verso, list of books *By The Same Author*), pp. (i, ii) ; Title-page, as above (verso blank), pp. (iii, iv) ; Dedication, *To / My Father* (verso blank), pp. (v, vi) ; List of *Contents* (verso blank), pp. vii, (viii) ; Text, pp. (1)-301 ; p. (302) has printers' imprint, *Printed By / Morrison And Gibb Limited, Edinburgh* There follow a blank leaf and a 40-page *Catalogue of Books*, dated *March* 1897.

Issued in red cloth, lettered across in gilt with gilt line panels on front cover and back. Back : *The / Plattner / Story / H. G. / Wells* (all in panel) / *Methuen* (in panel) Front cover : *The / Plattner / Story / By / H. G. / Wells* (all in panel, right centre of cover) Edges uncut. White end-papers.

Most of the seventeen stories in this volume were originally printed in various magazines in 1895 and 1896. Their titles are *The Plattner Story, The Argonauts of the Air, The Story of the Late Mr. Elvesham, In the Abyss, The Apple, Under the Knife, The Sea-raiders, Pollock and the Porroh Man, The Red Room, The Cone, The Purple Pileus, The Jilting of Jane, In the Modern Vein, A Catastrophe, The Lost Inheritance, The Sad Story of a Dramatic Critic,* and *A Slip under the Microscope.* The last was printed in The Yellow Book. The Idler, The New Budget, and The New Review each printed two or three, and Pearson's Magazine, The Unicorn, Truth, The Weekly Sun Literary Supplement, Black and White, The Pall Mall Gazette, and Phil May's Annual one each.

(11)

THE INVISIBLE MAN : 1897

The Invisible Man (*in red*) / A Grotesque Romance / By / H. G. Wells / Author of " The Time Machine," " The War of the Worlds," &c. / London / C. Arthur Pearson Limited / Henrietta Street, W. C. / (*short line*) / 1897

Crown 8vo ; pp. vi + 246, consisting of a blank leaf not reckoned in the pagination ; Half-title, *The Invisible Man* (verso, publisher's advertisement), pp. (i, ii) ; Title-page, as above (verso blank), pp. (iii, iv) ; List of *Contents*, pp. (v, vi) ; Text, pp. (1)-245 ; p. (246) has printers' imprint, *The Gresham Press / Unwin Brothers, / Woking And London* There follow 2 pages of publisher's advertisements.

Issued in red cloth, lettered in gilt across back and front cover, with gilt
panel on back and design in black on front cover. Back : *The /
Invisible / Man /* (short line) / *H. G. Wells* (all in panel) / *C. A.
Pearson / Ltd.* Front cover :   *The Invisible Man /* (design of the
Invisible Man in his dressing-gown) / *H. G. Wells* Edges all cut.
White end-papers.
P. (1) is incorrectly numbered with the figure 2.

This story was first printed serially in Pearson's Weekly (June and
July, 1897).
The story, as given in the edition collated above, ends with the death of
Griffin in Chapter XXVIII.   The American first edition (Edward Arnold,
New York.   1897), however, has a short *Epilogue* in which Thomas
Marvell, who has retained the papers of the dead man, is pictured as
proprietor of an inn, " The Invisible Man."   This *Epilogue* is printed in a
cheap edition with paper wrappers issued by Pearson (1900), where it
occupies four pages (pp. 247-250).
A music-hall sketch based on the idea of *The Invisible Man* was written
and produced some years ago, but it was not very successful and, apart
from the main conception, bore no relation to the novel at all.   Mr. Wells
is unable to recall any further particulars : he had no hand in either the
writing or production.

(12)

CERTAIN PERSONAL MATTERS :   1897

Certain Personal Matters. / A Collection Of Material, Mainly / Autobiographical. / By / H. G. Wells. / (*device*) / Lawrence & Bullen, Ltd., /
16, Henrietta Street, Covent Garden, W.C. / 1898.

Crown 8vo ; pp. viii + 278, consisting of Half-title, *Certain Personal
Matters.* (verso blank), pp. (i, ii) ; Title-page, as above (verso, in
centre, printers' imprint, *Bradbury, Agnew, & Co. Ld., Printers, /
London And Tonbridge.*), pp. (iii, iv) ; *Preface.* (verso blank), pp.
(v, vi) ; List of *Contents.*, pp. (vii),viii ; Text, pp. (1)-278 ; Printers'
imprint at foot of p. 278, *Bradbury, Agnew, & Co. Ld., Printers,
London And Tonbridge.*   There follow one blank leaf and a 32-page
List of Publications. dated *Spring Season,* 1897.
Issued in light blue cloth, lettered in gilt across back and front cover,
within gilt line panels.   Back : *Certain / Personal / Matters / H. G. /
Wells* (all in panel) / *Lawrence & Bullen* (in panel)   Front cover :
Certain / Personal / Matters / H. G. / Wells (all in panel, right upper
corner)   Top and fore edges uncut, lower edges untrimmed.   Cream
end-papers.

The thirty-nine short essays which make up this volume were all written
and printed during the three years 1893-5, at the very beginning of H. G.
Wells's career as author.   Some of them, no doubt, formed part of the

" string of facetious articles " which won him his first literary position
as a contributor to The Pall Mall Gazette. All but half-a-dozen were first
printed in that paper : of the others The New Budget printed three, and
The National Observer, The Saturday Review, and Black and White one
each.

(13)

THIRTY STRANGE STORIES : 1897

Thirty / Strange Stories / (*double lines*) / By H. G. Wells / Author Of /
" The Time Machine," " The Wheels of Chance," / " The Wonderful
Visit," Etc. / (*double lines*) / (*decoration*) / (*double lines*) / New York /
Edward Arnold / 70 Fifth Avenue / 1897 (*all in double line border, ruled
thrice across as indicated*)

  Crown 8vo ; pp. vi + 504, consisting of Half-title, (double lines) /
  Thirty Strange Stories / (double lines) (verso blank), pp. (i, ii) ; Title-
  page, as above (verso, in centre, (double lines) / *Copyright*, 1897, *by
  Edward Arnold* / (double lines), and at foot printers' imprint, (double
  lines) / *University Press : John Wilson and Son, Cambridge, U. S. A.* /
  (double lines), pp. (iii, iv) ; List of *Contents*, pp. (v), vi ; Text, pp.
  1-504. There follows one blank leaf.

  Issued in light green cloth, lettered across back and front cover in black,
  with design in black on back, and in black, green and gold on front
  cover. Back : (line) / *Thirty* / *Strange* / *Stories* / *Wells* / (line) /
  (design of skull) / (line) / *Arnold* / (line) Front cover : *Thirty* /
  Strange / *Stories* / (broken line) / *H · G · Wells* (all in right upper corner,
  the rest being filled by a design signed *F R K*, all enclosed within black
  line border.) Top edges gilt, others uncut. White end-papers.

This volume contains the ten best tales from *The Stolen Bacillus and
Other Incidents*, and the seventeen from *The Plattner Story and Others*.
There are three new stories, printed as the eleventh, the sixteenth, and the
twenty-first, *The Reconciliation, The Rajah's Treasure,* and *Le Mari
Terrible. The Reconciliation* was first printed in The Weekly Sun Literary
Supplement (Dec. 1st, 1895) under the title of *The Bulla.* This collection
has never been issued in Great Britain.

(14)

THE WAR OF THE WORLDS : 1898

The / War of the Worlds / By / H. G. Wells / Author of ' The Time
Machine,' ' The Island of Doctor Moreau,' / ' The Invisible Man,' etc. /
' But who shall dwell in these Worlds if they be inhabited ? / . . . Are we
or they Lords of the World ? . . . And / how are all things made for

man ? ' / Kepler (quoted in *The Anatomy of Melancholy*) / London /
William Heinemann / 1898

> Crown 8vo ; pp. viii + 304, consisting of Half-title, *The War / of the
> Worlds* (verso, publisher's advertisement of *Popular Six Shilling
> Novels*), pp. (i, ii) ; Title-page, as above (verso, *All rights reserved*),
> pp. (iii, iv) ; Dedication, *To / My Brother / Frank Wells, / This
> Rendering Of His Idea.* (verso blank), pp. (v, vi) ; List of *Contents*,
> pp. (vii), viii ; Text, pp. 1-303 ; Printers' imprint at foot of p. 303
> under a line, *Billing and Sons, Printers, Guildford.* ; p. (304) blank.
> There follow 16 numbered pages of publisher's announcements, dated
> *mdcccxcvii*
> Issued in grey cloth, lettered in black across back and front cover, with
> the publisher's mark in black on the back cover.   Back : *The War /
> Of The / Worlds / H. G. / Wells / Heinemann* Front cover :   *The
> War / Of The Worlds / H. G. Wells*   Top and fore edges uncut.   White
> end-papers.

This story was first printed serially in Pearson's magazine (April-Dec.
1897), with illustrations by Warwick Goble, 15 of which were reproduced
in the American first edition (Harper & Bros., New York. 1898). A
condensation of the novel, by H. G. Wells himself, was printed in The
Strand Magazine (Feb. 1920) with an *Introduction, An Experiment in
Illustration.* It is under 4000 words in length, and is illustrated by five
drawings by Johan Briede, a Dutch artist. In the introduction Mr. Wells
discusses the origin of the story : " The book was begotten by a remark
of my brother Frank. We were walking together through some particularly
peaceful Surrey scenery. ' Suppose some beings from another planet were
to drop out of the sky suddenly,' said he, ' and began laying about them
here ! ' . . . That was the point of departure. . . . And the value of the
story to me lies in this, that from first to last there is nothing in it that is
impossible."
He mentions also the attraction which this particular book has always
had for artists. Chief among the illustrated editions actually published
may be noted the French translation issued by Vandamme, Brussels, in
1906, with illustrations by a Belgian artist, Alvim-Corrêa.

(15)

WHEN THE SLEEPER WAKES :   1899

When the / Sleeper Wakes / *(line)* / By H. G. Wells, Author / of " The
Invisible Man " / " The War of the Worlds " / *(line)* / With Illustrations /
(line) / (device) / (line) / Harper & Brothers Publishers / London And New
York / 1899 *(all in line border, ruled four times across as indicated)*

> Crown 8vo ; pp. viii + 330, consisting of Half-Title, *When the / Sleeper
> Wakes* (verso blank), pp. (i, ii) ; Frontispiece, not reckoned in the

pagination ; Title-page, as above (verso, at foot, *Copyright*, 1899, *by Harper & Brothers* / (short line) / *All rights reserved*), pp. (iii, iv) ; List of *Contents* (verso blank), pp. (v, vi) ; *List of Illustrations* (verso blank), pp. (vii, viii) ; Text, pp. (1)-(329) ; Printers' imprint at foot of p. (329), *Printed by Balla tyne, Hanson & Co. / Edinburgh & London* ; p. (330) blank ; blank leaf follows.

Issued in red cloth, lettered in gilt across back and front cover. Back : *When / The Sleeper / Wakes / H. G. Wells / Harpers* Front cover : *When / The Sleeper Wakes / A Story Of The Years / To Come / H. G. Wells* All edges cut. White end-papers.

This story of the future was first printed serially in The Graphic (1898-9). H. G. Wells calls it " one of the most ambitious and least satisfactory of my books," and tells how it was written against time in 1898 when he was " overworked, and badly in need of a holiday " (*Preface to The Sleeper Awakes*). Circumstances prevented the rewriting which took place in the case of *Love and Mr. Lewisham*, and it was not until 1910 that a revised edition was published in Nelson's Sevenpenny Library with a preface and the new title *The Sleeper Awakes*. A collation of this reissue is given below.

(15a)

The Sleeper / Awakes / A Revised Edition of " When the / Sleeper Wakes " / H. G. Wells / Thomas Nelson And / Sons (*printed in brown within a decorative design in brown*)

12mo (6 1/10" x 4") ; pp. 288, consisting of List of books *Uniform With This Volume* in *Nelson's Library* (verso, Frontispiece), and Title-page, as above (verso, device), neither reckoned in pagination ; *Preface To The New Edition*, pp. (i), ii ; List of *Contents*, pp. (iii), iv ; Text, pp. (5)-288.

Issued in red cloth, lettered across back in gilt with gilt designs, and with blind device and double line border on front cover. Back : *The / Sleeper / Awakes / H. G. / Wells* (all within panel decorated top and bottom) / (design) / *Nelson's / Library* / (decorated panel) All edges trimmed. White end-papers.

The revision in this edition consists mainly of omission, about 6000 words being cut out, though the story is in twenty-five chapters as compared with twenty-four in the original edition (the original Chapter XXIII being divided into two). The main deletions are in Chapters XIV, XVI, XXI, and XXIII. Apart from these very little is altered, the most noticeable change being the use of the word " monoplane " for the earlier word " aeropile." In the *Preface* the author explains that he has eliminated all idea of a " sexual interest " between Helen Wotton and Graham, also " certain dishonest and regrettable suggestions that the People beat Ostrog. My Graham dies, as all his kind must die, with no certainty of either victory or defeat."

A cheap paper-covered edition of the original story and with the original title was issued by Collins, London in 1921 with a short new *Preface*.

(16)

TALES OF SPACE AND TIME: 1899

Tales of Space / and Time / (*line*) / By H. G. Wells, Author / of " When the Sleeper Wakes " / " The War of the worlds " / etc. / (*line*) / (*device*) / (*line*) / Harper & Brothers Publishers / London And New York / 1900 (*all enclosed in line border, ruled thrice across as indicated*)

> Crown 8vo ; pp. vi + 358, consisting of blank leaf not reckoned in the pagination ; Half-title, *Tales of Space / and Time* (verso blank), pp. (i, ii) ; Title-page, as above (verso, at foot, *Copyright*, 1899, *by Harper & Brothers* / (short line) / *All rights reserved*), pp. (iii, iv) ; List of *Contents* (verso blank), pp. (v, vi) ; Text, pp. 1-358 ; Printers' imprint at foot of p. 358, *Printed by Ballantyne, Hanson & Co. / Edinburgh & London*   There follow 2 numbered pages of publishers' advertisements.
>
> Issued in light brown cloth, lettered across the back in brown and the front cover in gilt, with device and lines in brown on the front cover. Back : *Tales / Of / Space / And / Time / H. G. / Wells / Harpers*   Front cover : *Tales of Space / and Time* / (device) / *H. G. Wells* (all enclosed in double line border)   Top edges cut, others uncut.   White end-papers.

The five stories in this volume were all printed in various magazines during 1897 and 1898, as follows : *The Crystal Egg* (The New Review), *The Star* (The Graphic), *A Story of the Stone Age* (serially in The Idler), *A Story of the Days to Come* (serially in The Pall Mall Magazine), and *The Man who could Work Miracles* (The Illustrated London News).   *The Star*, which in its immensity of conception and imaginative vividness of execution must be reckoned one of the author's most powerful short stories, was reprinted alone in 1913 by Pitman & Sons, as follows :

(16a)

The Star / Bi / H. G. Wells / London : Sir Isaac Pitman & Sons, Ltd. / No. I Amen Corner, E.C. . . . 1913

> Crown 8vo ; pp. 28, consisting of Title-page, as above (verso, *Alfabetical List ov Simplified Spelingz*), pp. (1, 2) ; Text, pp. 3-27 ; Note at foot of p. 3, *Isyud in Simplified Speling with the ciend permishon / ov the Author.* ; p. 28 has list of officials of the *Simplified Speling Sosieti* (H. G. Wells's name appearing as that of a *Vies-Prezident*).
>
> Issued as a pamphlet in paper wrappers.   Front cover is blue-grey with white panels, lettered across and with lines in dark blue, *The / Star* (on white panel within triple-line border) / *Bi / H.G.Wells* / (ornament) (all within white circle with triple-line border) / *London : Sir Isaac Pitman & Sons, Ltd. / No. I Amen Corner, E.C.* . . . . .

Back cover and inside of covers white : Printers' imprint on p. (ii), *The Riverside Press Limited, Edinburgh.* ; p. (iii) has advertisement of *The Pioneer / (ov Simplified Speling)* ; p. (iv) has advertisement of publishers' books. All edges cut.

A reissue of this pamphlet was made in 1917, by *The Simplified Speling Sosieti / 44 Great Russell Street / London, W.C.*, this replacing the previous publishers' name on Title-page and front cover. There are other minor differences in the advertisements and in the printers' imprint (which is on verso of Title-page).

(17)

LOVE AND MR. LEWISHAM : 1900

Love and / Mr. Lewisham / *(line)* / By H. G. Wells, Author of / " Tales of Space and Time " / " When the Sleeper Wakes " / " The War of the Worlds " / etc. / *(line)* / *(device)* / *(line)* / Harper & Brothers Publishers / London and New York / 1900 *(all enclosed in line border, ruled thrice across as indicated)*

> Crown 8vo ; pp. iv + 324, consisting of blank leaf and Half-title, *Love And Mr. Lewisham* (verso blank), neither reckoned in the pagination ; Title-page, as above (verso, at foot, printers' imprint, *Printed by Ballantyne, Hanson & Co. / At the Ballantyne Press*), pp. (i, ii) ; List of *Contents*, pp. (iii), iv ; Text, pp. 1-323 ; p. (324) has printers' imprint, *Printed by Ballantyne, Hanson & Co. / Edinburgh & London* There follow 4 pages of publishers' advertisements.
> Issued in red cloth, lettered in gilt across back and front cover, with a mauve border line on front cover. Back : *Love / And / Mr. Lewisham / H·G·Wells /* Harpers Front cover : *Love And / Mr. Lewisham / H·G·Wells* (all within border line) Top edges trimmed, others uncut. White end-papers.

This " Story of a Very Young Couple " was first printed serially in The Weekly Times (Nov. 1899-1900).

It was written in 1898, simultaneously with the very different story *When the Sleeper Wakes.* Both were finished during a period of ill-health and the author recalls " the impotent rage and strain of my attempt to put some sort of finish to my story of Mr. Lewisham with my temperature at a hundred and two " *(Preface to The Sleeper Awakes).* But, more fortunate with this than with the romance, Mr. Wells was able to rewrite that part of the novel, and both author and many of his critics combine in agreeing that *Love and Mr. Lewisham* is among his five or six best books.

Referring to the question of autobiography in fiction, H. G. Wells has somewhere made a remark to the effect that it is not so much what one has done which counts, as where one has been, and the truth of that statement is particularly evident in this novel. The emotional experiences of Mr. Lewisham are not to be confused with those of Mr. Wells, nor the Mr.

Bonover of fiction with the **Mr.** Byatt of fact, but it is true that both **Mr.**
Lewisham and **Mr.** Wells were, at the age of eighteen, assistant masters at
country schools, and that three years later both were commencing their
third year at The Normal School of Science, South Kensington, as teachers
in training under Huxley.   The accounts of the school, of the students
there and of their social life and interests, may be taken as true descriptions
of those things during the period 1883-1886.

(18)

THE FIRST MEN IN THE MOON : 1901

The First Men / in the Moon / By / H. G. Wells / Author of " Tales of
Space and Time," / " Love and Mr. Lewisham," / and " Anticipations " /
" Three thousand stadia from the earth to the / moon. . . . Marvel not,
my comrade, if I appear / talking to you on super-terrestial and aerial
topics. / The long and the short of the matter is that I am / running over
the order of a journey I have lately / made."—Lucian's *Icaromenippus* /
London / George Newnes, Limited / Southampton Street, Strand / 1901

> Crown 8vo ; pp. viii + 342, consisting of Half-title, *The First Men
> In / The Moon* (verso blank), pp. (i, ii) ; Frontispiece with leaf of
> tissue, not reckoned in the pagination ; Title-page, as above (verso
> blank), pp. (iii, iv) ; List of *Contents*, pp. v, vi ; *List Of Illustrations*
> (verso blank), pp. vii, (viii) ; Text, pp. (1)-342 ; Printers' imprint
> at foot of p. 342, *George Newnes, Limited, London*   There follows one
> blank leaf.
> Issued in dark blue cloth, lettered across back and front cover in gilt,
> with gilt decorations.   Back : *The First / ·Men· / in the / ·Moon·*
> (ornament) / *·H·G· / ·Wells.· / Geo. Newnes / Limited*.   Front cover :
> *The·First·Men / in·the·Moon /* (design) / *H·G·Wells*   All edges cut.
> Black end-papers.
> Later issues of the first edition were bound in light blue cloth, lettered
> in black.

This story was first printed serially in The Strand Magazine (Dec. 1900-
Aug. 1901), with many illustrations by the late Claude Shepperson, A.R.A.,
twelve of which were reproduced in the edition collated above.

The First Men in the Moon was the first of H. G. Wells's works to be
filmed ; so far it remains the most venturesome and least satisfactory of
the various attempts in this direction.   It was produced in 1919 by J. V.
L. Leigh for the Gaumont Film Company, with a caste given as follows :

Cavor	Bruce Gordon
Bedford	Lionel D'Arragan
Hannibal Higben	Hector Abbas
The Grand Lunar	Cecil Morton York
Susan Cavor	Heather Thatcher

The film version mutilates the original story by the introduction of two
new characters and a " love-interest."   The main incidents, briefly, are

these : when the scheming Bedford attaches himself to Cavor, the scientist
is already assisted by a wireless operator with the quite unnecessary and
entirely un-Wellsian name of Hannibal Higben, who is in love with Susan,
a young relative of Cavor. The sphere in which the three men are to go
to the moon is completed, but Higben, somewhat absent-mindedly, is left
behind ! The two others reach the moon, are captured by the Selenites,
and escape. Bedford stuns Cavor, steals what he believes, incorrectly,
to be the Cavorite formula, and returns to the earth alone, there losing the
sphere. He tells Susan that Cavor, dying in his arms, wished her to marry
him (Bedford), but Higben receives wireless messages from the moon in
which the truth is told, and virtue triumphs in the dismissal of Bedford
and the marriage of Susan and Hannibal. The film showed a few inadequate scenes of the moon's interior, with a Grand Lunar who resembled a
giant baby strayed from *The Food of the Gods*.

(19)

ANTICIPATIONS : 1901

Anticipations / Of The / Reaction Of Mechanical And Scientific / Progress
Upon Human Life / And Thought / By / H. G. Wells / Author Of / " Love
And Mr. Lewisham," " The Island Of Dr. Moreau," / And " Tales Of Space
And Time." / London : Chapman & Hall, Ld. / 1902

> Crown 8vo ; pp. vi + 318, consisting of a blank leaf not reckoned in
> the pagination ; Half-title, *Anticipations* (verso blank), pp. (i, ii) ;
> Title-page, as above (verso blank), pp. (iii, iv) ; List of *Contents* (verso
> blank), pp. (v, vi) ; Text, pp. (1)-318 ; Printers' imprint at foot of
> p. 318 under a thin line, *Printed By William Clowes And Sons, Limited,
> London And Beccles*. There follows one blank leaf.
> Issued in red cloth, lettered in gilt across back and front cover, with gilt
> designs. Back : *Anticipations* / (design) / *H. G. Wells / Chapman
> & Hall* Front cover : *Anticipations* / (design) / *H. G. Wells* Top
> edges gilt, others uncut. White end-papers.

These nine papers were first printed serially in The Fortnightly Review
(Apr.-Dec. 1901) under the title, *Anticipations : An Experiment in Pro-
phecy. A New And Cheaper Edition / With Author's Specially-Written
Introduction* was issued by Chapman & Hall in 1914.

(20)

THE DISCOVERY OF THE FUTURE : 1902

The Discovery Of / The Future / A Discourse Delivered To The Royal
Institution / On January 24, 1902 / By / H. G. Wells, B.Sc. / Author Of
" Anticipations " / (*device*) / London / T. Fisher Unwin / Paternoster
Square / 1902

Crown 8vo ; pp. 96, consisting of blank leaf, pp. (1, 2) ; Half-title,
   The Discovery Of The Future (verso, advertisement of the fifth edition
   of *Anticipations*), pp. (3, 4) ; Title-page, as above (verso, at foot, *All
   Rights Reserved*), pp. (5, 6) ; Text, pp. (7)-95 ; p. (96) has advertisement of the publisher's cheap edition of *Certain Personal Matters* ;
   Printers' imprint at foot of p. 95, *Morrison And Gibb Limited, Edinburgh.*
Issued in red cloth, lettered in black on back and front cover. All
   edges cut. White end-papers.
Issued simultaneously in red paper wrappers, lettered in black across
   back and front cover. All edges cut.
The first issue of the first cloth edition has " Anticipations " misspelt
   as " Anticipation " on the front cover.

About 1906 the same sheets were issued in green paper wrappers by
Fifield, London. The title-page still bears the name of the original publisher. In 1921 this lecture was reprinted with *This Misery of Boots* in a
booklet by The Appeal Publishing Co., Girard, Kansas, as follows :

(20a)

People's Pocket Series No. 165 / Discovery of the / Future / By H. G.
Wells / This Misery of Boots / By H. G. Wells / Appeal To Reason /
Girard, Kans.

Pp. 64 (5″ x 3½″), consisting of Title-page, as above (verso blank), pp.
   (1, 2) ; Text, pp. (3)-59 ; pp. (60-64) have publishers' advertisements.
Issued in blue paper wrappers, pinned, lettered in black on front cover,
   *People's Pocket Series No. 165 / Discovery of the / Future / By H G.
   Wells /* (device) */ Edited by / E. Haldeman-Julius. / Appeal To Reason /
   Girard, Kans.* All edges cut.

This paper was read at the Royal Institute on Friday, Jan. 24th, 1902
and first printed in Nature (Feb. 6th, 1902).

(21)

THE SEA LADY : 1902

The Sea Lady / A Tissue Of Moonshine / By / H. G. Wells / Methuen &
Co. / 36 Essex Street W.C. / London / 1902

Crown 8vo ; pp. vi + 302, consisting of blank leaf not reckoned in the
   pagination ; Half-title, *The Sea Lady* (verso, list of books *By The
   Same Author*), pp. (i, ii) ; Title-page (verso blank), pp. (iii, iv) ; *The
   Chapters Are* (verso blank), pp. v, (vi) ; Text, pp. 1-301 ; p. (302) has
   printers' imprint, *Printed By / Morrison And Gibb Limited, / Edinburgh* There follow one blank leaf and a 40-page *Catalogue of Books*,
   dated *July* 1902.

Issued in red cloth, lettered in gilt across back and front cover, with gilt line panels. Back : *The / Sea / Lady / H. G. / Wells* (all in panel) / *Methuen* (in panel) Front cover : *The / Sea / Lady / By / H. G. / Wells* (all in panel) Top edges trimmed, others uncut. White end-papers.

The Sea Lady was first printed serially in Pearson's Magazine (July-Dec. 1901). The first American edition (Appleton, New York. 1902) has 8 illustrations by Lewis Baumer.

(22)

MANKIND IN THE MAKING : 1903

Mankind In The / Making / By / H. G. Wells / *(device)* / London : Chapman & Hall, Ld. / 1903

> Crown 8vo ; pp. x + 430, consisting of blank leaf not reckoned in pagination ; Half-title, *Mankind In The Making* (verso, list of books *By the Same Author*), pp. (i, ii) ; Title-page, as above (verso blank), pp. (iii, iv) ; *Preface*, pp. (v)-viii ; List of *Contents* (verso blank), pp. (ix, x) ; Text, pp. (1)-396 ; *Appendix* (Divisional fly-title, verso blank, pp. (397, 398), pp. (399)-420 ; *Index*, pp. 421-429 ; Printers' imprint at foot of p. 429 under thin line, *Printed By William Clowes And Sons, Limited, London And Beccles.* ; p. (430) blank.
> Issued in blue cloth, lettered in gilt across back and front cover, with gilt designs. Back : *Mankind / In The Making /* (design) / *H. G. Wells / Chapman & Hall* Front cover : *Mankind / In The Making /* (design) / *H. G. Wells* Top edges gilt, others uncut. White end-papers.

The eleven chapters in this book were first printed serially in The Fortnightly Review (Sept. 1902-Sept. 1903). *A New And Cheaper Edition / With Author's Specially-Written Introduction* was issued by Chapman & Hall in 1914 : in this the *Appendix* and *Index* are both omitted. *Appendix I* (pp. 399-417) was originally read before the Fabian Society in March, 1903 (H. G. Wells had joined the Society in February 1903), under the title *The Question of Scientific Administrative Areas in Relation to Municipal Undertakings*. In the book this paper bears no title, but in one copy it is headed, by Mr. Wells himself, *Locomotion and Administration*.

(23)

TWELVE STORIES AND A DREAM : 1903

Twelve Stories / And A Dream / By / H. G. Wells / London / Macmillan And Co., Limited / New York : The Macmillan Company / 1903 / All rights reserved

Crown 8vo ; pp. viii + 378, consisting of a blank page (verso, list of books *By The Same Author*), pp. (i, ii) ; Half-title, *Twelve Stories And A Dream* (verso, publishers' device), pp. (iii, iv) ; Title-page, as above (verso blank), pp. (v, vi) ; List of *Contents* (verso blank), pp. (vii, viii) ; Divisional fly-title, *Filmer* (verso blank), pp. (1, 2) ; Text, pp. 3-377 ; Printers' imprint at foot of p. 377, *Printed by R. & R. Clark, Limited, Edinburgh.* ; p. (378) blank. There follow 22 pages of publishers' advertisements dated 20/9/03.

Issued in sage green cloth, lettered in gilt across back and front cover, with blind design on front cover. Back : *Twelve / Stories / And / A Dream / H. G. Wells / Macmillan & Co.* Front cover : *Twelve / Stories / And / A Dream / H. G. Wells* (all within panel of design, left upper corner). Top edges gilt, others cut. White end-papers.

As the title indicates, this volume contains thirteen stories, the titles of which are *Filmer, The Magic Shop, The Valley of Spiders, The Truth about Pyecraft, Mr. Skelmersdale in Fairyland, The Story of the Inexperienced Ghost, Jimmy Goggles the God, The New Accelerator, Mr. Ledbetter's Vacation, The Stolen Body, Mr. Brisher's Treasure, Miss Winchelsea's Heart, A Dream of Armageddon.* All were printed between 1898 and 1903, eight of them in The Strand Magazine, two in The Graphic, and one each in Pearson's Magazine, Black and White, and The Queen.

(24)

THE FOOD OF THE GODS: 1904

The Food / Of / The Gods / And How It Came To Earth / By / H. G. Wells / London / Macmillan And Co., Limited / 1904 / All rights reserved

Crown 8vo ; pp. viii + 318, consisting of Half-title, *The Food Of The Gods / And How It Came To Earth* (verso, list of books *By The Same Author*), pp. (i, ii) ; Title-page, as above (verso blank), pp. (iii, iv) ; List of *Contents*, pp. v-vii ; p. (viii) blank ; Divisional fly-title, *Book I / The Dawn Of The Food* (verso blank), pp. 1, (2) ; Text, pp. 3-317 ; Printers' imprint at foot of p. 317, *Printed by R. & R. Clark, Limited, Edinburgh* ; p. (318) blank. There follow 18 pages of publishers' advertisements dated 20/7/04

Issued in sage green cloth, lettered in gilt across back and front cover, with blind design on front cover. Back : *The Food / Of / The Gods / And / How It Came / To Earth / H. G. Wells / Macmillan & Co.* Front cover : *The Food / Of / The Gods / And / How It Came / To Earth / H. G. Wells* (all within panel of design, left upper corner) Top edges gilt, others cut. White end-papers.

This story was first printed serially in Pearson's Magazine (Dec. 1903-June 1904).

(25)

A MODERN UTOPIA : 1905

A Modern Utopia / By / H. G. Wells / (*device*) / London / Chapman & Hall, Ld. / 1905

Crown 8vo ; pp. xii + 394, consisting of Half-title, *A Modern Utopia* (verso, list of books *By the Same Author*), pp. (i, ii) ; Frontisipece not reckoned in the pagination ; Title-page, as above (verso blank), pp. (iii, iv) ; *A Note To The Reader*, pp. v-viii ; List of *Contents*, pp. ix, x ; *List of Illustrations* (verso blank), pp. xi, (xii) ; Text, pp. 1-374 ; *Appendix / Scepticism Of The Instrument*, pp. 375-393 ; Printers' imprint at foot of p. 393 under thin line, *Printed By William Clowes And Sons, Limited, London And Beccles.* ; p. (394) blank. A blank leaf follows.

Issued in red cloth, lettered in gilt, with gilt designs, on back and front cover. Back : *A / Modern / Utopia / . . . / H. G. Wells /* (H.G.W. monogram design) / *Chapman & Hall* Front cover : *A Modern Utopia / H. G. Wells /* (design) Top edges gilt, others cut. White end-papers.

A Modern Utopia was first printed serially in The Fortnightly Review (Oct. 1904-April 1905). The illustrations in the first edition are by Edmund J. Sullivan. The *Appendix* is a revised extract from a paper read to the Oxford Philosophical Society on Nov. 8th, 1903, and printed in Mind, July, 1904.

(26)

KIPPS : 1905

Kipps / The Story Of A Simple / Soul / By / H. G. Wells / Author Of / " The Sea Lady " And " Love And Mr. Lewisham " / London / Macmillan And Co., Limited / 1905 / All rights reserved

Crown 8vo ; pp. viii + 426, consisting of Half-title, *Kipps* (verso, publishers' device), pp. (i, ii) ; Title-page, as above (verso, in centre, printers' imprint, *Printed By / William Clowes And Sons, Limited, / London And Beccles.*), pp. (iii, iv) ; Quotation of one sentence from "Manners and Rules of Good Society," / *By a Member of the Aristocracy.* (verso blank), pp. (v, vi) ; List of *Contents*, pp. vii, viii ; Divisional fly-title, *Book I / The Making Of Kipps* (verso blank), pp. (1, 2) ; Text, pp. 3-425 ; Printers' imprint at foot of p. 425 under a line, *Printed By William Clowes And Sons, Limited, London And Beccles.* ; p. (426) blank. There follows one blank leaf and 8 numbered pages of publishers' advertisements dated 16/8/'05.

Issued in sage green cloth, lettered in gilt across back and front cover, with blind design on front cover. Back : *Kipps / The Story / Of /*

A Simple / Soul / H. G. Wells / Macmillan & Co. Front cover : *Kipps / The Story / Of / A Simple / Soul / H. G. Wells* (all within panel of design, left upper corner) Top edges gilt, others cut. White end-papers.

A later issue of the first edition has 8 numbered pages of publishers' advertisements dated 10/10/'05

This novel was first printed serially in The Pall Mall Magazine (in 1905). Since its publication it has been adapted both for the stage and as a film. As a play it was adapted by Rudolf Besier, and produced at The Vaudeville Theatre, London, on March 5th, 1912, running until April 20th of the same year. The caste of the chief characters was as follows :

Edwin Shalford	Frederick Volpe
Our Mr. Kipps	O. B. Clarence
Chester Coote	Rudge Harding
Mrs. Walshingham . . .	Gertrude Scott
Helen Walshingham	. Helen Haye
Harry Chitterlow . . .	Leslie Carter
Ann Pornick	Christine Silver

There were eight other characters, four of whom bore names which do not appear in the novel at all. Apparently Coote in the play combined the parts of Coote, young Walshingham, and Mr. Bean in the novel. The film version, which presented the original story not unably, was produced by Harold Shaw for the Stoll Film Company in 1920. The part of Kipps was taken by George K. Arthur, that of Ann Pornick by Edna Flugrath (Mrs. Harold Shaw).

(27)

IN THE DAYS OF THE COMET : 1906

In The Days Of / The Comet / By / H. G. Wells / Author Of / " A Modern Utopia," " The Sea Lady," and " Love And Mr. Lewisham " / London / Macmillan And Co., Limited / 1906 / All rights reserved

Crown 8vo ; pp. viii + 306, consisting of Half-title, *In The Days Of The Comet* (verso, list of books *By The Same Author*), pp. (i, ii) ; Title-page, as above (verso, printers' imprint, *Printed By / William Clowes And Sons, Limited, / London And Beccles.*), pp. (iii, iv) ; Quotation of 6 lines from Shelley's " Hellas " (verso blank), pp. (v, vi) ; List of *Contents*, pp. vii, viii ; Divisional fly-title, *Prologue / The Man Who Wrote In The / Tower* (verso blank), pp. (1, 2) ; Text, pp. 3-305 ; p. (306) has printers' imprint as verso of Title-page. There follow 8 pages of publishers' advertisements dated 5.5.'06.
Issued in sage green cloth, lettered in gilt across back and front cover, with blind design on front cover. Back : *In / The Days / Of The / Comet / H. G. Wells / Macmillan & Co.* Front cover : *In / The Days /*

Of The | Comet | H. G. Wells (all within panel of design, left upper corner) Top edges gilt, others cut. White end-papers.

A later issue of the first edition has 8 pages of publishers' advertisements dated 20.8.'06.

This story was first printed in The Daily Chronicle in 1905-6.

(28)

THE FUTURE IN AMERICA: 1906

The Future In / America / A Search After Realities / By / H. G. Wells / Author Of / " The Time Machine," " Anticipations," " Kipps," / And " A Modern Utopia " / London / Chapman & Hall, Ltd. / 1906

Demy 8vo ; pp. x + 360, consisting of a blank leaf not reckoned in the pagination ; Half-title, *The Future In America* (verso, list of books *By The Same Author*), pp. (i, ii) ; Title-page, as above (verso blank), pp. (iii, iv) ; Dedication, *To / D.M.R.* (verso blank), pp. (v, vi) ; List of *Contents* (verso blank), pp. vii, (viii) ; *List Of Illustrations* (verso blank), pp. ix, (x) ; Divisional fly-title, *The Prophetic Habit | Of Mind* (verso blank), pp. (1, 2) ; Text, pp. (3)-359 ; Printers' imprint in centre of p. (360), *Printed By / William Clowes And Sons, Limited, / London And Beccles.*

Issued in light red-brown cloth, lettered in gilt across back and front cover, with gilt lines and dot on back and gilt dot and blind double line border on front cover. Back : (line) / *The / Future / In / America /* (dot) / *H. G. Wells | Chapman & Hall /* (gilt line) Front cover : *The Future In / America /* (dot) / *H. G. Wells* Top and lower edges cut, fore edges uncut. White end-papers.

Remainder copies of this edition are issued in still lighter red-brown cloth, with blind lettering on the front cover.

The text of this book was first printed serially in Harper's Weekly (July 14th-Oct. 6th, 1906).

(29)

FAULTS OF THE FABIAN: 1906

Private : For Members only. / Faults Of The Fabian. / *(introductory paragraph) / (text)*

Demy 8vo ; pp. 16, consisting of Text, headed on p. (1) as above, pp. (1)-16. The introductory paragraph begins : (*On Feb. 9th Mr. H. G. Wells read a paper to a meeting confined strictly | to members of the Fabian Society. It has been thought desirable to place it | before the*

D

24 THE BIBLIOGRAPHY

entire membership. . . .). The text begins: *Mr. Wells opened by declaring himself a socialist of long standing, / but only recently a Fabian. . . .* and ends on p. 16 : *Mr. Wells then proceeded to outline the committee he suggested / should develop the scheme he had in this broad manner sketched.*

Issued as a pamphlet without covers, and undated as to year: it was published by Edward R. Pease, the secretary of the Fabian Society, for private circulation ; the printer was Geo. Standring, 7 & 9 Finsbury St., E.C.

The criticism of the Fabian Society contained in the above paper was the main cause of the reconstruction of the Society which took place in 1906 and the early part of 1907. An account of the general circumstances, together with the full story of H. G. Wells's connection with the Society, will be found in *The History of the Fabian Society,* by Edward R. Pease (Fifield, 1916).

(30)

SOCIALISM AND THE FAMILY: 1906

Socialism And / The Family / By / H. G. Wells / Author of " In the Days of the Comet," " A Modern / Utopia," " Anticipations," etc / London / A. C. Fifield, 44, Fleet Street, E.C. / 1906

Crown 8vo ; pp. 60, consisting of Half-title, *Socialism And The Family* (verso, list of books *By The Same Author*), pp. (1, 2) ; Title-page, as above (verso, *All rights reserved*), pp. (3, 4) ; Text, pp. 5-60 ; Printers' imprint at foot of p. 60, under a thin line, *Butler & Tanner, The Selwood Printing Works, Frome, and London.* ; there follow four pages of advertisements.

Issued in green boards with brown ¼ cloth, lettered in black on back and front cover. Top edges gilt, others cut. White end-papers.

Issued simultaneously in red paper wrappers, lettered in black along back and across front cover. Back: *Socialism And The Family. H. G. Wells.* Front cover : *Sixpence Nett. / Also in quarter cloth, gilt top,* 1*s. nett. / Socialism / .And. / The Family / By / H. G. Wells / Author of / " Anticipations," " Mankind in the Making," / " In the Days of the Comet," etc. /* (4 lines of summary beginning *In this booklet* enclosed in black line border) / *London : A, C. Fifield.* The back cover and the insides of the covers are filled with publisher's advertisements. All edges cut.

This essay is a reprint of two articles, originally entitled *Socialism and the Middle Classes* and *Modern Socialism and the Family.* The former was read to The Fabian Society in Oct. 1906 and subsequently printed in The Fortnightly Review (Nov. 1906). The latter was first printed in The Independent Review (Nov. 1906).

(31)

RECONSTRUCTION OF THE FABIAN SOCIETY: 1906

Reconstruction Of The / Fabian Society. / *(two thin lines)* / *(there follows an introductory note to the eighth line from the bottom of the first sheet, where it ends,* In moving his resolution upon the Agenda of the meeting of / the Fabian Society upon December 7th, Mr. Wells said :— / *(text of speech by H. G. Wells)*

The text of this speech was issued on 6 sheets, printed on one side only, measuring 20½" x 4¾", pinned diagonally at the top left-hand corner. Sheet (1) is as above ; the text continues on sheets 2-6. There is no imprint.

Copies of the above were only issued privately to members of the Fabian Society. They were either sent out by H. G. Wells himself, or else placed on the seats at a meeting of the Society.

(32)

THIS MISERY OF BOOTS: 1907

This Misery of Boots. By / H. G. Wells. Reprinted with / alterations from the Indepen- / dent Review, December 1905 / London : The Fabian Society / 3 Clement's Inn, Strand, W.C. / 1907.

Flscp 8vo ; pp. 48, consisting of Half-title, *This Misery Of Boots* (verso blank), pp. (1, 2) ; Title-page, as above (verso, list of *Books By H. G. Wells / of interest to enquirers into Socialism.*), pp. (3, 4) ; Text, pp. (5)-42 ; Divisional fly-title, *Notices* (verso, list of *Dramatic Works / By Bernard Shaw*), pp. (43), 44 ; Notices of the Fabian Society, pp. 45-48.

Issued in sage green wrappers, with plate mounted on front cover. Back and back cover blank. The plate is lettered in dark red across a black and white design, signed *Arthur Watts*, within a thick black line border, as follows : *This Misery / Of / By / H. G. Wells. / Price 3d. / Boots.* Top edges trimmed, fore and lower edges unopened.

Later in the same year reissued as a 40-page pamphlet, pinned, with wrappers as above except that the lettering on the front cover plate is light red. The pages are numbered as in the edition collated above, with the omission of the Half-title leaf, pp. (1, 2), and the Notices at the end, pp. (43)-48. Also, verso of Title-page is blank.

This essay was originally read to the Fabian Society, and was first printed in The Independent Review (Dec. 1905). It was also reprinted in 1922 by The Appeal Publishing Company, Girard, Kansas, with other works by H. G. Wells (see notes under *The Discovery of the Future* and *The Country of the Blind*).

(33)

WILL SOCIALISM DESTROY THE HOME: 1907

Will / Socialism / Destroy (*double line*) / the Home (*all underlined by single red lines*) / By H. G. Wells. / (*device in red*) / Independent Labour Party / 23 Bride Lane, Fleet Street / (*line*) London, E.C. (*line*) / One Penny.

4to (8″ x 4″) ; pp. 16, consisting of Text (headed on p. (1), *Will Socialism Destroy* / " *The Home* " ?), pp. (1)-14 ; p. (15) has advertisements of *Books by H. G. Wells* ; p. (16) has a note on Socialism.

Issued in white wrappers, the front cover being the Title-page, as above (verso blank) ; pp. (iii, iv) of wrappers have I. L. P. advertisements. All edges cut.

This essay was first printed in The Grand Magazine (Dec. 1907) as the sixth of a series with the general title *New Worlds for Old* It is reprinted as Chapter VI of the book *New Worlds for Old*.

(34)   ·

NEW WORLDS FOR OLD: 1908

New Worlds / For Old / By / H. G. Wells / London / Archibald Constable & Co. Ltd. / 1908

Crown 8vo ; pp. viii + 356, consisting of Half-title, *New Worlds For Old* (verso, list of books *By The Same Author*), pp. (i, ii) ; Title-page, as above (verso, printers' imprint, *Richard Clay & Sons, Limited,* / *Bread Street Hill, E.C., And* / *Bungay, Suffolk.*), pp. (iii, iv) ; *Intro-ductory Remarks* (verso blank), pp. (v, vi) ; List of *Contents* (verso blank), pp. vii, (viii) ; Text, pp. 1-355 ; p. (356) has printers' imprint as on verso of title-page. There follow 4 pages of publishers' adver-tisements.

Issued in red cloth, lettered in gilt across back and front cover, with H. G. W. monogram in gilt on front cover. Back : *New* / *Worlds* / *For* / *Old* / *H. G.* / *Wells* / *Constable* / : *London* : Front cover : *New Worlds* / *For Old* / (monogram) / *H. G. Wells* Top edges trimmed, others uncut. White end-papers.

Chapters I-IX of this volume were first printed serially in The Grand Magazine (July 1907-March 1908). Some of the six other chapters appeared in various papers : one, Chapter XIV, *Some Arguments Ad Hominem*, was first delivered as a lecture by the author at the City Temple Hall, London, in November 1907, under the title *Every-Day Life In a Socialist State*.

In 1923 section 4 of Chapter I was reprinted, with the omission of about 40 words, under the title *A Walk Along The Thames Embankment*, as an Independent Labour Party Christmas card booklet. The collation is as follows :

(34a)

A Walk Along The / Thames Embankment / By H. G. Wells

Pp. 8 (5″ x 3½″), consisting of Title-page, as above, p. (1) ; Text, pp. (2-8).

Issued in brown paper wrappers, lettered in darker brown across the front cover within a decorative border, *A Walk Along / The Thames / Embankment / By H. G. Wells / From " New Worlds for Old " / by permission of the Author / I.L.P. Publication Department /* 308 *Gray's Inn Road, London* The back cover has the printers' imprint, *National Labour Press Ltd. /* 17/23 *Albion St., Leicester /* 13215 The booklet is sewn with brown silk.

(35)

THE WAR IN THE AIR: 1908

The War In The Air / And Particularly How Mr Bert / Smallways Fared While / It Lasted / By / H. G. Wells / With Illustrations By A. C. Michael / (*device*) / London / George Bell & Sons / 1908

Crown 8vo ; pp. viii + 390, consisting of Half-title, *The War In The Air* (verso, list of books *By The Same Author*), pp. (i, ii) ; Frontispiece, not reckoned in the pagination ; Title-page, as above (verso, at foot, printers' imprint, *Chiswick Press : Charles Whittingham And Co. / Tooks Court, Chancery Lane, London.*), pp. (iii, iv) ; List of *Contents* (verso, *The publishers are much indebted to the proprietors / of the " Pall Mall Magazine " for their kind per- / mission to use Mr. Michael's drawings.*), pp. v, (vi) ; List of *Illustrations* (verso blank), pp. (vii, viii) ; Text, pp. (1)-389 ; p. (390) has printers' device, followed by imprint as on verso of title-page. There follow 2 pages of advertisements.

Issued in blue cloth, lettered in gilt with gilt designs across back and front cover. Back : *The / War / In The / Air /* (short line) / *H. G. Wells /* (device) / *George Bell & Sons* Front cover : *The War In The Air* (upon a drawing of the rising sun, within double lines) Top edges trimmed, others uncut. White end-papers.

This story was first printed serially in The Pall Mall Magazine, with illustrations by A. C. Michael, sixteen of which are reproduced in the edition collated above. The American first edition (Macmillan Co., New York. 1908) has twenty illustrations by Eric Pape.

(36)

FIRST AND LAST THINGS: 1908

First & Last Things / A Confession of Faith / and Rule of Life / By / H. G. Wells / London / Archibald Constable & Co. Ltd. / 1908

Crown 8vo ; pp. xii + 246, consisting of Half-title, *First And Last Things* (verso, list of books *By The Same Author*), pp. (i, ii) ; Title-page, as above (verso blank), pp. (iii, iv) ; List of *Contents*, pp. v-vii ; p. (viii) blank ; *Introduction*, pp. ix-xii ; Divisional fly-title, *Book The First / Metaphysics* (verso blank), pp. (1, 2) ; Text, pp. 3-246 ; Printers' imprint on p. (246), *Printed by R. & R. Clark, Limited, Edinburgh* There follows one leaf, blank on recto (verso, advertisement of *New Worlds / For Old*

Issued in blue-grey cloth, lettered across the back in gilt with gilt lines, and across the front cover in black within black double border lines. Back: (2 lines) / *First / and / Last / Things / H. G. / Wells / London / Constable /* (2 lines) Front cover : *First & Last Things / A Confession of Faith / and Rule of Life / H. G. Wells* Back cover has blind double line border. Top and fore edges uncut, lower edges untrimmed. White end-papers.

Book I of this volume is mainly an expansion of the author's essay *Scepticism of the Instrument* (see *A Modern Utopia*) : sections 5, 6, 7, and 9 are mainly quotation from it. Portions of Books III and IV were first printed in The Independent Magazine (July and August 1908).

In 1917, after the publication of *God the Invisible King*, a new edition was issued by Cassell & Co., London, in Demy 8vo form with a new Preface and with a Title-page as follows :

(36a)

First and Last Things / A Confession of Faith and Rule of a Life / By / H. G. Wells / Revised and Enlarged Edition / Cassell and Company, Ltd / London, New York, Toronto and Melbourne

There were xviii + 234 pp., bound in dark blue cloth with gilt lettering and ornaments on back and front cover, blind ornamental border on front cover. All edges cut. White end-papers.

The main points of difference between this and the original edition are the omission in the later edition of sections 2 and 12 in Book I and section 15 in Book II, the addition of a Preface, of sections 2, 12, 13, 14, 15 in Book I and section 15 in Book II and of 2½ pages to section 11 in Book III, and a few minor deletions and alterations of words and phrases.

(37)

TONO-BUNGAY :   1909

Tono-Bungay / By / H. G. Wells / Macmillan And Co., Limited / St. Martin's Street, London / 1909

Crown 8vo ; pp. iv + 494, consisting of Half-title, *Tono-Bungay* (verso, titles, etc, of two *Other Novels By H. G. Wells*), pp. (i, ii) ; Title-page, as above (verso, in centre, publishers' device followed by : *Macmillan And Co., Limited | London. Bombay. Calcutta | Melbourne | The Macmillan Company | New York. Boston. Chicago | Atlanta. San Francisco | The Macmillan Co. Of Canada, Ltd. | Toronto*), pp. (iii, iv) ; Divisional fly-title, *Book The First | The Days Before Tono-Bungay | Was Invented* (verso blank), pp. (1, 2) ; Text, pp. 3-493 ; Printers' imprint at foot of p. 493 under a line, *Printed By William Clowes And Sons, Limited, London And Beccles.* ; p. (494) blank. There follow 8 pages of publishers' advertisements, dated 1.09.

Issued in light green cloth, lettered, with designs in gilt across back and front cover, with blind designs on front cover. Back : *Tono- | Bungay | (ornament) | H · G · | Wells* (all within design which continues almost to foot) | *Macmillan* (within decorative panel) Front cover : *Tono-Bungay | (ornament) | H · G · Wells* (all within panel of the blind design) Top edges gilt, others trimmed. White end-papers.

A later issue of the first edition has the pages of publishers' advertisements dated 2.09.

After being rejected by many big newspapers, this novel was first printed serially in The English Review (Dec. 1908-March 1909), being one (according to report) of the dozen or so works by various authors to publish each one of which that paper was specially founded !

(38)

ANN VERONICA : 1909

Ann Veronica / A Modern Love Story / By / H. G. Wells / London : T. Fisher Unwin / Adelphi Terrace. MCMIX

Crown 8vo ; pp. 352, consisting of Half-title, *Ann Veronica* (verso blank), pp. (1, 2) ; Title-page, as above (verso, Dedication, *To | A.J.*, and beneath, (*All Rights Reserved.*)), pp. (3, 4) ; List of *Contents*, pp. 5, 6 ; Text, pp. 7-352 ; Printers' imprint at foot of p. 352 under line, *Unwin Brothers, Limited, The Gresham Press, Woking And London.*

Issued in red brown cloth, lettered in gilt across back and front cover, with gilt design on front cover. Back : *Ann | Veronica | By | H. G. Wells | T · Fisher · Unwin* Front cover : *Ann Veronica | H. G. Wells | (design)* All edges cut. White end-papers.

It is amusing, if a little mystifying, to recall the stir caused by this book upon its original publication. One obscure Canon, doubtless with an eye on the " publicity " possibilities, declared that " I would as soon send a daughter of mine to a house infected with diphtheria or typhoid fever as put that book into her hands." The local demand rose immediately from no to several copies a day !

(39)

THE HISTORY OF MR. POLLY : 1910

The History / Of Mr. Polly / By H. G. Wells / (line) / (device) / (line) / Thomas Nelson And Sons / London, Edinburgh, Dublin, / . . And New York . . / Leipzig : 35-37 Königstrasse. Paris : 61 Rue des Saints Pères. (all enclosed in double line border, ruled twice across as indicated)

Crown 8vo ; pp. 374, consisting of Frontispiece, not reckoned in the pagination ; Title-page, as above (verso, First Published 1910.), pp. (1, 2) ; List of books By The Same Author. (verso blank), pp. (3, 4) ; List of Contents (verso blank), pp. (5, 6) ; Text, pp. (7)-374. There follow 10 pages of Notes on Nelson's New Novels, with imprint on the last, Established 1798 / (design) / T. Nelson / And Sons / Printers And / Publishers

Issued in green cloth, with white panel and gilt lettering and double line border on back. The lettering is across the panel as follows : The / History / Of Mr. / Polly / (decoration) / H. G. Wells / Nelson All edges cut. The end-papers are white, with designs and monogram in green.

(40)

THE NEW MACHIAVELLI : 1911

: : The New : : / Machiavelli / By / H. G. Wells / " A closer examination . . . shows that Abelard was a / Nominalist under a new name." / G. H. Lewes, Hist. Philos. / " It suffices for our immediate purpose that tender- / minded and tough-minded people . . . do both exist." / William James, Pragmatism. / John Lane The Bodley Head / Vigo Street London W. MCMXI

Crown 8vo ; pp. viii + 528, consisting of Half-title, The New Machiavelli (verso, list of books Mr. Wells has also written), pp. (i, ii) ; Title-page, as above (verso, at foot, printers' imprint, William Clowes And Sons, Limited, London And Beccles.), pp. (iii, iv) ; List of Contents (verso blank), pp. (v, vi) ; Fly-title, The New Machiavelli (verso blank), pp. (vii, viii) ; Divisional fly-title, Book The First / The Making Of A Man (verso blank), pp. (1, 2) ; Text, pp. 3-528. There follow 30 pages of publisher's advertisements.

Issued in red cloth, lettered in gilt across back with white border lines, and in white across the front cover with white lines. Back : The New / Machiavelli / by / H. G. Wells (all within panel, top line of which is ornamental, others plain) / (ornamented panel) / The Bodley Head (within panel) Front cover : The New / Machiavelli / By H. G. Wells. (all within ornamental double line panel) Top edges stained red to match binding, other edges uncut. White end-papers.

This novel was first printed serially in The English Review (May-Oct. 1910). When the book was published in January 1911 H. G. Wells was attacked for his alleged introduction into his story of prominent politicians and other well-known figures. This charge was definitely repudiated by Mr. Wells in an interview published in The Bodleian (Jan. 1911) under the title *A Select Conversation*, by Ralph Straus. At Mr. Wells's own suggestion a copy of this interview was sent out with each review copy of the book, but certain critics apparently saw fit to ignore it.

(41)

THE COUNTRY OF THE BLIND: 1911

The Country / Of The Blind / And Other Stories / By / H. G. Wells / (*line*) / ((*device*) / (*line*) / Thomas Nelson and Sons / London, Edinburgh, Dublin, / Leeds, and New York / Leipzig : 35-37 Königstrasse. Paris : 189, rue Saint-Jacques (*all within double line border, ruled twice across as indicated*)

Crown 8vo ; pp. 576, consisting of Frontispiece not reckoned in pagination ; Title-page, as above (verso blank), pp. (i ii) ; *Introduction*, pp. (iii)-ix ; p. (x) blank ; List of *Contents*, pp. (xi), xii ; Fly-title, *The Country Of The Blind / And Other Stories.* (verso blank), pp. (xiii, xiv) ; Text, pp. (15)-574 ; p. (575) has imprint, *Established* 1798 / (design) / *T. Nelson / And Sons / Printers And / Publishers* p. (576) blank.

Issued in dark blue cloth, lettered in gilt across back with blind design, and blind across front cover within panel of blind design. Back : *The / Country / Of The / Blind, / Etc. / H. G. Wells / Nelson* (within blind panels) Front cover : *The Country / Of The Blind. / And Other Stories / H. G. Wells* All edges cut. The end-papers are white, with designs and monogram in green.

This volume of thirty-three tales contains " all the short stories by me that I care for anyone to read again " (*Introduction*). Eight are reprinted from *The Stolen Bacillus and Other Incidents*, ten from *The Plattner Story and Others*, three from *Tales of Space and Time*, and seven from *Twelve Stories and a Dream*, while five (Nos. XXII, XXX, XXXI, XXXII, and XXXIII) are here printed in a book for the first time. These five are *A Vision of Judgment* (first printed in The Butterfly, Sept., 1899), *The Empire of the Ants* (The Strand Magazine, Dec. 1905), *The Door in the Wall* (The Daily Chronicle, Summer No., July 14th 1906), *The Country of the Blind* (The Strand Magazine, April 1904), and *The Beautiful Suit* (Collier's Weekly, in April 1909, under the title *A Moonlight Fable*).

The Door in the Wall is often selected as H. G. Wells's best short story, and has been reprinted in at least one anthology (*Thirty One Stories by Thirty and One Authors*, Edited by Ernest Rhys and C. A. Dawson Scott. Butterworth, London. 1923. Pp. 11-30).

The Country of the Blind, which comes close to it in favour, was printed in a booklet with *This Misery of Boots* by The Appeal Publishing Co., Girard, Kansas in 1922 as follows :

(41a)

People's Pocket Series No. 161 / Edited by E. Haldeman-Julius / The Country of / the Blind / By H. G. Wells / Appeal Publishing Company / Girard, Kansas.

> Pp. 64 (5″ x 3½″), consisting of Title-page, as above (verso blank, pp. (1, 2) ; Text, pp. (3)-40 ; Text of *This Misery of Boots,* pp. 41-62 ; Blank leaf.

> Issued in blue paper wrappers, pinned, lettered in black on front cover, *Appeal Pocket Series No. 161 / Edited by E. Haldeman-Julius / . . .* (as Title-page) . . . All edges cut.

About 1912 it was arranged that Ralph Straus should print a large quarto edition of *The Country of the Blind* on his private press and for private circulation. About one page was set up by Mr. Straus in great primer type, and Vernon Hill did several sketches for illustrations. But no more was done in the matter and the sketches and a proof-pull of the one page are all that are left of the endeavour. At Christmas, 1915, a privately printed edition of this one story with a photograph by A. L. Coburn was issued in New York. In 1922-3 Collins, London issued three cheap volumes containing altogether fifty-three short stories selected and arranged by J. D. Beresford from the various volumes of tales by H. G. Wells. The titles of the volumes are *Tales of the Unexpected, Tales of Life and Adventure,* and *Tales of Wonder.*

(42)

FLOOR GAMES :   1911

Floor Games / By / H. G. Wells / With Marginal Drawings By / J. R. Sinclair / *(device)* / London / Frank Palmer / 12-14 Red Lion Court *(all enclosed in blue border line)*

> Super Royal 8vo ; pp. 72, consisting of Half-title, *Floor Games* (verso, list of books *Mr Wells has also written*), pp. (1, 2) ; Frontispiece not reckoned in the pagination ; Title-page, as above (verso, in centre, *All Rights Reserved, First Published December* 1911), pp. (3, 4) ; List of *Contents* (verso, drawing), pp. (5, 6) ; Divisional fly-title, *Section I / The Toys To Have* (verso, drawing), pp. (7, 8) ; Text, pp. (9)-71 ; p. (72) has Printers' imprint, *Printed By / Neill And Company, Edinburgh.* There are seven plates (in addition to the frontispiece) : these face pp. 16, 24, 32, (40), 48, 56, (64).

Issued in dark blue cloth, lettered in buff along back and across front
cover, with a blind line border on front cover.   Back : *Floor Games :
H. G. Wells.*   Front cover : *Floor | Games |* (coloured plate reproduced
from photograph) / *H. G. Wells* All edges cut.   White end-papers.

The usual height of this book is just under $8\frac{1}{2}''$: some copies of it are
$\frac{1}{2}''$ taller, being otherwise identical.

The text of this book was first printed in The Strand Magazine (Dec.
1911).   A publisher's note states that it " was the description of the boy's
floor games " in *The New Machiavelli* which " led Mr. Palmer to suggest
a book on Floor Games to Mr Wells."   The eight photographs are by
H. G. Wells.   It may be noted that the two boys in the front cover plate
are Mr. Wells's sons, the G.P.W. (left) and F.R.W. mentioned in the text.

(43)

THE DOOR IN THE WALL : 1911

The Door / In The Wall / And Other Stories / By / H. G. Wells / Illustrated / With Photogravures From / Photographs By / Alvin Langdon
Coburn / *(device)* / New York & London / Mitchell Kennerley / MCMXI

Small Post Folio ; pp. iv + 156, consisting of a blank leaf not reckoned
in the pagination ; Half-title, *The Door In The Wall And Other
Stories* (verso blank), pp. (i, ii) ; Frontispiece, pp. (iii, iv) ; Title-page,
as above (verso, in centre, *Copyright* 1911 *by Mitchell Kennerley* and at
the foot, *The Village Press*), pp. (1, 2) ; Lists of *Contents* and of
Illustrations (verso blank), pp. (3, 4) ; Text, pp. (5)-153 ; p. (154)
blank ; Printers' imprint at head of p. (155), *THIS book has been set
up by Bertha S. Goudy at the Village Press, New | York, with types and
decorations designed by Frederic W. Goudy, under | whose supervision
it has been printed by Norman T. A. Munder & | Company, Baltimore,
U. S. A. | Six hundred copies printed on French hand-made paper, in
November, | 1911, and the types distributed.*   p. (156) blank ; one
blank leaf follows, not reckoned in the pagination.   There are 9
illustrations (in addition to the frontispiece) which are pasted on the
otherwise blank pp. 14, 31, 50, 79, 92, 100, 114, 131, 148.

Issued in reddish brown boards with grey canvas backing.   The back
is lettered in black along a white paper label, *The Door In The Wall*
The front cover is lettered across in gilt, *The Door in | the Wall | By
H·G·Wells And | Alvin Langdon Coburn* Top edges trimmed, others
uncut.   White end-papers.

As stated in the printers' imprint 600 copies of this book were printed in
Nov. 1911, and the types distributed.   In Jan. 1915, 60 of these 600 copies,
signed by both author and illustrator, were issued in Great Britain by
Grant Richards, Ltd., London, with a Title-page as follows :

(43a)

The Door / In The Wall / And Other Stories / By / H. G. Wells /
Illustrated / With Photogravures From / Photographs by / Alvin / Langdon Coburn / (*device*) / London / Grant Richards Ltd. / Publishers.

Otherwise the collation is exactly similar to that of the American issue
as given above, except that the verso of the blank leaf before the Half-title
has an inscription in ink : *This edition is limited to sixty copies / for the
United Kingdom. January* 1915. / No. . . . with the two signatures
beneath *H. G. Wells / Alvin Langdon Coburn* This British edition is,
however, issued in light brown boards.

All the eight stories in this volume were taken from previous collections,
every one, with one exception, having been included in *The Country of the
Blind and Other Stories.* The exception is *The Diamond Maker*, which is
reprinted from *The Stolen Bacillus and Other Incidents.* The stories are
*The Door in the Wall, The Star, A Dream of Armageddon, The Cone, A
Moonlight Fable* (original title of *The Beautiful Suit*), *The Diamond Maker,
The Lord of the Dynamos,* and *The Country of the Blind.*

(44)

THE GREAT STATE : 1912

The / Great State / Essays In Construction / By / H. G. Wells, Frances
Evelyn Warwick / L. G. Chiozza Money, E. Ray Lankester / C. J. Bond,
E. S. P. Haynes, Cecil Chesterton / Cicely Hamilton, Roger Fry, G. R.
S. Taylor / Conrad Noel, Herbert Trench, Hugh P. Vowles / (*device*) /
London and New York / Harper & Brothers / 45 Albemarle Street, W. /
1912

Crown 8vo ; pp. vi + 380, consisting of blank leaf not in pagination ;
Title-page, as above (verso, *Copyright*, 1911, 1912, *By Harper &
Brothers / Published May*, 1912), pp. (i, ii) ; List of *Contents* (verso
blank), pp. (iii, iv) ; *Prefatory Note*, signed *E.W. / G.R.S.T. / H.G.W.*,
pp. v, (vi) ; Divisional fly-title, *The Past And The Great State / By
H. G. Wells* (verso blank), pp. (1, 2) ; Text, pp. 3-(379) ; Printers'
imprint on p. (380), *Printed By / William Clowes And Sons, Limited, /
London And Beccles.*

Issued in red cloth, lettered in gilt across back, and in black across front
cover, with blind line borders on front and back covers. Back :
The / Great / State / Harpers Front cover : *The / Great State / H. G.
Wells* (ornament) / *Countess Of Warwick / L. G. Chiozza Money /
E. Ray Lankester / C. J. Bond* (ornament) / *E. S. P. Haynes / Cecil
Chesterton / Cicely Hamilton / Roger Fry* (ornament) / *G. R. S. Taylor /
Conrad Noel / Herbert Trench / Hugh P. Vowles* Top and fore edges
cut. White end-papers

H. G. Wells was one of the three editors of this symposium, and it was upon his essay that those of the other contributors were based. Here printed as the first in the book, under the title *The Past and the Great State*, and filling pp. (1)-46, it was originally published in Harper's magazine (in 1911) as *Socialism and the Great State*. It is again reprinted as the seventh essay in *An Englishman Looks at the World*. The American edition (Harper & Bros., New York, 1914) has the title *Socialism and the Great State*.

(45)

THE LABOUR UNREST : 1912

(*portrait*) / H. G. Wells. / The Labour / Unrest. / (*short line*) / By H. G. Wells. / (*short line*) / Price One Penny / (*short line*) / Reprinted from / " The Daily Mail." (*all enclosed in double line border*)

    4to (8″ x 4″) ; pp. 32, consisting of Text, pp. (1)-32, headed on p. (1), *Reprinted from* " *The Daily Mail.*" / *The Labour Unrest* / (short line) / *By H. G. Wells.* / (short line) / (unsigned introductory note) / (short line) / *I.—Distrust.* / (short line). Copyright note at foot of p. (1) under a thin line, *Copyright in U.S.A. Translation rights reserved.* ; Printers' imprint at foot of p. 32 under a thin line, *Printed and Published by the Associated Newspapers, Ltd.,* / *London. E.C.*

    Issued as a pamphlet in yellow paper wrappers, lettered across in black. P. (i) is Title-page, as above ; pp. (ii-iv) contain publishers' advertisements. All edges trimmed.

The six articles which make up this pamphlet were first printed under the general title of *The Labour Unrest* in The Daily Mail (May 13th, 14th, 15th, 16th, 18th and 20th, 1912). They were again reprinted, with the discussion which they provoked and with two new articles in the volume *What the Worker Wants* (q.v. in Bib. II, 1912), and also as the sixth essay in *An Englishman Looks at the World*.

(46)

MARRIAGE : 1912

Marriage / By / H. G. Wells / " And the Poor Dears haven't the shadow of a doubt they / will live happily ever afterwards." / *From a Private Letter* / Macmillan And Co., Limited / St. Martin's Street, London / 1912

    Crown 8vo ; pp. viii + 552, consisting of Half-title, *Marriage* (verso, list of books *Mr. Wells has also written*), pp. (i, ii) ; Title-page, as above (verso, in centre, *Copyright* and at the foot, *Printed By William Clowes And Sons, Limited, London And Beccles.*), pp. (iii, iv) ; Dedication,

Fraternally / To / Arnold Benn'tt (verso blank), pp. (v, vi) ; List of *Contents* (verso blank), pp. (vii, viii) ; Divisional fly-title, *Book The First / Marjorie Marries* (verso blank), pp. (1, 2) ; Text, pp. 3-551 ; Printers' imprint at foot of p. 551 under line as on verso of title-page ; p. (552) blank.   There follow 8 pages of publishers' advertisements.

Issued in sage green cloth, lettered in gilt across back and front cover, with blind designs on back and front cover.   Back : *Marriage / H. G. Wells / Macmillan & Co.*   Front cover : *Marriage / H. G. Wells*   Top edges gilt, other edges cut.   White end-papers.

(47)

WAR AND COMMON SENSE : 1913

War / And / Common Sense. / By H. G. Wells. / *(ornament) / Reprinted from the " Daily Mail."*

4to (8″ x 4″) ; pp. 24, consisting of Title-page, as above (verso blank), pp. (1, 2) ; unsigned Introduction, *Mr. Wells / And War.*, pp. 3, 4 ; Text, pp. 5-23 ; Printers' imprint in centre of p. (24), *Printed and Published by the Associated Newspapers, Ltd., / London, E.C.*

Issued as a pamphlet in light blue paper wrappers, front and back covers lettered in black.   Front cover : (portrait) */ H. G. Wells. / War / And / Common Sense. / By H. G. Wells. /* (short line) */ Price One Penny. /* (short line) */ Reprinted from / " The Daily Mail."* (all enclosed in a double line border).   Back cover has a publishers' advertisement. All edges trimmed.

The three articles which make up this pamphlet were first printed in The Daily Mail (April 7th, 8th, 9th, 1913).   They were again reprinted under the title *The Common Sense of Warfare* as the eighth essay in *An Englishman Looks at the World.*

(48)

LITTLE WARS : 1913

Little Wars (*in red*) / A Game For Boys / From Twelve Years Of Age To One Hundred And Fifty / And For That More Intelligent Sort Of Girls Who / Like Boy's Games And Books / With An Appendix On Kriegspiel / By / H. G. Wells / The Author Of / " Floor Games " / And Several Minor And Inferior Works / With Marginal Drawings By / J. R. Sinclair / (*device*) / London / Frank Palmer / Red Lion Court (*all enclosed in red line border*)

Super Royal Octavo ; pp. 112, consisting of Half-title, *Little Wars* (verso, advertisement of " Floor Games "), pp. (1, 2) ; Title-page, as above

(verso, *All Rights Reserved* / *First Published July* 1913), pp. (3, 4) ;
List of *Contents* (verso, *List Of* / *Full-Page Illustrations*), pp. (5, 6) ;
Text, pp. (7)-111 ; Printers' imprint at foot of p. 111 under a line,
Printed By Neill And Co., Ltd., Edinburgh. ; p. (112) blank.

Issued in dark red cloth, lettered in cream along back and across front
cover, with a blind line border on front cover. Back : *Little Wars :
By H. G. Wells* Front cover : *Little* / *Wars* / (coloured plate reproduced from photograph) / *H. G. Wells* All edges cut. White end-
papers.

As with *Floor Games*, the usual height of this book is just under 8½″ :
some copies are ½″ taller, being otherwise identical.

The contents of this volume were first printed in The Windsor Magazine
in two parts (Dec. 1912 and Jan. 1913). The nineteen photographs were
taken by Mrs. H. G. Wells.

(49)

THE PASSIONATE FRIENDS : 1913

The Passionate / Friends / A Novel / By / H. G. Wells / " There are at
least two sorts of women " . . . / Otto Limburger. / Macmillan And Co.,
Limited. / St. Martin's Street, London / 1913

Crown 8vo ; pp. viii + 356, consisting of Half-title, *The Passionate
Friends* (verso, list of books *Mr. Wells has also written*), pp. (i, ii) ;
Title-page, as above (verso, (device) / *Macmillan And Co., Limited* /
London . Bombay . Calcutta / *Melbourne* / *Copyright* / *Printed By
William Clowes And Sons Limited* / *London And Beccles*), pp. (iii, iv) ;
Dedication, *To* / *L. E. N. S.* (verso blank), pp. (v, vi) ; List of *Contents*
(verso blank), pp. (vii, viii) ; Text, pp. 1-356 ; Printers' imprint at
foot of p. 356 under a line, *Printed By William Clowes And Sons,
Limited, London And Beccles.* There follow 12 pages of publishers'
advertisements.

Issued in sage green cloth, lettered in gilt across back and front cover,
with blind designs on back and front cover. Back : *The* / *Passionate* /
Friends / *H. G. Wells* / *Macmillan & Co.* Front cover : *The* /
Passionate / *Friends* / *H. G. Wells* Top edges gilt, other edges cut.
White end-papers.

This story was first published serially in The Grand Magazine (March-
Nov. 1913).
A film version of the novel was produced by The Stoll Film Company
in 1922. The part of Stephen Stratton was taken by Milton Rosmer, and
other important characters by Mlle. Valia, Madge Stuart, Teddy Arundel
and Ralph Forster. Some stress was laid upon the " costliness " of the
stage settings.

(50)

AN ENGLISHMAN LOOKS AT THE WORLD: 1914

An Englishman Looks / at the World (*ornament*) Being a / Series of
Unrestrained Remarks / upon Contemporary Matters (*ornament*) / By /
H. G. Wells / (*ornament*) / Cassell and Company, Ltd / London, New York,
Toronto and Melbourne / 1914

> Demy 8vo ; pp. viii + 358, consisting of Half-title, *An Englishman
> Looks At / The World* (verso blank), pp. (i, ii) ; Title-page, as above
> (verso blank), pp. (iii, iv) ; Synopsis, pp. (v), vi ; List of *Contents*,
> pp. (vii), viii ; Text, pp. (1)-(357) ; p. (358) has printers' imprint,
> *Printed by / Cassell & Company, Limited, La Belle Sauvage, / London,
> E.C.* There follows one blank leaf.
> Issued in green cloth, lettered in gilt, with gilt designs, on back and front
> cover. Back : *An / Englishman / Looks at / the World / H. G. Wells /*
> (design) / *Cassell* Front cover : *An Englishman / Looks at the World /
> H. G. Wells /* (design) All edges cut. White end-papers.

Of these twenty-six essays one half (including the already published
series of articles on *The Labour Unrest* and *The Common Sense of Warfare*)
were first printed in The Daily Mail between 1904 and 1913 : ten more
appeared in nearly as many weekly and monthly papers between 1905 and
1914, while the three others had all had previous publication in volume
form, *The Great State* in the book of that name, *About Sir Thomas More*
as an introduction to an edition of More's Utopia (see Bib. III, 1905), and
The American Population in Harmsworth's Popular Educator (about 1909).
The American edition of this book (Harper & Bros., New York. 1914)
bore the title *Social Forces in England and America.*

(51)

THE WORLD SET FREE: 1914

The World Set / Free / A Story Of Mankind / By / H. G. Wells / Macmillan
And Co., Limited / St. Martin's Street, London / 1914

> Crown 8vo ; pp. viii + 286, consisting of Half-title, *The World Set Free*
> (verso, list of books *Mr. Wells has also written*), pp. (i, ii) ; Title-page,
> as above (verso, publishers' monogram) / (decorative line) / *Mac-
> millan And Co., Limited / London . Bombay . Calcutta / Melbourne /
> Copyright / Printed By William Clowes And Sons, Limited / London
> And Beccles*), pp. (iii, iv) ; Dedication *To / Frederick Soddy's / " Inter-
> pretation Of Radium " / This Story, Which Owes Long Passages / To
> The Eleventh Chapter Of / That Book, Acknowledges / And Inscribes /
> Itself* (verso blank), pp. (v, vi) ; List of *Contents* (verso blank), pp.
> (vii, viii) ; Text, pp. (1)-286. Printers' Imprint at foot of p. 286 under

thin line as follows : *Printed By William Clowes And Sons, Limited, London And Beccles.* There follow 2 numbered pages of publishers' advertisements of books *By H. G. Wells,* and 8 numbered pages of *Macmillan's / New Fiction*

Issued in green cloth, with blind designs on back and front cover, lettered across the back in gilt as follows : *The / World / Set Free / H. G. Wells / Macmillan & Co.,* and across the front cover in gilt as follows : *The / World / Set Free / H. G. Wells* Back cover blank. Top edges gilt fore and lower edges trimmed. White end-papers.

This story was first printed serially in The English Review (Dec. 1913-May 1914).

(52)

THE WIFE OF SIR ISAAC HARMAN : 1914

The Wife Of / Sir Isaac Harman / By / H. G. Wells / Macmillan And Co., Limited / St. Martin's Street, London / 1914

Crown 8vo ; pp. vi + 466, consisting of a blank leaf not reckoned in the pagination ; Half-title, *The Wife Of / Sir Isaac Harman* (verso, list of books *Mr. Wells has also written*), pp. (i, ii) ; Title-page, as above (verso, in centre, *Copyright* and at foot, *Printed By William Clowes And Sons, Limited, / London And Beccles.*), pp. (iii, iv) ; List of *Contents* (verso blank), pp. (v, vi) ; Text, pp. 1-465 ; Printers' imprint at foot of p. 465 under line, *Printed By William Clowes And Sons Limited, London And Beccles.* ; p. (466) blank. There follow 10 pages of publishers' advertisements.

Issued in sage green cloth, lettered in gilt, with blind designs, across back and front cover. Back : *The Wife / Of / Sir Isaac / Harman / H. G. Wells / Macmillan & Co.* Front cover : *The Wife / Of / Sir Isaac / Harman / H. G. Wells* Top edges gilt, other edges cut. White end-papers.

(53)

THE WAR THAT WILL END WAR : 1914

The War That / Will End War / By / H. G. Wells / Author of " The War of the Worlds," / " The War in the Air," etc. / (*design*) / London / Frank & Cecil Palmer / Red Lion Court, E.C.

Crown 8vo ; pp. 100, consisting of Half-title, *The War That / Will end War* (verso blank) ; pp. (1, 2) ; Title-page, as above (verso, in centre, *First Published September,* 1914), pp. (3, 4) ; List of *Contents* (verso blank), pp. (5, 6) ; Text, pp. (7)-99 ; p. (100) has a publishers' advertisement. There follow 2 leaves, the first 3 pages of which bear advertisements, the fourth being blank.

E

Issued in yellow paper wrappers, lettered in black on back and front cover. Back (along) : *The War That Will End War : H. G. Wells* (and then across) 1/- / *Net*; Front cover (across) : *The War | That Will | End War | By | H. G. Wells |* (short thick line) / (design) / *London : | Frank & Cecil Palmer, Red Lion Court.* (all within a thick line border). All edges cut.

The eleven articles which make up this volume all appeared in the London press between Aug. 7th and 29th, 1914 : six in The Daily Chronicle, three in The Nation, and one each in The Daily News and The War Illustrated

In 1915 Chapter XI, *The War of the Mind*, and the greater part of Chapter VII, *The Opportunity of Liberalism*, were reprinted as a pamphlet with a Title-page as follows :

(53a)

The War & / Socialism / By / H. G. Wells / One Penny. / The Clarion Press, / 44, Worship Street, London, E.C.

$7\frac{1}{4}''$ x $4\frac{3}{4}''$; pp. 12, consisting of Text, pp. (1)-(12) ; Printers' imprint at foot of p. (12) under a thin line, *The Utopia Press (T.U. and 48 hours)*, 44, *Worship Street, London, E.C.*

Issued in yellow paper wrappers, lettered in blue across covers. Front cover is Title-page, as above ; pp. (ii-iv) of covers have *Clarion Press* advertisements. All edges trimmed.

(53b)

Towards the end of 1914 a pamphlet by H. G. Wells, *End of the Armament Rings*, was issued by the World Peace Foundation, New York. I have never seen a copy of this, but have reason for believing it to be a reprint of one of the early War articles printed in the volume *The War that will End War*, probably that entitled *An Appeal to the American People*, or else *The Most Necessary Measures in the World*.

(54)

TIDSTANKAR : 1915

Tidstankar. / Af / H. G. Wells. / Från " The Nation." / London : / Harrison & Sons. / (*short line*) / 1915. (*all enclosed in double line border*)

$9\frac{2}{3}''$ x $6''$; pp. 16, consisting of Title-page, as above (verso blank), pp. (1, 2) ; Text, pp. (3)-15 ; p. (16) blank.

Issued as a pamphlet, without wrappers. All edges trimmed.

This pamphlet contains a Swedish translation of three articles first printed in The Nation in 1914. The contents are as follows : *Liberalernas Rädsla För / Ryssland.* (*The Liberal Fear of Russia*, Aug. 22nd), pp. (3)-7 ; *En Sinnenas Strid.* (*The War of the Mind*, Aug. 29th), pp. 7-11 ; *De Båda Vågarne.* (*The Two Ways*, Sept. 12th), pp. 12-15. The first two had already been reprinted in *The War That Will End War* ; the last is here reprinted for the first time.

(55)

THE PEACE OF THE WORLD: 1915

The Peace Of The / World / By / H. G. Wells / Author of / " The War of the Worlds," " The Time Machine," / and many Novels. / London / The Daily Chronicle / 12, Salisbury Square / Fleet Street, E.C.

Crown 8vo ; pp. 64, consisting of blank leaf, pp. (1, 2) ; blank page (publishers' design on verso), pp. (3, 4) ; Half-title, *The Peace Of The World* (verso blank), pp. (5, 6) ; Title-page, as above (verso blank), pp. (7, 8) ; Text, pp. 9-64 ; Printers' imprint at foot of p. 64 under a thin line, *United Newspapers, Ltd., Salisbury Square, London*

Issued in light grey paper wrappers, lettered in red across back and front cover. Back : *The / Peace / Of The / World / (ornament) / H. G. / Wells / The / Daily / Chronicle* ; Front cover : *The Peace / Of / The World / H. G. Wells.* / 6d. net All edges trimmed.

The first issue was on April 16th 1915, as above. On November 23rd of the same year just over 2300 copies with the same sheets were bound in orange brown cloth, lettered in black along the back and across the front cover. Back : The Peace Of The World H. G. Wells Front cover : The Peace / of / the World / H. G. Wells

This essay was first printed in The English Review (March 1915), as one of a series of essays by various authors published under the general title of *The War of Liberation.*

(56)

BOON: 1915

Boon, The Mind of the / Race, The Wild Asses of the / Devil, and The Last Trump / Being a First Selection from the / Literary Remains of George Boon, / Appropriate to the Times / Prepared for Publication by / Reginald Bliss / Author Of " The Cousins Of Charlotte / Bronte," " A Child's History Of The / Crystal Palace," " Firelight Rambles," / " Edible Fungi," " Whales in Captivity," / And Other Works / With / An Ambiguous Introduction by / H. G. Wells / T. Fisher Unwin, Ltd. / London : Adelphi Terrace

Crown 8vo ; pp. 344, consisting of Half-title, *Boon, The Mind Of | The Race, The Wild | Ass s Of The Devil, | and The Last Trump* (verso blank), pp. (1, 2) ; Title-page, as above (verso has *First published in 1915* in centre, and (*All rights reserved*) at foot), pp. (3, 4) ; *Introduction*, pp. 5, 6 ; List of *Contents*, pp. 7, 8 ; Text, pp. 9-342 ; Printers' imprint on p. (343), *The Gresham Press | Unwin Brothers, Limited | Woking And London* p. (344) blank.

Issued in dark green cloth, lettered in gilt across back and front cover, with gilt lines and designs. Back : *Boon | By | Reginald | Bliss | Introduced | By | H. G. Wells* (all within line panel) | (line-drawing) | *T · Fisher · Unwin* (in panel) Front cover : gilt line-drawing. Top edges gilt, others trimmed. White end-papers.

(56a)

In 1920 a second edition of this book was published in which H. G. Wells acknowledged the authorship of the volume. The text was the same, though in 320 pp. instead of 344 pp. The Title-page is the same except for the rearrangement *Prepared for Publication | by Reginald Bliss* and the addition after *H. G. Wells* of (*Who is in Truth the | Author of the entire Book*)

Crown 8vo ; pp. 320, consisting of Half-title, as before (verso, advertisement of *Ann Veronica*), pp. (1, 2) ; Title-page, as above (verso, in centre, *First published in 1915 | Second Impression 1915 | Second Edition 1920* and at foot (*All rights reserved*)), pp. (3, 4) ; *Introduction*, pp. 5, 6 ; List of *Contents*, pp. 7, 8 ; Text, pp. (9)-320 ; Printers' imprint at foot of p. 320, *Printed in Great Britain by | Unwin Brothers, Limited, The Gresham Press, Woking And London*

Issued in dark green cloth, lettered in gilt across the back only, within gilt line panels, *Boon | By | H. G. Wells* (all in panel) | *T. Fisher Unwin* (in panel) Top edges trimmed, others uncut.

Parts of this book were written in 1911, put on one side, taken up again in 1914 and prepared for publication with additions. The 26 sketches are by H. G. Wells.

Certain passages of the book caused some annoyance to the late Henry James. His correspondence with H. G. Wells, with the latter's reply, will be found, reprinted, in *The Letters of Henry James* (Macmillan & Co., London. 1920), Vol. II, pp. 503-508.

(57)

BEALBY : 1915

Bealby | A Holiday | By | H. G. Wells | Methuen & Co. Ltd. | 36 Essex Street W.C. | London

Crown 8vo ; pp. viii + 336, consisting of Half-title, *Bealby* (verso, list of books *By The Same Author*), pp. (i, ii) ; Title-page, as above (verso, *First Printed in* 1915), pp. (iii, iv) ; *Dedication And Note To The*

Reader, pp. v, vi ; List of *Contents* (verso blank), pp. vii, (viii) ; Text, pp. 1-336 ; Printers' imprint at foot of p. 336, *Printed by Morrison & Gibb Limited, Edinburgh* ; There follow 4 pages of publishers' advertisements dated *Spring*, 1915, and 31 numbered pages (p. (32) blank) of the publishers' *Selection Of Books*.

Issued in violet cloth, lettered in gilt across back with gilt design, and with blind lettering and design on the front cover. Back : *Bealby | By | H. G. | Wells* (all within line panel decorated top and bottom) | *Methuen* Front cover : *Bealby | By | H. G. | Wells* (all within circle design. Top and fore edges trimmed. White end-papers.

This story was first printed serially in The Grand Magazine (Aug. 1914— March 1915).

(58)

THE RESEARCH MAGNIFICENT : 1915

The Research / Magnificent / By / H. G. Wells / Macmillan And Co., Limited / St. Martin's Street, London / 1915

Crown 8vo ; pp. vi + 406, consisting of blank leaf not reckoned in the pagination ; Half-title, *The Research Magnificent* (verso, list of books *Mr. Wells has also written*), pp. (i, ii) ; Title-page, as above (verso, in centre, *Copyright* and at foot, *Printed By William Clowes And Sons, Limited, | London And Beccles.*), pp. (iii, iv) ; List of *Contents* (verso blank), pp. (v, vi) ; Divisional fly-title, *The Prelude* (verso blank), pp. (1, 2) ; Text, pp. 3-406 ; Printers' imprint at foot of p. 406 under a thin line, *Printed By William Clowes And Sons, Limited, London And Beccles.* There follow 2 numbered pages of publishers' advertisements of other books *By H. G. Wells* and 8 numbered pages of *New & Recent | Works Of Fiction* dated 15.8.15.

Issued in sage green cloth, lettered in gilt, with blind designs, across back and front cover. Back : *The | Research | Magnificent | H. G Wells | Macmillan & Co.* Front cover : *The | Research | Magnificent | H. G. Wells* All edges trimmed. White end-papers.

(59)

WHAT IS COMING ? : 1916

What is Coming ? / A Forecast of Things after the War / By / H. G. Wells / (*ornament*) / Cassell and Company, Ltd / London, New York, Toronto and Melbourne / 1916

Crown 8vo ; pp. vi + 296, consisting of blank leaf not reckoned in pagination ; Half-title, *What Is Coming ?* (verso, list of books *Mr. Wells has also written*), pp. (i, ii) ; Title-page, as above (verso blank),

pp. (iii, iv) ; List of *Contents* (verso blank), pp. (v, vi) ; Text, pp. 1-295 ; Printers' imprint on p. (296), *Printed by / Cassell & Company, Limited, La Belle Sauvage, / London, E.C. / F* 60.416 Issued in green cloth, lettered, with ornament, in gilt across back, and with blind lettering, ornament and line border on front cover. Back : *What / Is / Coming? /* (ornament) */ H. G. Wells / Cassell* Front cover : *What Is Coming? / A Forecast of Things / After the War /* (ornament) */ H. G. Wells* (all within blind single line border). All edges cut. White end-papers.

This book is in twelve chapters, of which I, III, V, IX, XII and XI were first printed serially in that order in Cassell's Magazine (Jan.-June 1916). II, IV and X appeared in The Daily Chronicle, and VII and VIII in The Daily News, all between January and May, 1916.

(60)

MR. BRITLING SEES IT THROUGH : 1916

Mr. Britling Sees It / Through / By / H. G. Wells / *(ornament) /* Cassell And Company, Ltd / London, New York, Toronto and Melbourne

Crown 8vo ; pp. vi + 434, consisting of blank leaf, not reckoned in the pagination ; Half-title, *Mr. Britling Sees It Through* (verso, list of books *Mr. Wells has also written*), pp. (i, ii) ; Title-page, as above (verso, *First Published* 1916), pp. (iii, iv) ; List of *Contents* (verso blank), pp. (v, vi) ; Divisional fly-title, *Book I / Matching's Easy at Ease* (verso blank), pp. (1, 2) ; Text, pp. (3)-433 ; Printers' imprint in centre of p. (434), *Printed by / Cassell & Company, Limited, La Belle Sauvage, / London, E.C. / F.*100.716 There follows one blank leaf. Issued in green cloth, lettered in gilt and blind across back, and blind across front cover, with blind designs on back and front cover. Back : *Mr. Britling / Sees It / Through / H. G. / Wells* (all gilt) */ Cassell* (blind) Front cover : *Mr. Britling / Sees It Through / H. G. Wells* (all within panel of blind design) Top and fore edges cut. White end-papers.

This story was first printed serially in The Nation (May-Oct. 1916). The scene of the incidents in this novel is, quite obviously, H. G. Wells's home in Essex, while many of the characters are drawn from actual people and are easily recognisable.

(61)

THE ELEMENTS OF RECONSTRUCTION : 1916

The Elements Of / Reconstruction / A Series Of Articles / Contributed In July / And August 1916 To / The Times / With An Introduction By /

Viscount Milner / (*device*) / London / Nisbet & Co. Ltd. / 22 Berners Street / W.

> Foolscap 8vo ; pp. 120, consisting of Half-title, *The Elements / Of Reconstruction* (verso blank), pp. (1, 2) ; Title-page, as above (verso, *First Published in* 1916), pp. (3, 4) ; List of *Contents* (verso blank), pp. (5,6) ; *Introduction*, pp. 7-26 ; Text, pp. 27-(120) ; Printers' imprint beneath thin line at foot of p. (120), *Spottiswoode, Ballantyne & Co. Ltd., Printers, London, / Colchester, and Eton.*

Issued in green paper wrappers, lettered in black. The back is lettered across at the foot 1/- / *Net* and then along, *The Elements Of Reconstruction* The front cover is lettered across within a double line border, *One Shilling Net / The Elements Of / Reconstruction / Reprinted From / The Times / With An Introduction / By / Viscount Milner / Nisbet & Co. Ltd.* Pp. (iii, iv) of covers have publishers' advertisements. All edges cut.

The contents of this volume were first printed in The Times (July 17th, 19th, 24th, 29th, Aug. 1st and 4th, 1916) as a series of letters to the editor, signed *D.P.* The first two impressions were anonymous, but in the third the authorship is acknowledged. Chapter I states that the book is the work of " two friends," and in the *Introduction* Viscount Milner refers to the " authors," but as a matter of fact the whole series was written by H. G. Wells only.

(62)

WAR AND THE FUTURE : 1917

War and the Future / Italy, France and Britain at War / By / H. G. Wells / (*ornament*) / Cassell And Company, Ltd / London, New York, Toronto and Melbourne / 1917

> Demy 8vo ; pp. vi + 298, consisting of blank leaf not reckoned in pagination ; Half-title, *War And The Future* (verso, list of books *Mr. Wells has also written*), pp. (i, ii) ; Title-page, as above (verso blank), pp. (iii, iv) ; List of *Contents* (verso blank), pp. (v, vi) ; Divisional fly-title, *The Passing Of The Effigy* (verso blank), pp. (1, 2) ; Text, pp. 3-297 ; Printers' imprint on p. (298), *Printed by / Cassell & Company, Limited, La Belle Sauvage, / London, E.C. / F* 40.117 There follows one leaf, recto of which bears an announcement of the author's forthcoming book " God the Invisible King " (verso blank).

Issued in dark red cloth, lettered, with ornament, in gilt across back, and with blind lettering and ornament on front cover. Back : *War / And The / Future / H. G. / Wells /* (ornament) / *Cassell* Front cover : *War / & / The Future / H. G. / Wells /* (ornament) All edges trimmed. White end-papers.

This book is in four parts. Part I was first printed in Cassell's Magazine (Dec. 1916), while portions of Parts III and IV appeared in The Daily Chronicle (Nov. 1916) and The Daily News (Dec. 1916-Jan. 1917) respectively.

The American edition (Macmillan Co., New York. 1917) is called *Italy, France and Britain at War.*

(63)

GOD THE INVISIBLE KING: 1917

God / The Invisible King / By / H. G. Wells / Cassell And Company, Ltd / London, New York, Toronto and Melbourne / 1917

Medium 8vo ; pp. xx + 206, consisting of Half-title, *God The Invisible King.* (verso, list of books *Mr. Wells has also written*), pp. (i, ii) ; Title-page, as above (verso blank), pp. (iii, iv) ; *Preface*, pp. v-xvii ; p. (xviii) blank ; List of *Contents* (verso blank), pp. (xix, xx) ; Text, pp. 1-206 ; Printers' imprint at foot of p. 206 under a thin line, *Printed by Cassell & Company, Limited, La Belle Sauvage, London, E.C.4* / F90.417 There follows one blank leaf.

Issued in dark blue cloth, lettered in gilt across back and front cover, with gilt lines on back and blind border line on front cover. Back : (2 lines) / *God The* / *Invisible* / *King* / *H. G. Wells* / *Cassell* / (2 lines) Front cover : *God* / *The Invisible* / *King* / *H. G. Wells* All edges cut. White end-papers.

(64)

A REASONABLE MAN'S PEACE: 1917

A / Reasonable / (*thick line*) / Man's Peace / (*thick line*) / By H. G. Wells. / (2 *lines*) / Reprinted from The Daily News & Leader, / Tuesday, August 14th, 1917. / (2 *lines*) / Price 1d. / Special quotation for quantities on application. / (2 *lines*) / The Daily News Limited, / London and Manchester. (*all within line border*)

Issued as a four page folder. Title-page, as above, p. (1) ; Text, pp. (2-4).

This leaflet was printed by The Daily News for The National Council for Civil Liberties, which distributed over 200,000 copies. The article was reprinted later as a four page folder 8⅛″ × 5⅜″ for The International Free Trade League, 28 Victoria Street, London, S.W.1. In this there is only a brief heading on p. (1), the text beginning immediately beneath and running on to the foot of page (4): printed at The Pelican Press, Gough Square, E.C.4. It was reprinted again as section 2 of Chapter 5 of *In the Fourth Year.*

(65)

THE SOUL OF A BISHOP: 1917

The / Soul of a Bishop / A Novel (with Just a Little Love in It) / about Conscience and Religion / and / The Real Troubles of Life / By / H. G. Wells / (ornament) / Cassell And Company, Ltd / London, New York, Toronto and Melbourne

Crown 8vo ; pp. viii + 320, consisting of Half-title, *The Soul Of A Bishop* (verso has list of books *Mr. Wells has also written*), pp. (i, ii) ; Title-page, as above (*First Impression September* 1917 in centre of verso), pp. (iii, iv) ; Quotation, " *Man's true Environment is God* " / J. H. Oldham in " The Christian Gospel " / (Tract of the N. M. R· and H.) (verso blank), pp. (v, vi) ; List of *Contents* (verso blank), pp. (vii, viii) ; Text, pp. (1)-320. Printers' imprint at foot of p. 320 under a thin line as follows : *Printed by Cassell & Company, Limited, La Belle Sauvage, London, E.C.4.* / *F*300.717

Issued in green cloth, lettered in gilt and blind across the back, blind lettering across the front cover, and blind designs on back and front cover. Back : *The Soul* / *Of A* / *Bishop* / *H. G.* / *Wells* (all gilt) / *Cassell* (blind) Front cover : *The Soul* / *Of A Bishop* / *H. G. Wells* (all within blind design) Top and fore edges cut, lower edges untrimmed. White end-papers.

This novel was first printed serially in Collier's Weekly (in 1917).

(66)

IN THE FOURTH YEAR: 1918

In the Fourth Year / Anticipations Of A World Peace / By / H. G. Wells / Author Of " Mr. Britling Sees It Through," / " The War And The Future," " What Is Coming ? " " The War That Will / End War," " The World Set Free," " In The Days Of / The Comet," And " A Modern Utopia " / London / Chatto & Windus / 1918

Crown 8vo ; pp. xii + 156, consisting of Half-title, *In The Fourth Year* (verso, list of books *Mr. Wells has also written*), pp. (i, ii) ; Title-page, as above (verso, in centre, Printers' imprint, *Printed In England By* / *William Clowes And Sons, Limited* / *London And Beccles* and at foot, *All rights reserved*), pp. (iii, iv) ; *Preface*, pp. v-x ; List of *Contents* (verso blank), pp. xi, (xii) ; Text, pp. (1)-156 ; Printers' imprint at foot of p. 156 under a thin line, *Printed In England By* / *William Clowes And Sons, Limited, London And Beccles.* There follow 32 numbered pages of the publishers' *Alphabetical Catalogue Of Books*

Issued in dark green cloth, lettered in lighter green across back and front cover, with blind lines on back and blind line border on front cover. Back : (line) / *In* / *The* / *Fourth* / *Year* / (dot) / *H. G.* / *Wells* / *Chatto* / *& Windus* / (line) Front cover : *In The Fourth Year* / *Anticipations Of A World Peace* / *H. G. Wells* Top and fore edges cut. White end-papers.

Most of the eleven chapters of this book were first printed under various titles in The Daily Mail, The Daily Chronicle, The Daily News, etc., in 1917 and the early months of 1918. Section 2 of Chapter V is a reprint of the Daily News article issued in 1917 as the pamphlet *A Reasonable Man's Peace* (q.v.).

In Nov. 1918 Chatto & Windus issued a small book of selections from *In the Fourth Year* for The League of Free Nations Association with the title of *Anticipations of A World Peace*, collated below :

(66a)

Anticipations / Of A World Peace / Selected And Abbreviated / From / " In The Fourth Year " / By / H. G. Wells / London / Chatto & Windus

Crown 8vo ; pp. vi + 78, consisting of Half-title, *Anticipations* / *Of A World Peace* (verso, list of books *Mr. Wells has also written*), pp. (i, ii) ; Title-page, as above (verso, *In The Fourth Year* / *First Published* . . . *June 6, 1918* / *Second Impression* . . . *June, 1918* / *Third Impression* . . . *July, 1918* / *Abridged Edition* (*Anticipations of a World Peace*) / *First published November,* 1918 / *All rights reserved* / *Printed In England By William Clowes And Sons, Limited,* / *London And Beccles*), pp. (iii, iv) ; List of *Contents* (verso blank), pp. (v, vi) ; Text, pp. (1)-73 ; pp. (74-78) have announcements of the objects, members, committees, publications, etc, of *The* / *League Of Free Nations* / *Association* Printers' imprint at foot of p. (78) under a thin line, *Printed In England By* / *William Clowes And Sons. Limited, London And Beccles.*

Issued in light blue-grey paper wrappers, lettered in red along back and across front and back covers, with red double line borders on front and back covers. Back : *A World Peace · H. G. Wells* Front cover : *Anticipations* / *Of A World Peace* / *Selected And Abbreviated* / *From* / *" In The Fourth Year "* / *By* / *H. G. Wells* (facsimile of signature) / *1/3* / *Net* / *Chatto & Windus* / *The League Of Free Nations Association* Back cover : publishers' list of *New And Important Publications* All edges trimmed.

This propaganda volume contains most of Chapter I of *In the Fourth Year*, about half of II, all of III, the gist of V, most of VI and VIII, and a fragment of XI. It was published at 1/3 net, but soon remaindered at 6d. In some copies p. (78) is so badly printed as to be almost blank.

(67)

JOAN AND PETER: 1918

Joan And Peter / The Story of an Education / By / H. G. Wells / (*decoration*) / Cassell And Company, Ltd / London, New York, Toronto and Melbourne

Crown 8vo ; pp. viii + 748, consisting of Half-title, *Joan And Peter* (verso, list of books *Mr. Wells has also written*), pp. (i, ii) ; Title-page (verso *First Published* 1918 in centre), pp. (iii, iv) ; Dedication *To* / *P & J* (verso blank), pp. (v, vi) ; List of *Contents* (verso blank), pp. (vii, viii) ; Text, pp. (1)-748. Printers' imprint at foot of p. 748 beneath a thin line, *Printed by Cassell & Company, Limited, La Belle Sauvage, London, E.C.4* / *F.150.818*
Issued in green cloth, with blind designs on back and front cover. The back is lettered across as follows : *Joan* / *And* / *Peter* / *H. G. Wells* (all gilt) / *Cassell* (blind) The front cover has blind lettering within the design as follows : *Joan And Peter* / *H. G. Wells* All edges trimmed. White end-papers.

Parts of this story were first printed serially in The New Republic (in 1918) : two excerpts appeared in The Daily News under the title *Peter Flies*.

(68)

THE UNDYING FIRE: 1919

The Undying Fire / A Contemporary Novel / By / H. G. Wells / Cassell And Company, Ltd / London, New York, Toronto and Melbourne

Crown 8vo ; pp. viii + 254, consisting of Half-title, *The Undying Fire* (verso has list of books *Mr. Wells has also written*), pp. (i, ii) ; Title-page (verso blank), pp. (iii, iv) ; Dedication *To* / *All Schoolmasters and Schoolmistresses* / *and every* / *Teacher in the World* (verso blank), pp. (v, vi) ; List of *Contents* (verso blank), pp. (vii, viii) ; Text, pp. (1)-253. Printers' imprint in centre of p. (254) as follows : *Printed by* / *Cassell & Company, Limited, La Belle Sauvage,* / *London, E.C.4* / *F. 200419*
Issued in green cloth, with blind designs on back and front cover. The back is lettered across as follows : *The* / *Undying* / *Fire* / *H. G.* / *Wells* (all gilt) / *Cassell* (blind) The front cover has blind lettering within the design as follows : *The* / *Undying Fire* / *H. G. Wells* Top and fore edges are trimmed, lower edges untrimmed. White end-papers.

This story was first printed serially in The International Review (March-June 1919).

(69)

HISTORY IS ONE: 1919

History Is One / By / H. G. Wells (*all within decorative and double-line borders*)

8vo (8⅜ " x 5⁹⁄₁₀ ") ; pp. 16, consisting of Title-page, as above (verso, in centre, *Reprinted by Ginn And Company | From the Saturday Evening Post | (Copyright, 1919, by the Curtis Publishing Company)*, and at foot, *This article has been reprinted through the courtesy | of Mr. H. G. Wells, who kindly revised the proof | 704-11, 19*), pp. (1, 2) ; Text, pp. (3-15) ; p. (16) is blank.
Issued as a pamphlet, without covers. All edges trimmed. None of the pages are numbered in any way.

This article was first printed in the first two numbers of John o' London's Weekly (April 12th and 19th, 1919). It is reprinted with one or two minor alterations, but none of practical value.

(70)

THE OUTLINE OF HISTORY : 1920

The Outline / Of History / Being A Plain History / Of Life And Mankind / By H. G. Wells / (*double line*) / Written with the advice and / : editorial help of : / Mr. Ernest Barker / Sir H. H. Johnston / Sir E. Ray Lankester / and Professor Gilbert / Murray. / (*double line*) / London / George Newnes Limited / Southampton St. Strand W.C.2. (*all within ornamental border, ruled twice across with double lines as indicated*)
(*Title-page of Volume II as that of Volume I, given above, with the addition of the words* Volume Two *immediately beneath* Murray.)

2 Vols., Demy 4to.
Volume I : pp. viii + 384, consisting of Frontispiece, pp. (i, ii) ; Title-page, as above (verso blank), pp. (iii, iv) ; List of *Contents Of Volume One*, pp. (v, vi) ; List of *Colour Plates To Volume One* (verso blank), pp. (vii, viii) ; *Introduction*, pp. 1-3 ; Text, pp. 4-384.
Volume II ; pp. viii + 396, consisting of Frontispiece, pp. (i, ii) ; Title-page, as above (verso blank), pp. (iii, iv) ; List of *Contents Of Volume Two* (verso blank), pp. (v, vi) ; List of *Colour Plates To Volume Two* (verso blank), pp. (vii, viii) ; Text, pp. 385-761 ; *Notes And Errata* and *Key To Pronunciation*, p. 762 ; *Index*, pp. 763-780 ; Printers' imprint at foot of p. 780 under a thin line, *Printed by Hazell, Watson & Viney, Ld., London and Aylesbury.*
Issued in green linen, half morocco, lettered in gilt across back, with plain and decorated gilt line panels : (gilt line) / (decorated panel) / The / Outline / Of / History (all in panel) / (decorated panel) / H. G. Wells / (short line) / Vol. I (Vol. II.) (all in panel) / (decorated panel) / (decorated panel) / (2 gilt lines) All edges cut. Light green marbled end-papers.

This history was first printed serially in 24 fortnightly parts by George Newnes, Ltd., (Nov. 1919–Nov. 1920). Volume I, as above (Parts I-XII) was published in July 1920, and Volume II, as above (Parts XIII-XXIV) in Nov. 1920. This edition, which consists of the sheets of the parts bound together, contains some hundreds of photographic illustrations, many drawings, maps, and time-diagrams by J. F. Horrabin, and 47 coloured drawings by various artists. This is the Library Edition.

In Sept. 1920, Cassell & Co., London, issued the full text of *The Outline of History* (with certain minor revisions) in one volume, retaining the drawings, etc. by J. F. Horrabin but omitting the illustrations and coloured plates, which were supplied by the publishers of the first edition. This one-volume text, known as the Reader's Edition, is fully collated below.

(70a)

The Outline / Of History / Being a Plain History of Life and Mankind / By / H. G. Wells / Written with the Advice and Editorial Help of / Mr. Ernest Barker, Sir H. H. Johnston, / Sir E. Ray Lankester, and Professor / Gilbert Murray / And Illustrated by J. F. Horrabin / Revised And Corrected Edition / (With Several New Maps and Diagrams) / Cassell And Company, Ltd / London, New York, Toronto and Melbourne / 1920 (*all within black line border*)

Imperial 8vo ; pp. xx + 652, consisting of Half-title, *The Outline Of History* (verso, list of books *Mr. Wells has also written*), pp. (i, ii) ; Title-page, as above (verso blank), pp. (iii, iv) ; *Introduction*, pp. (v)-vii ; p. (viii) blank ; *Scheme Of Contents*, pp. (ix)-xv ; *List Of Maps And Illustrations*, pp. (xvi)-xx ; Divisional fly-title, *Book I / The Making Of Our World* (verso blank), pp. (1, 2) ; Text, pp. (3)-608 ; Divisional fly-title, *Time Charts / And / Chronological Table* (verso blank), pp. (609, 610) ; Text, pp. (611-625) ; Divisional fly-title. *Index* (verso, *Key To Pronunciation*), pp. (627, 628) ; *Index*, pp. 629-652 ; Printers' imprint at foot of p. 652 under a thin line, *Printed by Cassell & Company, Limited, La Belle Sauvage, London, E.C.4.* / F.150.820

Issued in black cloth, lettered in gilt across back and front cover, with gilt lines on back and blind line border on front cover. Back: (2 lines) / The / Outline / Of / History / H·G·Wells / Cassell / (2 lines) Front cover : *The Outline / Of History / H·G·Wells* All edges cut. White end-papers.

Several new editions with further revisions were published in the next two years in England and America, some of them being specially illustrated or bound in more volumes. The most important of all these reissues was that of the Definitive Edition of the Cassell's Reader's Edition in 1923, this containing the final corrections and rearrangements. It is fully collated below.

(70b)

The Outline / Of History / Being a Plain History of Life and Mankind / By / H. G. Wells / Written with the Advice and Editorial Help of / Dr. Ernest Barker, Sir H. H. Johnston, / Sir E. Ray Lankester, and Professor / Gilbert Murray / And Illustrated by J. F. Horrabin / The Definitive Edition / Revised and Rearranged by the Author / (With Several New Illustrations) / Cassell And Company, Ltd / London, New York, Toronto and Melbourne (*all within black line border*)

> Imperial 8vo ; pp. xx + 632, consisting of Half-title, *The Outline Of History* (verso, list of books *Mr. Wells has also written*), pp. (i, ii) ; Title-page, as above (verso, in centre, *First published September* 1920 / *Reprinted February* 1921. / *Definitive Edition January* 1923. and at foot *Printed in Great Britain*), pp. (iii, iv) ; *Introduction*, pp. v, vi ; *Scheme Of Contents*, pp. vii-xiii ; p. (xiv) blank ; *List Of Maps And Illustrations*, pp. xv-xix ; p. (xx) blank ; Divisional fly-title, *Book I / The Making Of Our World* (verso blank), pp. (1, 2) ; Text, pp. 3-590 ; Divisional fly-title, *Chronological Table / And / Time Charts* (verso blank), pp. (591, 592) ; Text, pp. 593-606 ; Divisional fly-title, *Index* (verso, *Key To Pronunciation*), pp. (607, 608) ; Index, pp. 609-631 ; Printers' imprint in centre of p. (632), *Printed by / Cassell & Company, Limited,* / *London,* E.C.4. / 50.1222
>
> Issued exactly as the Reader's Edition, collated above.

The Outline of History has also been published in several volumes in Braille type for the blind.

For several years before he began it, H. G. Wells had had the idea of such a history in his mind, but he was brought to the actual writing of it by his work as a member of the League of Nations Union. Convinced of its necessity he tried to persuade other people to attempt the production of the history, but finding that no one else would do so he at last decided to write it himself, an enterprise which took over two years of hard work.

(71)

RUSSIA IN THE SHADOWS: 1920

Russia in the / Shadows / (*line*) / By / H. G. Wells / (*line*) / Hodder And Stoughton / Limited London (*all in thin line border ruled twice across as indicated*)

> Crown 8vo ; pp. 154, consisting of Half-title, (line) / *Russia in the Shadows* / (thin line) (verso blank), pp. (1, 2) ; Frontispiece, not reckoned in pagination ; Title-page, as above (verso blank), pp. (3, 4) ; List of *Contents* (verso blank), pp. (5, 6) ; Divisional fly-title, (line) / *I. Petersburg in Collapse* / (thin line) (verso blank), pp. (7, 8) ; Text, pp. 9-153 ; Printers' imprint in centre of p. (154), *Printed In Great*

Britain By | Richard Clay and Sons, Limited, | Brunswick Street, Stamford Street, S.E. 1, | And Bungay, Suffolk. There follows one blank leaf. In addition to the frontispiece there are photographic illustrations facing pp. 24, 40, 48, 60, 64, 104, 120, 136, and between pp. 72, 73.
Issued in red cloth, lettered and lined in black across back and front cover. Back: (line) *Russia | In The | Shadows | H. G. | Wells | Hodder & | Stoughton |* (line) Front cover: *Russia | In The Shadows | H. G. Wells* (all within line border). All edges trimmed. White endpapers.

The contents of this book, with the exception of Chapter V, were first printed serially in The Sunday Express (Oct. 31st-Nov. 28th, 1920).

(72)

THE SALVAGING OF CIVILISATION : 1921

The Salvaging / Of Civilisation / By / H. G. Wells / (*ornament*) / Cassell And Company, Limited / London, New York, Toronto and Melbourne / 1921

Demy 8vo ; pp. vi + 202, consisting of Half-title, *The Salvaging Of Civilisation* (verso, list of books *Mr. Wells has also written*), pp. (i, ii) ; Title-page, as above (verso blank), pp. (iii, iv) ; List of *Contents* (verso blank), pp. (v, vi) ; Text, pp. (1)-198 ; *Index*, pp. 199-202 : Printers' imprint at foot of p. 202 under a line, *Printed by Cassell & Company, Limited, La Belle Sauvage, London, E.C.4 | F.*100.221
Issued in light green cloth, lettered in gilt across back, and in dark green across front cover. Back: *The | Salvaging | Of | Civilisation | H. G. | Wells | Cassell* Front cover: *The Salvaging | Of Civilisation | H. G. Wells* All edges cut. White end-papers.

The first chapter of this book was originally printed as a series of four monthly articles in The Review of Reviews (Oct. 1920-Jan. 1921). The other chapters were prepared to be delivered by the author during an American lecture-tour in January 1921, but ill-health following upon his visit to Russia he was compelled to cancel his arrangements and to go, instead, to Spain for a rest-cure. The lectures were then printed as weekly articles in The Sunday Times (March 27th-May 22nd, 1921).

(73)

THE NEW TEACHING OF HISTORY : 1921

The New Teaching / Of History / With a Reply to some Recent Criticisms / of *The Outline of History* / By / H. G. Wells / (*ornament*) / Cassell and Company, Ltd / London, New York, Toronto and Melbourne / 1921

Demy 8vo ; pp. 36, consisting of Title-page, as above (verso, *Copyright in U.S.A.—H.G.W.*), pp. (1, 2) ; Text, pp. 3-35 ; Printers' imprint in centre of p. (36), *Printed by | Cassell & Company, Limited, | La Belle Sauvage, London, E C. | F30.621*

Issued as a pamphlet in grey paper covers, printed with blue. The front cover is lettered as follows within a thin blue border : *The New Teaching | of History. With a | Reply to some Recent | Criticisms of The Outline | of History. By H. G. Wells | Cassell & Company, Ltd | London, New York, Toronto and Melbourne | Price One Shilling Net* The back cover has publishers' design in centre.

This essay was first printed in The Fortnightly Review (June 1921), under the title *History for Everybody : A Postscript to " The Outline of History."*

(74)

WASHINGTON AND THE HOPE OF PEACE : 1922

Washington / And The Hope Of Peace / by / H. G. Wells / In an appendix are given ver- / batim reports of the Speeches of / Mr. Hughes and M. Briand / *(device)* / London : 48 Pall Mall / W. Collins Sons & Co. Ltd. / Glasgow Melbourne Auckland

Crown 8vo ; pp. viii + 272, consisting of blank leaf not reckoned in the pagination ; Half-title, *Washington | And The | Hope Of Peace* (verso, publishers' announcement concerning *Mr Wells's Novels* and at the foot *Copyright, 1922*), pp. (i, ii) ; Title-page, as above (verso, list of books *Mr Wells has also written* and at foot *Manufactured in Great Britain*), pp. (iii, iv) ; List of *Contents*, pp. v, vi ; *Introduction*, pp. vii, viii ; Text, pp. 1-232 ; *Appendix*, pp. 233-272. The leaf following p. 272 has Printers' imprint in centre of recto, *Glasgow : W. Collins Sons And Co. Ltd.* (verso and 2 following leaves have advertisements of *Messrs | Collins' | Latest Novels*

Issued in red cloth, lettered in black across back and front cover, with line border and device on front cover. Back : *Washington | And The | Hope Of | Peace | H. G. | Wells | Collins* Front cover : *Washington | And The | Hope Of Peace | H. G. Wells |* (device in lower right corner) (all within line border). All edges trimmed. White endpapers.

The twenty-nine articles in this book were all first printed almost daily in The New York World, as whose special correspondent H. G. Wells attended the Conference, and The Chicago Tribune (Nov. 7th-Dec. 20th, 1921). In Great Britain thirteen of the first fourteen were published simultaneously by The Daily Mail, which in consequence of certain comments concerning the attitude of France began to suppress first passages and then one whole article (*France in the Limelight*), finally ceasing publication. Three articles were missed, but on Dec. 1st, The Daily Express, The Manchester Guardian, and The Glasgow Herald began simultaneous publication with the seventeenth, *Ebb Tide at Washington*, and continued to the end.

The American edition (Macmillan Co., New York. 1922) omits the *Appendix*.

(75)

THE MIND IN THE MAKING : 1922

What / H. G. Wells / thinks about / The Mind in / the Making / by James Harvey Robinson / from the New York Times / Book Review and Magazine / Feb. 26, 1922

Issued as a small 4-page folder, p. (1) as above, by Harper & Bros., New York.

A revised version of this article was printed as the *Introduction* to the English edition or The Mind in the Making (Cape, London. 1923)—see Bib. III.

(76)

THE SECRET PLACES OF THE HEART : 1922

The Secret Places / of the Heart / By / H. G. Wells / (*ornament*) / Cassell and Company, Ltd / London, New York, Toronto and Melbourne

Crown 8vo ; pp. vi + 312, consisting of blank leaf not reckoned in pagination ; Half-title, *The / Secret Places Of The Heart* (verso, list of books *Mr. Wells has also written*), pp. (i, ii) ; Title-page, as above (verso, *First published* 1922), pp. (iii, iv) ; List of *Contents* (verso blank), pp. (v, vi) ; Text, pp. 1-311 ; Printers' imprint on p. (312), *Printed in England by / Cassell & Company, Limited, / London, E.C.4. / F 200 422*

Issued in green cloth, lettered in gilt across the back, with blind lettering across the front cover, and with blind designs on back and front cover. Back : The / Secret / Places / Of The / Heart / H. G. / Wells / Cassell Front cover : The Secret Places / Of The Heart / H. G. Wells (all within panel of blind design) Top and fore edges trimmed. White end-papers.

This story was first published serially in Nash's and Pall Mall Magazine (Dec. 1921–July 1922).

F

(77)

A SHORT HISTORY OF THE WORLD: 1922

A Short / History of The World / By / H. G. Wells / Illustrated / Cassell
And Company, Ltd / London, New York, Toronto and Melbourne / 1922

> Super Royal 8vo ; pp. xvi + 432, consisting of Half-title, *A Short
> History Of The World* (verso blank), pp. (i, ii) ; Title-page, as above
> (verso, at foot, *Printed in Great Britain*), pp. (iii, iv) ; *Preface* (verso
> blank), pp. (v, vi) ; List of *Contents*, pp. vii-ix ; p. (x) blank ; *List Of
> Illustrations*, pp. xi-xvi ; Text, pp. (1)-405 ; p. (406) blank ; *Chrono-
> logical Table*, pp. 407-413 ; p. (414) blank ; *Index*, pp. 415-432 ;
> Printers' imprint at foot of p. 432 under a thin line, *Printed in England
> by Cassell & Company, Limited, London, E.C.4. / F.150.1022*

Issued in dark blue cloth, lettered with ornaments in gilt across back
and front cover, with blind double line border on front cover. Back :
A Short / History / Of The / World / H. G. Wells / (ornament) /
Cassell Front cover : *A Short History / Of The World / H.G.Wells /*
(ornament) All edges cut. White end-papers.

In a brief *Preface* Wells states that the " especial end " of this book
" is to meet the needs of the busy general reader, too driven to study
the maps and time charts " of *The Outline of History* "in detail, who
wishes to refresh and repair his faded or fragmentary conceptions of the
great adventure of mankind. It is not an abstract or condensation of
that former work."

(78)

UNIVERSITY OF LONDON ELECTION: 1922

120, Whitehall Court, / S.W. / University Of London Election. / (*double
lines*) / Dear Sir (or Madam), (*text follows*)

> A 4-page folder (10¼″ x 8⅜″), consisting of Heading, as above, pp. (1) ;
> Text, signed *H. G. Wells*, pp. (1-4) ; p. (4) has also a list of supporters
> and at the foot beneath a thin line, the printers' imprint as follows ,
> *Printed by St. Clements Press, Ltd., Portugal Street, London, W.C.2.:
> and Published by H. Finer for the London School of Economics, / Clare
> Market, London, W.C.2.*

In October 1922, at very short notice, H. G. Wells was asked, and agreed,
to stand as Labour candidate for the University of London constituency.
His original election address, collated above, was withdrawn owing to Post
Office disqualification due to the fact that it mentions both publisher and
price as well as title of *The Elements of Reconstruction* (incidentally giving
its date of first publication incorrectly as 1919). Also, some annoyance
was caused by the printers' imprint, which through an error gave the
publisher as H. Finer, " for the London School of Economics." The
pamphlet, *The World, Its Debts and the Rich Men,* was substituted as an
emergency election address.

(79)

THE WORLD, ITS DEBTS AND THE RICH MEN : 1922

The World, / Its Debts / And The / Rich Men / *(short line)* / *A Speech
by* / H. G. Wells / *(short line)* / Published by / H. Finer, 127, Queen's Road,
Finsbury Park, N. (*all within a double, decorative and line, border*)

8¼″ x 6⅔″ ; pp. 16, consisting of Text, headed *The World, its Debts,* /
and the Rich Men / (line) / *Report Of A Meeting At Millbank School* /
(line) / (text follows), pp. (1)-14 ; *List of Supporters.,* p. 15. Printers'
imprint in centre of p. (16) as follows : *Printed by* / *St. Clements Press,
Ltd.,* / *Portugal Street,* / *Kingsway, W.C.*2.

Issued as a pamphlet in grey-tinted paper covers, p. (i) of which is Title-
page, printed as above in black ; p. (ii) has two notes concerning the
University of London Election ; pp. (iii, iv) are blank. All edges
trimmed.

This report of a meeting held at Millbank School on Friday, Nov. 3rd,
1922, under the auspices of the London University Labour Party, was
substituted for H. G. Wells's original election address (q.v.).

(80)

MEN LIKE GODS : 1923

Men Like Gods / By / H. G. Wells / *(ornament)* / Cassell and Company,
Ltd / London, New York, Toronto and Melbourne

Crown 8vo ; pp. viii + 304, consisting of Half-title, *Men Like Gods*
(verso, list of books *Mr. Wells has also written*), pp. (i, ii) ; Title-page,
as above (verso, *First published* 1923 / *Printed in Great Britain*), pp.
(iii, iv) ; Dedication, *To* / *Florence Lamont* / *in whose home at Engle-
wood this story* / *was christened* (verso blank), pp. (v, vi) ; List of
Contents, pp. vii, viii ; Divisional fly-title, *Book The First* / *The
Irruption of the Earthlings* (verso blank), pp. (1, 2) ; Text, pp. 3-304 ;
Printers' imprint at foot of p. 304 under a thin line, *Printed by Cassell
& Company, Limited, La Belle Sauvage, London, E.C.*4. / F.200.123

Issued in green cloth, lettered across back in gilt, and blind across front
cover, with blind designs on back and front cover. Back : *Men* /
Like / *Gods* / *H. G.* / *Wells* / *Cassell* Front cover : *Men Like Gods* /
H. G. Wells (all within panel of blind design) Top and fore edges cut.
White end-papers.

This story was first printed serially in The Westminster Gazette (Dec.
1922-Feb. 1923).

(81)

SOCIALISM AND THE SCIENTIFIC MOTIVE : 1923

Socialism / And The / Scientific Motive / By / H. G. Wells

A 4-page leaflet (10″ x 7½″), consisting of Title-page, as above, p. (1) ; Text, in double columns, pp. 2-(4) ; Printers' imprint at foot of p. (4) under a thin line, *Co-operative Printing Society, Tudor Street, London, E.C.4.*—28622.

This is the text of a *Speech delivered at a Dinner at the University of London Club on March 21st, 1923.*

(82)

UNIVERSITY OF LONDON ELECTION : 1923

To The Electors Of / London University / (*thin line*) / (*text follows*)

A 4-page folder (10″ x 7½″), consisting of p. (1) as above ; Text, signed *H. G. Wells*, continues in double columns on pp. (2, 3) ; p. (4) blank except for printers' imprint at foot, *Printed at the Pelican Press, 2 Carmelite Street E.C.* and beneath, rubber-stamped, *Published By / M. Craig, / 5, Paulton's Square, S.W.2.*

This letter was issued not long before the announcement of the 1923 General Election.

(83)

UNIVERSITY OF LONDON ELECTION : 1923

To The Electors / Of London University / General Election, 1923, From / H. G. Wells, B.Sc. (Lond.) / (*thin line*) / (*text follows*)

A 4-page folder (10″ x 7½″), consisting of p. (1) as above, with text continuing in double columns on pp. (2, 3) ; p. (4) has a *Preliminary List Of Supporters*, and the imprint at the foot, *Printed at the Pelican Press, 2 Carmelite Street, London, E.C., and published by M. Craig, 162 Buckingham Palace Road, London, S.W.*

(84)

THE LABOUR IDEAL OF EDUCATION : 1923

The London University Labour Party Has in Preparation A / Pamphlet On The Labour Ideal of Education. The Following / Preliminary Statement Of Views Prepared By Mr. Wells / Under The Instruction Of The

Pamphlet Committee May Be / Of Interest To You At This Juncture. /
(*text follows*)

   Issued as a leaflet (7⅓" x 5"), the text filling pp. (1, 2) ; Printers' imprint
   at foot of p. (2), *Printed at the Pelican Press, 2 Carmelite Street, London,
   E.C.4., and published by* / *M. Craig, 162 Buckingham Palace Road,
   London, S.W.*

This leaflet was sent out to the electors of London University with the
1923 election address.

(85)

THE STORY OF A GREAT SCHOOLMASTER : 1924

The Story Or / A Great Schoolmaster / Being A Plain Account Of The
Life And Ideas / Of Sanderson Of Oundle / By / H. G. Wells / London /
Chatto & Windus / 1924

   Crown 8vo ; pp. viii+152, consisting of Half-title, *The Story Of* / *A
   Great Schoolmaster* (verso, list of books *Mr. Wells has also written*),
   pp. (i, ii) ; Frontispiece, not reckoned in the pagination ; Title-page,
   as above (verso, Printers' imprint, *Printed In Great Britain By* / *T.
   And A. Constable Ltd. Edinburgh* / *All Rights Reserved*), pp. (iii, iv) ;
   List of *Contents* (verso blank), pp. (v, vi) ; List of *Illustrations* (verso
   blank), pp. (vii, viii) ; Text, pp. 1-(151) ; p. (152) blank.
   Issued in dark green cloth, lettered in lighter green across back and front
   cover, with blind lines on back and blind line border on front cover.
   Back :   (line) / *The* / *Story* / *Of A* / *Great* / *School-* / *Master* / *H. G.* /
   Wells / *Chatto &* / *Windus* / (line)   Front cover : *The Story Of A* /
   Great Schoolmaster / *By* / *H. G. Wells*   Top edges light green, fore
   edges cut.   White end-papers.

This, the author's only " biographical effort," was first printed serially
in The New Leader and The New Republic.   In the former periodical it
appeared weekly, Sept. 14th-Oct. 26th, 1923, some 15000 words being
omitted, mainly from the latter part of the work.   It has been said that
H. G. Wells would make an excellent member of a committee—as long as
it consisted of himself only ! and this essay is, indeed, by way of being a
minority report written to supplement the earlier biography by various
hands, *Sanderson of Oundle* (Chatto & Windus, 1923).   " This present book
is, as it were, a simplified diagram of the teachings less luminously and more
fully set out in the official Life."

(86)

THE DREAM : 1924

The Dream / A Novel by / H. G. Wells / (*publisher's device*) / Jonathan
Cape / Eleven Gower Street London

Crown 8vo ; pp. 320, consisting of a leaf blank on recto (verso, list of books *Mr Wells has also written*), pp. (1, 2) ; Half-title, *The Dream* (verso blank), pp. (3, 4) ; Title-page, as above (verso, at head, *First Published* 1924 / *All Rights Reserved*, and at foot Printers' imprint, *Printed In Great Britain By Butler And Tanner Ltd., Frome And London*), pp. (5, 6) ; List of *Contents* (verso blank), pp. (7, 8) ; Divisional fly-title, *Part I / How Harry Mortimer Smith Was Made* (verso blank), pp. (9, 10) ; Text, pp. 11-320.

Issued in dark red cloth, lettered and lined in gilt across back, with blind border line on front cover and publisher's blind design on back cover. Back : (three lines) / *The* / *Dream* / (decoration) / *H. G. Wells* / *Jonathan Cape* / (three lines) Top edges stained to match covers ; other edges trimmed. White end-papers.

This story was first printed serially in Nash's and Pall Mall Magazine (Oct. 1923–May 1924).

(87)

THE P.R. PARLIAMENT : 1924

The P.R. / Parliament / (*short line*) / By / H. G. Wells. / (*short line*) / (Reprinted by permission of the *Westminster Gazette* / and the McClure Newspaper Syndicate.) / (*short line*) / Published by the / Proportional Representation Society, / 82, Victoria Street, London, S.W.1. / Price One Penny. (*all enclosed within thin line, this enclosed within thick line, border*)

Pp. 8 (8½″ x 5½″), consisting of Title-page, as above (verso, *A Note On Mr. Athelstan Rendall's P.R. Bill.*, signed *J.H.H.*), pp. (1, 2) ; Text, pp. (3)-6 ; pp. (7, 8), quotations from The New Leader on *Government under P.R.* by H. N. Brailsford and Ramsay Macdonald. At foot of p. (8) under a thin line, *Gaylard & Son, Printers, London, S.E.*14 19 *ax*-6-24

Issued as a pamphlet, without covers. All edges trimmed.

A reprint, with the addition of about 50 words, of the article *Proportional Representation*, printed in The Westminster Gazette (May 31st, 1924).

(88)

A YEAR OF PROPHESYING : 1924

A Year of Prophesying / By H. G. Wells (3 *decorative leaflets*) / T. Fisher Unwin Ltd. / London : Adelphi Terrace

Demy 8vo ; pp. 272, consisting of Half-title, *A Year Of Prophesying* (verso, announcement of the *Atlantic Edition Of Mr. Wells's Works* and list of books *Mr. Wells has also written*), pp. (1, 2) ;

Title-page, as above (verso, in centre, *First published in* 1924 and at foot, (*All rights reserved*), pp. (3, 4) ; *Foreword*, with list of *Contents* on verso and following leaf, pp. 5-8 ; Text, pp. 9-(272) ; Printers' imprint at foot of p. (272), *Printed in Great Britain by Hazell, Watson & Viney, Ld., / London and Aylesbury.*

Issued in dark blue cloth, lettered in gilt across back, with double blind lines at head and foot of back, and double blind line border on front cover. Back : *A Year / Of / Prophesying / (short gilt line) / H. G. Wells / T. Fisher Unwin* Top and fore edges trimmed. White end-papers.

Of the fifty-five articles in this volume fifty-four were written weekly from Sept. 1923 to Sept. 1924 for the McClure Newspaper Syndicate and printed in newspapers throughout the English-speaking world ; in London by The Westminster Gazette. The remaining one, *The Future of the British Empire,* appeared in The Empire Review.

(89)

THE ATLANTIC EDITION

Issued in Great Britain by T. Fisher Unwin Ltd., and in America by Charles Scribner's Sons, New York, in twenty-eight uniform volumes, strictly limited to 1670 sets, the first volume of each set being autographed by H. G. Wells. The edition is printed directly from type on pure rag deckle-edge paper specially made for it and bearing the watermark *H.G.W.* Each volume contains about 400-500 pages and a photogravure frontispiece, and is bound with fine buckram. The text throughout is read and revised by the author, who has written a special preface to each volume as well as a general introduction to the set. A collation of the first volume only is given below, followed by particulars of the contents of the remaining volumes.

Vol. 1.

The Time Machine / The Wonderful Visit / And Other Stories (*all in red*) / By / H. G. Wells / (*device*) / London / T. Fisher Unwin Ltd. (*in red*) / MCMXXIV

Medium 8vo (8⅘ ″ x 6″) ; pp. xxiv + 468, consisting of a blank page bearing on its verso the following certificate : *The Works Of / H. G. Wells / Atlantic Edition / This edition, printed from type which has / been distributed, is strictly limited to six / hundred and twenty sets for Great Britain / and Ireland, of which six hundred are for / sale and twenty are for presentation / This is number . . . . . / The edition for America is limited to one thou- / sand and fifty sets, of which one thousand /*

are for sale and fifty are for presentation | *H. G. Wells* (autograph signature in ink), p.p. (i, ii) ; Half-title, *The Works Of* | *H. G. Wells* | *Atlantic Edition* | *Volume I* (verso blank), pp. (iii, iv) ; Frontispiece, photograph of Wells signed *Very sincerely yrs* | *H. G. Wells*, with paper shield, not reckoned in pagination ; Title-page, as above (verso, copyright notices and beneath, under a short line, *Printed in the United States of America*), pp. (v, vi) ; List of *Contents* | *Volume I* (verso blank), pp. (vii, viii) ; *A General Introduction* | *To The Atlantic Edition*, pp. ix-xx ; *Preface To Volume I*, pp. xxi-xxiii ; p. (xxiv) blank ; Divisional half-title, *The Time Machine* (verso blank), pp. (1, 2) ; Text, pp. 3-118 ; Divisional half-title, *The Wonderful Visit* (verso blank), pp. (119, 120) ; Text, pp. 121-275 ; p. (276) blank ; Divisional half-title, *Other Fantastic Stories* (verso blank), pp. (277, 278) ; List of *Contents* (verso blank), pp. (279, 280) ; Text, pp. 281-467 ; p. (468) blank.

Issued in red buckram, with lettering and lines in gilt on front cover and back. Back : (2 lines) | *The Works of* | *H. G. Wells* | *Vol. I* | *The Time Machine* | *The Wonderful Visit* | *and other Stories* | *Atlantic Edition* | (2 lines) Front cover has the letters *H.G.W.* within a single circular line. Top edges gilt ; others uncut. White end-papers with design in light grey.

The *Other Fantastic Stories* included in this volume are *The Jilting of Jane, The Cone, The Flowering of the Strange Orchid, Æpyornis Island, The Remarkable Case of Davidson's Eyes, The Lord of the Dynamos, The Moth, The Story of the Late Mr. Elvesham, Under the Knife, The Plattner Story, The Purple Pileus.*

Vol. 2.

The Island of Doctor Moreau and *The Sleeper Awakes.*

Vol. 3.

The Invisible Man, The War of the Worlds, and *A Dream of Armageddon.*

Vol. 4.

Anticipations, Introduction to 1914 edition of *Anticipations, Locomotion and Administration* (reprint of Appendix I in *Mankind ;* original title, *The Question of Scientific Administrative Areas in Relation to Municipal Undertakings*), *The Problem of the Birth Supply, The Case for Republicanism* (the first half of *Political and Social Influences*), *Thought in the Modern State* (the last paragraph only of the chapter bearing that title), *The Discovery of the Future*, and *This Misery of Boots.*

Vol. 5.

The Food of the Gods and *The Sea Lady.*

Vol. 6.

The First Men in the Moon, The Euphemia Papers, A Slip under the Microscope, and *Miss Winchelsea's Heart.*

The Euphemia Papers are 22 essays from *Certain Personal Matters,* as follows : *Thoughts on Cheapness and my Aunt Charlotte, The Trouble of Life, On the Choice of a Wife, The House of Di Sorno, In a Literary Household, On Schooling and the Phases of Mr. Sandsome, The Poet and the Emporium, The Literary Regimen, House-Hunting as an Outdoor Amusement, The Veteran Cricketer, Concerning a Certain Lady, The Shopman, Dunstone's Dear Lady, For Freedom of Spelling, The Theory of Quotation, On the Art of Staying at the Seaside, The Book of Essays Dedicatory, Through a Microscope, The Pleasures of Quarrelling, The Amateur Nature-Lover, The Mode in Monuments, How I Died.*

Vol. 7.

The Wheels of Chance and *Love and Mr. Lewisham.*

Vol. 8.

Kipps.

Vol. 9.

A Modern Utopia, Scepticism of the Instrument, The Contemporary Novel, About Chesterton and Belloc, The American Outlook (previously printed as *The American Population*), and *The Ideal Citizen.*

Vol. 10.

In the Days of the Comet, The Red Room, The Reconciliation, The Man who could Work Miracles, Jimmy Goggles the God, The Magic Shop, The Valley of Spiders, The New Accelerator, A Catastrophe, The Truth about Pyecraft, The Empire of the Ants, The Crystal Egg, A Vision of Judgment, The Star, The Door in the Wall, The Country of the Blind, The Beautiful Suit, The Pearl of Love.

Vol. 11.

The Undying Fire, First and Last Things (with the omission of 11 sections, mainly from *Of General Conduct*), and *God the Invisible King.*

Vol. 12.

Tono-Bungay.

Vol. 13.

Ann Veronica and *Boon* (with the omission of *The Mind of the Race*).

Vol. 14.

The New Machiavelli.

Vol. 15.

Marriage

Vol. 16.

The Wife of Sir Isaac Harman and Socialism and the Family.

Vol. 17.

The History of Mr. Polly, and *Bealby.*

Vol. 18.

The Passionate Friends, Divorce, The Endowment of Motherhood, and *The Great State.*

Vol. 19.

The Research Magnificent.

Vol. 20.

The War in the Air, The Land Ironclads, The Coming of Bleriot, My First Flight, Off the Chain, Of the New Reign, Will the Empire Live ?, *The Common Sense of Warfare, The Possible Collapse of Civilisation.*

Vol. 21.

The World Set Free, The Peace of the World, The League of Free Nations (chapters 1-8 of *In the Fourth Year*), *A Memorandum on Peace Propaganda* (previously printed as *Memorandum on Propaganda Policy against Germany*), and *Democracy* (chapters 9-11 of *In the Fourth Year*).

Vol. 22.

Mr. Britling. (The last three words of the original title are purposely omitted for reasons explained in the preface.)

Vol. 23.

Joan and Peter (chapters 1-11).

Vol. 24.

Joan and Peter (Chapter 12 to end), and *The Story of a Great Schoolmaster.*

Vol. 25.

The Soul of a Bishop, and *The Secret Places of the Heart.*

Vol. 26.

The Future in America, War and the Future (a few chapters omitted), *Russia in the Shadows, The Project of a World State* and *The Enlargement of Patriotism to a World State* (as one essay under former title), *The Schooling of the World* and *College Newspaper and Book* (as one essay under former title), *Washington Conference Papers* (from *Washington and the Hope of Peace*, chapters 12, 17, 18, 20, 21, 24, 25 being omitted), and *Articles written in* 1923-1924 (*The Beauty of Flying, The Singapore Arsenal, Aviation of the Half-Civilised, The Future of the British Empire, Cosmopolitan and International, Parliament and Real Electoral Reform, The Extinction of Party Government, The Reconstruction of the League of Nations, An Open Letter to M. Anatole France, Youth and the Vote, The Schools of a New Age, Sex Antagonism, The Creative Passion* and *A Year of Journalism*—the last a reprint of *After a Year of Journalism.*).

Vol. 27.

History is One, A Short History of the World, What is Success? a Note on *Lord Northcliffe, The Gifts of the New Sciences, The Ten Great Discoveries,* and *The Human Adventure.*

Vol. 28.

Men Like Gods, and *The Dream.*

PART II

1897

The Humours of Cycling : stories and pictures by Jerome K. Jerome, H
  G. Wells, . . . etc., etc. (James Bowden, London. 1897. 4to.)
  (H. G. Wells's contribution was a short story, *A Perfect Gentleman on
  Wheels*, pp. 5-14. This slight tale in the style of *The Wheels of
  Chance* was first printed in Woman at Home (April, 1897) with the
  title, *A Perfect Gentleman on Wheels, or, the Humours of Cycling*.)

1900

For Britain's Soldiers. Edited by C. J. Cutcliffe Hyne (Methuen & Co.,
  London. 1900).
  (Contains, pp. 253-281, the first reprint of *Miss Winchelsea's Heart*,
  after the original publication in The Queen (Oct. 1898). It was later
  reprinted as the twelfth story in *Twelve Stories and a Dream*.)

1902

The Hampstead Braille Magazine. (The London Society for Teaching the
  Blind. Vol. I, No. 2, Dec. 1902.)
  (Contains, in Braille type, the first reprint of *The Story of the Inexperienced
  Ghost*, originally published in The Strand Magazine (March, 1902) and
  later reprinted as the sixth story in *Twelve Stories and a Dream*.)

1906

The Fabian Society. Report of the Special Committee appointed in
  February, 1906, to consider measures for increasing the scope, influence,
  income, and activity of the Society. Together with the Executive
  Committee's Report and resolutions thereon. To be submitted to the
  Members at Essex Hall, on Fridays, 7th and 14th December, 1906, at
  7.30 p.m. The Fabian Society, 3 Clement's Inn, Strand, London, W.C.
  November 1906.
  (The Report itself ends on p. 17 of this 48-page pamphlet, and is sub-
  scribed by ten signatories, in alphabetical order, ending with the name
  of H. G. Wells.)

1907

Sociological Papers, Volume III. By (eleven authors) (Published for The
Sociological Society by Macmillan & Co., London. 1907.)
(H. G. Wells's contribution to this volume is his essay *The So-Called Science
of Sociology*, read before a meeting of The Sociological Society at The
School of Economics and Political Science (University of London), Clare
Market, W.C., on February 26th, 1906, with Professor Patrick Geddes
in the Chair. With the discussion which followed, the essay occupied
pp. (355)-377. The essay alone was printed in The Independent Review
(May, 1905), and later reprinted as the fourteenth paper in *An Englishman
Looks at the World*.)

Election Addresses. Printed at the expense of the Candidates, and
circulated with " Fabian News " by authority of the Executive Committee. (Issued for members of the Fabian Society only, no publisher's
imprint. 4-page folder, folio. 1907.)
(The text begins *To The Members Of The Fabian Society. We beg to
present ourselves* . . . etc. and this introductory section is signed with
the names of Sidney Ball, Maud Reeves, R. Mudie Smith, and H. G.
Wells. The rest of the document is occupied by the addresses of other
individual candidates.)

The Book of the Queen's Fete. (Carl Hentschel, London. June, 1907)
(This souvenir programme contains a one-page drawing, *A Study of Six*,
by H. G. Wells, being caricatures of six Socialist leaders, the artist among
them).

1911

The H. G. Wells Calendar. A Quotation from the Works of H. G. Wells
for every day in the year selected by Rosamund Marriot Watson.
(Frank Palmer, London. 1911. 12mo. Pp. 102, with photographic
frontispiece, and printed throughout in green and black. Issued in
vellum wrappers, lettered in dark green on back and front cover.)

1912

What the Worker Wants : The *Daily Mail* Enquiry. By H. G. Wells (and
many others) (Hodder & Stoughton, London. 1912. 8vo. In paper
wrappers).
(This volume consists of articles and letters on the subject of the labour
unrest reprinted from the columns of The Daily Mail (May and June,
1912). The discussion was started by the six articles by H. G. Wells
which were reissued as the pamphlet, *The Labour Unrest*. These articles
are reprinted here, pp. (9)-30, together with two more, *The Craving for
One Simple Cheap Remedy* (first printed June 5th), pp. 105-108, and
Syndicalism or Citizenship (June 7th), pp. 116-120. These eight articles,
the seventh renamed *Social Panaceas*, are reprinted together as the sixth
es say in *An Englishman Looks at the World*.)

1913

Thoughts from H. G. Wells. Selected by Elsie E. Morton. (Harrap &
    Co., London. 1913. 32°. No. 47 of The Sesame Booklets. Pp. 64,
    with photographic frontispiece. Issued in stiff paper wrappers and in
    soft leather, the latter lettered in gilt on back and front cover.)

1915

The Blinded Soldiers and Sailors Gift Book.   Edited by George Goodchild
    (Jarrold & Sons, London. 1915. 8vo.).
    (Contains the first reprint in book-form of H. G. Wells's story *The Land
    Ironclads*, which originally appeared in The Strand Magazine (Dec. 1903).
    It was again printed in The Strand Magazine (Nov. 1916) after the appear-
    ance of the Tanks in France. It occupies pp. 93-122.)

The Book of France : In aid of The French Parliamentary Committee's
    Fund for the Relief of the invaded Departments. Edited by Winifred
    Stephens (Macmillan & Co., London, and Edouard Champion, Paris.
    1915.).
    (H. G. Wells's contribution to this volume is a short translation. *Debout
    Pour La Derniere Guerre !* par Anatole France, pp. 55, 56 : *Let Us Arise
    and End War !* English translation by H. G. Wells, pp. 57,58.)

1916

Princess Marie-José's Children's Book (Cassell & Co., London, for the
    Vestiaire Marie-José, a Society for providing Milk Food and Clothes to
    the Babies behind the firing line in Flanders. 1916.).
    (Contains, pp. 13-16, a very short story, *Master Anthony and the Zeppelin*,
    written and illustrated by H. G. Wells.)

1917

Shakespeare Day : Report of Meeting held May 3rd, 1917, at King's
    College, University of London. (Chatto & Windus, London. 1917).
    (Speech by H. G. Wells, pp. 26-30.)

1918

The W. E. A. Education Year Book, 1918. (The W. E. A., London, 1918).
    (Contains a 22-line quotation entitled *The War And The Workers*
    from a letter from H. G. Wells to the editors, p. 66.)

Natural Science and the Classical System in Education. Essays new and
    old, edited for the Committee on the Neglect of Science by Sir Ray
    Lankester (Wm. Heinemann, London. 1918).
    (H. G. Wells contributes Chapters VI and VII, *The Case against the
    Classical Languages* (originally appeared in The Fortnightly Review,
    April 1917, as the second of two articles printed under the general title

Our Educational Future, the first being by Lord Bryce), pp. 183-195, and
A Modern Education (delivered as a speech to The British Science Guild
at the Mansion House), pp. 196-206.)

1919

Report 1916 to 1918 of The League for the Promotion of Science in Education. (Harrison & Sons, London. 1919.)
(Speech by H. G. Wells made at the meeting held May 3rd, 1916, pp.
34-36.)

The Idea of the League of Nations : Prolegomena to the Study of World-
Organisation. By the Research Committee of the League of Nations
Union (Humphrey Milford, Oxford University Press, 1919).
(This essay was first printed in The Atlantic Monthly (Jan. and Feb. 1919).
It was the result of the collaboration of the nine members of the Research
Committee of the (then) League of Nations Free Association, these being
H. G. Wells (chairman), Viscount Grey, Gilbert Murray, J. A. Spender,
A. E. Zimmern, H. Wickham Steed, Lionel Curtis, William Archer
(secretary), and Viscount Bryce.)

The Way to the League of Nations : A brief sketch of the Practical Steps
needed for the formation of a League. By the Research Committee of
the League of Nations Union (Humphrey Milford, Oxford University
Press, 1919).
(The Research Committee responsible for this essay was similar to that
detailed in the previous item, with the omission of Viscount Bryce and
the addition of Ernest Barker, G. Lowes Dickinson, John Hilton, and
L. S. Woolf).

1920

Frank Swinnerton, Personal Sketches ; together with notes and comments
on the novels of Frank Swinnerton. By H. G. Wells, Arnold Bennett
and G. M. Overton. (Doran Co., New York. 1920. Privately printed.)

Debs and the Poets. Edited by Ruth Le Prade (Upton Sinclair, Pasa-
dena, Cal., 1920.)
(Contains a 7-line prose appreciation of Eugene Debs by H. G. Wells
on p. 6. The English edition published by Henderson's, London, 1921.)

Secrets of Crewe House. By Sir Campbell Stuart, K.B.E. (Hodder &
Stoughton, London. 1920).
(Contains, pp. 61-81, a *Memorandum on Propaganda Policy against
Germany*, written by H. G. Wells as First Director of the German Section
of the Enemy Propaganda Committee in May 1918, and used as the basis
of the British Propaganda campaign policy in the last months of the
War.)

Twenty-Four Portraits. By William Rothenstein, with critical appreciations by various hands (Allen & Unwin, London. 1920).
(One of the appreciations in this book is by H. G. Wells, but the name
of the subject is a secret still so closely guarded that one hesitates even
to suggest which it might be.)

1921

The Evolution of World Peace. Essays arranged and edited by F. S. Marvin (Oxford University Press, London. 1921. The Unity Series, No. 4).
(The tenth chapter is *An Apology for a World Utopia*, by H. G. Wells, pp. 159-178.)

1922

The University of London : its history and work. From . . . speeches made . . . at the 26th annual reunion of University Correspondence College, Wednesday, November 15th, 1922 (8-page pamphlet with no publisher's or printer's name).
(Speech by H. G. Wells on proposing the toast " University Correspondence College.", pp. 7, 8.)

1923

Yea And Nay : A series of lectures and counter-lectures given at the London School of Economics in aid of the Hospitals of London (Brentano's Ltd., London. 1923.).
(Lecture I, *Should History be Taught on a National or an International Basis ?*, was delivered by H. G. Wells and E. B. Osborn. The former's speech, here printed for the first time, occupies pp. 15-19. A photograph of Mr. Wells faces p. 18.)

1924

What is Socialism ? A Symposium. Edited by Dan Griffiths (Grant Richards, Ltd., London, 1924.).
(H. G. Wells's six-line definition of Socialism is printed at the top of p. 81.)

These Eventful Years ; the Twentieth Century in the Making. By J. L. Garvin and others (Encyclopædia Britannica Co., London. 1924. 2 volumes.).
(The second volume begins with Chapter XXXVI, *A Forecast of the World's Affairs*, by H. G. Wells, pp. 1-17. This essay was written specially for this work.)

PART III

1905

Underground Man. By Gabriel Tarde (Duckworth & Co., London. 1905. 8vo.). *Preface*, pp. 1-19.

Utopia. By Sir Thomas More (Blackie & Son, London. 1905. 8vo. In The Red Letter Library. Reprinted in 1923 in The " Wallet " Library of English Prose). *Introduction*, pp. iii-viii. (Wells's *Introduction* was reprinted as *About Sir Thomas More* in *An Englishman Looks at the World*).

1910

George Meek, Bathchairman. By Himself (Constable & Co., London. 1910. 8vo.). *Introduction*, pp. vii-xx. (At the end of this autobiography George Meek, full of hope, is about to sail to a newer country and a brighter future. After some difficulties with the emigration authorities he and his family reached Canada. But the work there proved too hard for his health and natural tastes, and he returned to Eastbourne and bathchairing. He wrote another book which has never been published, and to the end of his life contributed verse and prose to the local papers. He died at Eastbourne in March 1921.)

New York. By Alvin Langdon Coburn (Duckworth & Co., London. 1910. Folio.). *Foreword*, pp. 9, 10. (The volume contains twenty photogravures from photographs by A. L. Coburn.)

1912

Shop Slavery and Emancipation. By William Paine (King & Son, London. 1912. 8vo.). *Introduction*, pp. (vii)-x.

1915

Friendly Russia. By Denis Garstin (T. Fisher Unwin, London. 1915. 8vo.). *Introduction*, pp. 9-12. (This introduction was first printed in The Book Monthly [1915].)

Kultur Cartoons. By Will Dyson (Stanley Paul & Co., London. 1915. Folio.). *Introduction*.

1917

The Journal of a Disappointed Man. By W. N. P. Barbellion (Bruce F. Cummings) (Chatto & Windus, London. 1917. 8vo.). *Introduction*, pp. vii-x.

Pictures of War Work in England. By Joseph Pennell (Wm. Heinemann, London. 1917. 4to.). *Introduction*, pp. v-viii.

71　　　　　　　　　　　　　　　G

Catalogue of Paintings and Prints of the Earliest and Latest Types of Aircraft Collected and Arranged by the Countess of Drogheda In Aid of the Flying Services Fund (administered by the Royal Aero Club) and the Irish Hospital Supply Depôts for the British Red Cross, Exhibited at the Grosvenor Gallery, 51a New Bond Street, W. 1917. *Preface*, pp. 7, 8.

The Gods in the Battle. By Paul H. Loyson, translated from the French by Lady Frazer (Hodder & Stoughton, London. 1917. 8vo.). *Introduction*, pp. xxii-xxiv.

L'Angleterre, Sa Politique Intérieure. Par Edouard Guyot (Librairie Delagrave, Paris. 1917. 8vo.). *Preface*, pp. (v)-ix.

1918

The Quaint Companions. By Leonard Merrick (Hodder & Stoughton, London. 1918. 8vo.). *Introduction*, pp. v-viii.

Nocturne. By Frank Swinnerton (Secker, London. 1918. 8vo.). *Intro duction*, pp. 1-(8).
(This introduction was written for the first American edition, and first published in Great Britain in the second English edition.)

Keeling Letters and Recollections. Edited by E. T. (Allen & Unwin, Ltd., London. 1918. 8vo.). *Introduction*, pp. ix-xiv.

1919

The Gay-Dombeys. By Sir H. H. Johnston (Chatto & Windus, London 1919. 8vo.). *Preface*, pp. v-ix.

The Peculiar Major. By Keble Howard (Hutchinson & Co., London. 1919. 8vo.). *Preface* (6-line note) p. vi.

1922

The Pivot of Civilisation. By Margaret Sanger (Brentano's, New York. 1922. 8vo.). *Introduction*, pp. ix-xviii.

Youth in the Universities. By Ivison S. Macadam (No publisher's name or address given. 1922. Pamphlet, 8½″ x 5½″.). *Preface*, p. (3).

1923

The Mind in the Making. By James Harvey Robinson (Cape, London. 1923. 8vo.). *Introduction*, pp. 7-10.
(The Mind in the Making was first published by Harper & Bros., New York, in 1921. This had no introduction by H. G. Wells. The 1923 issue by Cape is a new and revised edition.)

Estaines Parva : A Venture. By R. L. Gwynne (Silas Birch, Ltd., London. 1923.). Foreword, pp. (5), 6.

APPENDIX

I

CHRONOLOGICAL LIST OF UNREPRINTED WRITINGS

(NOTE: *This list, combined with that of the volumes and pamphlets in order of publication, will provide a guide, not only to the full extent of Wells's literary activities, but to the general development of his art and ideas.*)

1887

Mammon.
A Talk with Gryllotalpa.
Protylian Vapourings.
A Tale of the Twentieth Century.

1888

The Chronic Argonauts.
Walcote.

1889

The Lamias.
Entre Nous.
Something Good from Birmingham.
Holiday Science.
The North Sea.

1890

The Lay of the Sausage Machine.
Cricket.

1891

The Subtle Examinee.
The Rediscovery of the Unique.
That Problem !
Zoological Retrogressions.

1892

Concerning our Pedigree.
Comenius.
The Future of Private Teaching.
Ancient Experiments in Co-operation.
Examinations.

1893

Biology for the Intermediate, etc.
What is Cram ?
On Extinction.
The Examiner Examined.
Animal Specialists.
Concerning Mr. Welsted.
The Literature of the Future.
The Education of an Elizabethan Gentleman.
The Pure and Natural Man.
Angels.
The Peculiar Danger of New Year's Eve.

1894

I Skate.
The Very Fine Art of Microtomy.
Concerning Lodging-house Keepers.
Jellygraphia.
Before the Fancy Dress Ball.
A Family Elopement.
The Education of the Novelist.
The Intangible Man.
In a Little Shop.
The Inert Person.
The Advantage of Toothache.
The Science Library, South Kensington.
Episode.
Hints on Visiting the Academy.
The Foundation Stone of Civilisation.
The Transfiguration of Porchuck.
The Holiday of the Draper's Assistant.
My Abominable Cold.
The Degeneration of the Ravensbourne.
Popularising Science.
Mahatma, M.A.
Stray Thoughts in an Omnibus.
The Story of the Stamps.
The Pains of an Imagination.
Science in School and after School.
The Cultivation of the Family.
A.D. 1900 Application for leave to give a Dinner.
The Disreputableness of Authorship.
The " Cyclic " Delusion.
The Transit of Mercury.
The Island of Opera.
Peculiarities of Psychical Research.
Fallacies of Heredity.

Of Horses.
The Hygienic Country.
The Rate of Change in Species.
Further Glove Buying.
Another Basis for Life.
Sequence of Studies.
The Biological Problem of To-day.

1895

The Vain Man and his Monument.
The Limits of Individual Plasticity.
The Newly Discovered Element.
The Centre of Terrestial Life.
The Duration of Life.
Discoveries in Variation.
Death.
Of Readers in General.
Our Little Neighbour.
Insects and Flowers.
Excelsior.
In the New Forest.
Protean Gas.
Of the Difficulties of Reviewing.
Ubiquitous Gold.
Of a Neighbour and a Garden.
Bio-optimism.
On the Visibility of Change in the Moon.
Huxley.
The Threatened University.

1896

On Elementary Science Teaching.
The Nose.
Intelligence on Mars.
Certain Critical Opinions.
The Possible Individuality of Atoms.
Cheap Microscopes and a Moral.
Human Evolution an Artificial Process.
The Well at the World's End.

1897

On Morals and Civilisation.
Human Evolution : a reply.

The London University Bill.
On the Novels of George Gissing.
The Presence by the Fire.
The British Schoolmaster.
Grant Allen's " Idea of God."
About the Principia.
Book-keeping a la Maitre d'Ecole.
Sums.
Stinks.

1898

The Evolution of God Idea.

1899

Is Britain on the Down-grade ?

1900
On Stephen Crane
The Cyclist Soldier.

1901

English Cities in A.D. 2000.
Truth and the Teetotaler.

1902

The Loyalty of Esau Common.

1903

H. G. Wells, Esq., B.Sc.
The Nature of Man.
Other Worlds' Inhabitants.

1904

From a Study Fireside : Religion is not Altruism.
The Birth Rate Decline.
George Gissing : an Impression.

1905
Garden Cities.
A Cottage in a Garden.

State Babies.
Joint Households.
A Woman's Day in Utopia.
About Landlords.

1906

True Fortune Telling.
Socialism and Free Love.
Race-Prejudice.

1907

The Good Man.

1908

The Two Chief Dangers.
The Things that Live on Mars.
An Answer.
Why Socialists Should Vote for Mr. Churchill.
Socialism and Politics.
Conciliatory Socialism.

1910

My First Aeroplane.
Little Mother up the Mörderburg.
Bunyan for Busy Men.
The Case Against Socialism.
The Real Source of the Labour Trouble.

1911

My Lucky Moment.
Dull Work.
Mr. Wells Explains Himself.

1912

The Truth about Gissing.

1913

The Labour Revolt.
What are the Liberals to Do ?
The Future is as Fixed and Determinate as the Past.

1914

Russia and England : a study in Contrasts.
The Great Community.
The War that will end War.
We, at the Base.
The Need for Strength and Clearness at Home.
America the Peacemaker.
The Most Splendid Fighting in the World.
The Two Ways.
The War of Material.
The Reckoning for the War.
If England is Raided.
The Future of the North of Europe.
Muddleheadedness and Russia.

1915

Scientific War.
A Convert to Protection.
The Organisation of Foresight in Great Britain.
A Suggestion for the Penalising of Germany's Commerce.
Holland's Future.
The Allied Zollverein.
Will the War Change England ?
Every Man's War.
The Perversion of Germany.
The Liberal Aim in the War.
The Logic of the U39.
The Quick Way to Essen.
Ideals of Organisation.
After a Year of War.
The Imperfection of Democracy.
A Testimonial to Books.

1916

War Economics.
Tidying Up the Language Question.
Liberty and Mr. Belloc.
Why the War will be Over by next June.
Free Trade is Peace : Tariffs are War.
Nationalism and Nationality.
The Idea of Allied Combines.

1917

As the World Lives On.
A Crusty Dawn.
The Right Method in Elections.
The First Class Air Fighter.

1918

The Soldiers' Message.
Our Ignorance of the U.S.A.
Man and the Machine.
The Great Power Idea.
No More Secret Treaties.

1920

An Experiment in Illustration.
The Next Stage in History.
Nationalisation and a New Magna Charta.
Mr. Wells Hits Back.

1921

The Grisly Folk.

1922

The Six Greatest Men in the World.
The Mystery of the Perennial Paragraph.
Education for Creative Service.

1923

Is our World Collapsing ?
What Everyone should Read.
A Book on Bolshevik Russia.
Modern Reviewing.
The Reviewers Again.
Of G. B. and Peasants and Cuckoos.
What Everyone should Learn at School.
French Economic History.

1924

The Teacher as Statesman.
The Launching of Sons and Daughters.

II
LETTERS TO THE PRESS

This list gives only a brief selection from the numerous letters which Wells has addressed to various papers and magazines in the last thirty years :

Advice to Grocers' Assistants. Grocer's Assistant, February, 1900.
Message to Young Man. August, 1903. With a portrait.
Is Sociology a Science. Fortnightly Review, October, 1905.
Mr. Wells' Economics. A Reply to Sir R. K. Wilson. Tribune, August 20th and 23rd, 1906.
Liberalism and the Fabian Society. Daily News, March 13th, 1907.
On the Alleged Diabolical Influences in the Fabian Society. Nation, April 6th, 1907.
A Note in Methods of Controversy. New Age, June 27th, 1907.
Socialism and the Business World. Magazine of Commerce, September, 1907.
Mr. Wells and Free Love. A Personal Statement. New Age, October 17th, 1907.
On an anti-Socialist pamphlet by J. H. Bottomley. Times, October 24th, 1907.
Mr. Wells and Free Love. New Age, October 31st, 1907.
Ought Socialists to Live Poor : How I Live. Labour Leader, February 14th, 1908.
Reply to a Challenge. New Age, April 18th, 1908.
Why Every Socialist should Vote for Mr. Keir Hardie. Socialist Torch, October 21st, 1908.
On Censorship of the Drama. Times, August 13th, 1909.
On the Relation of Socialism to Liberalism. Times, May 14th, 1910.
Sex and the Short Story. Bystander, January 18th, 1911.
The Discussion of Marriage. Times, June 24th, 1911.
On Labour and the Coal Dispute. Times, March 7th, 1912.
Nonsense about Eugenic Babies. Daily Mail, October 13th, 1913.
My Attitude to the Socialist Movement. Labour Leader, October 23rd, 1913.
Shaw v. Blatchford. Little Douglas Intervening. Clarion, July 3rd, 1914.
By Little Douglas. Clarion, July 10th, 1914.
On the European War. Times, August 8th, 17th, 20th, 24th, September 22nd, 23rd, October 31st, December 5th, 1914, and January 9th, 1915.
The Tariff as an Instrument of War. Daily Chronicle, February 4th, 1915.
Reply to Mr. Bland's " Self-Appointed Statesmen." Nineteenth Century, April, 1915.

On the European War. Times, May 14th, June 11th, 22nd, July 8th, September 3rd, 1915.

Trade Unions. Independent Review, June, 1915.

The Incoherence of Liberalism. Daily News, in June, 1915.

The New Englishman. Daily News, February 8th, 1916.

Mr. H. G. Wells and Mr. Henry James. Daily News, March 3rd, 1916.

On the European War. Times, May 10th, 11th, 23rd, August 2nd, 1916.

On Premium Bonds. Times, March 3rd, 1917.

On Proportional Representation. Times, March 30th, 1917.

On Republican Society for Great Britain. Times, April 21st (leading article deals with the letter), and 23rd, 1917.

On the Attitude of the Bolshevists to the League of Nations. Times, March 15th, 1918.

On the Doctrine of a Finite God. Times Literary Supplement, May 2nd, 1918.

On Lord Haldane and Preparations for the Great War. Times, May 13th, 1918.

On the League of Nations. Times, June 29th, 1918.

On the General Election : Candidates and Proportional Representation. Times, November 30th, 1918.

On Conscientious Objectors. Times, December 1st, 1919.

On American Studies : Suggestion of Travelling Studentships. Times, December 9th, 1919.

On American Journalism. Times, April 5th, 1920.

A Footnote to Hueffer. English Review, August, 1920.

III

TRANSLATIONS INTO FOREIGN LANGUAGES

As a whole, perhaps, the works of H. G. Wells have been more generally translated into foreign languages than have those of any other living author. In France practically every volume of the least importance has been issued, in some cases in various editions, while the short stories have been published in several collections of differing contents and titles. No other country approaches this record, though in Italy, Spain, Germany, Austria and Holland the earlier works, and particularly the scientific romances, have had a considerable popularity. The Scandinavian countries seem to favour the more serious novels, and the books on Socialism, religion and the war. A series of Russian translations were issued about 1909, and for this Wells wrote a general introduction (printed in England as *Mr. Wells Explains Himself*). Japan was first attracted by *A Modern Utopia*, but *God the Invisible King* and *The Outline of History* were translated almost immediately after publication here. In China a translation of the *Text-Book of Zoology* (a revised version of the *Text-Book of Biology*) was printed as long ago as 1907.

IV

PARODIES BY VARIOUS WRITERS

The War of the Wenuses, by C. L. Graves and E. V. Lucas (Arrowsmith, Bristol. 1898).

The Food of the Dogs and what became of it : a Travesty, by G. E. Farrow, illustrated by Harry Furniss (Brimley Johnson, London. 1904).

A Christmas Garland, by Max Beerbohm (Heinemann, London, 1912). 4. *Perkins and Mankind*. (An earlier parody by Beerbohm will be found in the 1896 Christmas Number of the Saturday Review ; a story of a man who defossilises a cannon-ball and makes it into a Christmas pudding.)

Tricks of the Trade, by J. C. Squire (Secker, London. 1917). *How They Do It*, No. 9.

Rather Like, by Jules Castier (Jenkins, London. 1919). *The Finding of Laura*.

Heavens, by Louis Untermeyer (Harcourt, Brace, New York. 1922). *The Heaven of the Time-Machine*.

These Liberties, by E. V. Knox (Methuen, London. 1922). Contains a brief parody which mingles Wells's various styles.

CRITICAL STUDIES OF H. G. WELLS

(NOTE: *In each of the following sections the list represents a selection only, though in the first at any rate it is hoped that nothing of the least importance is omitted.*)

(a) BOOKS

H. G. Wells, by J. D. Beresford (Nisbet, London. 1915. Writers of the Day Series).

The World of H. G. Wells, by Van Wyck Brooks (Unwin, London. 1915).

L'Europe Future: Réponse à M. H. G. Wells, par Jean de la Hire (Albin-Michel, Paris. 1916).

Letters to Mr. Britling, by F. G. Worsley (R. Scott, London. 1917).

Mr. Britling's Finite God, by T. A. Lacey (Mowbray, London. 1917).

God and Mr. Wells, by William Archer (Watts, London. 1917).

Mr. Wells's Invisible King, by L. Elliott Binns (S.P.C.K., London, 1918).

That " Dance a trois " Mr. Wells: a few remarks on " God the Invisible King," by Aylmer D. T. Hunter (Caxton Press. 1917).

I See Through Mr. Britling, by Rev. Philip Norton (Count, Market Place, Dereham, 1918).

H. G. Wells, par Edouard Guyot (Payot, Paris. 1920).

Some Errors of H. G. Wells, by Richard Downey, D.D. (Burns, Oates, London. 1921).

Mr. Wells as Historian, by A. W. Gomme (MacLehose, Jackson, Glasgow. 1921).

Footnotes to H. G. Wells (Outline of History), by F. H. Drinkwater (Longmans, Green, London. 1921).

Mr. Wells and the New History, by Carl Becker (American Historical Review. 1921).

Symposium of Opinions upon The Outline of History by H. G. Wells: Views of Historians. (National Civic Federation, New York, 1921).

My Dear Wells, by Henry Arthur Jones (Nash, London. 1921).

The Outline of H. G. Wells: the Superman in the Street, by Sidney Dark (Parsons, London. 1922).

H. G. Wells: Personality, Character, and Topography, by R. Thurston Hopkins (Palmer, London. 1922).

Bibliography of H. G. Wells, with a Prologue, by Fred. A. Chappell (Covici-McGee, Chicago. 1924). Neither complete nor reliable ; no collations.

H. G. Wells, by Ivor Brown (Nisbet, London. 1924. Writers of the Day Series, written to replace Beresford's essay, now out of print).

(b) ESSAYS IN BOOKS

Heretics, by G. K. Chesterton (Lane, London. 1905). V. *Mr. Wells and the Giants*, pp. 68-91.

The Religion of H. G. Wells and other Essays, by Rev. Alexander H. Crauford (Unwin, London. 1909). I. *The Religion of H. G. Wells*, pp. 11-115

Romance and Reality, by Holbrook Jackson (Richards, London.   1911).
   H. G. Wells.
English Literature, 1880-1905, by J. M. Kennedy (Swift, London, 1912).
   VII. *H. G. Wells*, pp. 206-252.
Personality in Literature, by R. A. Scott-James (Secker, London.   1913).
   Part 3, section 2.   *H. G. Wells*, pp. 151-169.
The Pillars of Society, by A. G. Gardiner (Dent, London.   1913).   *H. G.
   Wells*, pp. 285-292.
The Moderns, by John Freeman (Scott, London.   1916).   *H. G. Wells.*
Horizons : a Book of Criticism, by Francis Hackett (Huebsch, New York.
   1918).   *H. G. Wells*, pp. 101-138.
Modern English Writers, by Harold Williams (Sidgwick & Jackson, London.
   1918).   *H. G. Wells.*
Some Modern Novelists, by H. T. Follett and Wilson Follett (Allen &
   Unwin, London.   1920).   One chapter on *H. G. Wells.*
Reputations, by Douglas Goldring (Chapman & Hall, London.   1920).
   IV. *Mr. Wells and the War.*
Adventures in Interviewing, by I. F. Marcosson (Lane, London.   1920).
   Interview with Wells, pp. 257-259.
Secrets of Crewe House, by Sir Campbell Stuart (Hodder & Stoughton,
   London.   1920).   Account of Wells's work on the Enemy Propaganda
   Committee, with a reprint of his *Memorandum on Propaganda Policy
   Against Germany*, pp. 61-81.
Writers of Three Centuries, 1789-1914, by Claude Williamson (Richards,
   London.   1920).   LXVIII. *The Religion of H. G. Wells.*
Authors and I, by C. Lewis Hind (Lane, London. 1921).   LV. *H. G. Wells*,
   pp. 300-305.
Prejudices : First Series, by H. L. Mencken (Cape, London.   1921).   *The
   Late Mr. Wells.*
*Bibliographical Catalogue of First Loan Exhibition Held by The First
   Edition Club* (First Edition Club, London.   1922).   Contains an in-
   complete and not always accurate list of the first editions of Wells's
   works, with collations.
Some Impressions of My Elders, by St. John G. Ervine (Allen & Unwin,
   London.   1923).   IV. *H. G. Wells*, pp. 226-247.
On Contemporary Literature, by S. P. Sherman (Holt, New York.   1923).
   The Utopian Naturalism of Wells.
First Essays in Literature, by Edward Shanks (Collins, London.   1923).
   The Work of Mr. H. G. Wells.
A Gallery, by Philip Guedalla (Constable, London.   1924).   *H. G. Wells*,
   pp. 63-71.

(c) ESSAYS IN PERIODICALS

A New Writer (illustrated).   Bookman, August, 1895.
The Latest Apocalypse of the End of the World, by W. T. Stead.   Review
   of Reviews, April, 1898.
H. G. Wells : Portraits at Different Ages.   Strand Magazine, December,
   1898.

H. G. Wells, by G. B. Burgin. Weekly Sun, June 3rd, 1899.
H. G. Wells and his Work, by E. A. Bennett. Cosmopolitan, August, 1902.
Mr. Wells as a Sociologist, by J. B. Crozier. Fortnightly Review, September, 1905.
The New Aristocracy of H. G. Wells, by J. A. Hobson. Contemporary Review, April, 1906.
An Open Letter to Modern Utopias, by Vernon Lee. Fortnightly Review, December, 1906.
Persuasive Socialism, by W. H. Mallock. Nineteenth Century, May, 1908.
Conciliatory Socialism, by G. H. Paley. New Quarterly, October, 1908. (Wells's reply to this essay is printed in the same issue under the same title.)
Author and Artist Too (illustrated), by Walter Emmanuel. Strand Magazine, April, 1911.
H. G. Wells, by Thomas Seccombe. Bookman, April, 1914.
Self-Appointed Statesmen, by J. O. P. Bland. Nineteenth Century, March, 1915. (Criticism of the " Shaw and Wells School " of apologists for Germany. Correspondence by Wells and Bland, April, May, June.)
What Mr. Wells Thinks is Coming, by G. B. Shaw. Nation, July 22nd, 1916.
A Very Invisible God, by Frederic Harrison. Nineteenth Century, October, 1917.
Big Little H. G. Wells, by Edwin Pugh. New Witness, July 4th to August 15th, 1919, weekly.
Doubts on Modern Biography, by G. K. Chesterton. New Witness, August 22nd, 1919.
Mr. Wells and Bolshevism, by Winston Churchill. Sunday Express, December 5th, 1920.
Mr. Wells's Outline of History, by Hilaire Belloc. London Mercury, November, 1920.
H. G. Wells, by C. F. G. Masterman. Review of Reviews, June 15th, 1922.
H. G. Wells, by Wyatt Tilby. Edinburgh Review, January, 1923.

THE DICTIONARY

Throughout the Dictionary each story, essay, etc., is numbered against its final title; these numbers are used for reference in the Subject-Index which follows.

A

1. ABOUT CHESTERTON AND BELLOC. New Age, Jan. 11th, 1908 ; the 11th essay in *An Englishman.* Chesterton, Belloc, and the writer are closely akin in many of their ideas, diverging more in expression than in spirit ; politically anti-capitalists they should combine, leaving the settlement of their minor points of dispute until the achievement of their main and similar ideals.

2. ABOUT LANDLORDS. Daily Mail, in Nov., 1905.

3. ABOUT SIR THOMAS MORE. Printed as introduction to More's " Utopia " (see Bib. III, 1905) ; the 12th essay in *An Englishman.* An account and criticism of More and his " Utopia," a work which is " in reality . . . very unimaginative."

4. ABOUT THE PRINCIPIA : Dead Languages that should be buried. Daily Mail, Dec. 4th, 1897.

5. ADMINISTRATIVE SOCIALISM. 12th chapter of *New Worlds.* Account of the Fabian Society's application of the administrative spirit in British politics to Socialism, of the works and ideas of the Society, and of its " dominant intelligence," Sidney Webb.

ADULT EDUCATION. Sunday Times, May 22nd, 1921 ; reprinted as *College, Newspaper and Book* (q.v.).

6. ADVANCEMENT OF SOCIALISM, THE. 15th and final chapter of *New Worlds.* Summary of previous arguments, statement of the three channels for Socialist effort, and the connection between constructive Socialism and politics and the Labour Party.

7. ADVANTAGE OF TOOTHACHE, THE. Pall Mall Gazette, Apr. 24th, 1894.

ADVENT OF THE FLYING MAN, THE. Pall Mall Gazette, Dec. 8th, 1893. Reprinted as *The Flying Man* (q.v.).

ADYE, COLONEL. Chief of the Port Burdock Police, he organizes the pursuit of Griffin, who getting him alone takes his revolver from him, and shoots and presumably kills him. *Invisible Man.*

8. A.D. 1900 APPLICATION FOR LEAVE TO GIVE A DINNER. Pall Mall Gazette, Oct. 12th, 1894.

9. ÆPYORNIS ISLAND. Pall Mall Budget, Christmas No. 1894 ; 10th story in *Stolen Bacillus,* 6th in *Country of the Blind ;* also Pearson's Magazine, Feb., 1905. Butcher, an orchid collector, is stranded upon an atoll off the coast of Madagascar. He has with him an æpyornis egg which hatches. In his loneliness he grows quite fond of his strange companion, but it becomes so vicious that he has to kill it. He is rescued and sells the bones.

AEROPILES. The name given to the smaller flying machines in *When the Sleeper Wakes* : in the revised edition, *The Sleeper Awakes*, they are called monoplanes.

AFRICAN RIDDLE, THE. Daily Mail, Jan. 30th, 1918 ; reprinted as *The Labour View of Middle Africa* (q.v.).

10. AFTER A YEAR OF JOURNALISM : AN OUTBREAK OF AUTO-OBITUARY. Westminster Gazette, Sept. 20th, 1924. 55th and last article in *Year of Prophesying*. In this " outbreak of auto-obituary " Wells, looking back over his series of articles for the McClure Syndicate, and over his life's work in the proof sheets of the *Atlantic Edition*, reviews and summarizes his endeavour and faith as a " creative revolutionary."

11. AFTER A YEAR OF WAR (Looking Ahead). Daily Chronicle, Aug. 2nd, 1915. Survey of obvious changes brought about in England by the war, with a prophecy concerning the changed relative financial position of England and America in the future.

12. AGE OF SPECIALISATION, AN. Daily Mail, Apr. 20th, 1904 ; 19th essay in *An Englishman*. There is a popular idea that the present age is one of specialisation, arising through the confusion of specialisation with division of labour. " This is most distinctly *not* an age of specialisation."

13. AIR ARMAMENT : THE SUPREMACY OF QUALITY. Westminster Gazette, May 3rd, 1924 ; 35th article in *Year of Prophesying*. The numerical supremacy of the

French air-force does not necessarily mean victory for it ; in the air that depends more upon individual quality than upon quantity.

ALEXIEVNA, ANNA. A Russian prostitute, daughter of an Englishwoman. Prothero falls in love with her in Moscow, but not sufficiently to stay with her or to take her with him. *Research Magnificent.*

ALIMONY, AGATHA. The " deep-voiced, stirring Agatha," " one of that large and increasing number of dusky grey-eyed ladies who go through life with an air of darkly incomprehensible significance." She is a novelist and leader of a " section of the suffrage movement. . . . It was one of the less militant sections, but it held more meetings and passed more resolutions than any two others." When Lady Harman leaves her husband she appeals to Agatha for advice, but is only told to return and fight out her battle in the home. *Marriage* and *Sir Isaac Harman.*

14. ALLIED ZOLLVEREIN, THE. Some Objections Considered. Daily Chronicle, Feb. 13th, 1915.

15. AMATEUR NATURE-LOVER, THE. See *Out Banstead Way*. 36th essay in *Personal Matters*. Description of an autumn walk over Epsom Downs through Banstead to Sutton, with humorous interludes concerning golfers, puff-balls, and old boots.

16. AMERICA AND ENTANGLING ALLIANCES. See *Dogmas that are Dying*. 18th chapter in *Washington*. Disarmament can be made possible and world peace ensured

only by America's entry into protective alliances with certain countries. She has always shirked such
alliances and their responsibilities,
but to-day such a policy is "entirely unworthy of a republic which
has now become the predominant
state in the world."

17. AMERICAN POPULATION, THE.
See *Social Conditions and the Social
Future in the United States of
America.* 22nd essay in *An Englishman.* Discussion and weighing
of certain arguments for and against
" the belief that these ninety million
people who constitute the United
States of America are destined to
develop into a great distinctive
nation with a character and culture
of its own." Wells analyses the
social system, considers the American tradition and lack of a " sense
of the state," and the trend of
national self-criticism, and discusses the " four sets of possibilities " which will play a great part
in the moulding of the future—the
plutocracy, the universities, the
Socialist movement, and the women.
He touches upon the question of
government and concludes this
pessimistic essay with the words,
" It is quite possible that the
American John Smiths may have
little to brag about in the way of
national predominance by A.D.
2000. It is quite possible that the
United States may be sitting meekly
at the feet of at present quite un-
anticipated teachers."

AMERICA'S LIVING PROJECT. Sunday Express, Dec. 4th, 1921 ; reprinted as *An Association of Nations*
(q.v.).

18. AMERICA'S ROLE IN WORLD
PEACE. See *The Voice of America.*

24th chapter in *Washington.* Wells
hears President Harding address
the reassembled Congress, Dec. 9th,
1921 ; describes the occasion, the
men themselves, Harding's position
as the voice of America, and his
speech. He finds the ceremony
" simple, fine, dignified."

19. AMERICA THE PEACEMAKER.
Daily News, Sept. 7th, 1914.

ANARCHIST, THE. In *The Stolen
Bacillus.* A nervous, haggard, pale-
faced man, who steals a tube of
what he believes to be a cultivation
of cholera bacteria, thinking to
desolate London with it.

20. ANCIENT EXPERIMENTS IN CO-
OPERATION. Gentlemen's Magazine,
Oct., 1892.

AND NOW ? Daily Mail, June
26th, 1911, reprinted as the first
half of *Of the New Reign* (q.v.).

ANGEL, THE. Whose adventures
in the village of Siddermorton are
related in *The Wonderful Visit.* He
is beautiful in an effeminate way,
short and slight, with iridescent
wings, " the angel of Italian art,
polychromatic and gay. He comes
from the land of beautiful dreams,"
in a glare of golden light and amid
the sound of music. When the
Vicar shoots him down he is clad
in a saffron robe, but adopts one
of his host's suits. After the fatal
fire at the vicarage, a cross is
erected over " the ashes of the
Vicar's stuffed ostrich," and in-
scribed " Thomas Angel."

21. ANGELS. Pall Mall Gazette,
late 1893.

22. ANIMAL SPECIALISTS. Globe, Sept. 29th, 1893.

23. ANN VERONICA : A Modern Love Story. See Bib., No. 38. Ann Veronica Stanley lives with her father and aunt at Morningside Park, a London suburb on the L.S.W.R. Chafing under restrictions continually imposed upon her, she runs away to London, and refuses to return. Her money dwindles away, she cannot find work, and has to pawn her more valuable possessions. She comes into contact with some London Socialists and goes to a meeting of the Fabian Society. Then she accepts a loan of £40 from Ramage, a neighbour of the Stanleys, and becomes a student in the biological laboratory of the Central Imperial College. Ramage takes her out occasionally, and one night tries to kiss her. She, in love with Capes, a demonstrator at the College, repulses him, and is reminded of her debt. Next day she sends him £20, and when he returns the notes burns them in a fit of temper. Desperate now, she joins the suffragettes in a House of Commons raid and is sent to Cannongate Prison for a month. During this period she thinks things over, and upon her release returns to her home, but still attends the lectures at the College. In spite of her love for Capes, she allows herself to be engaged to Manning, a middle-aged civil servant who is sincerely in love with her. Then, realising the impossibility of such a marriage, she breaks the engagement and tells Capes that she loves him. He is a married man living apart from his wife, and for a time he tries to resist his love for her, but at the end of the session they go to Switzerland, spending their holiday together in the mountains. Four years later Capes, now a successful playwright, and Ann Veronica, now his wife and soon to be a mother, entertain Mr. and Miss Stanley at their flat.

24. ANOTHER BASIS FOR LIFE. Saturday Review, Dec. 22nd, 1894. A scientific speculation on the possibility of another and quite different atomic basis for life.

25. ANSWER, AN. New Age, Mar. 28th, 1908. A reply to some criticisms.

26. ANTAGONISM OF SEX, THE. Westminster Gazette, August 30th, 1924 ; reprinted as *Sex Antagonism* (q.v.). A comment on " Ancilla's Share," by Elizabeth Robins ; protests against a tendency expressed in it towards a vast feminine movement against co-operation with men.

27. ANTICIPATIONS OF A WORLD PEACE : Selected and Abbreviated from *In the Fourth Year*. See Bib. No. 66a. The chapter-titles are : 1, *The Way to Concrete Realization ;* 2, *The League must be Representative ;* 3, *The Necessary Powers of the League ;* 4, *League and Empire ;* 5, *Three Vital Questions ;* 6, *The War-Aims Controversy ;* 7, *The Plain Necessity for a League ;* 8, *The Propaganda of the League.*

28. ANTICIPATIONS OF THE REACTION OF MECHANICAL AND SCIENTIFIC PROGRESS UPON HUMAN LIFE AND THOUGHT. See Bib. No. 19. The chapter-titles are : 1, *Locomotion in the Twentieth Century ;* 2, *The Probable Diffusion of Great Cities ;* 3, *Developing Social Elements ;* 4, *Certain Social Reactions ;*

5, *The Life-History of Democracy ;*
6, *War in the Twentieth Century ;*
7, *The Conflict of Languages ;* 8,
The Larger Synthesis ; 9, *Faith,
Morals, and Public Policy in the
Twentieth Century.*

29. APOLOGY FOR A WORLD-
UTOPIA, AN. Printed as Chapter
10 of *Evolution of World Peace*
(see Bib. II, 1921).

APOSTLE OF NATURE, THE. A
native of Utopia who overtakes the
Owner of the Voice and the botanist
as they are descending into the
Zermatt valley. He wears sandals
and has no hat, professes himself a
Nazarite, and advocates a " return
to Nature." He spends all his
leisure travelling and lecturing on
" The Need of a Return to Nature "
and " Simple Foods and Simple
Ways." The essence of his creed
is that " a natural death is better
than an artificial life," and he
criticises Utopia as being " over-
managed." The Owner of the Voice
describes him as " a poseur beyond
question, a conscious Ishmaelite
in the world of wit, and in some
subtly inexplicable way . . . a most
consummate ass." *Modern Utopia.*

30. APPEAL TO THE AMERICAN
PEOPLE, AN. Daily Chronicle, Aug.
24th, 1914 ; 9th chapter in *War
that will End War.* A protest
against certain American proposals
to purchase German ships lying in
American harbours and to use them
to supply Germany with war
material and food ; appeals to
America as a great free nation not
to " make difficulties for us out
of our world perplexities, snatch
advantages, carp from your infinite
security at our allies, and perhaps
in the crisis of our struggle pick

a quarrel with us upon some second-
ary score." Rather should America
take the lead her greatness war-
rants, and when the war is over
come into a general conference to
ensure world-peace.

31. APPLE, THE. Idler, Oct.,
1896 ; 5th story in *Plattner Story.*
Mr. Hinchcliffe, a young assistant
master journeying to take up a new
position at Holmwood Grammar
School, is given an apple from the
Tree of Knowledge by a fellow-
traveller who explains how it came
into his possession. The young
man takes it, but finding it awk-
ward to carry and fearing to appear
ridiculous, throws it away untasted.

32. ARE WE STICKING TO THE
POINT ? A Discussion of War Aims.
Daily Mail, Dec. 26th, 1917 ; reprinted as section 3 of *Getting the
League Idea Clear in Relation to
Imperialism.* In this article, written at the request of the editor,
Wells holds that the real issue of
this war is that of " freedom versus
imperialism, the League of Nations
versus that net of diplomatic
roguery and of aristocratic, pluto-
cratic, and autocratic greed and
conceit which has dragged us all
into this vast welter of bloodshed
and loss."

33. ARGONAUTS OF THE AIR, THE.
Phil May's Annual, 1895 ; 2nd
tale in *Plattner Story.* Monson, a
millionaire, exhausts his wealth in
the building and testing of flying
machines. Smarting under a casual
phrase uttered by a woman, he
makes his first and last flight, in
the company of Woodhouse, his
assistant. For a few moments the
machine swoops Londonwards from
his grounds in Worcester Park,

then crashes in South Kensington, killing them both.

34. ARMAMENTS : The Futility of Mere Limitation. Daily Mail, Nov. 9th, 1921 ; 2nd chapter of *Washington*. Derides the idea that limitation of armaments will prevent warfare. The only solution of the problem lies in the settlement of international disputes, the conversion of the armament interests, and the bringing into being of an " organised international co-operation."

ART EXISTS FOR JOY. See *What Everyone Should Read*.

ARTILLERY MAN, AN. In *War of the Worlds*. He spends the first night of the Martian offensive in the narrator's house on Maybury Hill, and tells how his battery was wiped out by the Fighting Machines. In the morning he and the narrator start Londonwards together, but are separated at Shepperton Lock. After the exodus from London they meet again on Putney Hill, and he is full of plans for the preservation of Man and his ultimate victory against the Martians. But he prefers planning to execution, and the narrator leaves him after a day or two.

35. ART OF BEING PHOTO-GRAPHED, THE. Pall Mall Gazette, late 1893 ; 4th of the *Select Conversations*.

36. ASSOCIATION OF NATIONS, AN. See *America's Living Project*. 19th chapter in *Washington*. Suggests that out of the Conference may grow an Association of Nations which will create a World Parliament functioning through commissions sitting in various countries.

37. AS THE WORLD LIVES ON. Independent Magazine, Jan. 8th, 1917. An article.

AT A WINDOW. Black and White, Aug. 25th, 1894 ; reprinted as *Through a Window* (q.v.).

38. AT WASHINGTON. 14th chapter of *The Future in America*. Comments on the lack of ideas and concentration that Wells finds in Washington during his visit there. He has a talk with President Roosevelt, " a very symbol of the creative will in man."

AUTHOR, AN. The hero of *The Wild Asses of the Devil*, a prosperous popular novelist who writes stories " of an acceptable nature . . . carefully offending no one and seeking only to please." There are several sketches of him.

39. AVIATION OF THE HALF-CIVILISED, THE. Westminster Gazette, Oct. 27th, 1923 ; 6th article in *Year of Prophesying*. Criticism of the present air-services of Europe. Private enterprise will never run them successfully, also " it is impossible to control (them) on nationalist lines."

40. AWAKENING OF PASSION FOR THE WORLD STATE, THE (Probable Future of Mankind, 4). Review of Reviews, Jan., 1921 ; reprinted as section 4 of *Probable Future of Mankind* (q.v.). Unless mankind is to perish, self-destroyed, world-peace must be accomplished. Teaching is the " initial and decisive factor in the future of mankind," and it is the duty of everyone who has ability and opportunity to teach this vision of a single world-state. So far the movement towards it has lacked passion, but that will come.

AZUMA-ZI. The part negroid, part Asiatic assistant at the Camberwell power station. In his ignorance he worships the large dynamo as a god and at last sacrifices the bullying Holroyd to it. He attacks the electrician who takes the dead man's place, but, unsuccessful, throws himself upon the machine and is killed. *Lord of the Dynamos.*

B

BABBLE MACHINES. Mechanisms which replace the newspaper in the 22nd century, bellowing the news from their "foolish trumpet faces." The largest of them, the General Intelligence Machine, is fifty feet in height. *Sleeper Wakes.*

41. BAGARROW. Pall Mall Gazette, about 1894 ; 32nd essay in *Personal Matters.* Portrait of a man, Bagarrow, who is "born good, a congenital good example, a sufferer from atrophy of his original sin." His ambition is to be a True Gentleman ; he is "without the lust or pride of life, without curiosity or adventure, a mere timid missionary of a religion of 'Nicer Ways.'" Forcible trepanning seems the only remedy.

42. BAGSHOT'S MURAL DECORATIONS. Pall Mall Gazette, May 17th, 1894 ; 5th of the *Select Conversations.* The uncle protests against the fashion of decorating walls with reproductions of famous paintings.

BAILEY, ALTIORA. Wife of Oscar Bailey, a "tall commanding figure, splendid but a little untidy in black silk and red beads, with dark eyes that had no depths, with a clear hard voice that had an almost visible prominence, aquiline features and straight black hair that was apt to get astray," a high tenor voice, and an authoritative manner. Before her marriage she is prominent as one of the "little shoal of young women who were led into politico-philanthropic activities by the influence of the earlier novels of Mrs. Humphrey Ward— the Marcella crop." It is through her writings on social questions that she meets Oscar when she is thirty-three ; after her marriage she makes their house in Chamber Street a centre of political and social activity. Their first book, "The Permanent Official," in three volumes, is mentioned as an "enduring achievement." Altiora plans the marriage of Remington and Margaret, and brings them together as much as possible. *New Machiavelli.*

BAILEY, OSCAR. A "short, sturdy figure with a rounded protruding abdomen and a curious broad, flattened, clean-shaven face that seemed nearly all forehead." He goes to Balliol "bristling with extraordinary degrees and prizes captured in provincial" universities, and makes a name there "as the most formidable dealer in facts the rhetoricians of the Union had ever had to encounter." Enters the Civil Service and becomes a political journalist. After his marriage he gives up everything to collaborate with his wife. He is a member of the Pentagram circle. An acquaintance describes him as an "infernal Bottle-Imp." *New Machiavelli.*

43. BALANCE OF PRESENT AND FUTURE, THE. Daily Mail, Apr.

9th, 1913 ; 3rd article in *War and Common Sense*. Prophecies that if war with Germany does not come before 1933 or so, the next war will be fought on the borders of Poland by Britain, France and Germany. against Russia and Asia. This consideration must have its effect on our war policy ; education must be better organised ; " make men, that is the only sane permanent preparation for war."

BALLADE OF THE BEDROOM SUITE. A fragmentary poem (16 lines only) read by the Poet in *The Poet and the Emporium*.

BANGHURST. An unscrupulous London journalist, owner of The New Paper, mentioned in *Filmer*, *In the Days of the Comet*, *The Sea Lady*. His motto is, " Stuff that the public won't believe aren't facts."

BARDLET'S ROMANCE, A. Truth, Mar. 8th, 1894 ; reprinted as *In the Modern Vein* (q.v.).

BARNET, FREDERICK. Son of wealthy parents, well educated, left penniless after his father's bankruptcy and suicide in 1956. He starves in the intervals between teaching and writing, but upon the outbreak of war is sent to France as an infantry officer. Transferred to Holland he sees the smashing of the dykes, but saves himself and his men. With the peace he returns to England and is employed at the Winchester wireless station. In 1970 he publishes " Frederick Barnet's Wander Jahre," an account of his life and thoughts between his nineteenth and twenty-third years, the period of the " last war." *World Set Free*.

BARNSTAPLE, ALFRED. " Sub-editor and general factotum of the *Liberal*, that well-known organ of the more depressing aspects of advanced thought." He is " a man of strong natural affections ; he loved his family extremely so that he knew it by heart," but he is depressed by the " unvarying pessimism of Mr. Peeve, his chief," and " when he was in these jaded moods it bored him acutely." Before he starts on his holiday he is " night and day now . . . worrying about the world at large." He has a wife, whose " competent devotion " he so carefully evades, and three sons. *Men Like Gods*.

BARRACK, DR. ELIHU. (Elihu the son of Barachel the Buzite of the kindred of Ram). The Sundering on Sea doctor consulted by Job Huss, a " round-headed young man with a clean-shaven face, a mouth that was determinedly determined and slightly oblique, a short nose, and a general expression of resolution." He is " hard, competent," and has lost a leg in the war. He suggests an examination and operation by Sir Alpheus Mengo, and on the morning of the operation comes in to see that his patient is ready, getting so interested in the discussion that he forgets to meet Sir Alpheus. He is an " Agnostic by habit and profession. A Doubting Thomas, born and bred," putting his faith in Fact and believing in a Process, something beyond and outside Man. His motto is " Be yourself." In Huss's dream he is Elihu the son of Barachel, sitting " with an air of false humility insolently judging them all." *Undying Fire*.

BARRALONGA, LORD. Owner of the grey touring car which is the first to enter Utopia. He is a "youngish, baldish, undersized man, who suffers very gravely from a disordered liver and kidneys," and has made a fortune "partly by accident, partly by the unscrupulous cheating of various inventors. ... So he was able to buy the noble title." "His skull was very low and broad above his brows ... his little brown eyes were alert and wary as those of a wicked urchin in the hands of a policeman." He is killed on Quarantine Crag. *Men Like Gods.*

BATHWICK, MISS. Boon's amanuensis, a "large, cool, fresh-coloured permanently young lady." Every morning he dictates to her, she typing his words and intimating when his imagination carries him into "regions outside the tastes and interests of that enormous ante bellum public it was his fortune to please." *Boon.*

BAYNES, EDWIN PEAK. A young poet who has his work typed by Ethel Lewisham ; he comes several times to the house and meets her once in the street. When Lewisham sends the roses to his wife she thinks that Baynes has sent them and throws them under the dressing-table. Lewisham thinks that his work might be "spoken of collectively as Bosh." *Mr. Lewisham.*

BEACH-MANDARIN, LADY. "A broad, abundant, billowing personality ... altogether less like a woman than an occasion of public rejoicing. Even her blue eyes projected, her chin and brows and nose all seemed racing up to the front of her as if excited by the clarion notes of her abundant voice, and the pinkness of her

complexion was as exuberant as her manners. She is a friend of Mr. Brumley, and through him of Lady Harman, in whose coming out she plays a considerable part and whose rescue she attempts unsuccessfully. Sir Isaac Harman hates and fears her. *Sir Isaac Harman ;* mentioned in *Bealby* and *Research Magnificent.*

44. BEALBY ; A Holiday. See Bib. No. 57. This book is dedicated to "that real Lord Chancellor who not only reads Hegel but who gave his country an army to be proud of, fit and ready when the moment came."—Lord Haldane. Sir Peter and Lady Laxton are giving an important week-end party at Shonts, the chief guest being the Lord Chancellor, Lord Moggeridge. On the Saturday night, after his host has retired, Lord Moggeridge creeps downstairs in search of whisky and cigars. He is discovered through the rebellion and flight from lower regions of the latest and very youthful addition to the staff of servants at Shonts, Arthur Bealby, who collides with him on the stairs and then, in the confusion, finds refuge in a priest hole behind the wall of the Lord Chancellor's room. All night long Lord Moggeridge is kept awake by movements behind the wall, and in the morning chances to discover Mergleson, the stately butler, about to enter the passage leading to the hole. He jumps to the conclusion that Captain Douglas, a fellow-guest, has bribed the servants to annoy him. By this time Bealby is some miles away from Shonts, and that morning joins a caravan party consisting of Mrs. Bowles, Mrs. Geedge, and Madeleine Philips, an actress who is engaged to Captain

Douglas. For two days he travels with them, until, on the Tuesday, the ladies are joined by their husbands and Captain Douglas, when, hearing them speak of Shonts and fearing recapture, he runs away. He meets a tramp, William Bridget, who next day forces him to take part in a burglary. On Thursday morning, he gets away from his unpleasant companion, only to find notices everywhere offering £5 reward for his return to Shonts. In the village of Crayminster he is recognised and pursued by a great crowd right across the sacred strawberry fields of Mr. Benshaw, a local farmer. He escapes and hides in a shed until the next morning. Meanwhile, Captain Douglas, anxious to clear himself of the Lord Chancellor's charge and realising that Bealby is the cause of all the trouble, sets out in pursuit of him after considerable delay caused by Madeleine, with whom he quarrels. On the Friday morning, Bealby comes upon Captain Douglas, who whirls him off to London on his motor-cycle. Through his uncle, Lord Chickney, he gains immediate access to the Lord Chancellor and attempts an explanation. Bealby starts confessing his part in the burglary in a way most compromising to the captain, who gives everything up and goes to France. Bealby returns to Shonts with the determination to do better work in the future.

BEALBY, ARTHUR. Step-son of the gardener at Shonts. He is a boy of romantic disposition, with an objection to work in general and " service " in particular. At one time he is persuaded that, in reality, he is the rightful " Earl Shonts." *Bealby*.

BEAST PEOPLE, THE. The grotesque inhabitants of Dr. Moreau's island, numbering about sixty at the time of Prendick's arrival. Altogether Moreau made over one hundred, but many died or were killed. Certain of the females bear offspring, which generally die ; those which survive are pink hopping creatures with long hind legs, about the size of cats. They inherit none of the acquired human characteristics of their parents. Those of the Beast People mentioned by name are the Ape-Man, the Bear-Bull Man, three Bull Men (the boat-pullers), a Footless Thing (a limbless creature which broke loose while still unfinished and in " infuriating pain " ; " it travelled in a rollicking way like a porpoise swimming "), the Hyæna- Swine, the Leopard Man (these two were the first of the rabbit-killers and leaders of the revolt), M'ling (Montgomery's personal attendant, " a bear tainted with dog and ox "), the Saint Bernard Dog Man, the Sayer of the Law (also called the Hairy Grey Thing and the Silvery Hairy Man ; he leads the rest of the People in the saying of Moreau's Law), and the Wolf-Bear Man. *Dr.Moreau*.

45. BEAUTIFUL SUIT, THE. See A Moonlight Fable. 33rd story in *Country of the Blind*. A " little man " has a beautiful suit made for him by his loving mother. One moonlit night he wakes and dons his suit, tearing away the cuff and elbow guards and revealing it in all its precious perfection. He goes out into the garden, wading the duck-pond, " a great bowl of silver moonshine," and so on to the high road, rejoicing in the sweetness of the night, at last to fall into a stone pit, breaking his neck.

BEAUTY OF FLYING, THE. 2nd article in *Year of Prophesying ;* see *H. G. Wells on the Beauty of Flying.*

BECHAMEL, GEORGE. A distinguished London art critic. Under the pretence of helping her to Live Her Own Life he persuades Jessica Milton to leave home with him, hoping to compromise her and so achieve his desire. But he soon begins to feel that " this romantic business of seduction " is " unexpectedly tame," and when she runs away from him he does not trouble to pursue her. His wife is mentioned as a woman of " peculiar moral views " who measures " marital infidelity largely by its proximity to herself." *Wheels of Chance.*

BEDFORD. Narrator of *The First Men in the Moon.* An undischarged bankrupt, hard pressed by one creditor, he takes a bungalow at Lympne and lives on credit while writing a play. Here he meets Cavor and forces himself upon the inventor. In the moon he causes trouble by his too-hasty temper. After the loss of the sphere he goes to Amalfi to write the story of his adventures and to complete his play, being now in comfortable circumstances from the sale of the moon-gold. When messages are received from Cavor he goes to Wendigee's observatory on Monta Rosa. While disposing of the gold he assumes the name of Blake to avoid any risks of annoyance from his " cantankerous creditor."

46. BEFORE THE FANCY DRESS BALL. Pall Mall Gazette, in March, 1894. Article.

47. BEGINNINGS OF MIND AND LANGUAGE, THE. 4th chapter of *Mankind.* In three sections, the first of which discusess the " ideal environment " for a child, the second the beginnings of speech and the present inefficient teaching of English, and the last the knowledge which the average child should have acquired by the end of his fifth year.

48. BEHIND THE FRONT. 3rd chapter of *The War in Italy.* Discusses the effect of the war upon Italy, and the Italian attitude to her allies and enemies.

BEHRENS. A young Oxford don, " one of those vividly clever energetic people who are the despair of originative men." Beginning as Trafford's " pupil and sedulous ape," he goes on to imitate his work in a way and " with an intensity which most marvellously simulated originality." He becomes known as an authority upon molecular physics, and enrages Trafford by the " solemn mess he's making of it." It is owing to Behrens's advertised assertion that he has solved the problem of synthesising india-rubber that Trafford works it out himself. *Marriage.*

BELLOWS. Narrator of *Le Mari Terrible, The Poet and the Emporium, The Remarkable Case of Davidson's Eyes, The Triumphs of a Taxidermist.*

BENHAM, WILLIAM PORPHYRY. The main character in *The Research Magnificent,* son of a clergyman and schoolmaster. His mother runs away with a rich man, Nolan, who leaves most of his fortune to her son in compensation, and Benham takes advantage of his circumstances to devote his life to a study of the collective life of the world, to a " research after aristocracy." He is ruled from his schooldays to his death by his attempt to live the aristocratic life. His religious belief develops from an " atheistical republicanism " to a belief in " God the immortal adventurer in me." He is a physical coward, and hates all animals, particularly horses ; he rides with such " joylessness of bearing " that he is called the " Galvanised Corpse." All his life he battles with what he calls the four limitations. Fear, Indulgence, Jealousy, Prejudice. He marries Amanda Morris.

BENSINGTON. An " eminent scientist," Fellow of the Royal Society, and a former president of the Chemical Society. A short, bald man with gold-rimmed spectacles and slashed cloth boots, who has risen to eminence by his researches upon Toxic Alkaloids. The public take him to be the sole inventor of the Food of the Gods, and an attempt is made to lynch him at his flat. Whereupon he retires, with Jane, his cousin and housekeeper, to Tunbridge Wells. *Food of the Gods.*

49. BIBLE OF CIVILISATION, THE. See *The New Bible.* 4th and 5th chapters of *The Salvaging of Civilisation.* A revival of an idea first suggested by Comenius, that of " a common book . . . which should form the basis and framework for the thoughts and imaginations of every citizen in the world." This he models on the Bible, suggesting a modern equivalent for each of the old Jewish books. The New

Bible would contain an outline history of the world and of mankind, the rules of life and health, the facts of sex, the moral code, the fundamentals of economics, and, in place of the later books, groups of anthologies containing the best thought of the world in prose and poetry.

BINDON. " One of the most influential shareholders " in the London flying-stage company of the 22nd century, a middle-aged man with a fondness for pleasure which he indulges to such an extent that it kills him. When Elizabeth Mwres elopes with Denton he uses his influence to drive them to the lowest level, and then at the last minute leaves all his money to her, hoping at least to impress her with his magnanimity. *Story of the Days to Come.*

50. BIOLOGICAL PROBLEM OF TO-DAY, THE. Saturday Review, Dec. 29th, 1894. Unsigned article.

51. BIOLOGY FOR THE INTERMEDIATE SCIENCE AND PRELIMINARY SCIENTIFIC EXAMINATIONS ; Hints for Practical Work. University Correspondent, Feb. 25th, 1893.

52. BIO-OPTIMISM. Nature, Aug. 29th, 1895. Review of " The Evergreen," a semi-annual periodical issued from St. Andrew's University, Edinburgh.

53. BIRTH RATE DECLINE, THE. Daily Mail, May 19th, 1904.

BLACK SMOKE, THE. A highly poisonous vapour used by the Martians in their advance upon London. It is discharged from great canisters fired rocket-wise from guns. *War of the Worlds.*

54. Blame the Newly Rich Adventurers. Penny Pictorial, Oct. 25th, 1919. A 200-word note on an article by Shaw Desmond, "Is Labour Sinking the Ship?" in the same issue.

Blandish, Mr. Hero of *The Spoils of Mr. Blandish;* a man "pretty completely taken from the James ideal." A drawing shows him "going delicately through life. Oh no! Oh no! But *yes!* and *This is it!*"

55. Bleak March in Epping Forest. Pall Mall Gazette, Mar. 16th, 1894; 27th essay in *Personal Matters.* Description of visit paid to Epping Forest in March by the writer and his wife.

56. Blinkers for Free Youth : Young America Asks to Hear and See. Westminster Gazette, June 14th, 1924; 41st article in *Year of Prophesying.* Comments on elementary and university education in America, with a protest against the attempts of the authorities to keep students from full knowledge and "mental freedom."

Bliss, Reginald. Friend of George Boon and his literary executor; he edits and "prepares for publication" the volume of Boon's literary remains. He is a writer too, the title-page of *Boon* (see Bib. No. 56) naming several of his books, and suggests to Boon the idea which develops into *The Mind of the Race.* There are two sketches of him printed in the volume.

Blundering Bolshevism (Russia in the Shadows, 3). Sunday Express, Nov. 14th, 1920; reprinted as *The Quintessence of Bolshevism* (q.v.).

Bonover, George. Headmaster of the Whortley Proprietary School. He dismisses Lewisham for telling lies about Ethel Henderson after the Scandalous Ramble. *Mr. Lewisham.*

Booch, Mrs. One of Lady Drew's pensioned servants, and trustee for a favourite Skye terrier. She has "a small set of stereotyped remarks that constituted her entire mental range." *Tono-Bungay.*

57. Book-Keeping a la Maitre D'Ecole. Daily Mail, Dec. 17th, 1897.

58. Book of Curses, The. See *On Swearing.* 18th essay in *Personal Matters.* Professor Gargoyle holds that swearing is a "thoroughly hygienic and moral practice"; he travels about the world "culling flowers of speech." He bemoans the decay of cursing in England, contrasting it with the East.

59. Book of Essays Dedicatory, The. See *My Last Book.* 33rd essay in *Personal Matters.* Asked by a publisher for a book of verse, the author decides on the title "Lichens," and passes on to consideration of the dedication. Three months later he looks through his still unsatisfactory attempts, and decides to make a book of them as they stand.

60. Book on Bolshevik Russia, A. Adelphi, June, 1923 (Contributors' Club). Review of Odette Kean's "My Adventure in Bolshevik Russia."

61. Boon, the Mind of the Race, the Wild Asses of the Devil, and the Last Trump. See

Bib. No. 56. After the death of George Boon, a popular novelist, in Dec., 1914, Reginald Bliss, his literary executor, finds that his literary remains are fragmentary, that the secret works of which Boon talked so much exist only in incomplete scraps. He resolves " at least one experimental volume " by editing certain of these (to make) fragments and linking them by recorded conversations between Boon and his friends. There are three stories ; throughout the book there is much discussion of a collective mind of the race, of contemporary thought and literature, and of contemporary writers. It is illustrated with 26 sketches of characters and writers mentioned. See also *The Mind of the Race, The Wild Asses of the Devil, The Story of the Last Trump.*

BOON, GEORGE. A writer of popular books and plays, known throughout the world. But the George Boon of Reginald Bliss is not " George Boon the Great Writer, but the one who was known only to his little circle of intimate friends—Bliss, Dodd, F. M. Hueffer, Wilkins—to whom he was an earnest and serious thinker. Bliss recalls " his round, enigmatical face, an affair of rosy rotundities, his very bright, active eyes, his queer, wiry, black hair that went out to every point in the heavens." He dies towards the end of 1914 from pneumonia brought on by bathing by moonlight in October, in an attempt to distract his mind from the war. Among the " remains " not printed in *Boon*—some being unpublishable—are mentioned a small MS. volume of Limericks, " Jane in Heaven," and " An Account of a Play " (imitations of

Villiers de l'Isle Adam), an " extraordinarily offensive " interview with Raymond Blathwayt, an unfinished study of the " Literary Statesmen of the Transition Years from the Nineteenth to the Twentieth Centuries," a general index to the works of Plato and Aristotle, several long pieces of Vers Libre, the draft of a novel, and great quantities of sketches of his friends and contemporaries. Only one of Boon's " popular " novels is mentioned— " Captain Clayball." Mrs. Boon is described as an " extraordinarily irrelevant person," who resents the publication of the " remains."

BOTANIST, THE. Companion of the Owner of the Voice in his visit to *A Modern Utopia.* He is a man of thirty-nine, lean and tall and grave and dyspeptic and " weakly handsome," who constantly intrudes his " poor little love-affair " upon the Utopian speculations of his friend. While in Utopia he sees Mary, the woman he loves, and in a moment of anger and passion bursts the bubble that the Owner of the Voice has spun about them, bringing them back to reality.

62. BRAINTREE, BOCKING, AND THE FUTURE OF THE WORLD (Looking Ahead). Daily Chronicle, Feb. 19th, 1916 ; 4th chapter in *What is Coming ?* A stretch of road, foolishly planned, together with the administration of the two villages, Braintree and Bocking, through which it runs, is taken as a " sample of the general human way of getting things done." The writer predicts that after the war, if there is no increase in efficiency, there will be revolution and bloodshed. This article was commented upon in The Essex Review, April, 1916.

BRIDGET, WILLIAM. The tramp
with whom Bealby joins company
after leaving the caravan. A dirty,
ugly, unshaven man, with great
experience of the more unpleasant
side of life ; self-named a Socialist,
he is a thief and an expert in
simulating epilepsy. He mentions
his wife as a " bad and spiritless
person " who was " born scared."
Bealby.

BRIGGS. A young man at a motor
works. He blows the celestial trumpet by attaching it to a powerful
foot blow-pipe. *Story of the Last
Trump.*

63. BRITISH SCHOOLMASTER, THE.
Daily Mail, Nov. 18th, 1897.

BRITLING, HUGH. The central
character in *Mr. Britling.* At the
time of the outbreak of the Great
War he is a prominent British
thinker and writer. Beginning with
" a Pembroke fellowship and a prize
poem " he becomes an art-critic
and leader-writer. As a Kahn
scholar he tours the world, returning
to write for The Times and to
produce books on national relation-
ships and social psychology. He
is, mentally and physically, an
energetic, active man. " His moustache, his hair, his eyebrows bristled;
his flaming freckled face seemed to
bristle too. His little hazel eyes
came out with a ' ping.' " His
" naturally irritable " and " active
and encyclopaedic " mind teems
with ideas upon every subject. His
first passionate marriage to Mary,
the mother of his son Hugh, took
place when he was a fellow of
Pembroke, and their life together,
cut short by her death, is an un-
forgettable memory. His love for
Edith is cooler and calmer, insufficient to hold him altogether ;

when Mr. Direck visits him he is
involved in his eighth love affair,
this time with a Mrs. Harrowdean.
Books and pamphlets mentioned
are " American Impressions," " And
Now War Ends," " The Anatomy
of Hate," " An Examination of
War," " The Better Government
of the World," and—an unfinished
volume of verse—" The Silent
Places." Edith, his second wife, is
a " tall, freckled woman with
pretty brown hair and preoccupied
brown eyes." She is a B.Sc. of
London University and " several
things like that," a woman of calm
watchful serenity. She and her
husband no longer love one another,
but they are bound together by an
" habitual affection " and by their
two children. The elder of these
two boys is not mentioned by name ;
the younger is Gilbert, a small
bright bristling boy.

BRITLING, HUGH. Mr. Britling's
eldest son, the only child of his first
wife. He is a lanky, shock-headed
boy of seventeen, whose ambitions
are divided between science and
art. Soon after the outbreak of
war, though not yet eighteen years
old, he enlists as a private, and in
due course is sent to France. His
letters to his father give vivid
accounts of his army life in training
and in the trenches. He is killed
by a stray bullet in October, 1915.

BRITTEN. Remington's chief
friend at the City Merchants School,
a clever but rather slovenly boy.
He goes on to Oxford, and though
he and Remington correspond they
are not brought continuously together until the founding of the
" Blue Weekly," of which he becomes sub-editor. He plays a great
part in Remington's secession from
the Liberal Party ; at the last

I

crisis he does his best to persuade Remington to part with Isabel Rivers rather than ruin his career. *New Machiavelli*.

64. BROTHERHOOD OF PEOPLES. Daily Express, Dec. 16th, 1921 ; 28th chapter of *Washington*. Comments on the part Japan has played in helping towards a Pacific settlement. He outlines necessary future conferences, and foresees the political future of mankind as " a great system of associated States locked and interlocked together by . . . treaties . . . ruling jointly the still barbaric regions of the earth and pledged to respect, keep, and at last welcome to their own ranks the now politically enfeebled regions of the old civilisation."

BRUMLEY, GEORGE. A " stout, medium-sized gentleman," with " a round, ruddy, rather handsome, amiable face, a sort of bang of brown hair coming over one temple, and a large silk bow under his chin and a little towards one ear. . . . His profile was regular and fine, his eyes expressive, his mouth, a very passable mouth." He is the author of a series of " Euphemia " books, and volumes of essays and travel notes, distinguished by their " gay yet steadfast superficiality." About the time of his first meeting with Lady Harman, three years after the death of his wife, he is discontented, new ideas are coming to him, reality is forcing itself upon him. He wishes to sell Black Strand, his old home, and to start afresh in new surroundings. His one son, a schoolboy, is mentioned. *Sir Isaac Harman*.

65. BUBBLE BURSTS, THE. 11th and final chapter in *A Modern Utopia*. The botanist, seeing the woman he had loved on earth

happy in Utopia with her husband' flies into a passion and bursts the imaginative bubble which the Owner of the Voice has spun about them, bringing them back to the London of reality. The Owner of the Voice leaves the botanist and gets on a bus. He states his belief that some day out of all these dreams of Utopia there will come the " final World State, the fair and great and fruitful World State, that will only not be a Utopia because it will be in this world."

BUGGINS. A young man with a " very wise face," assistant at the Folkestone Drapery Bazaar. One of Kipps's special friends. *Kipps*.

BULLA, THE. Weekly Sun Literary Sup., Dec. 1st, 1895 ; reprinted as *The Reconciliation* (q.v.).

BUMPUS, BEATRICE. A " slender young woman of about five and twenty," a woman's suffrage worker, who has the drawing-room floor at Matilda Good's house. She urges Harry Smith to avoid Blind Alley occupations. *Dream*.

BUNTHORNE, EDNA. Bert Smallway's " girl " ; he returns to her from America and marries her after killing a rival suitor. *War in the Air*.

BUNTINGS, THE RANDOLPH. The family who " rescue " the Sea Lady near their villa on the beach between Folkestone and Sandgate, and invite her to remain with them as a " paying guest." The family consists of Mr. and Mrs. Randolph Bunting, and three children, Fred, Betty, and Nettie. *Sea Lady*.

BUNTING, REVEREND MR. Vicar of Iping. Griffin burgles his house in the early hours of Whit-Monday. Later he and Mr. Cuss examine

Griffin's papers, but are interrupted by the Invisible Man, who takes the vicar's clothes. Mr. Bunting subsequently makes a dash up the village street clad only in a newspaper. *Invisible Man.*

66. BUNYAN FOR BUSY MEN. Bellman, April 2nd, 1910.

BURLEIGH, CECIL. "The great Conservative leader," "not only distinguished as a politician" but "eminent as a private gentleman, a philosopher and a man of universal intelligence." He is "tall, slender, grey-headed." "On earth he had done little and been intelligently receptive with the happiest results." The Utopians propose to return him to the earth. *Men Like Gods.*

BURNET, SUSAN. An independent young woman who comes regularly to the Harman's Putney house to renovate the furniture; she is one of the "disturbing influences" which lead to Lady Harman's revolt and flight from Black Strand. Later she gives much advice concerning the management of the International Hostels to Lady Harman, but becoming one of the chief malcontents at the Bloomsbury Hostel, she is forced to leave. *Sir Isaac Harman.*

BURROWS, SIR ELIPHAZ (Eliphaz the Temanite). A governor of Woldingstanton School, "a slender old man, with an avid vulturine head poised on a long red neck," scholarly, refined, and courteous. With Dad and Farr he plans to remove Huss from the headmastership. During the discussion in Huss's rooms he expresses his belief in immortality and spiritualism, and that "God does not strike men needlessly," implying that Huss's misfortune's are due to his wrong-

doing. He is a manufacturer of Temanite building blocks. In Job Huss's dream he becomes Eliphaz the Temanite. His nephew, Kenneth Burrows, is head of a committee of old boys formed to prevent the dismissal of Huss, his letter to whom is quoted. *Undying Fire.*

BUTTERIDGE, ALFRED. Inventor of a very successful though simple aeroplane, a man "singularly free from . . . modesty of any kind." He is continually talking about his mother, who is "largely Scotch," and about a lady with whom he has "a love affair of large and unusual dimensions and irregular circumstances." It is rumoured that he is actually a South African hotel-keeper who has robbed a young inventor. Bert Smallways meets him at Dymchurch, and subsequently, in Germany, is mistaken for him. *War in the Air.*

C

CADDLES, ALBERT EDWARD. One of the Giant Children. He is the child of two Cheasing Eyebright villagers, and grandson of Mrs. Skinner, who feeds him with Herakleophorbia. He grows up lonely and unhappy, unintelligent but possessed by a continual wonder. "What are ye for, ye swarming little people? What are ye all doing, what are ye all for?" He works for several years in a local chalk-pit, running it single-handed; in the end he makes a tragic trip to London, and is killed. His father is described as Lady Wondershoot's "ideal lower-class person, dishonest, faithful, abject, industrious, inconceivably incapable of responsibility." *Food of the Gods.*

CAPES, GODWIN. Demonstrator in the biological laboratory of the Central Imperial College at Westminster, a blonde young man of thirty or so, and a Fellow of the Royal Society. He has married young, but his wife, a woman of "very serene and proud and dignified temperament," will not live with him after he has been cited as co-respondent in a divorce case. Despite the impossibility of marriage, for his wife refuses to divorce him, he and Ann Veronica Stanley decide to live together. He gives up his work at the College and takes to writing. A few years later his wife seemingly changes her mind and sues for divorce, and he (now a successful dramatist writing under the pseudonym Thomas More) and Ann Veronica marry. *Ann Veronica.* Also mentioned in *Marriage.*

CARETAKER, A. Who looks after the house and garden described in W. H. Mallock's "The New Republic," revisited in *The Mind of the Race* by several men of letters who hope to hold a Summer Congress there. He is "morose, elderly . . . greatly embittered" and resents the intrusion : he makes several surprising revelations concerning the characters of "The New Republic."

CARNABY, THE EARL OF. A great sportsman, a man who has "sinned all the sins . . . and laid waste the most magnificent political debut of any man of his generation." Beatrice Normandy, despite her love for George Ponderevo, becomes his mistress. *Tono-Bungay.* Mentioned in *New Machiavelli.*

67. CASE AGAINST SOCIALISM, THE. Daily Mail, June 27th, 1910.

68. CASE AGAINST THE CLASSICAL LANGUAGES, THE. Fortnightly Review, Apr., 1917 ; Chapter 6 of Natural Science and the Classical System in Education (see Bib. II, 1918). In a criticism of "A Defence of Classical Education," by R. W. Livingstone (Macmillan, 1916), states the case against classical education.

69. CASE OF UNAMUNO : THE FEEBLE REPUBLIC OF LETTERS, THE. Westminster Gazette, Apr. 12th, 1924 ; 31st article in *Year of Prophesying* Taking as example the case of the exiling of Don Miguel Unamuno for criticism of the King of Spain, comments on the lack of any solidarity among modern intellectuals, they having made no organised or even general protest.

CASTON. An American artist, during the war V. V. Grammont's lover. He was a "very rotten sort of man," and was shot for "calculated, cold-blooded cowardice." *Secret Places.*

70. CATASTROPHE, A. New Budget, Apr. 4th, 1895 ; 14th tale in *Plattner Story.* Winslow, a small draper, is faced by bankruptcy. News comes of the sudden death of his wife's uncle and uncle's family. She is sole heir to the dead man's property, the value of which will more than save her husband from ruin.

CATERHAM, JOHN. A prominent English politician who constantly advocates the total suppression of Herakleophorbia. It is his proclamation which the Giant Children answer by organised revolt. *Food of the Gods.*

CATSKILL, RUPERT. Secretary of State for War, a "slow-moving, intent, sandy-complexioned figure in a grey top hat with a black band "; he has " some slight impediment in his speech, the little brother of a lisp, against which his voice beat gutturally," but he has also " the knack of the plausible phrase and that imaginative touch which makes for eloquence." He scorns Utopia as a Golden Lotus Land whose people have " drunken the debilitating draught of Socialism," and presses his plan for the conquest of Utopia upon the other Earthlings. He survives the defeat of his party, and is presumably returned to the earth in due course. *Men Like Gods.* Commenting on this book in a later article, Wells admits that " one of the characters got out of my control, and began to act and speak in a way so like Mr. Churchill's that even I could see the resemblance. I was shocked and alarmed. I had to stun that character and hustle it out of the way, but not before it had made a long characteristic speech and started a war." *Winston.*

CAVOR. A scientist who conducts researches " because he has to." He manufactures Cavorite (a substance " opaque " to gravity) but sees none of its possibilities until Bedford points them out to him. He is a short, round-bodied little man, a water-drinker, a vegetarian, and " all those logical disciplining things." He has one habit, that of making a constant buzzing noise as he walks. *First Men in the Moon.*

CEMENT OF EMPIRE. Everybody's Weekly, Mar. 11th, 1911 ; reprinted as *Will the Empire Live ?* (q.v.).

71. CENTRE OF TERRESTIAL LIFE, THE. Saturday Review, Feb. 16th,

1895. Unsigned. Speculation on " where did terrestial animals come into being ? " ; decides on some northerly place with slow spreading to the south.

72. CERTAIN CRITICAL OPINIONS. Saturday Review, July 11th, 1896. Unsigned. Comments on Andrew Lang's objection to glossary of Scotch words in " The Weir of Hermiston."

73. CERTAIN PERSONAL MATTERS. See Bib. No. 12. The titles of the 39 stories and essays in this volume are : 1, *Thoughts on Cheapness and My Aunt Charlotte ;* 2, *The Trouble of Life ;* 3, *On the Choice of a Wife ;* 4, *The House of di Sorno ;* 5, *Of Conversation ;* 6, *In a Literary Household ;* 7, *On Schooling and the Phases of Mr. Sandsome ;* 8, *The Poet and the Emporium ;* 9, *The Language of Flowers ;* 10, *The Literary Regimen ;* 11, *House-Hunting as an Outdoor Amusement ;* 12, *Of Blades and Bladery ;* 13, *Of Cleverness ;* 14, *The Pose Novel ;* 15, *The Veteran Cricketer ;* 16, *Concerning a Certain Lady ;* 17, *The Shopman ;* 18, *The Book of Curses ;* 19, *Dunstone's Dear Lady ;* 20, *Euphemia's New Entertainment ;* 21, *For Freedom of Spelling ;* 22, *Incidental Thoughts on a Bald Head ;* 23, *Of a Book Unwritten ;* 24, *The Extinction of Man ;* 25, *The Writing of Essays ;* 26, *The Parkes Museum ;* 27, *Bleak March in Epping Forest ;* 28, *The Theory of Quotation ;* 29, *On the Art of Staying at the Seastde ;* 30, *Concerning Chess ;* 31, *The Coal Scuttle*; 32, *Bagarrow ;* 33, *The Book of Essays Dedicatory ;* 34, *Through a Microscope ;* 35, *The Pleasure of Quarrelling ;* 36, *The Amateur Nature-Lover ;* 37, *From an Ob-*

servatory ; 38, *The Mode in Monuments* ; 39, *How I Died.*

74. CERTAIN SOCIAL REACTIONS. 4th chapter in *Anticipations.* Considers " certain general ways in which the various factors and elements in the deliquescent society of the present time will react upon one another," and speculates therefrom upon the homes, morals, and general culture of the future.

75. CERTAIN WHOLESALE ASPECTS OF MAN-MAKING. 3rd chapter in *Mankind.* In two sections ; the first discusses the minimum conditions necessary to ensure that the new-born child shall not start life handicapped by ill-health or under-development ; the second considers the " problem of securing the maximum chance of life and health for every baby born into the world."

76. CERTAIN WORKERS. 6th chapter in *Future in America.* Discusses conditions of child-labour in the United States.

CHAFFERY, JAMES. Ethel Henderson's step-father, a plausible rogue who makes a living as a spiritualist medium. He is a " benevolent looking, faintly shabby gentleman, with bushy iron-grey side-whiskers, a wide thin-lipped mouth tucked in at the corners, and a chin like the toe of a boot." A fluent and persuasive speaker, " by nature tricky," he invents many new devices to assist his swindling. He marries Mrs. Henderson about the time of Ethel's visit to Whortley. Finally, after rooking Lagune of almost every penny, he leaves the country with his woman assistant. His wife, Ethel's mother, is a " queer little dust-lined woman" who appeals to Lewisham for aid when Chaffery deserts her. *Mr. Lewisham.*

CHARLOTTE, AUNT. A stern formidable Victorian lady with whom the narrator of the essays in *Certain Personal Matters* spent his youth. She appears prominently in *Thoughts on Cheapness and My Aunt Charlotte,* and is mentioned in *Of Cleverness, Of Conversation,* and *On Schooling and the Phases of Mr. Sandsome.*

CHATTERIS, HARRY. "The nephew of an earl and the hero of a scandal, and a quite possible candidate for the Hythe division of Kent." He is engaged to Adeline Glendower at the time of the coming of the Sea Lady, but this engagement, like his work, is broken off when he succumbs to the seductive charms of the mermaid. *Sea Lady.*

77. CHEAP MICROSCOPES AND A MORAL. Saturday Review, Sept. 12th, 1896. Compares prices and qualities of English and German microscopes, and comments on lack of English enterprise. Correspondence by Wells and others follows on Sept. 12th, 19th, 26th, Oct. 17th.

CHICKNEY, LORD. Cousin of the mother of Captain Douglas, who calls him Uncle ; he is a general with " a very tall, very drooping, grizzled old-veteran picturesqueness about him that kept him distinguished," but he is old, deaf, and his articulation is not clear. He cannot get rid of the idea that the trouble between Douglas and Lord Moggeridge is in some way connected with Madeleine Philips, and plays a part in the confusion of the final interview. *Bealby.*

78. CHINA IN THE BACKGROUND. Daily Mail, Nov. 17th, 1921 ; 8th chapter in *Washington*. A brief account of present-day conditions in China. The Chinese must be allowed to reconstruct their country unrestricted by foreign influences.

CHINA : THE LAND OUT OF THE LIMELIGHT. 34th article in *Year of Prophesying ;* see *Importance of China*.

CHITTERLOW, HARRY. A buoyant, garrulous playwright who, while cycling in the dark, runs Kipps down, takes him home for repairs, and becomes his lasting friend. He has an inexhaustible fund of stories about the stage and women, and an equally inexhaustible enthusiasm for "good old Methusaleh" whisky. He draws Kipps's attention to the advertisement which brings Kipps his fortune ; subsequently Kipps buys a share in his play "The Pestered Butterfly," which is a tremendous success. *Kipps.*

CHRISTABEL. The good-looking red-haired schoolgirl who sits on the wall of the school-garden and talks to Mr. Polly, to whom she becomes the personification of all Romance. Day after day he comes and talks to her until at last he tells her that he loves her ; some girls hidden behind the wall begin to giggle, and she attacks them, finally running off through the trees never to return. Fifteen years later Mr. Polly passes the wall again and wonders if she has quite forgotten. *Mr. Polly.*

CHRISTIAN, LADY MARY. A woman of "sweet and beautiful

possibilities," who despite her wisdom and nobility lacks the courage to face poverty with Stephen Stratton, or the power to deny her love for him. After a life of unhappiness and thwarted love, she commits suicide, killed by the "animal jealousies" of Stratton and Justin, her husband. Her brother, Philip Christian, fights Stratton on the steps of a London club when he hears that Justin proposes to divorce his sister. *Passionate Friends.*

78a. CHRISTINA ALBERTA'S FATHER. A novel. See *Sargon King of Kings*. Printed serially in Daily Telegraph, 1925 ; to be published in Sept., 1925 by Jonathan Cape, Ltd., London and The Macmillan Co., New York.

79. CHRONIC ARGONAUTS, THE. Science Schools Journal, Apr., May, June, 1888. The most important of the college magazine contributions, a fantastic story the main idea of which afterward became that of *The Time Machine*. Dr. Moses Nebogipfel comes to the Welsh village of Llyddwdd, there, in the loneliness of a supposedly haunted house, to construct the "Chronic Argo," a machine which travels through time. The superstitious villagers suppose him to be a wizard, and gather to attack the house. The local vicar comes to warn the inventor of his peril and the two men are forced to escape on the machine. The inventor tells the vicar that he, travelling into the past, committed the crime which caused the house to be haunted. They have various adventures in the far future (A.D. 4003 and 17,901), but these are not related. About 8,000-9,000 words in length.

80. COAL-SCUTTLE, THE. Pall Mall Gazette, end of 1893 ; 31st essay in *Personal Matters*. Discusses the problem of the coal-scuttle in the " dainty and delightful home," and describes Euphemia's experiments with various types of coal-boxes and coal-cupboards.

81. COLLEGE, NEWSPAPER AND BOOK. Reprint, with some additions. of *Adult Education* (q.v.) ; 7th chapter of *Salvaging of Civilisation*. " The key to all our human disorder is education, comprehensive and universal." The writer outlines a scheme of adult education to be carried out through college, book and newspaper.

82. COMENIUS. University Correspondent, Mar. 15th, 1892.

83. COMING OF BLERIOT, THE. See *Of a Cross Channel Passage*. 1st essay in *An Englishman*. Written July, 1909, upon the occasion of Bleriot's cross-channel flight. Concludes that the British are " hopelessly behindhand " in aeronautics, in science, and in education.

84. COMMON SENSE AND THE BALKAN STATES (Looking Ahead). Daily Chronicle, Aug. 28th, 1914 ; 10th chapter in *War that will End War*. With the Balkan States unsettled there can be no permanent peace in Europe. Suggests a council, upon which England, Russia and Italy would be represented, for the formation of a rehabilitated Balkan League.

85. COMMON SENSE OF CONSCRIPTION, THE. Daily Mail, Apr. 7th, 1913 ; 1st article in *War and Commonsense*. Conscription is not only impossible but needless in Great Britain. The average townsman cannot be converted into an efficient soldier in the space of a year or two, we have not the necessary officers, and large armies are useless in modern war. The need is for small bodies of scientifically trained and officered men armed with the newest weapons.

COMMON SENSE OF WARFARE, THE. 8th paper in *An Englishman*, a reprint of the pamphlet *War and Common Sense*.

86. CONCERNING A CERTAIN LADY. Black and White, Sept. 29th, 1894 ; 16th essay in *Personal Matters*. Describes a certain energetic lady of whom the writer goes in daily terror. Whenever he sees her she bumps him with her umbrella, or stands on his feet, or pushes him into a corner. He warns her that his patience is exhausted.

87. CONCERNING CHESS. Pall Mall Gazette, Feb. 1st, 1895 ; 30th essay in *Personal Matters*. Chess attracts people, but gives no real happiness. Recollects the " only game of chess that I recall with undiluted pleasure."

88. CONCERNING FREEDOMS. 2nd chapter of *A Modern Utopia*. The two visitors to Utopia come down from the mountain pass, pick up a gold coin, dine at an Urserenthal inn where later they spend the night, and go for a walk in the evening darkness. The botanist tells the story of his love-affair, and the Owner of the Voice discusses individual liberty, prohibitions, personal privacy, freedom of movement, travel, and the drink question, in a modern Utopia.

89. CONCERNING LODGING-HOUSE KEEPERS. Pall Mall Gazette, Feb. 10th, 1894.

90. CONCERNING MR. MAXIMILIAN CRAFT. Daily News, Aug. 14th, 1914 ; 4th article in *War that will End War*. Attacks a certain type of naturalised Englishman, who is very anxious to tell everyone how the war should be waged by "breaches of neutrality, national treacheries . . . a perfect world-organisation of super-sneaks."

91. CONCERNING MR. WELSTEAD. University Correspondent, Oct. 7th, 1893.

92. CONCERNING OUR PEDIGREE. Gentleman's Magazine, about 1891 or 1892.

93. CONCILIATORY SOCIALISM. New Quarterly, Oct., 1908. Replies to articles on Socialism by G. A. Paley and W. H. Mallock. States that the controversy between Socialists and anti-Socialists has reached a stage in which, under present circumstances, it is impossible to argue further. It has "resolved itself into terms that demand a critical digest of as yet uncollected and unclassified historical and contemporary facts."

94. CONE, THE. Unicorn, Sept. 18th, 1895 ; 10th tale in *Plattner Story*, 2nd in *Country of the Blind*, 4th in *Door in the Wall*. Horrocks a Five Towns ironmaster, discovers that his wife and a friend, Raut, are in love. Taking Raut to see the blast furnaces by moonlight, he seizes an opportunity as they stand upon a platform overhanging a furnace and throws him down into the cone. Raut hangs by a chain, shrieking in agony, until Horrocks puts an end to it by tilting a truck of coal down upon him.

95. CONFLICT OF LANGUAGES, THE. 7th chapter in *Anticipations*. Discusses the causes of present political boundaries, foresees the disappearance of the smaller, less important languages, and argues the respective claims of English, French, German and Chinese to be the world-languages of the future.

96. CONSTRUCTIVE IDEAS AND THEIR RELATION TO CURRENT POLITICS. Westminster Gazette, May 17th, 1924 ; 37th article in *Year of Prophesying*. The Labour Party has no "monopoly of creative ideas," indeed, under present electoral conditions "there is no political party in the world that dare do more than fumble and prevaricate about any of them."

97. CONSTRUCTIVE SOCIALISM. 13th chapter of *New Worlds*. Discusses the part and place of Socialism in the collective mind of the world, the publication of books and newspapers in the Socialist state, and the programme of modern constructive Socialism.

98. CONTEMPORARY NOVEL, THE. Fortnightly Review, Nov., 1911 ; Atlantic Monthly, Jan., 1912 ; 9th essay in *An Englishman*. Originally read as a lecture at the Times Book Club, London, in May, 1911, under the title *The Scope of the Novel*. Considers the general trend of the modern novel and states "just what I think the novel is, and where, if anywhere, its boundary-line ought to be drawn." In his opinion the novel should present

the whole of human life. " Before we have done, we will have all life within the scope of the novel."

99. CONVERT TO PROTECTION. A. Daily Express, in Jan., 1915.

COOTE, CHESTER. A " young man of semi-independent means," a " local house-agent, and a most active and gentlemanly person, a conscious gentleman, equally aware of society and the serious side of life. From amateur theatricals of a nice refined sort to science classes, few things were able to get along without him." He also "read Mrs. Humphrey Ward, and took an interest in social work." After Kipps has inherited a fortune and left the shop, Coote takes him under his wing and chaperons him into local society. In the 1917 edition of *First and Last Things*, Wells, admitting a certain priggishness in some of his heroes (Remington, Stratton, Trafford, Benham), says that they " have all a flavour of distant cousinship with Mr. Chester Coote." Coote's sister, a maiden lady who " had painted a picture to be exhibited at the Royal Academy," specialises in Kipp's artistic development. *Kipps.*

CORNER, CECILY. A pretty, dark-haired girl, sister of Mrs. Teddy and a very distant cousin of Mr. Direck, who meets her at Mr. Britling's house and falls in love with her. She, intelligent, active-minded, is dissatisfied with his lack of real purpose in life. After he has joined the Canadian Army she admits her love for him. *Mr. Britling.*

100. CORRUPTION. 7th chapter in *Future in America.* Discusses

the ethical system of the average American and the principles of political and social graft.

101. COSMOGONY OF MODERN RELIGION, THE. 1st chapter of *God the Invisible King.* Statement of the main doctrines of the modern renascent religion which Wells sees dawning about the world among peoples of all races and faiths. The True God is finite, a Captain of Mankind who exists in every human soul. The Creator, the Veiled Being is not God. God is within, a " still, small voice " which comes to a man when he is distressed with the futility of individual life, bringing comfort and purpose to him.

COSMOPOLITAN AND INTERNATIONAL. 16th article in *Year of Prophesying;* see *Some Fine Words and Bad Passports.*

COSSAR. A civil engineer, a " large-bodied man with gaunt inelegant limbs . . . and a face like a carving abandoned at an early stage." A friend of Redwood and Bensington, he organises the destruction of the Experimental Farm. He gives the Food to his three sons, and in after years plans the fortress at Chislehurst where the giants gather for the decisive battle. The three Cossar boys are prominent figures in the latter part of the story. *Food of the Gods.*

COTHOPE. A self-educated man, " one of the best and handiest working engineers alive." Assists George Ponderevo in his aerial navigation experiments. *Tono-Bungay.*

102. COTTAGE IN A GARDEN, A. (Utopianisms, 2). Daily Mail, Mar. 30th, 1905.

**103. COUNTRY OF THE BLIND,
THE.** Strand Magazine, Apr., 1904;
32nd story in *Country of the Blind;*
8th in *Door in the Wall;* as pamphlets, see Bib. No. 41a and note.
Nunez, a mountaineer, whilst climb-
ing amid the Andes of Ecuador,
comes upon the legendary Country
of the Blind. He enters the valley,
thinking to make himself king of
the blind inhabitants. But he
quickly finds that he is at a dis-
advantage, their other senses
having been sharpened by need and
use in the passing generations,
and he is made a slave. After
some time he wishes to marry his
master's daughter, and consent is
given on condition that his eyes
be removed. He agrees, but on
the last day realises that sight
is too precious a thing to lose even
for love; he climbs up out of the
valley back to the open world.

**104. COUNTRY OF THE BLIND
AND OTHER STORIES, THE.** See
Bib. No. 41. The 33 tales in this
volume are : 1, *The Jilting of Jane;*
2, *The Cone;* 3, *The Stolen Bacillus;*
4, *The Flowering of the Strange
Orchid;* 5, *In the Avu Observatory;*
6, *Æpyornis Island;* 7, *The Re-
markable Case of Davidson's Eyes;*
8, *The Lord of the Dynamos;*
9, *The Moth;* 10, *The Treasure in
the Forest;* 11, *The Story of the
Late Mr. Elvesham;* 12, *Under the
Knife;* 13, *The Sea Raiders;* 14,
The Obliterated Man; 15, *The
Plattner Story;* 16, *The Red Room;*
17, *The Purple Pileus;* 18, *A Slip
Under the Microscope;* 19, *The
Crystal Egg;* 20, *The Star;* 21,
The Man who could work Miracles;
22, *A Vision of Judgment;* 23,
Jimmy Goggles the God; 24, *Miss
Winchelsea's Heart;* 25, *A Dream
of Armageddon;* 26, *The Valley of

Spiders;* 27, *The New Accelerator;*
28, *The Truth about Pyecraft;* 29,
The Magic Shop; 30, *The Empire
of the Ants;* 31, *The Door in the
Wall;* 32, *The Country of the
Blind;* 33, *The Beautiful Suit.*

**CRAVING FOR ONE SIMPLE CHEAP
REMEDY, THE.** Daily Mail, June
5th, 1912; reprinted in *What the
Worker Wants* (see Bib. II, 1912),
and again as *Social Panaceas* (q.v.).

**105. CREATIVE EDUCATIONAL
SCHEME FOR BRITAIN, A.** Westminster Gazette, Feb. 23rd, 1924;
24th article in *Year of Prophesying.*
A "Tentative Forecast" of the
new Labour Government's "treatment of national education."

**106. CREATIVE EFFORT IN RUS-
SIA, THE.** See *Toilers in the
Wreckage.* 4th chapter in *Russia.*
Describes the efforts of the Bol-
shevik government to build a new
Russia amid the ruins of the old.
Deals with the lack of efficiency
in the government offices and gives
an account of the Petersburg schools
and general educational work.

107. CREATIVE PASSION, THE.
Westminster Gazette, Sept. 13th,
1924; 54th article in *Year of
Prophesying.* The creative passion,
the desire for a "better world," is
constantly dominant in few, if
any, of us. Only "true education"
can make it so, submerging our
"fear, jealousy, vanity."

CREATURES OF THE ABYSS. Who
inhabit the ocean-bed. They are
grotesquely human, vertebrated,
intelligent bipeds, with globular
bodies, frog-like legs, a tail, and
fore-limbs which terminate in an
almost human "hand." The face

is reptilian, but with a high fore-head and large brain-case. It is suggested that they are " des-cendants like ourselves of the great Theriomorpha of the New Red Sandstone Age." They live in large cities of roofless houses built of water-logged wood, iron spars, and the bones of dead men. *In the Abyss.*

108. CRICKET. Henley House Magazine, Dec., 1890. Unsigned.

CRUMP, DR. The Siddermorton doctor. Called in to attend to the Angel's wound, he tells the vicar that the patient is only an abnormal man ; later he calls him a swindler. Finally, as " medical adviser of the parish," he orders the Angel to leave it at once. *Wonderful Visit.*

108a. CRUSTY DAWN, A. A Series of Sketches by Mr. H. G. Wells, showing the enthusiastic reception given in his household to Mr. E. V. Lucas's " England Day by Day " immediately after its arrival. Bookman, Feb., 1917. Page of sketches.

CRYSTAL. A Utopian boy. He is " reading history in a holiday stage of his education," and has many discussions with Mr. Barn-staple during the latter's convales-cence. *Men Like Gods.*

109. CRYSTAL EGG, THE. New Review, in 1897 (Vol. 16, p. 556 ; 1st story in *Tales of Space ;* 19th in *Country of the Blind.* Cave, a Seven Dials antique dealer, purchases a crystal egg. He dis-covers that by gazing into it at a certain angle from a ray of light he can distinguish a living and shifting picture of a spacious countryside

laid out with great buildings and beautiful gardens, and populated by strange unearthly beings. He takes the egg to Wace, a scientific acquaintance, who believes that this strange world must be Mars. Wace assists Cave to carry on his investigations. Cave does not call upon him for some time ; Wace calls at the shop to find that the dealer is dead and that the egg has been sold. He searches for it unsuccessfully.

110. CULTIVATION OF THE FAM-ILY, THE. Pall Mall Gazette, Oct. 3rd, 1894.

111. CULTIVATION OF THE IMAG-INATION, THE. 8th chapter in *Mankind.* A discussion of sex and of the manner in which adolescents arrive at an interpretation of sexual things.

112. CULTURE. 13th chapter in *Future in America.* Wells visits Boston, the home of American culture, and finds it " obsessed by the scholarly prestige of mere knowledge and genteel remoteness."

CURATE, A. Who spends nine days with the narrator of *The War of the Worlds,* watching the Martians from their hiding-place, a ruined house at Sheen. He goes mad and the narrator has to kill him to prevent him from attracting the Martians' attention. The narrator hides in the cellar, and when he ventures out two days later the body of the curate has disappeared.

CUSPARD, BUNNY. A pupil, with Joan and Peter, at the School of St. George and the Venerable Bede. From boyhood he loves Joan, whom he meets again at Cambridge. In

August, 1914, he enlists at once, fearful (so he tells Joan) lest he should go " Pacifist right out—out of funk." He writes regularly to Joan until he is shot by a Dublin sniper in the Sinn Fein rebellion at Easter, 1916. *Joan and Peter.*

Cuss, Dr. The Iping general practitioner. After Griffin's flight he and the Rev. Mr. Bunting examine the Invisible Man's papers. Griffin returns and takes Cuss's trousers from him. *Invisible Man.*

113. " Cyclic " Delusion, The. Saturday Review, Nov. 10th, 1894. An inquiry into and destruction of the idea that all things move in cycles. Unsigned.

114. Cyclist Soldier, The. Fortnightly Review, Dec., 1900. Criticism of " Cyclist Drill," by Lieut.-Col. E. Balfour (a War Office publication). Wells points out the inadequate official conception of the possibilities of cyclists as a new arm " which may even be destined to be the predominant arm in the European warfare of the future." He considers these possibilities, discusses the composition and equipment of a cycling force, and gives an imaginative account of such a force in action against a body of War Office cyclists. Correspondence, Feb., 1901, and reply from Wells, March, 1901.

D

Dad, William (Bildad the Shuhite). A governor of Woldingstanton School, an " industrial fox-terrier from the Midlands," silver-haired but alert and keen ; before the war manufacturer of the Dad

and Showite car, now a leading aeroplane contractor and immensely rich. He believes in a " simple, straightforward, commercial and technical education," and regards Job Huss as incompetent, faddy and " history mad." In everything he seeks the " practical value," and prefers not to discuss his religion. " Give me the Bible and the simple religion I learnt at my mother's knee. . . . Can't we just have faith and leave all these questions alone ? " In Huss's dream Dad becomes Bildad. *Undying Fire.*

Dale, Dr. A harsh-voiced, lean, dark young man, with a " distinctly sceptical " eye, who, coming from Cambridge with the highest testimonials, temporarily takes the place of Scrope's regular doctor while the latter is in France. He gives patients not narcotics to sooth but tonics to stimulate, and from him Scrope obtains the opalescent fluid which induces the visions. Later the other doctor calls Dale a " dangerous lunatic " and says that he has " shattered the practice of years." He is killed at the front in France. *Soul of a Bishop.*

Dangle. Friend and admirer of Mrs. Milton, and a member of the Rescue Party. *Wheels of Chance.*

Dawn in the Darkness. Daily Express, Dec. 1st, 1921 ; reprinted as *Ebb Tide at Washington* (q.v.).

115. Deal in Ostriches, A. Pall Mall Gazette or Budget, about 1894 ; 5th tale in *Stolen Bacillus.* Told by the Taxidermist. The incidents take place on board a homeward bound East Indiaman. An ostrich, which may be any one

of five, is alleged to have swallowed a valuable diamond belonging to Sir Mohini Padishah. Potter, a fellow-passenger, buys the birds and puts them up for auction at a starting price of £80 each. They are sold at prices averaging £227 each and are taken away by their purchasers to be killed after landing. Later the narrator sees Padishah and Potter in Regent Street, " arm in arm and having a purple time of it."

116. DEATH. Saturday Review, March 9th, 1895. Unsigned. Through the whole range of life it is the same : " the individuals perish . . . the type alone persists."

DEBENHAM, JOAN. The illegitimate daughter of Will Sydenham; after her mother's death adopted by Arthur and Dolly Stubland and brought up under their name as Peter's sister. She is a pretty black-haired, black-eyed child, whose beauty increases with every year. In 1914 she discovers that Peter is not her half-brother, and that she is in love with him ; they are married during the war. *Joan and Peter.*

117. DEBS AND THE POETS. See Bib. II, 1920.

118. DEGENERATION OF THE RAVENSBOURNE, THE. Pall Mall Gazette, July 12th, 1894.

119. DEMOCRACY. 9th chapter in *Fourth Year.* Defining the modern meaning of the word democracy as " selective democracy " rather than " delegate democracy," advocates the adoption of Proportional Representation as a solution of electoral difficulties.

DENTON. A good-looking young attendant on a London flying-stage, in love with Elizabeth Mwres. *Story of the Days to Come.*

120. DEVELOPING SOCIAL ELEMENTS. 3rd chapter in *Anticipations.* Discusses the evolution of the social order of to-day and the main social elements of the future.

DEVIL, A. One of " the very lowest types of infernal denizen," a weak, nerveless, egotistical character. He allows a herd of wild asses to escape from Hell while listening to Gladstone's arrival speech, and is sent into the world in search of them. *Wild Asses of the Devil.*

121. DIAMOND MAKER, THE. Pall Mall Budget, about 1894 ; 9th tale in *Stolen Bacillus ;* 6th in *Door in the Wall ;* also in Pearson's Magazine, March, 1905. The narrator meets a ragged, hungry man on the Embankment. This man tells him that he can make diamonds, and explains his method and shows some samples. He offers to sell a large uncut stone for £100 and the narrator, a little doubtful, asks him to call at his office next morning. They never meet again.

122. DICTATORS OR POLITICIANS ? THE DILEMMA OF CIVILISATION. Westminster Gazette, March 22nd, 1924 ; 28th article in *Year of Prophesying.* Comments on the appearance of dictators in several European countries. Warns Britain that if she does not cleanse her parliamentary methods and educate the masses to " political efficiency," it is not impossible that this country may have its dictator before long.

DIMPLE, MR. The "perfect vicar" of Matching's Easy, "plump and genial." *Mr. Britling.*

DIRECK; MR. Secretary of The Massachusetts Society for the Study of Contemporary Thought, on behalf of which he visits Mr. Britling in the summer of 1914. He is "a type of man not uncommon in America . . . clean and pleasant-looking . . . that agreeable person who smiles and says, 'Good, it's Fizgig Brand,' or 'Yes, it's a Wilkins, and that's the best,'" in the advertisement pages of American magazines. *Mr. Britling.*

123. DISCOVERIES IN VARIATION. Saturday Review, Mar. 9th, 1895. Unsigned. Scientific article.

124. DISCOVERY OF THE FUTURE, THE. See Bib. No. 20. In this lecture the author contrasts two types of mind : (1) that which bases all its actions and ideas upon the past, and (2) that which looks to the future. Man's knowledge of the past comes to him in three ways ; there is the personal past, the historical and traditional past, and the far greater and more distant past of geological time, the inductive past. Is it, asks the author, hopeless to think that by "seeking for operative causes instead of fossils," and by criticising them as thoroughly as the geological records have been criticised "it may be possible to throw a searchlight of inference forward instead of backward ? " A knowledge of the future is more important than of the past. He mentions the peculiarly limited views of the nineteenth century positivists, and makes certain pro-

phecies concerning the general trend of the world during the next few generations. Fundamental beliefs he says, are set on faith. Man does not believe that he can utterly end ; " Worlds may freeze and suns may perish, but there stirs something within us now that can never die again."

125. DISEASE OF PARLIAMENTS, THE. Cassell's Magazine, Feb. and Mar., 1914 ; 21st essay in *An Englishman.* Parliament has ceased to be representative ; with the methods of voting in use " almost any result may be got out of an election except the production of a genuinely representative assembly." Proportional Representation, the working of which is outlined, is suggested as the one possible remedy.

126. DISREPUTABLENESS OF AUTHORSHIP, THE. National Observer, Nov. 8th, 1894.

127. DISTRUST (The Labour Unrest, 1). Daily Mail, May 13th, 1912 ; see *The Labour Unrest.*

128. DIVORCE. Cassell's Magazine, Apr., 1912 ; reprinted as 15th essay in *An Englishman.* Wells, to whom the family is the one justification of marriage, discusses certain main points which call for alteration in the existing divorce laws, indicating what these alterations should be.

129. DOCTORS. Daily Mail, Oct. 7th, 1905 ; 18th essay in *An Englishman.* Under the existing system of " competitive scramble " the majority of doctors are so reduced to " mere fee-hunting " that they have no time to keep informed

upon progress and discovery in medical science. Modern research is disjointed and unorganised, and scientific and medical investigators are underpaid and insufficiently equipped.

DODD, EDWIN. A " leading member of the Rationalistic Press Association, a militant agnostic and a dear, compact man." He has his suspicions of Boon's idea of the collective mind of the race. One of the best sketches in Boon shows him sitting upon a flower-pot. *Boon.*

DOGMAS THAT ARE DYING. Daily Express, Dec. 2nd, 1921 ; reprinted as *America and Entangling Alliances* (q.v.).

130. DOOR IN THE WALL, THE. Daily Chronicle, July 14th, 1906 (Summer No.) ; 31st story in *Country of the Blind* 1st in *Door in the Wall.* Lionel Wallace, a prominent politician, tells this story to his friend Redmond, the narrator. He relates how as a child of five, wandering through West Kensington, he came upon a door set in a long white wall. He goes through it into an enchanted garden where all is sweet and beautiful. When he talks of it at home he is thrashed for telling lies. Some years later, hurrying to school, he comes upon the door again ; returning next day to look for it, he cannot find it. Twice more he sees it and passes by, and then after a long interval he comes upon it thrice in one year, each time when upon most urgent business. But the desire for the sweetness and infinite peace of the garden so grows upon him that he swears that next time, whatever the circumstances, he will enter it. A few months later

he is found dead, having walked through an accidentally unfastened door in a white hoarding, to fall into a deep shaft.

131. DOOR IN THE WALL AND OTHER STORIES, THE. See Bib. No. 43.

132. DO THEY REALLY THINK AT ALL ? (How People Think about the War, 1). Daily News, Dec. 15th, 1916. See *How People Think about the War.*

DOUGLAS, ALAN. A cousin of Lady Laxton, and a captain in the " Bistershires " ; he is intelligent and of an enquiring turn of mind, being specially interested in flying problems, but in appearance a pink blushing young man. He goes to Shonts by the same train as Lord Moggeridge, who suspects him of being his brother Eric, also an army captain and a notorious practical joker. *Bealby.*

DRACHENFLIEGER. One-man-flying machine used by the Germans for bomb-throwing ; three or four are attached to each airship. *War in the Air.*

133. DREAM, THE. See Bib. No. 86. Sarnac and Sunray, comrades of some twenty centuries hence, take a holiday from their work to " wander among the lakes and mountains " together. At a guest-house they meet a brother and sister, and two other women, Radiant and Starlight, Willow and Firefly, bent upon a similar expedition. Together they go through some recently excavated ruins, relics of the Age of Confusion. Sarnac cuts his hand upon broken glass and the wound does not heal ; that night he is feverish and the

next day in the open air he falls
asleep again, waking to tell his
friends that he has dreamed
" through a whole life in that old
world." Thereupon, with one interval for adjournment to a guest-
house as night comes on, he tells
his dream. In it he was Henry
Mortimer Smith, youngest child
of a greengrocer in Cherry Gardens,
a south coast town between Sand-
bourne and Lowcliff. He tells of
his early life and surroundings, of
the Smith family, of school and
church, and of his Sunday evening
walks to Chessing Hanger, where
his Uncle John Julip is gardener
to Lord Bramble. Each week he
and his father bring back stolen
produce for the shop until he,
quite innocently, reveals the fact
and the uncle is dismissed. Julip
and Harry's father take to betting
and drinking, Fanny, Harry's favourite sister, runs away with her
lover, and the father is killed in an
accident. Ernest, the elder son,
ejects Uncle John from the house,
and Harry, his mother, and the
other sister, Prudence, go to help
Matilda Good at her boarding-
house in Pimlico. Encouraged by
one of the boarders, Harry determines to educate himself while
working as an errand boy. Ernest,
a motor-driver, has a letter from
Fanny, brings the news to his
mother, and Harry goes to see
his sister. She is the mistress of
Newberry, the man she left home
with and who wishes to marry her
if his wife would divorce him.
At her suggestion Harry finds work
at Thunderstone House, the office
of Crane and Newberry, wholesale
' popular " publishers, and gets
on well there. He is about eighteen
years old when the war breaks out ;
he joins the army and while on

leave meets and later marries
Hetty Marcus. After the armistice
he comes back to her and to
Thunderstone House. Hetty is soon
to have a child, but the birth is
delayed until he knows that it
cannot be his. Before the birth
he accuses her, she tells how she
was seduced in his absence by a
soldier, and he leaves her. She
goes back to her mother's farm ;
after the divorce she marries Sumner, the co-respondent. More in
reaction than in love, Harry
marries Milly Kimpton, an old
office friend. Many months later
he meets Hetty again, quite by
chance, and she tells him how unhappy Sumner, a drunken black-
guard, has made her. Still loving
her, he, with Fanny, helps to send
her to America, where she has
friends. Sumner believes that
Harry is hiding her, threatens him
and at last shoots him. He dies
in his house, with Milly near him,
and wakes to find himself once
more in the world of the future, in
Sunray's arms.

134. DREAMER IN THE KREMLIN,
THE. (Russia in the Shadows, 5).
Sunday Express, Nov. 28th, 1920 ;
6th and 7th chapters of *Russia,
The Dreamer in the Kremlin* and
The Envoy. A brief description
of conditions in Moscow, and an
account of an interview with Lenin,
who discusses the future of Russia
under Communism. In *The Envoy*
Wells prophecies the relapse of
Russia into " peasant barbarism "
if the blockade continues. Advocates the formation of a national
or international trust for trading
with Russia.

135. DREAM OF ARMAGEDDON.
A. Black and White, in 1901 ; 13th

K

tale in *Twelve Stories ;* 25th in *Country of the Blind ;* 3rd in *Door in the Wall.* A Liverpool solicitor relates this story to the writer in the train between Rugby and Euston. He tells how, night after night, he dreams of some other life in the future, when he is a man wielding world-power, who has thrown away his high position to live with his mistress at Capri. He is begged to return to the north and save the world from war, but he refuses. War breaks out and the two fly from Capri to be overtaken by battle at Pastium, where the woman is killed by shrapnel. He stays by her body until he is killed by an officer whose intrusion he resists.

DREW, LADY. Her " leddyship " of Bladesover House, a shrivelled old woman " with a wonderful memory for genealogies." *Tono-Bungay.*

136. DRIFT AND SALVAGE. See *Russia in Collapse.* 2nd chapter of *Russia.* Account of the life and position of Russian writers, artists and scientists under the Bolshevik rule. Gorky, Shalyapin, Glazounov and Pavloff are mentioned particularly. The attitude of the Bolshevik Government toward art and science is discussed. The writer insists upon the fact of the total collapse of Russia.

137. DULL WORK. Daily Mail, about 1911 ; French translation in the Paris Journal, July 14th, 1911.

DUNKERLEY. Senior assistant master and Lewisham's sole colleague at Whortley Proprietary School. He dispises Mr. Bonover, who has only a Durham degree,

because he, " having none, inclined to be particular." Later, when an assistant master in London, he becomes one of the Friends of Progress. He holds that it is the part of woman to join with man in the struggle for existence, and it is partly under the influence of his words that Lewisham asks Ethel Henderson to marry him. *Mr. Lewisham.*

138. DUNSTONE'S DEAR LADY. Pall Mall Gazette, in 1894 ; 19th story in *Personal Matters.* Dunstone marries a visiting governess, a small thin girl, nervous and refined. Five years pass, and the narrator returns to find her " rapidly developing an extremely florid vulgarity." Yet Dunstone still speaks of her as his Dainty Little Lady.

DUPONT, EMILE. A French journalist and publicist, " a dark, smartly dressed man, with an imperfect command of English." He enters Utopia as one of Lord Barralonga's party. *Men Like Gods.*

139. DURATION OF LIFE, THE. Saturday Review, Feb. 23rd, 1895. Discusses the duration of life in men and animals. Unsigned.

E

EADHAMITE. An artificial substance resembling toughened glass which is used for road surfaces. First made by a man named Eadham ; Warming acquires the patent, and the consequent fortune he makes forms the basis of Graham's wealth. *Sleeper Wakes ;* mentioned in *Story of the Days to Come.*

EASTON, SIR PHILIP. A handsome young man who loves Amanda Benham. She is very friendly with him in her husband's absence, and ultimately becomes his lover. When they are surprised together by Benham, Easton asks him to divorce Amanda that he may marry her. *Research Magnificent.*

140. EBB TIDE AT WASHINGTON. See *Dawn in the Darkness.* 17th chapter in *Washington.* Comments upon the dying down of the spirit of hopefulness at the Washington Conference ; but Wells sees certain signs which promise a revival of the original enthusiasm and desire for peace.

141. ECONOMIC PROCESS, THE. 4th chapter in *Future in America.* General study of the social and economic process in America, which is seen as one of " systematically concentrating wealth on the part of an energetic minority, and of a great insurgence of alarm, of waves of indignation and protest and threat on the part " of the majority.

142. EDUCATION FOR CREATIVE SERVICE. New Leader, Oct. 6th, 1922. A brief article on the work of " Sanderson of Oundle " and its importance to the Labour movement.

143. EDUCATION OF AN ELIZABETHAN GENTLEMAN, THE. University Correspondent, Oct. 14th, 1893.

144. EDUCATION OF THE NOVELIST, THE. Pall Mall Gazette, March 9th, 1894.

145. ELECTION ADDRESS. Fabian Society, 1907. See Bib. II, 1907.

146. ELECTION ADDRESS. University of London Election, 1922. See Bib. No. 78.

ELECTION ADDRESS. University of London Election, 1922. See *The World, its Debts, and the Rich Men.*

147. ELECTION ADDRESS. University of London Election, 1923. See Bib. No. 82.

148. ELECTION ADDRESS. University of London Election, 1923. See Bib. No. 83.

149. ELEMENTS OF RECONSTRUCTION, THE. See Bib. No. 61. The six chapters in this volume are : 1, *Science in Education and Industry;* 2, *Scientific Agriculture and the Nation's Food;* 3, *The Long View and Labour;* 4, *Problems of Political Adaptation;* 5, *An Imperial Constitution;* 6, *Higher Education in the Empire.*

ELOI, THE. The delicate child-like race which the Time Traveller finds inhabiting the earth's surface in the year 802,701 A.D. They are only about four feet in height, with curly hair and a Dresden China type of prettiness. Descendants of the old capitalist classes, they have lost all power, and are preyed upon by the Morlocks for food. They eat only fruit, and fear the night. *Time Machine.*

ELPHINSTONES, THE. The brother of the narrator meets Mrs. Elphinstone and her sister-in-law during the Exodus from London. He comes upon them in a lane near High Barnet, and rescues them from the attack of three men. They escape with him to Ostend, though Mrs. Elphinstone wishes to return to her husband George at Stanmore. *War of the Worlds*.

150. EMPIRE OF THE ANTS, THE. Strand Magazine, Dec., 1905 ; 30th tale in *Country of the Blind*. Captain Gerilleau of the Brazilian Navy is sent to Badama to help the inhabitants of the district against a plague of large and intelligent ants. They are wonderfully organised, possess knowledge of fire and implements, and are capable of marvellous engineering feats. After a brief encounter with them in which one officer is killed, the captain fires his big gun twice and retreats. Holroyd, the Lancashire engineer of the gunboat, tells the story to the writer.

151. ENDING OF THE WAR, THE. (How People Think about the War, 6). See *Ideas for a World Peace*. Also *How People Think about the War*.

152. END OF MILITARISM, THE. Chicago Tribune, Aug. 19th, 1914. Possibly an article printed under another title in Great Britain.

153. END OF THE ARMAMENT RINGS. See Bib. No. 53b.

154. END OF THE WAR, THE. (Looking Ahead). Daily Chronicle, Jan. 17th, 18th, 1916 ; 2nd chapter in *What is Coming?* Shows how the prophecies of Bloch have been fulfilled in this war, and forecasts a campaign of continued deadlock in which the combatants will undergo a process of gradual exhaustion, coming at last to peace through neutral negotiation.

155. ENDOWMENT OF MOTHERHOOD, THE. Daily Mail, June 22nd, 1910 ; 17th essay in *An Englishman*. With every civilised race drifting towards race-suicide, it is imperative that some remedy should be found. Advocates the endowment of motherhood, and suggests a fair and reasonable method.

ENGLAND IN A.D. 2100. Villages and country towns have long since disappeared, while the cities have grown to enormous dimensions, London alone having a population of 33 millions. Labourers employed in the country live in the cities, going out to work each day and returning each night. The whole of the countryside is given over to agriculture and to the herds and flocks of the British Food Trust, the cities being linked together by broad Eadhamite roads. All the commerce of the world is in the hands of a few huge trusts, most of which are owned by Graham ; those mentioned are the British Food Trust, Consolidated African Companies, International Creche System, Labour Company, Sanitary Company, Public Schools Company, Wind Vanes Control, and the Euthanasy Company. It is by virtue of the power wielded by these companies and syndicates that Graham is Master of the World. *Sleeper Wakes*.

156. ENGLISH CITIES IN A.D. 2000. Daily Mail, Apr. 27th, 1901.

157. ENGLISHMAN LOOKS AT THE WORLD, AN. See Bib. No. 50. The 26 essays in this volume are : 1, *The Coming of Bleriot ;* 2, *My First Flight ;* 3, *Off the Chain ;* 4, *Of the New Reign ;* 5, *Will the Empire Live? ;* 6, *The Labour*

Unrest; 7, *The Great State;* 8, *The Common Sense of Warfare;* 9, *The Contemporary Novel;* 10, *The Philosopher's Public Library;* 11, *About Chesterton and Belloc;* 12, *About Sir Thomas More;* 13, *Traffic and Rebuilding;* 14, *The So-called Science of Sociology;* 15, *Divorce;* 16, *The Schoolmaster and the Empire;* 17, *The Endowment of Motherhood;* 18, *Doctors;* 19, *An Age of Specialisation;* 20, *Is There a People?;* 21, *The Disease of Parliaments;* 22, *The American Population;* 23, *The Possible Collapse of Civilisation;* 24, *The Ideal Citizen;* 25, *Some Possible Discoveries;* 26, *The Human Adventure.*

ENLARGEMENT OF PATRIOTISM, THE. (Salvaging of Civilisation, 2). Sunday Times, April 3rd, 1921; reprinted as the 1st part of *The Enlargement of Patriotism to a World State* (q.v.).

158. ENLARGEMENT OF PATRIOTISM TO A WORLD STATE, THE. See *The Enlargement of Patriotism* and *The World State — An Outline Sketch.* 3rd chapter of *Salvaging of Civilisation.* There must be no compromise with the nationalist patriotic idea; the League of Nations is such a compromise. The World State is the only possible common idea which will save the world, and modern propaganda facilities make the establishment of such a state quite possible. The bringing of the World State into being is "the most important work before men and women to-day." Follows an outline of the organisation and administration of the writer's World State, with an account of the life of its average citizen.

159. EN ROUTE. 2nd chapter of *Future in America.* Written on board the Cunard liner " Carmania " as it nears New York. Discusses the evolution of ocean-travel, and compares the onward driving ship to the United States, to the world.

160. ENTRE NOUS. Henley House Magazine, March, 1889, p. 209. Unsigned; part only.

161. ENVOY, THE. To *Future in America.* Written after the writer's return. Summary of general conclusions.

162. ENVOY, THE. To *God the Invisible King.* Traces the origin of the views set forth in the preceding chapters. Modern religion, he concludes, " comes as the dawn comes, through whatever clouds and mists may be here or whatever smoke and curtains may be there. It comes as the day comes to the ships that put out to sea. It is the Kingdom of God at hand."

163. ENVOY, THE. To *Russia in the Shadows.* 7th chapter, reprinted from part of *The Dreamer in the Kremlin* (q.v.).

164. ENVOY, THE. To *Salvaging of Civilisation.* A " summing up and underlining " of the chief points of the book. The writer insists upon the primary importance of education.

165. EPISODE. Pall Mall Gazette, May 9th, 1894. 8 lines of verse.

EUPHEMIA. The wife of the narrator of several of the short stories and essays written about 1894. She comes prominently into *The Coal-Scuttle, Euphemia's New Entertainment, The House of di*

Sorno, In a Literary Household, The Jilting of Jane and *The Parkes Museum.* Mr. Brumley (in *Sir Isaac Harman*) is the author of a series of Euphemia books. " Euphemia was my wife," he tells Lady Harman, " at least, my wife gave her to me—a kind of exhalation."

166. EUPHEMIA'S NEW ENTERTAINMENT. Pall Mall Gazette, May 9th, 1894 ; 20th essay in *Personal Matters.* Describes the pleasures and humours of clay-modelling as an after-dinner amusement.

166a. EUROPEAN KALEIDOSCOPE : THE GERMAN WILL IN DEFAULT, THE. Westminster Gazette, Apr. 3rd, 1924 ; 33rd article in *Year of Prophesying.* Comments on Poincare's new " liberal " policy and probable result of coming French elections : regrets the apparent absence of any will in Germany either to help herself or those who would help her.

EVERY-DAY LIFE IN A SOCIALIST, STATE. Lecture delivered at the City Temple Hall, London, in Nov., 1907 ; printed as *Some Arguments Ad Hominem* (q.v.).

167. EVERY MAN'S WAR. Illustrated Sunday Herald, March 21st, 1915.

EVESHAM. A prominent politician who is attracted to Remington by one of the latter's books. Remington writes of " his tall, bent body, his little-featured almost elvish face, his unequal mild brown eyes, his gentle manner, his sweet amazing oratory. . . He brought political art to the last triumph of naturalness. Always for me he has been the typical aristocrat, so typical and above the mere forms of aristocracy, that he remained a commoner to the end of his days." *New Machiavelli.* He is mentioned or appears briefly in *Marriage, Passionate Friends, Sir Isaac Harman, Bealby, Research Magnificent.*

168. EVOLUTION OF GOD IDEA, THE. Saturday Review, Feb. 12th, 1898. A review of Grant Allen's " The Evolution of the Idea of God."

EWART, SIDNEY. Illegitimate son of Rickman Ewart, a great artist. At school with George Ponderevo, who meets him again in London after an interval of six years. He attempts painting, but finding that he is colour-blind he takes up sculpture ; but he is too indolent to succeed, lacking the necessary gift of application, and becomes in the end a monumental mason. He is excessively talkative and talks well ; " commonness vanished before Ewart, at his expository touch all things became memorable and rare." *Tono-Bungay.*

169. EXAMINATIONS. Education Review, Nov., 1892.

170. EXAMINER EXAMINED, THE. University Correspondent, Sept. 23rd, 1893.

171. EXCELSIOR. Saturday Review, April 13th, 1895. Essay on the disadvantages of "getting on;" passing out of one's original element, the loss of one's friends, the loneliness ; " it is fun to struggle but tragedy to win."

EXPERIMENTAL FARM, THE. A poultry farm at Hickleybrow in

Kent, set up by Mr. Bensington for experimental purposes because his sister will not allow him to keep tadpoles. It is started in October, but it is May before the first signs of success become apparent. The Skinners, who are in charge of it, scatter Herakleophorbia about quite carelessly, and the house becomes a centre of giant rats, wasps and vegetation. In the end the Farm has to be burnt to the ground after the destruction of the rats and wasps. *Food of the Gods*.

172. EXPERIMENT IN ILLUSTRA-TION, AN. Strand Magazine, Feb., 1920. An introduction to the condensed version of *The War of the Worlds*. Discusses the origin of the story and the various artists who have done illustrations for it. Those mentioned are Alvim-Correa, Johan Briede (5 of whose drawings are here reproduced), Warwick Goble, R. A. M. Stevenson, and York Powell.

173. EXTINCTION OF MAN, THE. Pall Mall Gazette, Sept. 25th, 1894 ; 24th essay in *Personal Matters*. Reminds the reader that for all man's self-confidence his hold upon this earth may not be as secure as he believes. He suggests the extinction of man by sudden invasion of the land by terrible and as yet unimagined deep-sea dwellers, by the advance of myriads of intelligent ants, or by the incursions of new and devastating plagues.

EXTINCTION OF PARTY GOVERN-MENT, THE. 39th article in *Year of Prophesying* see *Proportional Representation*.

F

174. FAILURE IN A MODERN UTOPIA. 5th chapter in *Modern Utopia*. Discussion of the way in which a modern Utopia will deal with its inferior types, criminals and lunatics, and with unemployment and idleness. The Owner of the Voice and the botanist visit the Public Office at Wassen, and explain their position to an official. He sends them on to Lucerne, where they work at a wood-carving factory while investigations are being made. This leads to the question of a universal identification system. Eventually their Utopian doubles are traced.

175. FAITH, MORALS, AND PUBLIC POLICY IN THE TWENTIETH CENTURY. 9th and last chapter in *Anticipations*. Considers and discusses the " primary conception of life, the fundamental, religious, and moral ideas of these predominant men of the new time."

176. FALLACIES OF HEREDITY. Saturday Review, Dec. 8th, 1894. Unsigned.

FALLING STARS, THE. A name given to the ten cylinders fired from Mars to this earth ; they fall to the west and south-west of London on ten successive nights, each one in its passage through the air leaving a greenish streak which glows for some seconds. The positions of the first seven cylinders are : Horsnell Common, north-west of Woking, Pyrford, Bushey Park, Sheen, Wimbledon, Primrose Hill. Each of the cylinders is about 30 yards in diameter. *War of the Worlds*.

177. FAMILY ELOPEMENT, A. St. James' Gazette, March 3rd, 1894.

178. FANTASIES OF MR. BELLOC AND THE FUTURE OF THE WORLD, THE. Westminster Gazette, Feb. 16th, 1924 ; 23rd article in *Year of Prophesying*. A criticism of Belloc's book on America, " The Contrast."

FARR, JOSEPH. (Zophar the Naamathite). Head of the technical staff of Woldingstanton School and aspirant for the position of headmaster. He is a big man with a " large, round, white, shiny, clean-shaven face and uneasy hands." He scorns " educational theories." Huss says that his mind " is no more opened than the cricket professional's," that for him the empire " is no more than a trading conspiracy, fenced about with tariffs. It goes on to nothing. . . . He has no religion, no faith, no devotion." In Huss's dream he is Zophar, a man in unclean linen with an eager, coarse face. *Undying Fire.*

179. FAULTS OF THE FABIAN. See Bib. No. 29.

180. FEW UTOPIAN IMPRESSIONS, A. 7th chapter of *Modern Utopia*. After some days in Lucerne, the Owner of the Voice and the botanist go to London to meet their Utopian doubles. Describes a Utopian city and railway journey, and discusses the absence of domestic animals.

181. FIFTEEN - YEAR - OLD MR. AMERY. THE. Westminster Gazette, Oct. 13th, 1923 ; reprinted as *The Singapore Arsenal* (q.v.). Criticism of Mr. Amery, then First Lord of the Admiralty, and of the proposal for the establishment of a naval base at Singapore.

182. FILMER. Graphic, in 1901 ; 1st tale in *Twelve Stories*. A biography of Filmer, the inventor of the first successful flying-machine. He is " taken up " by Banghurst, a newspaper proprietor, and boomed extensively. Preparations are made for the first flight, but Filmer, fearing the ordeal of actual ascent, commits suicide. In his anger and disappointment Banghurst sells the machine for half-a-crown to Mac-Andrew, Filmer's assistant. Next morning, when all England is reading of Filmer's failure, Mac-Andrew is soaring over Epsom and Wimbledon.

183. FIRST AND LAST THINGS. See Bib. No. 36. This volume consists of four Books, with an Introduction, as follows : Book 1, *Metaphysics ;* 2, *Of Belief ;* 3, *Of General Conduct ;* 4, *Some Personal Things. ;* It " stands now the frank confession of what one man of the early Twentieth Century has found in life and himself, a confession just as frank as the limitations of his character permit ; it is his metaphysics, his religion, his moral standards, his uncertainties and the expedients with which he has met them."

184. FIRST CLASS AIR FIGHTER, THE. Daily Mail, Oct. 3rd, 1917.

185. FIRST MAIN GENERALISATION OF SOCIALISM, THE. Grand Magazine, Sept. 1907 ; 3rd chapter in *New Worlds*. States that to the Socialist the care and education of the child is the most vital thing in the social scheme. Proof is given of the failure of private individual parentage under contemporary conditions, and Wells insists upon the necessity for making the community responsible for every child born into it.

186. First Meeting, The. Daily Mail, Nov. 14th, 1921 ; 6th chapter in *Washington*. Account of the first meeting of the Washington Conference. Again and again Wells refers to the atmosphere of a theatrical first night which seems to infect everyone.

187. First Men in the Moon, The. See Bib. No. 18. Bedford, the narrator, goes to Lympne in Kent to write a play. There he meets Cavor, a scientist, and seeing a possibility of money in one of his projects, joins him as foreman. On the 14th of Oct., 1899, Cavorite, an "incredible substance opaque to all forms of radiant energy," is made for the first time. By the spring a specially manufactured metal sphere, coated on the exterior with Cavorite, is completed and one evening the two men set off on their journey to the moon. Landing in a desolate crater just before sunrise, they witness the full splendour of the lunar dawn and find that there is both air and vegetable life upon the moon. Venturing out from the sphere, they wander through the swiftly springing vegetation, moving in great leaps of twenty yards or more until they realise that they have lost all sense of direction and that the sphere is out of sight. While searching for it they see their first Selenites driving the moon-calves out to pasture. They eat a red fungus, become intoxicated, and are captured by the Selenites. They are taken beneath the surface of the moon and wake to find themselves chained in a vast cavern. After a fight they escape and reach the sunlight again. They separate to seek the sphere, but it is not until sunset that Bedford comes upon it, and when he returns to their meeting-place it is to find that Cavor has been recaptured. Night comes on ; Bedford takes refuge in the sphere and eventually reaches the earth, falling into the sea near Littlestone. He leaves the sphere on the beach while he breakfasts ; a small boy climbs into it, plays with the controlling studs, and shoots off into space. Bedford has brought some gold bars with him from the moon, and with the money brought by the sale of these he settles down in Italy. Presently he hears from a Dutch electrician, Julius Wendigee, who is experimenting with inter-planetary wireless communication, and is receiving messages from Cavor, he being alive and well in the interior of the moon. He tells how he was captured the second time, and how the Selenites took him into the moon, right down to the Central Sea. Altogether he sends eighteen long accounts of lunar affairs, dealing with the various types of Selenites, their natural history, and their social system. The last long message details an interview with the Grand Lunar, the master of the moon, to whom he gives an account of life upon earth, foolishly adding that he is the only man who possesses the secret which allows communication between the two worlds. Then "like a cry in the night" comes the last message, an unsuccessful attempt to give the Cavorite formula.

Flo, Aunt. The "plump woman" of the Potwell Inn, a kind, comfortable, placid, trustful woman, whose one fear in life is Uncle Jim. She and Mr. Polly get on remarkably well together. *Mr. Polly.*

188. FLOOR GAMES. See Bib.
No. 42. This brief book tells of
the endless games which may be
played upon a clear floor with an
adequate supply of lead soldiers,
bricks, boards and planks, and
clockwork railway rolling stock.
Incidentally he girds " improvingly
and usefully " at the toy manu-
facturers for their lack of enterprise.
There are eight photographs and
many marginal drawings, the latter
by J. R. Sinclair. The volume is
in four parts : 1, *The Toys to Have ;*
2, *The Game of the Wonderful
Islands ;* 3, *Of the Building of
Cities ;* 4, *Funiculars, Marble
Towers, Castles and War Games, but
very little of War Games.*

**189. FLOWERING OF THE STRANGE
ORCHID, THE.** Pall Mall Budget,
Aug. 2nd, 1894 ; 2nd tale in *Stolen
Bacillus ;* 4th in *Country of the
Blind ;* also in Pearson's Magazine,
Apr., 1905. Winter-Wedderburn,
who bewails the uneventfulness of
his life, buys an unidentified orchid
root. He is engrossed in its progress, and on the day of its flowering, standing before it in admiration, he is overpowered by its scent
and falls fainting on the floor. His
cousin finds him lying there, the
aerial rootlets of the orchid clinging
to his flesh and sucking his blood.
She smashes the hot-house windows
and drags him away. Next morning the orchid is dead, " but Wedderburn himself was bright and
garrulous upstairs in the glory of
his strange adventure."

190. FLYING MAN, THE. See *The
Advent of the Flying Man.* 8th tale
in *Stolen Bacillus.* An incident
in a Northern Indian frontier campaign. It is narrated by a lieu-

tenant who, in command of nine
men, is sent to visit a village
supposedly friendly to the British
forces. They are attacked by the
natives and cornered without water
on a ledge. After two days the
lieutenant, desperate, makes a para-
chute with the tent canvas and
escapes to bring help. A legend
arises among the natives of a
flying man with great black wings,
who hovers by night over the
mountain crests.

**191. FOOD OF THE GODS AND
HOW IT CAME TO EARTH, THE.** See
Bib. No. 24. Two scientists, Bensington and Redwood, manufacture
a substance, Herakleophorbia, the
Food of the Gods, which stimulates
growth to six or seven times the
normal. An experimental farm at
Hickleybrow, in Kent, completely
establishes the success of their
discovery, but owing to the care-
lessness of Mr. and Mrs. Skinner,
the caretakers, the Food is scattered
and the countryside made dangerous
by plagues of giant wasps, insects
and rats, while plants grow to
enormous dimensions. With the
aid of Cossar, an engineer, the farm
is burnt down and the more dangerous creatures destroyed. The Skinners have already fled, Mrs. Skinner
to her married daughter's home in
Cheasing Eyebright, Mr. Skinner
into a never illuminated obscurity.
The Food is given to several children ; Redwood's boy, Cossar's
three sons, a Princess of Weser
Dreiburg, young Caddles (Mrs. Skinner's grandson) and others in
different parts of England. The
years pass and they grow to manhood, forty - foot giants. Young
Redwood and the Cossars are companions ; Caddles is brought up in
wondering isolation at Cheasing

Eyebright and set to work in Lady Wondershoot's chalk quarry; the Princess has no idea that there are other beings like herself, until she meets young Redwood and they fall in love. The Anti-Boom-food Party (Boomfood is the popular name for Herakleophorbia) led by Caterham, introduces bill after bill in Parliament to restrict the liberty of the giants. Driven to desperation, they rise in revolt, and gather in the fortress-camp of the Cossars at Chislehurst. Unaware of these events, Caddles chooses this time to stop his work in the chalk-pit and come to London, seeking the wherefore of things. He spends the night in Regent's Park, and is killed the next day by the rat-police, the first of the giants to fall. Redwood and the Princess are with the others at Chislehurst. For the two days the giants hold their own, firing great canisters of the Food upon London, and Caterham calls for a truce. He sends Professor Redwood, who has been held under arrest, with the terms of peace, these being that the making of the Food shall cease and that the giants shall beget or bear no children. The giants refuse, resolving to fight to an end, until they or the little people be overwhelmed.

192. FORECASTING THE FUTURE. Cassell's Magazine, Jan., 1916; 1st chapter in *What is Coming?* Wells touches upon certain of his more successful past prophecies, and goes on to discuss the possibility of establishing a permanent world-peace after the war. He points out the very great difficulties which hamper such a project. Forecasting post-war conditions, he says that this war will leave three world-

powers—the anti-German allies, the Central Europeans, and the Pan-Americans—and that among these three may be formed the nucleus of the World State, the one hope of permanent peace.

193. FORECAST OF THE WORLD'S AFFAIRS, A. See Bib. II, 1924.

194. FOREWORD to "Estaines Parva: A Venture." See Bib. III, 1923.

195. FOREWORD to "New York." See Bib. III, 1910.

196. FOR FREEDOM OF SPELLING. Pall Mall Gazette, Oct. 23rd, 1893; 21st essay in *Personal Matters*. Protests against the modern insistence on uniform spelling, and argues for complete freedom.

197. FOUNDATION STONE OF CIVILISATION, THE. Pall Mall Gazette, May 22nd, 1894.

198. FRANCE AND ENGLAND—THE PLAIN FACTS OF THE CASE. See *Future of the Entente*. 20th chapter in *Washington*. Deals with the Franco-British clash over treatment of Germany. Gives reasons for each country's policy, and suggests reconciliation through the intervention of America, the financial restoration of Germany, and the establishment of a protective alliance between France, Germany, Britain and America.

199. FRANCE IN THE LIMELIGHT. 11th chapter of *Washington*. Printed in America by the New York World and the Chicago Tribune, but suppressed in England by the Daily Mail; dated Nov. 21st, 1921. Comments on the speech of M. Briand at the third session of the

Conference, and on the attitude of France toward disarmament. Accuses France of militarist ambitions, and remarks that France can only want more submarines for use against British commerce.

FRAPP, NICODEMUS. A Chatham baker, the cousin of George Ponderevo. He is a slow, narrow-minded, chapel-going man, an example of "the servile tradition perfected," beset by small debts which ultimately overwhelm him. He has a wife, "young, plump, prolific, malingering," and some very detestable children. George is sent to him after the fight with Archie Garvell, but runs away. *Tono-Bungay*.

200. FREE TRADE IS PEACE : TARIFFS ARE WAR. (Some Liberal Ideals, 1). Daily Chronicle, Sept. 18th, 1916.

201. FRENCH ECONOMIC HISTORY. Adelphi, Nov., 1923 (Contributors' Club). A nine-line note.

FRENSHAM, THE COUNTESS OF. A "constitutionally triumphant" woman, "strong upon the Irish question," who visits Lady Homartyn at Claverings Park. *Mr. Britling*.

FRIENDS OF PROGRESS, THE. An informal association of certain students at the Normal School of Science, formed after the reading of a paper on Socialism by Mr. Lewisham. "It was understood that strenuous things were to be done to make the world better, but so far no decisive action had been taken." They meet in Parkson's rooms and talk about things in general. *Mr. Lewisham*.

202. FROM AN OBSERVATORY. Saturday Review, Dec. 1st, 1894 (unsigned) ; 37th essay in *Personal Matters*. Points out how easily we might never have seen the stars, and discusses the difference that this would make to our science, our philosophy, and our everyday life.

203. FROM A STUDY FIRESIDE : RELIGION IS NOT ALTRUISM. Daily Mail, March 24th, 1904.

FROM WASHINGTON TO EUROPE. Daily Mail, Nov. 25th, 1921 ; reprinted as *The Larger Question Before the Conference* (q.v.).

204. FUNDAMENTAL IDEA OF SOCIALISM, THE. Grand Magazine, Aug., 1907 ; 2nd chapter in *New Worlds*. Wells finds certain parallels in the socialistic and scientific systems of ideas. The object of each is to make an orderly plan, the one of the " wilderness of fact," the other of the " wilderness of human effort."

205. FURTHER GLOVE BUYING. Pall Mall Gazette, Dec. 17th, 1894. A sequel to *The Shopman*.

206. FUTURE IN AMERICA, THE. See Bib. No. 28. An account of a visit to the United States in the spring of 1906, the author's main object being to discover what he could of the true spirit and will of America, and from that to trace her destiny in the coming years. But after the first chapter, written before arrival, the book is mainly an interesting and illuminating record of impressions. Wells visits New York, Boston, Chicago, Washington, talks with various prominent men, studies with critical

mind the conditions which sur-
round him. There are 14 chapters
and an envoy. Chapter 1 and the
Envoy were written in Sandgate,
Chapter 2, on board the " Carmania " ; the remainder, with the
exception of certain paragraphs
inserted at a later date, were com-
posed in America. There are 12
illustrations by Vernon Howe Bailey
and another artist. The chapters
are : 1, *The Prophetic Habit of
Mind ;* 2, *En Route ;* 3, *Growth
Invincible ;* 4, *The Economic Process ;* 5, *Some Aspects of American
Wealth ;* 6, *Certain Workers ;* 7,
Corruption ; 8, *The Immigrant
9, State-Blindness ;* 10, *Two Studies
in Disappointment ;* 11, *The Tragedy
of Colour ;* 12, *The Mind of a
Modern State ;* 13, *Culture ;* 14,
At Washington ; The Envoy.

207. FUTURE IS AS FIXED AND
DETERMINATE AS THE PAST, THE.
Cassell's Magazine, July, 1913.

208. FUTURE OF JAPAN, THE.
Daily Mail, Nov. 19th, 1921 ; 9th
chapter in *Washington.* Considers
the future of China and Japan.
Japan's problem is that of population ; Wells advocates judicious
birth-control.

209. FUTURE OF MONARCHY, THE·
7th chapter of *Fourth Year.* Foresees the break-down of the dynastic
system of monarchy in Europe as
one result of the war, believing
however that the British monarchy
may survive in a modified form.

210. FUTURE OF PRIVATE TEACH-
ING, THE. University Correspondent, May 15th, 1892.

211. FUTURE OF THE BRITISH
EMPIRE, THE. Empire Review,
Oct., 1923 ; 8th article in *Year of*

Prophesying. Wells judges the Empire " critically as a possible half-
way house or a possible obstacle
to a more comprehensive and enduring synthesis." Analyses the
Empire and points the way toward
world-federation. See *Winston.*

FUTURE OF THE ENTENTE. Daily
Express, Dec. 5th, 1921 ; reprinted
as *France and England—the Plain
Facts of the Case* (q.v.).

212. FUTURE OF THE NORTH OF
EUROPE, THE. (Looking Ahead).
Daily Chronicle, Dec. 18th, 1914.
Considers the positions of Norway,
Sweden, Denmark and Finland
with relation to the war. Wells
warns these countries against the
German claim that this war is a
struggle between German and Slav
for world-ascendancy, saying that
it is rather " a revolt of the nations
against military imperialism." G.
B. Shaw replied to this article
Dec. 23rd, and a letter from F. M.
Hueffer on " G. B. Shaw and H. G.
Wells ; a Rejoinder " was printed
Dec. 24th.

G

213. GARDEN CITIES. (Utopianisms, 1). Daily Mail, Mar. 18th,
1905.

GARVELL, ARCHIE. Half-brother
of Beatrice Normandy. He taunts
George Ponderevo with not being a
gentleman ; they fight, and George
is sent to his cousin, Nicodemus
Frapp, as a consequence. *Tono-
Bungay.*

GEORGE. To whom the uncle's
Select Conversations are addressed ;
he is Euphemia's husband and the

narrator, not only of the *Conversations*, but of *The Jilting of Jane* and presumably most of the essays in *Personal Matters*.

214. GEORGE GISSING : AN IMPRESSION. Monthly Review, Aug. 1904. Written as a preface to Gissing's unfinished novel " Veranilda," but never printed as such.

215. GETTING THE LEAGUE IDEA CLEAR IN RELATION TO IMPERIALISM. 5th chapter of *Fourth Year* : in three sections : 1, Letter printed in Daily Chronicle under the heading *Wanted, a Statement of Imperial Policy ;* 2, a Daily News article, *A Reasonable Man's Peace ;* 3, a Daily Mail article, *Are We Sticking to the Point ?—a Discussion of War Aims.* See these three titles.

GIDDING. A wealthy young American, a man of action and unlimited enterprise who, like Stephen Stratton, conceives the idea of a World State as a desirable possibility. He and Stratton meet on a liner in the Mediterranean and again, three years later, in New York ; their conversations result in the establishment of a great publishing business for the distribution of translations and cheap editions of all the world's finest books. *Passionate Friends*.

216. GIFT OF THE NEW SCIENCES, THE. Strand Magazine, Feb., 1924. In the next hundred years material changes will be more detailed than sweeping ; the real innovations will be in the mental sciences and so in education, the legal system and so on. In 500 years, say, travelling, for example, will be very much the same as it is now ; it is the schools which will be

altered beyond recognition, and prisons and lunatic asylums " almost completely swept away."

GLENDOWER, ADELINE. The elder of two half-sisters who live with the Randolph Buntings as paying guests. She is an heiress who takes a very serious view of life, " very keen and obvious in public affairs," Melville asserts that she is " attempting the incarnation " of Mrs. Humphrey Ward's Marcella. She is engaged to Chatteris and is deeply distressed by his obvious love for the Sea Lady. *Sea Lady*.

GOD. Appears in *A Vision of Judgment* and in the Prologue to *The Undying Fire*. He is seen in a dream by Huss in the latter story, by Scrope in *Soul of a Bishop*, and by Peter in *Joan and Peter*.

217. GOD THE INVISIBLE KING. See Bib. No. 63. In this volume Wells sets forth, briefly and forcibly, his religious beliefs. He declares himself an adherent of " modern religion," a believer in a finite God who fights through mankind against the " confusion and evil within us and without," against the cold indifference of the Veiled Being, the unknown and the unknowable Creator. The book is in 7 chapters and an envoy : 1, *The Cosmogony of Modern Religion ;* 2, *Heresies, or the Things that God is Not ;* 3, *The Likeness of God ;* 4, *The Religion of Atheists ;* 5, *The Invisible King ;* 6, *Modern Ideas of Sin and Damnation ;* 7, *The Idea of a Church ; Envoy.*

GOLFER, A. " Astray from some adjacent course — and he had lunched." He is " a big heavy man with a short-cropped moustache a great deal of neck and dewlap, and a solemn expression," and a " richly excessive " voice. He comes " simly coring " upon Madeleine Philips at the caravan ("Simly orny arínoon cor. . . . No wish 'trude. No wish 'all.") and Bealby battles valiantly with him. *Bealby.*

GOOD, MATILDA. A Pimlico boarding-house keeper who invites Martha Smith and the children to come and live with her. She is an amiable, kind-hearted woman, with a "breadth and variety of contour like scenery rather than like a human being; the thought of her veins being varicose, indeed of all her anatomy being varicose and fantastic, seemed a right and proper one. . . . Her face had the same landscape unanatomical quality as her body; she had a considerable moustache, an overhung slightly mischievous mouth and two different large dark-grey eyes with a slightly vertical caste in them and very marked eyelashes. . . . One eye looked at you sidelong, the other seemed to watch something over your head. She spoke in a whisper which passed very easily into wheezy, not unkindly laughter." *Dream.*

218. GOOD MAN, THE. Cosmopolitan Magazine, in 1907.

219. GOOD WILL IN MAN, THE. Grand Magazine, July, 1907; 1st chapter in *New Worlds*. Explains Wells's objects and intentions in writing this series of papers on Socialism. He sees through all the evils of life a gradual advancement, a growing good will, in mankind.

GORDON-NASMYTH. A " lank, sunburnt person in tweeds with a yellow-brown, hatchet face and one faded blue eye," a " queer blend of romance and illegality," an adventurer, explorer and author. He tells the Ponderevos of the quap on Mordet Island, but is prevented from accompanying the expedition by an accident. *Tono-Bungay.*

GORE, BILL. Leader of a band of bullies which dominates the country about Horsham after the War in the Air. He forces himself upon Edna Bunthorne. Bert Smallways shoots him and assumes the leadership of his band. *War in the Air.*

GOTCH, SIR JOHN. A Siddermorton land-owner, who has several clashes with the Angel. On the last day the Angel thrashes Gotch with a riding-whip. *Wonderful Visit.*

220. GRADES OF WAR, THE. (The Western War, 2). Daily Chronicle, Nov. 20th, 1916; 2nd chapter of *The Western War* (q.v.).

GRAHAM. A politician, a man of thirty or so, who, suffering from overwork and insomnia, falls into a trance which lasts for 203 years, waking to find himself, by virtue of his accumalated wealth, Master of the World. He is known as the Master, the Owner, the Proprietor. *Sleeper Wakes.*

GRAMMONT, V.V. An " extremely pretty " American girl whom Sir Richmond Hardy meets at Stonehenge; he is attracted to her by her " genuine historical imagination." The daughter of an

oil millionaire, she worked in the
Red Cross during the war, since the
end of which she has travelled about
Europe with Belinda Seyffert. During the war she had a love-affair
with Caston, and is now engaged to
Gunter Lake. Her father is a
" small-headed grey-haired gentleman with a wrinkled face " who
" has the jealousy of ten husbands "
for his daughter. *Secret Places.*

GRAND LUNAR, THE. Master of
the Moon, a highly intellectual being
with so huge a brain-case that his
body is but an appendage. Cavor's
penultimate message gives a detailed account of their meeting.
First Men in the Moon.

221. GRANT ALLEN'S " IDEA OF
GOD." Daily Mail, Nov. 27th,
1897. A review of Allen's book,
" The Evolution of the Idea of
God."

222. GREAT CHANGE, THE. Pall
Mall Gazette, in 1894 ; 11th of
the *Select Conversations.* The
uncle, strolling round the Zoo with
George, mentions his approaching
marriage and discusses the " human
metamorphosis " brought about by
marriage.

223. GREAT COMMUNITY, THE.
Nation, July 4th, 1914. Review of
" The Great Society," by Graham
Wallas.

224. GREAT POWER IDEA, THE.
Daily News, Nov. 17th, 1918.
On the League of Nations and the
Foreign Office.

225. GREAT STATE, THE. See
Socialism and the Great State and
The Past and the Great State. 7th
essay in *An Englishman.* Says
that the Normal Social Life is to-day

disintegrating ; most of the political
and social discussion has been an
attempt to " apprehend this de-
fensive struggle of the Normal
Social Life against waxing novelty
and innovation." Certain " key-
words of contemporary thought "
are considered in the light of this
generalisation, and modern thinkers
are divided into three classes : the
Conservators, the Planless Pro-
gressives, and the Constructors.
Wells briefly analyses the Socialist
movement ; Fabian Socialism is
dealt with as the " first systematic
movement to meet the fatal absence
of administrative schemes in the
earlier socialisms," though to-day
it is only an " interesting failure."
The greater social state—the Great
State—is not an inevitable thing ;
only strength and clearness of
purpose can bring it into being.
Concludes with some remarks upon
labour, administration and government, and women, in the Great
State.

226. GREAT STATE, THE. See
Bib. No. 44.

GREAT WORLD AT PEACE, THE.
Daily Express, Dec. 20th, 1921 ;
reprinted as the second half of
*What a Stably Organised World Peace
Means for Mankind.* (q.v.).

GREY, GREETA. A revue actress
who enters Utopia as one of Lord
Barralonga's party. She is a
" frankly blonde beauty " who carries herself " with the habitual
hauteur of a beautiful girl almost
professionally exposed to the risk of
unworthy advances." *Men Like
Gods.*

GRIFFIN. A " shabby, poverty-
stricken, hemmed-in demonstrator,
teaching fools in a provincial col-

lege," quick-tempered, utterly un-scrupulous. He devises a means of making himself invisible. His father is mentioned as having killed himself when Griffin stole some trust-funds the father held. *Invisible Man.*

227. GRISLY FOLK AND THEIR WAR WITH MEN, THE. Storyteller Magazine, Apr., 1921. An im-aginative account—half-story, half-essay—of the first European en-counters of the true men with the Neanderthal pseudo men—the grisly folk.

228. GROWTH INVINCIBLE. 3rd chapter of *Future in America.* Im-pressions of New York, Ellis Island, Boston, Niagara, and Chicago. Dwells upon the unwearying growth, for the most part loose and un-disciplined, which seems to be in progress everywhere.

GRUBB. A " pirate-souled young man," proprietor of a bicycle shop where Bert Smallways works. Their relations are " unsalaried and pallish and informal," and presently Grubb, in a moment of " financial elo-quence," gives Bert a half share in the business. But eventually it collapses altogether. *War in the Air.*

H

HALL, MRS. JENNY. Proprie-toress of the " Coach and Horses," Iping,where the Invisible Man stays for some time. She has several " skirmishes " with him upon matters of " domestic discipline," but he quiets her with money. When her bill is not paid promptly she refuses to take him his meals.

Hall, her husband, dislikes the strange lodger, and constantly urges her to get rid of him. *Invisible Man.*

HALLERY. The hero of Boon's story, *The Mind of the Race,* an intensely earnest man obsessed by the idea of the collective mind of the race. He joins the party in the Garden by the Sea, and opposes the taking of the villa as a conference-place. Finally he is made president of the conference and reads his address. In a fragment of the story not printed in Boon he murders Dr. Keyhole and gives himself up to the police. *Boon.*

HAMMERGALLOW, LADY. Owner of the greater part of Siddermorton village, where she rules autocratic-ally. She is " a dear old lady with a ropy neck, a ruddled countenance and spasmodic gusts of odd temper" who lives upon burgundy and scandal. She believes that the Angel is an illegitimate son of the Rev. K. Hilyer. *Wonderful Visit.*

229. HAMMERPOND PARK BUR-GLARY, THE. Pall Mall Budget, about 1894 ; 13th tale in *Stolen Bacillus ;* also reprinted Pearson's Magazine, Jan., 1905. Teddy Wat-kins, a professional burglar, visits Hammerpond as a rather startling artist, his object being to steal the wedding presents from Hammer-pond House. At nightfall he is joined by his assistant, but their expert operations are interrupted by the efforts of local amateurs. They all rush away in confusion and Watkins is attacked by the two villagers. He recovers conscious-ness to be thanked for his bold pursuit of the thieves, and is invited to spend the night at the House.

Next morning both Watkins and the more valuable presents and jewellery have vanished.

230. HANDS OFF THE PEOPLE'S FOOD. (Looking Ahead). Daily Chronicle, Aug. 13th, 1914 ; 3rd chapter in *War that will End War.* Advocates certain measures which should be taken for the distribution of food during the war.

HARBOROUGH, MRS. A young widow mentioned in several of the *Select Conversations.* The uncle eventually marries her.

HARDY, DELIA. Maid to the Vicar of Siddermorton ; the Angel is kind to her. *Wonderful Visit.*

HARDY, SIR RICHMOND. A tall, dark, gaunt man, passionate, impatient and irritable ; a munition manufacturer who has been "hit by a stray knighthood," and whose present ambition is to bring his work on the Fuel Commission to a triumphant conclusion. He is a coarse, violent man, acting selfishly towards both his wife and his mistress, Martin Leeds, but with a more than redeeming streak of fineness. Lady Hardy is a "frail little blue-eyed woman" with "that type of face that under even the most pleasant and luxurious circumstances still looks bravely and triumphantly enduring." Hardy calls her "a wonderfully intelligent and understanding woman. . . . I have no excuse for any misbehaviour —so far as she is concerned." They have three children, all grown up. *Secret Places.*

HARMAN, LADY. Before her marriage, which took place when she was eighteen, Ellen Sawbridge. At the opening of the story she is a tall young woman of twenty-five "with a big soft mouth, great masses of blue-black hair on either side of a broad, low forehead, and eyes of so dark a brown that you might have thought them black." She married Sir Isaac from pity and not at all from love ; when he dies she resolves never again to lose her freedom. *Sir Isaac Harman.*

HARMAN, SIR ISAAC. A "lean, grey-headed, obstinate-looking man with a diabetic complexion." The son of a bankrupt steam-miller, he makes a fortune in the catering trade and is given a knighthood for his financial assistance to the Liberal press. He is forty when he marries Ellen Sawbridge ; his ideas of marriage are "simple and strict" and utterly opposed to her demand for "autonomy." *Sir Isaac Harman.*

HARROWDEAN, MRS. With whom Mr. Britling is involved in the early part of 1914. She has a house not far from Matching's Easy and attracts him by "an intermittent vein of high spirits that was almost better than humour." When war breaks out Mr. Britling decides to see her no more. *Mr. Britling.*

231. HAS COMMUNISM A FUTURE ? THE POSSIBILITY OF A SOCIALIST RENASCENCE. Westminster Gazette, Aug. 9th, 1924 ; 49th article in *Year of Prophesying.* In America and Asia there may yet be widespread movements towards Communism, but Wells believes that in Europe "the Communist drive has passed its maximum and that the popular mind is moving onward to a more constructive and hopeful type of Socialism."

HEAT-RAY, THE. The chief offensive weapon of the Martians; it is a beam of heat projected from a parabolic mirror, so intense that anything combustible breaks into flame at its touch, even at great distances. The method of generation is a mystery. *War of the Worlds.*

HEINRICH, HERR. An "unmistakable young German, very pink, with close-cropped fair hair," and glasses. He is a student of philology preparing for his doctorate, and just before the outbreak of war tutor to the younger Britling boys, but more interested in "ideas of universal citizenship, in Esperanto and Ido . . . and such-like attacks upon the barriers between man and man." He dies in confinement as a Russian prisoner-of-war. *Mr. Britling.*

HENDERSON, ETHEL. Chaffery's step-daughter. Lewisham first meets her in Whortley, is dismissed on her account, and later in London comes across her again and marries her. *Mr. Lewisham.*

HENLEY HOUSE MAGAZINE, THE. Of which Wells was editor while assistant master at Henley House School in his early twenties; he traces five items actually written by himself for the magazine between March 1889 and August 1891. See *Cricket, Holiday Science, The North Sea, " That Problem ! " Entre Nous.*

232. HERESIES ; OR THE THINGS THAT GOD IS NOT. 2nd chapter of *God the Invisible King.* A clear statement of certain " misconceptions of God," repudiated by Modern Religion.

HEYDINGER, ALICE. A zoology student at the Normal School of Science who is secretly in love with Mr. Lewisham. She has optimistic opinions of his powers, and is distressed by his failure and still more by his love for Ethel Henderson. *Mr. Lewisham.*

H. G. WELLS. See Wells, H. G.

233. HIGHER EDUCATION IN THE EMPIRE. Times, Aug. 4th, 1916 ; 6th chapter in *Elements of Reconstruction.* A consideration of the education question. Condemns the opposition of the scientific and classical schools, and insists upon the necessity of a course of philosophy and world-history in any liberal education. " The backbone stuff must be a clear and critical knowledge of oneself in relation to the universe."

HILYER, REV. K. Vicar of Siddermorton and a prominent ornithologist. He shoots the Angel in the belief that he is a bird of some rare species, and then, discovering his mistake, invites him to the vicarage to have his wound tended. After the burning of the vicarage and the passing of the Angel he sinks into a state of apathy and dies within a year. *Wonderful Visit.*

HINKS. A Fishbourne saddler and a " sporting man." He is friendly with Mr. Polly until he begins to despise him for his objection to billiards and betting. *Mr. Polly.*

234. HINTS ON VISITING THE ACADEMY. Pall Mall Gazette, May 9th, 1894 ; Pall Mall Budget, May 17th, 1894.

**HISTORY FOR EVERYBODY : A POSTSCRIPT TO " The Outline of

History." Fortnightly Review, June, 1921 ; Yale Review, July, 1921 ; reprinted as a pamphlet with the title *The New Teaching of History* (q.v.).

235. HISTORY IS ONE. See Bib. No. 69. Insists on the uselessness of attempting to teach separately the history of individual countries, contending that history is " only to be properly understood as a whole." It is quite possible and practicable to teach in outline the history of all mankind from the beginning ; Wells points out the way in which this should be done.

236. HISTORY OF MR. POLLY, THE. See Bib. No. 39. This novel opens to discover Mr. Polly, a stout unhealthy draper of thirty-seven, sitting on a stile near Fishbourne in the throes of a despondency induced by insolvency, dyspepsia, and an east wind. From this it goes back to his infancy and childhood, telling of his inadequate education and of his discovery of the joys of reading. At fourteen he is apprenticed at the Port Burdock Drapery Bazaar, where he stays for six years. Here he has two friends, Platt and Parsons, also apprentices. The " three P's " have many good times together, tramping the countryside on Sundays and holidays, wandering about the streets after closing-time, and reading and talking about " everything in the world." The trio is ultimately broken up by the dismissal of Parsons. Mr. Polly leaves the Bazaar and passes from situation to situation. Then his father dies and leaves him three or four hundred pounds ; after a lively funeral he decides to take a holiday. He stays with Harold Johnson, his cousin,

and cycles about the neighbourhood. There he meets Christabel, a schoolgirl, and falls in love with her ; she pities him though she hardly understands, and treats him in a way which seems deliberately cruel. In his disappointment he proposes to and marries Miriam, one of his three Larkins' cousins. He purchases a shop at Fishbourne and settles down to fifteen years of growing dullness and semi-misery, of quarrelling with wife and neighbours. And year by year he drifts nearer to bankruptcy, until he can stand it no longer. Sitting upon the stile, pondering his past, present, and probable future, he decides to kill himself. One Sunday evening he sets fire to the house, hoping thus to conceal the fact of his suicide that his wife may receive his life-insurance money. But the fire so excites him that he forgets his primary object, and when it spreads so that several houses are involved he makes himself the hero of the hour by rescuing an old lady. He receives the fire-insurance money and leaving all but £20 to Miriam he deserts her to become a tramp. Presently he comes to the Potwell Inn in Sussex, and here, attracted by the inn and by the old lady who keeps it, he settles down once more as odd-job man. Uncle Jim, the old lady's nephew, disputes his right to this position, but after three attacks he steals Mr. Polly's clothes and goes away, to be found shortly afterwards drowned in the Medway, in Kent. The body is identified by the clothes, and Miriam receives the life-insurance. Five years later Mr. Polly, knowing nothing of this, returns to Fishbourne to see his wife. She has started a sweet-shop and tea-room with the money, and her main emotion upon seeing him is fear that it will have to be repaid. He returns to the Potwell Inn, there to live out the rest of his life (as far as the story takes it) in peace and comfort.

236a. HOLIDAY OF THE DRAPERS' ASSISTANT, THE. Pall Mall Gazette, June 5th, 1894.

237. HOLIDAY SCIENCE. Henley House Magazine, Aug., 1889. Signed H. G. Wells.

238. HOLLAND'S FUTURE. New York Times, Feb. 7th, 1915.

HOLROYD, JAMES. A Yorkshire engineer who " doubted the existence of God, but accepted Carnot's cycle, and . . . had read Shakespeare and found him weak in chemistry." He is a bully and a blackleg. *Lord of the Dynamos.*

HOLSTEN. A great chemist and mathematician ; in 1933 he sets up " atomic disintegration " in a particle of bismuth, the first man to accomplish this. He keeps a diary which is quoted. *World Set Free.*

HOMARTYN, LADY. Of Claverings Park ; one of Mr. Britling's nearest neighbours. *Mr. Britling.*

239. HONOURS PHYSIOGRAPHY. See Bib. No. 2. A text-book written in collaboration with R. A. Gregory.

HOOPDRIVER, J. E. A drapers' assistant, the rather pale young hero of *The Wheels of Chance* (q.v.).

240. HOUSE-HUNTING AS AN OUTDOOR AMUSEMENT. Pall Mall Gazette, Sept. 24th, 1894 ; 11th essay in *Personal Matters*. Describes the pleasures of " artistic house-hunting," not with the object of finding a house but for the fun of it. Mentions different types of landlords and landladies, and closes with an account of Hill Crest, a monstrous house with a curiously low rent.

241. HOUSE OF DI SORNO, THE. Pall Mall Gazette, Aug. 24th, 1894 ; 4th essay in *Personal Matters*. The writer, searching for a tie in his wife's box, discovers the MS. of a novel, " The House of di Sorno," written by his wife at the age of sixteen. He reads some parts of it ; then Euphemia comes in and snatches it away from him.

HOWARD. A " short, fat, and thick-set beardless man," appointed Graham's guardian by the White Council. *Sleeper Wakes.*

242. HOW FAR WILL EUROPE GO TOWARDS SOCIALISM ? Cassell's Magazine, Mar., 1916 ; 5th chapter in *What is Coming ?* Wells cites Germany's comparative success in the war as an example of the result of national syndication, contrasting it with the too individualistic British states. Great Britain now finds herself with all the more important industries nationalised, and he believes that " there will arise, there does even now arise . . . the framework of a new economic and social order based upon national ownership and service."

243. HOW I DIED. Probably printed in Pall Mall Gazette, about 1895 ; last essay in *Personal Matters*. Ten years before the narrator discovered that he had not long to live. He took to his bed, was visited by distressed friends, wrote last letters to them, made " memor-

able remarks." Until one spring day he goes out " to look once more —perhaps for the last time—on sky and earth." He meets a girl, and talking with her forgets that he is a Doomed Man. And he decides that he is not going to die.

244. HOW PEOPLE THINK ABOUT THE WAR. 4th and last section of *War and the Future*, consisting of six articles reprinted from the Daily News : 1, *Do They Really Think At All ? ;* 2, *The Yielding Pacifist and the Conscientious Objector ;* 3, *The Religious Revival ;* 4, *The Riddle of the British ;* 5, *The Social Changes in Progress ;* 6, *The Ending of the War.* Wells doubts (1) whether people really are thinking about the war and post-war conditions, considers (2) the conscientious objector, and (3) the part played in the war by the Anglican and Catholic Churches, with special reference to the National Mission of Repentance and Hope and to the political quibbling of the Vatican. He is confident (4) that Britain is finding her way out of the old ideas, despite the conservatism of the dominant military and administrative classes, seeing (5) a new spirit of collective service among the business and organising classes ; he says that this spirit must be turned to the serving of God. He sketches (6) the essentials of a world-peace, among which he includes a League of Peace and an International Tribunal for the discussion of international affairs. He looks to America to play a large part in reconciliation, and comes finally to the idea of God as the ultimate world-king.

245. HOW WE MUDDLE THROUGH THE YEARS OF DESTINY. Westminster Gazette, Jan. 5th, 1924 ; reprinted as *The Parliamentary Triangle* (q.v.). Criticism and forecast of the new Labour Government and of the modern parliamentary system in general.

HUB OF EUROPE : CZECHO-SLOVAKIA AND FRANCE, THE. 20th article in *Year of Prophesying ;* see *Is Czecho-Slovakia the Hub of Europe ?*

246. HUMAN ADVENTURE, THE. Daily Mail ; last essay in *An Englishman.* Traces very briefly the progress of Man from the earliest times to the present day, then looks into the future and sees the men of those days united, thinking and willing collectively. The essay is a brief but vivid word-picture of " Man on his planet, flying swiftly to unmeasured destinies through the starry stillnesses of space."

247. HUMAN EVOLUTION AN ARTIFICIAL PROCESS. Fortnightly Review, Oct., 1896. Suggests that man has undergone only an " infinitesimal alteration in his intrinsic nature since the age of polished stone," making a biological comparison between man and rabbit. He traces the apparent vast change to the development of speech and writing and the consequent creation of the artificial factor in man. He prophecies that man will win complete control of this factor and at last " attain and preserve a social organisation so cunningly balanced against exterior necessities on the one hand, and the artificial factor in the individual on the other, that the life of every human being . . . may be happy." A reply to this by F. H. P. Coste was printed in Natural Science, Mar., 1897 ; Wells

replied to this criticism in Natural Science, Apr., 1897, in an article, *Human Evolution : a Reply.*

248. HUMAN EVOLUTION : A REPLY. See *Human Evolution an Artificial Process.*

HUNKER. An American Cinema King ; he enters Utopia as one of Lord Barralonga's party. *Men Like Gods.*

HUNTLEY, GAVAN. A "blond young man with a strong profile, a hungry, scornful expression, and a greedy, large blue eye," a scornful, sarcastic egotist who spends his life pursuing women, among them Joan Debenham. He talks to her of sex and the "superstition of chastity," but without success. He is a well-known novelist and dramatic critic. During the war he is a conscientious objector. *Joan and Peter.*

HUSS, JOB. (Job). Headmaster of Woldingstanton School. After many years of conspicuous success he is suddenly beset by disaster. There are deaths in the school, he loses his money, his son is reported dead, his wife turns against him, he discovers that he is suffering from cancer and that an immediate operation is necessary, and the school governors wish to deprive him of his post and appoint a man who will undo all that he has done. Yet despite it all he holds fast to his faith in God. His wife is a dark and graceful, but untidy, emotional, effusive woman. Their son, Gilbert, is shot down while flying over the German lines, and apparently killed; later he is discovered to be still alive, though a prisoner. *Undying Fire.*

249. HUXLEY. Royal College of Science Magazine, probably in 1895, just after Huxley's death.

250. HYGIENIC COUNTRY, THE. Lika Joko, Dec. 15th, 1894.

I

251. IDEAL CITIZEN, THE. 24th essay in *An Englishman.* Wells's conception of the ideal citizen in the modern community.

IDEAL SCHOOL, THE. (Salvaging of Civilisation, 6). Sunday Times, May 15th, 1921 ; reprinted as the latter part of *The Schooling of the World* (q.v.).

252. IDEALS OF ORGANISATION. Nation, July 24th, 1915. Discussion of a pamphlet by Professor Van Gennep, "The Spirit of Organization ; A Contrast of the French and English Formula as Opposed to the German."

253. IDEA OF A CHURCH, THE. 7th chapter of *God the Invisible King.* Discusses the question of a Church for this modern religion which is dawning in the minds of men all about the world, raising several objections to "the church-forming disposition." But Wells sees no objection to the formation of organisations for the spreading of the faith as long as they do not seek to "restrict religious activities or the freedom of religious thought and teaching."

254. IDEA OF A LEAGUE OF NATIONS, THE. See Bib. II, 1919.

255. IDEA OF ALLIED COMBINES, THE. (Some Liberal Ideals, 3). Daily Chronicle, Oct. 2nd, 1916.

IDEAS FOR A WORLD PEACE. Daily News, Jan. 19th and 22nd, 1917 ; reprinted as *The Ending of the War* (q.v.).

256. IF ENGLAND IS RAIDED : THE CIVILIAN FORCES. Daily Chronicle, Dec. 12th, 1914.

257. IMMENSITY OF ISSUE AND THE TRIVIALITY OF MEN, THE. Daily Mail, Nov. 7th, 1921 ; 1st chapter in *Washington*. Points out the imminent dangers which face the world to-day, and that only some collective international action can save civilisation ; the Washington Conference is an affair almost of life and death. In this " phase of universal danger " we must " resolve to be charitable and frank with one another to the best of our ability, to be forgiving . . . seeking patience in hearing and generosity in action. High aims and personal humility may yet save mankind."

258. IMMIGRANT, THE. 8th chapter in *Future in America*. Discusses the case of the immigrant, viewing with some apprehension the " huge dilution " of the American people by ignorant peasants from Europe and the East.

259. IMPERFECTION OF DEMOCRACY, THE. Daily News, Aug. 5th, 1915. A reply to an article by Arnold Bennett printed Aug. 4th.

260. IMPERIAL CONSTITUTION, AN. Times, Aug. 1st, 1916 ; 5th chapter in *Elements of Reconstruction*. Criticism of contemporary parliamentary representation. Considers the possibility of an Imperial Parliament. Advocates the modernisation of the existing legislature, the Upper House representatives to be classified by function, while in the Lower House occupational constituencies to be substituted for local reference constituencies.

261. IMPORTANCE OF CHINA. Westminster Gazette, April 26th, 1924 ; reprinted as *China : the Land Out of the Limelight* (q.v.). Comments on the modern progress and educational development of China.

262. IMPUDENCE OF FLAGS : OUR POWER RESOURCES AND MY ELEPHANTS, WHALES, AND GORILLAS, THE. Westminster Gazette, Aug. 2nd, 1924 ; 48th article in *Year of Prophesying*. Taking the Prince of Wales's speech at the World Power Conference as his text, Wells insists upon the necessity for the international development (as opposed to national) of the world's power resources. For this, for the preservation of the " dwindling world fauna," for the extermination of diseases, " flag-worship " must be suppressed.

263. IN A LITERARY HOUSEHOLD. Pall Mall Gazette, Oct. 17th, 1894 ; 6th essay in *Personal Matters*. Describes the literary household in fiction and in fact.

264. IN A LITTLE SHOP. Pall Mall Gazette, about April, 1894.

265. INCIDENTAL THOUGHTS ON A BALD HEAD. See *Thoughts on a Bald Head*. 22nd essay in *Personal Matters*. Struck by the number of bald heads visible at a lantern lecture, the author reflects that man is slowly dwindling, " growing hairless, growing bald, growing toothless," and replacing his losses with artificial substitutes. He suggests that ultimately man will become

" a kind of hermit crab, the bulk of him a complex mechanism"; perhaps he may disappear altogether, leaving the world populated by " a democracy of honest machinery."

266. INCOMPATIBILITY OF INDIA : DIVORCE OR LEGAL SEPARATION, THE. Westminster Gazette, July 5th, 1924 ; 44th article in *Year of Prophesying*. A review of a recent libel case arising from native disturbances in India. Wells believes that the time has come for a separation from India.

267. INDIA'S PLACE IN THE WORLD. Daily Express, Dec. 9th, 1921 ; 23rd chapter in *Washington*. Considers the future of India. Every nation will have to pay its price for world peace and prosperity; that of the Empire will be the giving of complete political freedom to India.

268. INERT PERSON, THE. Pall Mall Gazette, April 18th, 1894.

269. INSECTS AND FLOWERS. Saturday Review, April 6th, 1895. Unsigned. A scientific article.

270. INTANGIBLE MAN, THE. Pall Mall Gazette, April 13th, 1894.

271. INTELLIGENCE ON MARS. Saturday Review, April 4th, 1896. Unsigned. Even should life exist on Mars, there is no reason why we should suppose any common measures of intelligence between ourselves and the Martians.

INTERVIEW WITH LENIN, AN. Westminster Gazette, Feb. 9th, 1924 ; reprinted as *Lenin : Private Capitalism against Communism* (q.v.).

INTERVIEWS. The following interviews with Wells are mentioned as being of some special interest : 1, *The Romance of the Scientist*, Young Man, August, 1897 ; 2, *What I Believe*, Puritan, Apr., 1898 ; 3, *The Novelist as Prophet*, Cassell's Saturday Journal, Apr., 26th, 1899 ; 4, *H. G. Wells*, New York Herald, Apr. 15th, 1906 ; 5, *A Select Conversation* (by Ralph Straus), The Bodleian, Jan., 1911 ; 6, *H. G. Wells as Historian*, Strand Magazine, Nov., 1919. 7, *History as Healer*, Observer, Jan. 18th, 1920 ; 8, *G. Bernard Shaw and H. G. Wells Disbelieve in Spiritualism*, Strand Magazine, Apr., 1920 ; 9, *The Human Commonwealth*, Observer, Aug. 29th, 1920 ; 10, *H. G. Wells on the Six Greatest Men in History*, Strand Magazine, Sept., 1922.

272. IN THE ABYSS. Pearson's Magazine, Aug., 1896 ; 4th tale in *Plattner Story*. Elstead descends to the ocean bed, some five miles down, in a steel sphere fitted with windows, electric light, and a clockwork weight release. There he finds a great city populated by beings curiously human in appearance. These creatures of the abyss tow the sphere to a temple and worship it ; the clockwork jams and the performance goes on for several hours. At last the cord connecting sphere and weights is worn through by rubbing against the altar edge, and the sphere shoots to the surface. After making certain improvements in the sphere, Elstead descends again, this time never to return.

273. IN THE AVU OBSERVATORY. Pall Mall Budget, Aug. 9th, 1894 ; 3rd story in *Stolen Bacillus*, 5th in

Country of the Blind. An assistant at an observatory in Borneo is attacked while on duty one night by a strange bat-like creature. He wounds it and drives it away.

274. IN THE DAYS OF THE COMET. See Bib. No. 27. A romance in three books with a prologue and epilogue. In the pro'ogue a "grey-haired man, a figure of hale age," is writing in a tower before a window; it is his manuscript which forms the bulk of the book. William Leadford (the man in the tower) is a clerk in a pot-bank office in the Four Towns, Stafford-shire, and "a Socialist out and out." He lives with his mother, who supports herself by taking lodgers. The whole district is passing through a period of industrial unrest which forms a striking background for the more personal matter of Leadford's love for Nettie Stuart, his cousin. A comet appears in the sky, coming hourly earthward. The colliers strike; Germany declares war on England. Nettie runs away with Verral, the son of a local land-owner. Leadford pursues them to Shaphambury, intending to kill them. He comes upon them unexpectedly on the beach, revolver in hand, while out at sea a naval battle is in progress. He shoots at them, and as they run a green mist closes over the world, and in the sky the comet's head, now close upon the earth, radiates innumerable shooting stars. The mist grows denser until "the green curtain was a black one, and the earth and I and all things ceased to be." Leadford wakens with the dawn to find a cleaner, finer earth about him, the nitrogen in the air having been changed by the comet into a respirable gas,

"differing indeed from oxygen, but helping and sustaining its action, a bath of strength and healing for nerve and brain." With this change in the air comes a change in the hearts of all mankind; selfish personal ends are forgotten in the work for a common good. Leadford meets Melmount, the prime minister, and for a time acts as his secretary. Men set about the building of a better world. The old towns are torn down, and the last of the old traditions go up with the smoke of the fires of the Beltane Festivals. Leadford meets Nettie and Verral, but now there is no anger in his heart. His mother dies and he marries Anna Reeves, her nurse. Nettie comes back to him and the four—Leadford, Anna, Nettie, Verral—live on happily together in a world of happiness.

275. IN THE FOURTH YEAR: ANTICIPATIONS OF A WORLD PEACE. See Bib. No. 66. A brief volume in 11 chapters, consisting of articles reprinted from the London Press. It is prefaced with a short account of the spreading of the idea of a World League of Nations and of the author's purpose in publishing this book. It is in two parts; the first, consisting of 8 chapters under the general title, The League of Free Nations, deals with the League, its constitution, duties, and problems, and with the "necessary sacrifices of preconceptions" that the idea of the League involves. The last three chapters, under the title Democracy, advocate Proportional Representation as the only possible electoral method of attaining democracy. The chapter-titles are: 1, *The Way to Concrete Realization;* 2, *The League must*

be *Representative ;* 3, *The Necessary Powers of the League ;* 4, *The Labour View of Middle Africa ;* 5, *Getting the League Idea Clear in Relation to Imperialism ;* 6, *The War Aims of the Western Allies Compactly Stated ;* 7, *The Future of Monarchy ;* 8, *The Plain Necessity for a League ;* 9, *Democracy ;* 10, *The Recent Struggle for Proportional Representation in Great Britain ;* 11, *The Study and Propaganda of Democracy.*

276. IN THE MODERN VEIN : AN UNSYMPATHETIC LOVE STORY. See *A Bardlet's Romance.* 13th tale in *Plattner Story.* A minor poet conceives a romantic passion for a girl he meets at a tennis party. She loves him, but when he refuses to leave his wife and go away with her, she says that she will not see him again.

277. IN THE NEW FOREST. Saturday Review, April 27th, 1895. Unsigned. Nature article.

278. INTRODUCTION to *Anticipations,* 1914 edition. The " H. G. Wells of forty-eight " discusses this work of the " H. G. Wells of thirty-three."

279. INTRODUCTION to *Boon.* Remarks that " Bliss is Bliss and Wells is Wells. And Bliss can write all sorts of things that Wells could not."

280. INTRODUCTION to *Country of the Blind.* A discussion of the art of the short story.

281. INTRODUCTION to *First and Last Things,* 1908 edition. Tells how the book came to be written, and comments on its contents and purpose.

282. INTRODUCTION to " Friendly Russia." See Bib. III, 1915.

283. INTRODUCTION to " George Meek, Bathchairman." See Bib. III, 1910.

284. INTRODUCTION to " The Gods in the Battle." See Bib. III, 1917.

285. INTRODUCTION to "The Journal of a Disappointed Man." See Bib. III, 1917.

286. INTRODUCTION to " Keeling Letters and Recollections." See Bib. III, 1918.

287. INTRODUCTION to " Kultur Cartoons." See Bib. III, 1915.

288. INTRODUCTION to " The Mind in the Making." See Bib. III. 1923 ; also Bib. No. 75.

289. INTRODUCTION to " Nocturne." See Bib. III, 1918.

290. INTRODUCTION to *The Outline of History.* Explains the purpose and scope of the book, acknowledges indebtedness, etc.

291. INTRODUCTION to " Pictures of War Work in England." See Bib. III, 1917.

292. INTRODUCTION to " The Pivot of Civilisation." See Bib. III, 1922.

293. INTRODUCTION to " The Quaint Companions." See Bib. III, 1918.

INTRODUCTION to Russian translations of Wells's works. See *Mr. Wells Explains Himself.*

294. INTRODUCTION to "Shop Slavery and Emancipation." See Bib. III, 1912.

295. INTRODUCTION to "Utopia." See Bib. III, 1905.

INTRUDERS AT WASHINGTON. Daily Express, Dec. 8th, 1921 ; reprinted as *Some Stifled Voices* (q.v.).

296. INVISIBLE KING, THE. 5th chapter of *God the Invisible King*. Modern religion is political ; it seeks to establish a world-theocracy with God as the Invisible King. The first purpose of God, working through Man, is the attainment of knowledge as a means to power. The first duty of Man is to serve God ; he must completely surrender himself to, and become merely an agent for, God. Certain difficulties are discussed, and the case of the barrister dealt with as an extreme example. Finally, considers "God and the love and status of women." Sex has no place in modern religion, and the love of husband and wife has no parallel in the love of God.

297. INVISIBLE MAN, THE. See Bib. No. 11. Griffin, a demonstrator of physics in a provincial college, while working upon the subject of optical density, discovers a method by which he may achieve invisibility. Believing that this will give him unlimited power, he carries out the experiment. It is completely successful, but at a critical moment his landlord interferes and he fires the house to destroy all traces of his work. Necessarily he is stark naked, and, it being midwinter, anything but comfortable. After some adventures he steals

clothes, and bandages, spectacles and a paste-board nose with which to cover his face, and goes to Iping, a village in Surrey, resolved to find some way of reversing the experiment. He takes a room at the "Coach and Horses" and spends the next two months in scientific work. Then his supply of money comes to an end, he robs the local vicarage, and when accused, escapes by tearing off his clothes. Pressing a tramp, Mr. Thomas Marvell, into his service, he returns, and between them they carry away his books and other possessions. They come through Port Stowe to Burdock, where the tramp takes refuge in the police-station. Griffin is injured in a fight and hides in a house which turns out to be that of an old fellow-student, now Dr. Kemp. Here he spends the night and in the morning tells Kemp the whole story. The doctor, contrary to his promise, sends word to Colonel Adye, chief of the local police. Adye comes to the house with two policemen, and again Griffin has a narrow escape. He institutes a Reign of Terror, and that evening murders a Mr. Wicksteed. The next morning, having eaten and slept, he makes an attack on Kemp's house ; Kemp slips out through a window, and makes for the town, where a gang of navvies comes to his rescue. There is a fight in which Griffin is killed, his head and chest smashed in by the whirling spades. After death his body becomes slowly visible once more.

ISBISTER. The young artist who meets Graham on the cliffs near Boscastle and who is with him when he falls into the trance. Some years later he invents an advertising process and makes a fortune. His two sons are drowned and he leaves his wealth to the Sleeper. This money, with that left by Warming, forms the nucleus of Graham's enormous wealth. *Sleeper Wakes.*

298. Is BRITAIN ON THE DOWN GRADE ? Young Man, July, 1899.

299. Is CZECHO-SLOVAKIA THE HUB OF EUROPE ? Westminster Gazette, Jan. 26th, 1924 ; reprinted as *The Hub of Europe* (q.v.). Masaryk, president of Czecho-Slovakia, and Benes, his chief minister, have a "splendid and civilised dream" of their country as the "meeting-place and reconciler of European interests," but their work is endangered by a "loud and irreconcilable body of ultra-patriots."

300. I SKATE. Pall Mall Gazette, in Jan., 1894 ; Pall Mall Budget, Jan. 11th, 1894.

301. ISLAND OF DR. MOREAU, THE. See Bib. No. 7. Dr. Moreau, a prominent physiologist and notorious vivisector, is "howled out" of England for wanton cruelty, but continues his experiments upon a lonely Pacific island. His aim is "to find out the extreme limit of plasticity in a living shape." With this object he attempts the conversion of animals into men, and to a certain extent succeeds. Edward Prendick, the narrator, is landed on the island after a series of adventures following on the wreck of the "Lady Vain" in 1887. He notices the strange deformities of the inhabitants of the island, and remembering the story of the "Moreau Horrors," jumps to the conclusion that these are men who have been subjected to some horrible experiments. Fearing a similar fate, he flies to the woods, there meeting the Ape-Man, who takes him to the huts of the Beast-People. They welcome him as one of themselves, the latest arrival from the "House of Pain." Moreau and Montgomery (the doctor's assistant) pursue Prendick with staghounds and at last persuade him to return with them ; Moreau then tells him the truth. At the time of Prendick's arrival Montgomery had let loose some rabbits upon the island ; several of these are found killed and half-eaten, certain of the Beast-People having broken the Law Moreau has imposed upon them. Fearing that the taste of blood will awaken their carnivorous instincts, Moreau determines to punish the offender. Guilt attaches itself to the Leopard Man, and he is shot. Six weeks pass. Then Moreau is killed by a mutilated puma ; Prendick's left arm is broken ; Montgomery gets drunk, gives whisky to the Beast-People, destroys the boats, and is killed by the Sayer of the Law. Moreau's house is burnt to the ground, and Prendick has perforce to live in the huts, where the Dog-Man, faithful to the last, is his only friend. During the next ten months the creatures slowly lapse towards their original condition, losing all power of speech and becoming quadrupeds once more. At last a small boat drifts up to the island, manned by two dead bodies ; Prendick sails away in it and is picked up by a San Francisco-bound brig. The first edition of this book has an introduction by Charles Edward Prendick, nephew of the narrator ; this is omitted in some later editions.

302. ISLAND OF OPERA, THE.
Lika Joko, Nov. 24th, 1894.

303. ISONZO FRONT, THE. 1st
chapter of *The War in Italy*. Account of the wonderful organization
of the Italian armies and of the
fighting upon the Isonzo front.

304. IS OUR WORLD COLLAPSING?
Daily Herald, Jan. 24th, 1923.
Review of " The Decay of Capitalist
Civilisation," by Sidney and Beat-
rice Webb.

305. IS THERE A PEOPLE ? See
There Is No People. 20th essay
in *An Englishman*. The writer
doubts the existence of a People,
" that impalpable monster to which
the world has consecrated its
political institutions for the last
hundred years." Brings forward
certain supporting facts and concludes, " Suppose there is no people
at all, but only enormous, differ-
entiating millions of men. All sorts
of widely accepted generalisations
will collapse if that foundation is
withdrawn."

ITALY, FRANCE AND BRITAIN AT
WAR. Title of the American edition
of *War and the Future* (see Bib.
No. 62).

J

JANE. Whose tragic love-affair
is related in *The Jilting of Jane*.
After her disappointment she is
" even careful " over her work.

JEHORAM, JESSICA. The widow
of a minor poet, she is the Siddermorton authority upon music and
art. She tries to flirt with the
Angel. *Wonderful Visit*.

JELALUDDIN, MIR. A Cam-
bridge undergraduate from India
who meets Joan Debenham at the
Club of Strange Faiths and falls
in love with her. After the outbreak of war he joins the French
air-force and by a coincidence kills
Von Papen, the German airman
who had shot Peter down. He
visits Peter in hospital and criticises
the British government's attitude
to Indians. *Joan and Peter*.

306. JELLYGRAPHIA. Pall Mall
Gazette, Feb. 28th, 1894.

JEWELL, ARTHUR. The " most
offensive member " of Hugh Britling's company. " Soldiers Three "
is his bible, and he imagines himself
to be very like Private Ortheris.
Various accounts of his progress
are given in Hugh's letters to Mr.
Britling. When he is killed by a
shell in France Hugh is peculiarly
distressed. *Mr. Britling*.

307. JILTING OF JANE, THE.
12th story in *Plattner Story ;* 1st
in *Country of the Blind*. Jane,
Euphemia's servant, is engaged to
William Piddingquirk, porter in a
drapery shop. Three years later,
having risen to the position of
counter-assistant, he jilts her and
marries a milliner. Jane goes to
the wedding and throws a boot at
the bride ; unfortunately it hits
William.

JIM, UNCLE. The worthless
nephew of Aunt Flo, the plump
woman of the Potwell Inn, and the
terror of her life. As a boy he is
sent to a reformatory, his aunt
being partly responisble for his
conviction. Upon his release he
comes back to torment her ; he
teaches Polly, his young niece, to

spit and swear. He disputes Mr. Polly's right to stay at the inn, and makes three attempts to " scoot " him. The third, the great battle of the Night Surprise, ends by Uncle Jim making off with Mr. Polly's clothes. Five years later Mr. Polly learns that Uncle Jim was drowned in the Medway, and when found was only recognisable by his clothes, which were the stolen ones. *Mr. Polly.*

308. JIMMY GOGGLES THE GOD. Graphic Christmas No., Dec., 1898 ; 7th tale in *Twelve Stories ;* 23rd in *Country of the Blind.* A party of white men, engaged in illegal salving operations off the coast of Papua, is attacked by natives and exterminated with the exception of one man, the narrator, who is under water. He makes for the shore, realising that something is wrong, and there the natives receive him as a god from the sea, never suspecting the presence of a man within the diving dress. He lives with the tribe for four months ; then, fearing exposure from an interfering missionary, he leaves the dress behind and makes along the coast for civilisation.

309. JOAN AND PETER : THE STORY OF AN EDUCATION. See Bib. No. 67. This novel, the longest yet published by Wells, tells in detail of the life and education of two children, Joan Debenham and Peter Stubland, from birth to maturity. Peter is the only child of Arthur and Dolly Stubland ; Joan, a year or so younger, is the illegitimate child of Will Sydenham, Dolly's brother, but she is brought up with Peter and bears the name Stubland for several years. Arthur and Dolly are drowned in Italy,

and by Arthur's will the guardianship of the children passes to his sisters Phœbe and Phyllis, and to Oswald Sydenham and Lady Charlotte Sydenham. Oswald is in Africa ; Lady Charlotte is too busy with her own affairs to interfere then, except upon one occasion when she has the two children secretly christened ; they remain in the care of the two sisters at Limpsfield and attend the nearby School of St. George and the Venerable Bede. When Peter is nearly ten he and Joan are kidnapped by Lady Charlotte and sent secretly to Windsor. Joan is left in the care of Mrs. Pybus, sister of Lady Charlotte's maid ; Peter is sent to High Cross Preparatory School, a particularly bad institution. After a few days he runs away and reaches home in safety. Oswald returns to England and at the same time it is proved that Dolly survived her husband by some minutes ; her will appoints Oswald sole guardian. He is disgusted and irritated by the small and narrow outlook of the majority of men, and has come to the idea of education as the essential thing, the one thing which will save the world from war and destruction. The children return to their Limpsfield School and Oswald begins a searching of schools and schoolmasters. The question of education from the points of view of schoolmaster and parent are discussed at some length. At last Peter is sent to a Margate preparatory school, and thence to Caxton, a modern public school, and thence again to Cambridge. Joan goes to Highmorton School and to Newnham. Peter grows up a handsome young man, Joan a very beautiful girl, each with many friends and detesting most of the other's friends. Chief among Joan's are Gavan Huntley, Wilmington, Bunny Cuspard, Winterbaum, Troop, and Mir Jelaluddin. Peter's great friend is Hetty Reinhart, a rather promiscuous girl with whom he frequents the London night-clubs. At the Christmas party at Pelham Ford, Oswald's home, in 1913, Joan learns the truth about her parentage and realises that she is in love with Peter ; she strives to outdo Hetty in every way. Early in 1914 Oswald takes Peter to Russia ; on their return they visit Ireland. In July Peter goes for a walking tour with Troop in the Bernese Oberland, but at the end of the month joins Hetty in Italy. War breaks out, and after a few hours' hesitation he leaves her, comes to England, and joins an infantry regiment as a private. Joan joins the Women's Legion and becomes a motor-driver for the Ministry of Munitions. Oswald goes to France as an officer in an African labour corps, but is wounded by a bomb and sent home. All their friends, excepting only Huntley and the Sheldricks, are engaged in war-work, and many are killed. Peter transfers to the R.F.C. ; after a period of training he flies to France, is engaged in bombing work, and is brought down in his first flight, badly wounded. His victor is driven off and killed by Mir Jelaluddin, now an airman in the French army. During a period of delirium which follows, Peter dreams that he interviews the Lord God. He comes home for twenty-one days leave, but tells Oswald that he has only fourteen days, that he may be able to spend a week with Hetty. As the train moves out of the station Joan

tells him that she knows he is lying, and that she loves him ; he gets out at the next station and walks back to her. They are married before his return to France, where he is attached as an observer in the kite-balloon section. Once again he is brought down, with leg and shoulder smashed by machine-gun fire. The last chapter opens in April, 1918. Oswald is despondent concerning the progress of the war. Peter, no longer fit for active service, moves to London with Joan to take up a minor adminis-trative post. He has decided that after the war he will go in for scientific research work ; Joan's in-terest is in house-building. Before their departure the three discuss life, religion, education. Peter says that there must be no " passive peace " after the war ; " Man can-not stagnate. It is forbidden. It is the uttermost sin."

JOHNSON, HAROLD. Mr. Polly's married cousin, ticket-clerk at Ease-wood Junction, and a melancholy, practical-minded man, though thoughtful (he reads The British Weekly). Mr. Polly's father lives with him for some time, and the funeral is from his house, where Polly, too, lives until his marriage and removal to Fishbourne. John-son's wife, Grace, is cheerful and talkative. *Mr. Polly.*

310. JOINT HOUSEHOLDS. (Uto-pianisms, 4). Daily Mail, May 25th, 1905.

311. JOYS OF BEING ENGAGED, THE. Pall Mall Gazette, in 1893 ; 7th of the *Select Conversations.* George comes upon his uncle pur-chasing a ring for Mrs. Harborough. The uncle discourses upon the

differences between being engaged and being married.

JULIP, UNCLE JOHN. Gardener to Lord Bramble, and Martha Smith's brother; "a cynical opinionated man" with a "smooth white face and a wise self-satisfied smile." After his dismissal for stealing he is too contemptuous to succeed as a jobbing-gardener and takes to drinking and betting. His wife, Aunt Adelaide, is a white-faced woman in constant bad health; she dies in hospital soon after he leaves Chessing Hanger. *Dream.*

JUSTIN. The "incredibly rich and powerful" financier who marries Lady Mary Christian. He is a hard, harsh man, yet, despite their estrangements, his love for his wife is very real and deep. *Passionate Friends.*

K

KARENIN, MARCUS. A Russian cripple, a dominating influence upon the world education committee established after the "last war"; he enforces "self-abnegation, self-identification with the world-spirit" as the basis of universal education. As he grows old he is troubled by pain, and has to undergo two serious operations, the second of which kills him. For some days before this fatal operation he talks with the patients and doctors of the Paran surgical station upon science, the world before the war, love, sex, and the future of the race. *World Set Free.*

KARL ALBERT, PRINCE. "That great and puissant Prince, the War Lord, the hero of two hemispheres . . . a handsome blond man, with deep-set eyes, a snub nose, upturned moustache, and long white hands." Leader of the German Imperialist Party and in command of the air-fleet which attacks America. He is shot and killed by Bert Smallways on Goat Island. *War in the Air.*

KEMP, DR. A "tall and slender young man, with flaxen hair and a moustache almost white," once a student at University College, London with Griffin, now engaged upon scientific research at his house near Port Burdock. Griffin enters his house by chance, recognises him, and tells him the whole story of his adventures. Kemp promises not to give him away, and then sends a message to the police. *Invisible Man.*

KEYHOLE, DR. TOMLINSON. An "eminent litterateur" mentioned several times in Boon; he praises George Boon's books in reviews written not only under his own name but also under those of Simon up to Snuff, The Silver Fish, and The True-Born Englishman. In The Mind of the Race he is one of the party which visits the villa by the sea; at the end of that incomplete work he is murdered in his Hampstead Villa by Hallery. An excellent portrait is given at the end of Chapter 1. *Boon.*

KIMPTON, MILLY. Harry Smith meets her in the counting-house at Thunderstone House; they are friends before the war, and he marries her after the divorce from Hetty. She has "a broad, candid face that never looked either angry or miserable"; a rather stolid placid woman "without much whim or humour." *Dream.*

312. KIPPS : The Story of a Simple Soul. See Bib. No. 26. Arthur Kipps, an illegitimate child,

M

is brought up by an uncle and aunt in New Romney, where he makes friends with Sid and Ann Pornick, the children of the village haberdasher. He leaves a small private school to be apprenticed to Mr. Shalford, a Folkestone draper, for a period of seven years. These past, Mr. Shalford keeps him on as an improver. One night he meets Chitterlow, gets drunk and does not return to the shop until the following morning, and is dismissed, only to be saved from a period of " crib-hunting " by the unexpected inheritance of a large fortune left him by his paternal grandfather. Under the guidance of Mr. Chester Coote he becomes a member of Folkestone society, and is engaged to Helen Walshingham, who belongs to a " County family, related to the Earl of Beaupres " and whom he has long loved from a distance. For some time he perseveres but at last, roused to desperation by the obvious futility of his efforts to make himself a " gentleman," he runs away with and marries Ann Pornick, now a Folkestone housemaid. They attempt an impossible social standard, but are saved from themselves by Young Walshingham, Helen's brother, who has had charge of Kipps's money and has lost it by speculating. With the thousand or so pounds left they open a bookshop in Hythe and settle down to the happiest time of their lives. Chitterlow's play, " The Pestered Butterfly," in which Kipps had previously purchased a share purely to oblige his friend, is staged and becomes an enormous popular success, bringing almost as much money to Kipps as did his inheritance. But, with his wife and child, he stays on at the book-shop, still the same honest, kindly " simple soul."

KIPPS, ARTHUR. The illegitimate son of a man named Waddy and of Margaret Euphemia Kipps, of whom he has only the faintest recollections. See summary above. His son is named Arthur Waddy Kipps.

KIPPS, EDWARD GEORGE. Arthur Kipps's uncle, who keeps a small general store in New Romney. He and his wife Molly have charge of Kipps from his infancy until he goes to Shalford's. *Kipps.*

KURT, LUFT-LIEUTENANT. With whom Bert Smallways shares a cabin on the " Vaterland." He is a pleasant young man, the son of an Englishwoman, and has been educated in England. He is killed in the destruction of the " Hohenzollern." *War in the Air.*

L

313. LA BELLE DAME SANS MERCI. Pall Mall Gazette, in Oct., 1894 ; 8th of the *Select Conversations.* The uncle discourses upon a neighbour who daily at her piano mutilates certain well-known musical compositions.

LABOUR AFTER THE WAR. Daily News, Jan. 15th, 1917 ; reprinted as the 2nd and 3rd sections of *The Social Changes in Progress* (q.v.).

LABOUR COMPANY, THE. An organization developed from the Salvation Army, which is brought up and reconstructed on business lines by Graham's trustees. In return for a day's food and shelter it demands not only a day's work but also that the labourer shall wear the blue canvas uniform of the Company. Conditions are such that once a man has worked for the Company he becomes almost inevitably its slave. *Sleeper Wakes* and *Story of the Days to Come.*

314. LABOUR IDEAL OF EDUCATION, THE. See Bib. No. 84.

315. LABOUR PARTY ON TRIAL: FOLLY OF THE FIVE CRUISERS, THE. Westminster Gazette, Mar. 15th, 1924 ; 27th article in *Year of Prophesying.* Criticises the Labour Government's decision to build five new cruisers.

316. LABOUR POLITICIANS : THE EVAPORATION OF THE INTELLIGENT-ZIA. Westminster Gazette, May 10th, 1924 ; 36th article in *Year of Prophesying.* Explains the alienation of the intelligentzia from the Labour Party now it has attained office ; "they are coming to realise how greatly they overrated the creative power and the creative will of Labour."

317. LABOUR REVOLT, THE. Everyman, Feb. 7th, 1913. Wells sympathises with the modern labour revolt, but disagrees with the views of many of its leaders. He protests against the idea of a specialised working class ruled by a bureaucracy, and suggests universal labour conscription as an alternative. All must belong to the working class that all may belong to the leisure class. He advocates the abolition of the obstructive Party System by the adoption of Proportional Representation.

LABOUR'S LITTLE HOUSES. Westminster Gazette, Aug. 16th, 1924 ; reprinted as *The Little House* (q.v.).

318. LABOUR UNREST, THE. See Bib. No. 45. The six articles

reprinted in this pamphlet are : 1, *Distrust.* 2, *The Lawyer's Tone.* 3, *The Spectacle of Pleasure.* 4, *What May Be Done.* 5, *A National Plan.* 6, *What Must Be Done Now.* The labour unrest is deepening and increasing. Labour distrusts the ruling classes, who spend too much time in pleasure ; this lack of confidence must be killed by a common devotion to the public good. At present the country is governed by lawyers, and "lawyer and working man are antipathetic types." Labour conscription is suggested ; "in making labour a part of everyone's life and the whole of nobody's life lies the ultimate solution of these industrial difficulties." There must be a national plan of social development, and economic and social questions must be studied by all. Proportional Representation must be introduced to restore a representative government, and the younger generation must be educated to take its part in the "living conflict." "We have all to think, to think hard and to think generously, and there is not a man in England to-day, even though his hands are busy at work, whose brain may not be helping in this great task of social arrangement that lies before us all."

319. LABOUR VIEW OF MIDDLE AFRICA, THE. See *The African Riddle.* 4th chapter of *Fourth Year.* A statement of the Labour Party's demand that Central Africa be placed under international control.

LAGUNE. An elderly and "enormously rich" student at the Normal School of Science ; he is an ardent spiritualist and editor of

" Hesperus : A Paper for Doubters."
After an argument he invites Alice
Heydinger, Smithers and Lewisham
to a séance, where the latter once
more meets Ethel Henderson, now
Lagune's typist. Despite an ex-
posure, Lagune still believes in
Chaffery's powers, and is finally
induced, while under hypnotic
influence, to sign a blank cheque.
This is filled up and cashed by
Chaffery for an amount within
17/6d. of Lagune's total balance.
Mr. Lewisham.

LAKE, GUNTER. A wealthy
American banker, in love with V. V.
Grammont ; they are engaged.
He thinks that " there could be no
lovelier thing in life than a wife
' in name only ' slowly warmed into
a glow of passion by the steadfast
devotion . . . of a mate at first
despised. Until at last a day
would come . . ." *Secret Places.*

320. LAMIAS, THE. Science
Schools Journal, Feb., 1889. A
" reverential attempt at a gloss "
upon Keat's " Lamia." A cynical
comment upon the supposed nature
of women.

321. LAND IRONCLADS, THE.
Strand Magazine, Dec., 1903, and
Nov., 1916 ; see also Bib. II, 1915.
Describes a battle between towns-
men and countrymen in which the
latter, despite their superior military
qualities, are defeated, the towns-
men routing them with steam-
driven land-ironclads which bear,
in essentials, a singular resemblance
to the actual " tanks " of 1916.

322. LANGUAGE OF THE FLOWERS,
THE. Pall Mall Gazette, June 25th,
1894 ; 9th essay in *Personal Matters.* An account of a book by

Thomas Miller upon the language
of flowers.

323. LARGER QUESTION BEHIND
THE CONFERENCE, THE. See *From
Washington to Europe.* 13th chapter in *Washington.* Summarises the
work of the Conference, and advocates the holding of a similar
conference in Europe for the more
particular consideration of European
affairs.

324. LARGER SYNTHESIS, THE.
8th chapter in *Anticipations.* Discusses the international movements
of to-day and the probability of a
still wider synthesis, and predicts
with the growth of education, the
coming of the New Republic, a
world-government by educated and
efficient citizens.

LARKINS SISTERS, THE. Whom
Mr. Polly meets at his father's
funeral, and afterwards visits frequently. Annie, the eldest, is a
lively, attractive girl ; finally she
goes into partnership with Miriam
in the tea-shop in Fishbourne.
Miriam, who marries Mr. Polly, is a
resolute, earnest girl with very little
" Joy de Vive " ; she and her
husband do not understand one
another, they quarrel frequently,
and her inclination to nag him
increases with the passing years.
Minnie, the youngest, is high-
spirited and affectionate ; Mr. Polly
nearly proposes to her and only
saves himself by rushing from the
room. *Mr. Polly.*

LARKINS, MRS. Their mother,
and Mr. Polly's maternal aunt ; she
is a genial talkative woman, elderly
and stout, and anxious to get her
daughters married. *Mr. Polly.*

325. LAST OF THE VICTORIANS, THE. See *H. G. Wells's Views of Free Trade.* 11th chapter of *Year of Prophesying* (misdated 24-11-23 ; see *The Other Side in France*). Criticism of Asquith's " scholarly evasion." Free Trade, Wells believes, is impossible in an armed and nationalist world.

326. LATIN AMERICA AND THE LEAGUE. See *Will Latin-America Leave the League ?* 15th chapter in *Year of Prophesying.* The League of Nations has become a " costume parade " a preposterous " mockery." Suggests the linking together of " kindred peoples " (Latins in one group, Anglo-Saxons in another, etc.), as a basis for a " real conference of peoples."

327. LAUNCHING OF SONS AND DAUGHTERS, THE. Good Housekeeping, Dec., 1924. Discusses modern parents' attitude to their children. Advocates on their part a control of " too-aggressive solicitude," and for the children a growing financial independence and responsibility. There must be companionship, not " possessiveness. ',

LAURIER. A wealthy young American who, learning that Bert Smallways has the plans of the Butteridge flying-machine, rushes him off in search of the President of the United States. *War in the Air.*

328. LAWLESSNESS OF AMERICA AND THE WAY TO ORDER, THE. Westminster Gazette, June 21st, 1924 ; 42nd article in *Year of Prophesying.* Analyses the causes of the " lack of civil order " in America in a note upon the American impressions of Rebecca West. The main need, he feels, is for an " educational effort."

329. LAWYER AND PRESS. 6th chapter in *What is Coming ?* Considers the problem of post-war government. Following the general outcry against the " lawyer politician," there must be some change, and in that change the Press will play a large part. Wells forecasts " firstly, a legal profession with a quickened conscience, a sense of public function and a reformed organisation, and, secondly, a Press which is recognised and held accountable in law and in men's minds, as an estate of the realm, as something implicitly under oath to serve the state."

330. LAWYER'S TONE, THE. (The Labour Unrest, 2). Daily Mail, May 15th, 1912 ; see *The Labour Unrest.*

LAXTON, SIR PETER. A babyfood manufacturer who has purchased a baronetcy, host at the week-end party at Shonts. Lucy, his wife, is much upset by the ill-success of her important party, but when she hears that Bealby is lost she realises the necessity for urgent measures. After a disastrous attempt to discover secret passages she has notices offering a reward for Bealby's return circulated about the countryside. *Bealby.*

331. LAY OF THE SAUSAGE MACHINE, THE. Science Schools Journal, Nov., 1890 ; Phœnix, May, 1912. A 45-line ballad of love, rivalry, murder, and sausages ; a footnote remarks that " like all modern poetry, it consists of the profoundest allegory."

LEADFORD, WILLIAM. Narrator of *In the Days of the Comet*, in the Prologue and Epilogue mentioned as The Man who Wrote in the

Tower. Born into the lower middle class, he is a clerk in a pot-bank office, and, with his friend Parload, "a Socialist out and out." His mother is a widow, very conservative and old-fashioned in her opinions : " hers was the accepted religion, her only social ideas were blind submissions to the accepted order . . . with her to believe was to fear."

LEAGUE AND EMPIRE. 4th chapter of *Anticipations of a World Peace.* Reprints the essential portion of section 1 of *Getting the League Idea Clear in Relation to Imperialism.*

332. LEAGUE MUST BE REPRESENTATIVE, THE. 2nd chapter of *Fourth Year ;* 2nd chapter (1500 words omitted) of *Anticipations of a World Peace.* A necessary preliminary to the Peace Conference is the organisation of an Allied League of Nations, to ensure that the Allies shall go to the conferences united among themselves. The people of the nations must directly p a r t i c i p a t e in the settlement through the " direct election for this particular issue of representative and responsible men."

333. LEAGUE OF FREE NATIONS, THE. Daily Mail, Feb. 20th and 28th. 1918 ; probably reprinted under another title in *Fourth Year.*

334. LEAGUE OF NATIONS AGAIN, THE. See *H. G. Wells on the League of Nations.* 5th article in *Year of Prophesying.* Reply to criticisms of *The League of Nations and the Federation of Mankind* ; concludes, " It's (the League's) past is contemptible, and the briefer its future the better for mankind."

335. LEAGUE OF NATIONS AND THE FEDERATION OF MANKIND, THE. Westminster Gazette, Sept. 22nd, 1923 ; 1st article in *Year of Prophesying.* Wells declares his hostility to the League because he feels that it is not " even likely to develop into an effective world confederation." He says that the series of articles of which this is the first will be, very largely, about the " coming of a world confederation and of the world civilisation it will make possible. " " My younger readers, at least, I hope to infect with that same idea of creative service for the new civilisation which possesses my own life."

LEBLANC. A " little bald spectacled man, inspired by that intellectual idealism which has been one of the peculiar gifts of France to humanity." He is the French ambassador in Washington at the time of the " last war," and as an " impassioned humanitarian " appeals for a meeting of the rulers of the world at Brissago to save civilisation. The ninety-three who answer his appeal become the first world-government of the Assembly of Brissago. *World Set Free.*

LEEDS, MARTIN. A young artist of " considerable genius," for four years mistress of Sir Richmond Hardy and mother of his young daughter. She does " humorous illustrations with a considerable amount of bite in them," and has " the face of a sensitive youth rather than the face of a woman " ; she is " short in proportion to her broad figure and her broad forehead " and has " fine brown eyes " and untidy clothes and hair. *Secret Places.*

336. LENIN : PRIVATE CAPITAL-
ISM AGAINST COMMUNISM. See *An
Interview with Lenin.* 22nd chapter
of *Year of Prophesying.* Written
just after Lenin's death ; recalls
Wells's interview with him in 1920,
and discusses the result of Communism in Russia.

LETTY. In Mr. Britling. See
Mrs. Teddy.

337. LET US ARISE AND END
WAR ! A brief translation from
Anatole France ; see Bib. II, 1915.

LEWISHAM, GEORGE EDGAR. The
youthful subject of *Love and Mr.
Lewisham.* In the first chapters
he is a boy of eighteen, an assistant
master who thinks " little of Love
but much on Greatness " ; the
walls of his room are decorated with
South Kensington certificates, a
portrait of Carlyle, and an ambitious
" Schema." His character is carefully and consistently developed
to the end of the book, where he
is left in dubious circumstances,
yet having come at last through
trial and worry to the end of
adolescence and the realisation
of manhood.

338. LIBERAL AIM IN THE WAR,
THE. Daily Chronicle, May 4th,
1915. A statement of the war-
aims of the mass of the British
people. Wells urges that the Allies
should openly discuss and settle
the peace-terms before the end of
the war, that there may be neither
dissension nor surprise at the final
conference.

339. LIBERAL FEAR OF RUSSIA,
THE. Nation, Aug. 22nd, 1914 ;
8th chapter in *War that will End
War.* Discussion of the exagger-
ated dread of the power and intentions of Russia which affects the
attitude of the British and American
liberals towards the continuation
of the war and its ultimate settlement. Wells states his reasons for
thinking that there is nothing to fear
from Russia either now or in the
future.

340. LIBERTY AND MR. BELLOC.
Daily News, July 24th, 1916.

341. LIFE-HISTORY OF DEMOC-
RACY, THE. 5th chapter in *Anticipations.* Discusses the evolution of modern democracy and
forecasts the passing of the present
system of government before the
reforms of the coming class of
intelligent and scientifically educated men.

342. LIKENESS OF GOD, THE.
3rd chapter of *God the Invisible
King.* Wells asserts four things :
that God is Courage ; that God is
a Person (though he does not exist
in matter or space, " he exists in
time just as a current of thought
may do ") ; that God is Youth,
always beginning, always looking
to the future ; that God is Love, the
austere love of a captain for his
men.

343. LIMITS OF INDIVIDUAL PLAS-
TICITY, THE. Saturday Review,
Jan. 19th, 1895 ; reprinted as part
of Chapter 14 of *Dr. Moreau.* Unsigned. Sets forth the general idea
upon which Moreau worked.

LINCOLN. The half-brother of
Ostrog ; he sees to Graham's comfort and welfare after the over-
throw of the White Council. *Sleeper
Wakes.*

344. LITERARY REGIMEN, THE.
Pall Mall Gazette, June 13th, 1894 ;
10th essay in *Personal Matters ;*
also (illustrated) in English Illustrated Magazine, Nov., 1901. Traces
an inevitable connection between
food and thought, and suggests the
varying diets necessary to the
literary man. He instances several
modern writers as examples of his
theory.

345. LITERATURE OF THE FUTURE
THE. Pall Mall Gazette, Oct. 11th,
1893.

346. LITTLE HOUSE : AS IT WAS,
IS NOW, AND APPARENTLY EVER
WILL BE, THE. See *Labour's Little
Houses.* 50th article in *Year of
Prophesying.* Reproves the Labour
Government for its lack of imagina-
tion in facing the housing problem.
What is needed is not a " multi-
tude " of small houses, but a num-
ber of " block buildings " each
" containing a great number of
houses."

347. LITTLE MOTHER UP THE
MÖRDERBURG. Strand, Apr., 1910.

348. LITTLE WARS : A GAME FOR
BOYS. See Bib. No. 48. This
small volume develops the ideas
set forth in *Floor Games* with special
application to war games ; it is
in six sections : 1, *Of the Legendary
Past ;* 2, *The Beginnings of Modern
Little Warfare ;* 3, *The Rules ;*
4, *The Battle of Hook's Farm ;* 5,
*Extensions and Applications of Little
War ;* 6, *Ending with a Sort of
Challenge.* An appendix, *Little
Wars and Kriegspiel,* suggests the
" possibility of developing Little
Wars into a vivid and inspiring
Kriegspiel," and gives a more com-
plete and complicated set of rules

than those set forth in section 3.
There are many marginal drawings
by J. R. Sinclair, and 19 photographs.

349. LIVING THROUGH : THE
TRUTH ABOUT AN INTERVIEW.
Westminster Gazette, September
6th, 1924 ; 53rd article in *Year of
Prophesying.* In these dark and
perplexing times we need " the
flexible reconciliations of humour " ;
" we must not simply ' live danger-
ously,' but humorously." Part of
the article comments on an inter-
viewer's distortion of Wells's statement to this effect.

350. LOAD OF WAR DEBT. Daily
Express, Dec. 14th, 1921 ; 27th
chapter of *Washington.* Considers
the problem of European war-debts
to America. Wells reminds the
American citizen in what cause
these debts were contracted, and
warns him that if he insists upon
payment it is his fellow-fighters who
will have to pay, and payment can
only bring disorganised business and
unemployment to America.

351. LOCOMOTION IN THE TWEN-
TIETH CENTURY. 1st chapter in
Anticipations. A " speculation upon the probable developments and
changes of the means of land locomotion during the coming decades."

352. LOGIC OF THE U39, THE.
(Looking Ahead). Daily Chronicle,
May 22nd, 1915. With the advent
of the submarine and aeroplane certain conditions of warfare are
changed ; it becomes more destructive but less conclusive. Progress
is not an inevitable thing, and
unless lasting peace follows this
war " revenge will become the

burthen of history," war follow upon war, and the world fall back into disorder. "The War Path or the World State; that is the choice for mankind."

353. LONDON UNIVERSITY BILL, THE. Saturday Review, July 31st, Aug. 7th, 1897.

354. LONG VIEW AND LABOUR, THE. Times, July 24th, 1916; 3rd chapter in *Elements of Reconstruction*. The " thesis of this chapter is that it is possible, desirable, and necessary to change the life of labour concurrently with this process of industrial nationalisation, and to replace the . . . publicly wasteful method of employment on a basis of weekly and even hourly wages by much longer and fairer forms of engagement." Wells insists upon the importance of scale in industrial problems, and touches upon the relations of employers and trade unions, and the way in which Guild Socialism is preparing the minds of the workers for the nationalisation of industries.

355. LOOKING AHEAD. The general title of a series of articles contributed to The Daily Chronicle, 1914-1916, all dealing with aspects of the war. The articles, in order of publication, are : 1, *Hands off the People's Food;* 2, *The Need of a New Map of Europe Now;* 3, *The Most Necessary Measures in the World;* 4, *Common Sense and the Balkan States;* 5, *We, at the Base;* 6, *The Most Splendid Fighting in the World;* 7, *The Future of the North of Europe;* 8, *The Organisation of Foresight in Great Britain;* 9, *A Suggestion for Penalising Germany's Commerce;* 10, *The Logic*

of the U39; 11, *After a Year of War;* 12 and 13, *The End of the War* (in two parts); 14, *Braintree, Bocking, and the Future of the World;* 15, *The United States, France, Britain, and Russia;* 16, *World Languages.* Nos. 1-4 were reprinted in *War that will End War;* Nos. 12-16 in *What is Coming?*

356. LORD OF THE DYNAMOS, THE. Pall Mall Budget, Sept. 6th, 1894; 12th tale in *Stolen Bacillus;* 8th in *Country of the Blind.* Holroyd (during a strike chief attendant of three dynamos at Camberwell) bullies his helper Azuma-zi, an African Asiatic half-caste, and tells him of the power of the biggest dynamo to hurt and kill. The ignorant stoker bows before it as to a great god, the Lord of the Dynamos, and serves it as priest and slave. In his frenzy he sacrifices Holroyd by throwing him suddenly against some exposed live wires. The engineer's death is explained as suicide or accident and a substitute is sent. He too is attacked by Azuma-zi, but is rescued; the fanatic, to escape capture, clutches the naked terminals in his hands and is instantly killed.

357. LOST INHERITANCE, THE. 15th tale in *Plattner Story.* For years a man visits his rich uncle, who on his death-bed gives the nephew a copy of his latest book. The only will which can be found leaves every penny to another nephew, who squanders the whole fortune and is sent to prison. Three years later the first nephew finds a later will leaving everything to himself—placed between the pages of his uncle's book, which he has never opened before.

358. LOVE AND MR. LEWISHAM.
See Bib. No. 17. At the time of
Lewisham's first encounter with
love he is eighteen years old, and
an assistant master at Whortley
Proprietary School, in Sussex. By
chance he meets Ethel Henderson.
a visitor from London who is staying
in Whortley with her aunt. On
the last day of her visit they go
for a long walk—The Scandalous
Ramble—as one consequence of
which Mr. Lewisham is dismissed.
Two and a half years elapse and
the story resumes with Lewisham
beginning his third year as a
student at the Normal School of
Science, South Kensington, having
been granted a scholarship. He
is invited to a séance by Lagune,
a fellow-student, and there meets
Ethel again. She is Lagune's typist
and occasionally assists her step-
father Chaffery, a medium, in his
séances. Each night Lewisham
walks home with her from Lagune's,
much to the distress of Alice
Heydinger, another student, who is
in love with him. He finds that
his work is getting behind and
tells Ethel that he cannot see her
every evening ; she thinks that his
love is dying and, yielding to family
pressure, breaks the promise she
has made to him never to take
part in a séance again. When he
discovers what she is doing she
tells him that she must do as
Chaffery wishes or else leave home.
Clutching at the only alternative,
Lewisham asks her to marry him.
They are married and go to live
in two small rooms in Chelsea, he
searching for employment by which
to add to his insufficient income,
she trying to help with her type-
writer. At first he is unsuccessful ;
amid their poverty the glamour of
love fades and they come to petty

quarrelling. These troubles distract him and in the final examination, " the examination that sig-
nalised the end of his income of a
weekly guinea " he does badly.
Miss Heydinger still writes to
Lewisham, not knowing that he is
married, and her letters are a constant source of jealousy to Ethel.
One day she and Lewisham have a
bitter quarrel over these letters
and over a misunderstanding arising
from some flowers he sends her,
but at last are reconciled. Chaffery
disappears, taking with him several
thousand pounds belonging to Lagune but deserting his wife, with
whom Mr. and Mrs. Lewisham go
to live. He obtains employment
and the reader leaves him with his
mother-in-law, his wife, and a
coming child dependent upon him.
But at last he has come to a realisation of his manhood, to " the end of
adolescence, the end of empty
dreams."

359. LOYALTY OF ESAU COMMON,
THE. Contemporary Review, Feb.,
1902. An unfinished story of Common, the son of a furniture dealer
and a native of Aurelia, who wishes
to enter the army but becomes a
journalist ; he criticises the organization of the Aurelian Army,
but with no effect. One day he is
invited to come to Marantha (Aurelia's great rival), where his talents
will be appreciated, but he refuses
to desert his country. Suddenly
war between the two countries
becomes inevitable. . . . " Here
the fragment ends. The impossibility of keeping up the tone of
careless geniality dawned upon the
author." A footnote states that
this was " intended to open a series
of kindly but instructive stories
about the British Army. This pro-

ject was abandoned. The fragment remains the picture of a point of view."

LYCHNIS. Who looks after the Earthlings from the time of their arrival in Utopia, and nurses Mr. Barnstaple through his illness. She is a brown-eyed woman of thirty or so, " a rather backward-minded woman. . . . One of Utopia's educational failures." " She had rediscovered the lost passion of pity, first pity for herself and then a desire to pity others. . . . She did not want to talk to Mr. Barnstaple of the brightness of Utopia ; she wanted him to talk to her of the miseries of earth and of his own miseries. That she might sympathise." *Men Like Gods.*

M

MACKRIDGE, MRS. One of Lady Drew's old servants. She, with Mrs. Booch and Mrs. Latude-Fernay, comes to Bladesover each year for a holiday ; she is remarkable for her caustic wit, her bald head, and the hair which is painted upon her forehead beneath her cap. *Tono-Bungay.*

360. MAGIC SHOP, THE. Strand Magazine, June, 1903 ; 2nd tale in *Twelve Stories ;* 29th in *Country of the Blind.* The writer and his little son, Gip, visit the Genuine Magic Shop, where the magic is uncomfortably real.

MAGNET, WILL. A writer of humorous books ; " one of those quiet, deliberately unassuming people who do not even attempt to be beautiful . . . a fairish man of forty, pale, with a large protuberant,

observant grey eye . . . and a face of quiet animation warily alert for the wit's opportunity." Marjorie Pope reluctantly engages herself to him ; after her marriage to Trafford (who calls Magnet " a beastly little area sneak ") he marries Daphne Pope. *Marriage.*

361. MAHATMA, M.A. Pall Mall Gazette, Aug. 1st, 1894.

362. MAMMON. Science Schools Journal, Jan., 1887. A study of the significance of Watts's painting, " Mammon," signed with the pseudonym Walker Glockenhammer. 800-900 words.

363. MAN AND THE MACHINE. Daily News, Sept. 10th, 1918.

364. MANDARINS AT THE GATE : THE REVIVAL OF THE OLD LEARNING, THE. See *The Revival of the Old Learning.* 21st article in *Year of Prophecy.* Wells fears the revival of the folly of classical learning ; in a modern education dead languages can play only a subordinate part.

MAN FROM PRISON, A. A convict (" his crime is no concern of ours ") who, pardoned after twenty years, comes out from prison to find the country to the south-east of London altered suddenly and amazingly by the spread of Herakleophorbia ; he is astounded by his first sight of the Cossars. He and his brother go to an anti-Boomfood meeting and hear Caterham speak. *Food of the Gods.*

365. MANKIND IN THE MAKING. See Bib. No. 22. In 1914 Wells wrote of this book as " something between an overflow and a continua-

tion of its far superior predecessor, *Anticipations.*" " It is an attempt to deal with social and political questions in a new way and from a new starting-point, viewing the whole social and political world as aspects of one universal evolving scheme, and placing all social and political activities in a defined relation to that." The chapter-titles are : *Preface ;* 1, *The New Republic* ; 2, *The Problem of the Birth Supply* ; 3, *Certain Wholesale Aspects of Man-Making ;* 4, *The Beginnings of Mind and Language ;* 5, *The Man-making Forces of the Modern State ;* 6, *Schooling ;* 7, *Political and Social Influences ;* 8, *The Cultivation of the Imagination ;* 9, *The Organization of the Higher Education ;* 10, *Thought in the Modern State ;* 11, *The Man's Own Share ; Appendix ; Index.*

366. Man-making Forces of the Modern State, The. 5th chapter of *Mankind.* " A careful analysis . . . of the great complex of circumstances which mould the vague possibilities of the average child into the reality of the citizen of the modern state." Considers the influence of home and school upon the growing child.

Manning. A London journalist who has a cottage at Matching's Easy ; on Aug. 3rd, 1914, he brings the news of the German invasion of Belgium. *Mr. Britling.*

Manning, Hubert. A rather handsome man of thirty-seven, a civil servant of some standing and a poet in his leisure hours ; nephew of Lady Palsworthy. He asks Ann Veronica Stanley to marry him, and they are engaged for a time after her return from London. *Ann Veronica.*

Man of the Year Million, The. Pall Mall Gazette, Nov. 9th, 1893 ; reprinted with slight alterations as *Of a Book Unwritten* (q.v.).

367. Man's Own Share, The. 11th and last paper in *Mankind.* Prophesies the coming of the New Republic. " At a thousand points," he writes, " it already starts into being."

368. Man Who Could Work Miracles, The. Illustrated London News, Summer No., July, 1898 ; 5th story in *Tales of Space ;* 21st in *Country of the Blind.* Fotheringay, an unimaginative village clerk, is suddenly endowed with the power to work miracles. At first he uses it for purely minor purposes, until in a moment of anger he sends a policeman to Hades. He repents and consults Mr. Maydig, a local preacher. That night, at Mr. Maydig's suggestion, they wander about the village in the small hours, reforming drunkards, turning beer to water, draining swamps and so on. Until Fotheringay, impatient at the swift passage of the hours, stops the rotation of the earth, forgetting, however, the " trifling removables " on its surface. These fly on, and all mankind—save only Mr. Fotheringay—is killed in the consequent hurricane and smash. But he is tired now of his gift and in his last miracle wills himself back in the bar of the Long Dragon " just before I drank my last pint," with everything as it was then and he without his abnormal powers.

369. Man With a Nose, The. 2nd of the two other reminiscences included in *Select Conversations ;* probably originally printed as *The Ugliest Thing in London* (q.v.).

The man with a nose tells a chance companion what a terrible burden an unshapely or ill-coloured nose can be.

MARAYNE, LADY. A " blue-eyed and very delicately-complexioned " woman, " quick-moving, witty, given to little storms of clean enthusiasm : she loved handsome things, brave things, successful things, and the respect and affection of all the world." She is the first wife of the Rev. Harold Benham and mother of William Porphyry Benham, but leaves her husband and child to run away with Nolan. After the latter's death, " being a woman of great spirit, enterprise and sweetness," she marries Godfrey Marayne, a distinguished surgeon who later receives a title. While Benham is a boy she is allowed to see him only five times a year, but when he is at Cambridge they meet more frequently. She has temporary control of the money left him by Nolan (which privately she thinks should have been hers) and makes plans for his future which are all upset by his quest. She dislikes his friends and his wife. *Research Magnificent.*

MARCUS, HETTY. " A clever girl, an elementary school teacher and bookish and enterprising for a country place. . . . Dark-eyed, warm-skinned, wayward and fragile." She is the daughter of a farmer's widow who lives near Chessing Hanger. Harry Smith marries her while on leave ; after he has divorced her she marries Sumner because there seems to be nothing else to do. *Dream.*

MARGARET. In *New Machiavelli ;* see Margaret Remington.

370. MARI TERRIBLE, LE. 21st tale in *Thirty Strange Stories ;* not printed in any English collection. A very slight sketch (with Bellows as narrator) of a flirtatious wife and a cynical husband.

371. MARRIAGE. See Bib. No. 46. Marjorie Pope, after a visit to friends, joins her family at Buryhamstreet Vicarage, which her father has taken for the summer holidays. He is a retired leader of the coachbuilding trade and a well-known publicist ; the other members of the family are Mrs. Pope, three girls, Daphne, Sydney and Romola, and Theodore, the only son. On the evening of her arrival, Will Magnet, a prominent humorous writer, and his friend, Wintersloan, have supper with the Popes. A few days later, at Lady Petchworth's garden party, Magnet asks Marjorie to marry him ; she refuses, but when he proposes again at a picnic given by him in honour of Theodore's birthday she, urged on by mother and aunt and by the thought of a large sum of money owed to various tradesmen, consents to marry him, though she tells him she does not love him. Then one day a monoplane crashes to earth on the vicarage lawn ; its pilot is Trafford, a young professor engaged in scientific research—he specialises in molecular physics and is an authority upon crystallography. He and Marjorie, who already know one another slightly, meet once or twice in the village, and he calls upon the Popes every day. They arrange a meeting in the shrubbery, where Mr. Pope finds them kissing and assaults Trafford. At Marjorie's request Trafford goes away, but two months later, she being now twenty-one, they elope, are married, and go to Italy for

their honeymoon. They return to London and settle down, he to his research work, she to housekeeping. (Mr. Magnet, after recovering from his disappointment, marries Daphne.) Trafford's income amounts to £600 a year, all too little for Marjorie's expensive tastes. A daughter is born and he has to find lecturing work, thus sacrificing to a certain extent his researches. Things get worse; he is overworked—she does not know how to fill her time. In an attempt to solve their difficulties they go for a walking tour in Switzerland; on the eleventh day they meet a party of London friends with whom they remain for a few days. At their host's house Trafford sees what a man owes his wife and children; he decides to give up his research work and accept the proposal of his friend Solomonson to market a synthesised rubber he has made. Seven years later Trafford is a "rich and influential man," but without much satisfaction in his life. He decides to go to Labrador, out into the solitudes, there to think things over; his mother advises him to take his wife with him, and so he and Marjorie go to Labrador together, leaving their four children behind. They travel inland with five guides, who return to the coast after the building of Lonely Hut. Trafford is badly mauled and has one leg broken in a fight with a lynx, but Marjorie drags him back to the hut and nurses him through fever to health and strength. Through the long Northland winter they talk things over together, coming to a conception of humanity as an instrument, imperfect and incomplete, of something beyond itself. On their return to England, they decide, Trafford is to take up the study of contem-

porary thought and the writing of criticism; Marjorie is to help by reading and writing with him. In January a half-breed trapper visits the hut, and with his help they make their way to the sea and so to England.

MARTIANS, THE. The strange, unhuman inhabitants of Mars described in *War of the Worlds*. They have followed the line of evolution foretold for the people of this world in *Of a Book Unwritten* and other essays. A detailed description of their life and habits is given in Chapter 2 of Book 2.

MARTINEAU, DR. A "distinguished Harley Street physician," a specialist in nervous cases, "also a philosophical writer." Hardy finds him "humanly plump, his face . . . round and pink and cheerfully wistful, a little suggestive of the full moon." He is writing a book on "The Psychology of the New Age" which he quotes to Hardy. *Secret Places*.

MARVEL, THOMAS. A tramp with a "copious, flexible visage, a nose of cylindrical protusion, a liquorish, ample, fluctuating mouth, and a beard of bristling eccentricity." The Invisible Man comes upon him on the roadside near Adderdean and, without consulting him, enlists his services as a luggage carrier. Finally he runs away from Griffin and takes refuge in the Port Burdock Police Station. In an epilogue he appears as proprietor of an inn called "The Invisible Man." *Invisible Man*.

MARY. A "sweetly beautiful woman," loved by the botanist from childhood; she marries an older man who has "the habit and

quality of achieving his ends."
Years later the botanist meets her
again to find her very changed,
ill-treated by her husband. They
meet in the world of Utopia but do
not speak ; there her husband is
one of the Samurai, and she a
follower of the Lesser Rule. *Modern
Utopia*.

MASSINGHAY, WESTON. A Conservative politician who appears
casually in *New Machiavelli, Marriage, Passionate Friends, Sir Isaac
Harman, Research Magnificent*.

372. MASTER ANTHONY AND THE
ZEPPELIN. See Bib. II, 1916. A
very short tale for children, with
more illustration (also by Wells)
than text, of a small boy who
reformed a Zeppelin by teaching it
to build a nest and lay eggs.

MASTERMAN. A middle-aged con-
sumptive Socialist who lodges with
Sid Pornick and his wife in London.
He " talks Socialism " to Kipps
when the latter goes to see Sid.
Kipps.

" MATERIALIST SINGS. THE." A
12-line poem by Phœbe Stubland
quoted in *Joan and Peter*. Lady
Charlotte Sydenham considers it
blasphemous.

MEDINA-SAROTÉ. The youngest
daughter of Yacob, " little esteemed
in the world of the blind, because
she . . . lacked that satisfying,
glossy smoothness that is the blind
man's ideal of feminine beauty."
Nunez thinks her " the most beautiful thing in the whole creation " and
wishes to marry her. *Country of
the Blind*.

MELMOUNT. Prime Minister of
Britain in the Days of the Comet.

After the awakening, Leadford comes
upon him in a field and helps him to
his house, he having twisted his
ankle. Melmount calls a cabinet
meeting at which Leadford is present
as a temporary secretary. *Days of
the Comet*.

MELVILLE. Second cousin to the
narrator of *The Sea Lady*. Mrs.
Bunting confides in him from the
beginning, and he has a talk with
Chatteris upon the night of the
latter's death.

373. MEMORANDUM ON PROPA-
GANDA POLICY AGAINST GERMANY.
See Bib. II, 1920. Written in May
1918, when Wells was a member of
the Enemy Propaganda Committee
and first director of the British
propaganda campaign policy against
Germany. A preface analyses the
German mind and summarises the
subject-matter of the memorandum,
which is a plain statement of the
war-aims of the Allies. In all the
world outside Germany there has
arisen " a will to a world peace "
which crystallises in the idea of a
League of Free Nations. The idea
of, and the work and power of, such
a league is outlined. The co-operation of Germany in the League is a
fundamental necessity. And since
the Germany of 1914 would not
honestly co-operate in such a
scheme, the " changing of Germany " becomes *the* primary war-
aim of the Allies.

MENDHAM, REV. GEORGE. Curate
at Siddermorton, " a cadaverous
man with a magnificent beard " who
could " bully his Vicar cheerfully
enough." He succeeds Hilyer as
vicar. His wife, Minnie, is a " young
woman of immense will, who used
to play tennis on the vicar's lawn,

and cut his roses, differ from him on doctrinal points, and criticise his personal behaviour all over the parish." She thinks the Angel's original dress most " suggestive and improper." *Wonderful Visit.*

MENGO, SIR ALPHEUS. The distinguished specialist who operates on Job Huss; he is a quick-tempered little man, " with active brown eyes in a tan face, a toothbrush moustache of iron-grey, and a protruded lower jaw." *Undying Fire.*

374. MEN LIKE GODS. See Bib. No. 80. Mr. Barnstaple, a Liberal journalist in need of a holiday, leaves his home at Sydenham surreptitiously in his small car, and sends a telegram from London to tell his wife that the doctor has ordered a complete rest and that it may be some time before he writes. Presently he is motoring along the Maidenhead Road beyond Slough when he is passed by a grey touring car and then by a limousine. Following them round a near corner he is amazed to find the road before him entirely clear. Then he seems to skid, there is a sound " sharp like the snapping of a lute-string " and he pulls up on an entirely different road with the limousine a little way ahead. He joins the occupants of this other car (Cecil Burleigh, Lady Stella, Father Amerton, Rupert Catskill, Freddy Mush, and Penk) and they come to the conclusion that they are no longer on the earth but in, as Burleigh names it, Utopia. Nearby a burning building and the dead bodies of a very beautiful man and woman make it clear that this is the scene of some scientific experiment. Other Utopians approach and the party of Earthlings

is taken in aeroplanes to a Conference Place. There Serpentine, a Utopian scientist, explains to them the means by which they were, quite accidentally, transferred from the earth to this other world, and also something of the history of and government in Utopia since the Age of Confusion, a period which very closely resembled " the present time on earth." Their criticisms are heard and answered. Then they learn that the grey touring car and its occupants (Lord Barralonga, Hunker, Emile Dupont, Greeta Grey, and Ridley) are also in Utopia and are being brought to the Conference Place. Next day it is discovered that the Earthlings are spreading disease in " a world which has known nothing of germs for many centuries," and the Utopians isolate them upon a high and lonely crag, a headland between two convergent canyons. Left temporarily alone the Earthlings, urged on by Catskill, decide upon the conquest of Utopia, Mr. Barnstaple being the only active dissentient. An attempt to capture Serpentine and Cedar as hostages is frustrated by Mr. Barnstaple (though one Utopian is killed, the other wounded), who in turn is pursued by his angry companions and forced to take refuge upon the open cliff-face where they can only roll down ineffectual rocks in the hope of hitting him. After twenty or so hours in which death, swift or lingering, seems more than once inevitable, he reaches the foot of the crag by means of rope ladders fixed by a party of Utopians who are busily at work upon the cliff-face, fixing cables about it. Just after dawn, as the Earthling's flag flies out above, " great flashes of violet light " leap from cable to cable and the crest of Quarantine Crag vanishes, " swung out of the Utopian universe altogether." (Later Mr. Barnstaple learns that when the " rotation " was completed and the crag returned into Utopia several of the Earthlings were found " asphyxiated and frozen but not dead ; " some, however, rushed down its side into the outer darkness.) Mr. Barnstaple is found by the Utopians, nursed through an illness, and allowed to remain, learning the ways and customs of Utopia. At last, feeling himself the " one useless soul " in this world of service, he offers to put himself at the Utopians' disposal to do anything they might wish, " to risk death—to take the danger of going into some strange place." The Utopians desire to reverse the experiment by which the Earthlings came into Utopia ; he gets into his car upon the road on which he first found himself, and drives away. There is a jerk, a sound like a snapping string, and he is on earth again, beside the Maidenhead Road. He returns to his home " bitterly sorrowful " for the lost world of beauty, but refreshed in body and in brain, and with faith and hope for the future renewed.

MERGLE, MISS. Once Jessica Milton's schoolmistress, she tells the girl when leaving school to live " fearlessly and truly." Remembering this, Jessica writes to her after she has run away from Bechamel, asking for assistance that she may live her own independent life. Instead of replying Miss Mergle communicates with Mrs. Milton and joins the Rescue Party. *Wheels of Chance.*

MERGLESON. Butler at Shonts, " an ample man with a large nose,

a vast under lip and mutton-chop whiskers. His voice would have suited a succulent parrot." *Bealby.*

375. METAPHYSICS. Book 1 of *First and Last Things ;* mainly an expansion of *Scepticism of the Instrument.* Wells insists upon the fact of individual uniqueness, and rejects the classifactory assumption and the use of empty and negative terms. Logic is static and life is kinetic ; the mind is an imperfect instrument, moving within limits determined by individual character and experience. " Most minds are similar . . . but none are absolutely alike." Words and ideas must be accepted with reserve. In the 1917 edition the new section 2 criticises current metaphysical teaching ; the other new sections discuss the idea of the two aspects of every man— he is himself, the individual, and he is Man.

MIDDLE CLASS BETWEEN THE MILL-STONES, THE. Independent Magazine, May 9th, 1907 ; Rapid Review, May, 1907 ; printed in England as *The Middle Class Man, the Business Man, and Socialism.*

376. MIDDLE CLASS MAN, THE BUSINESS MAN, AND SOCIALISM, THE. Grand Magazine, Feb., 1908 ; 8th chapter in *New Worlds.* Outlines the process of " grinding-out " which faces the middle classes of to-day. Suggests the alternative attractions of Plutocracy and Socialism, and in a letter to the Magazine of Commerce defines the position of the business man in the modern Socialist state.

MILLY. A woman of the streets who loves Ewart. She poses for

N

him and they go for holidays together in the country, she paying the greater part of the expenses. She is a pretty blonde woman of thirty. *Tono-Bungay.*

MILLY. A married woman of thirty-three or four whom Remington meets during his first visit to Italy; she compares herself to George Moore's "Woman of Thirty" and comes to his room to lend him a book. Willersley, Remington's companion, objects to their intrigue. Her husband is twenty years her senior. *New Machiavelli.*

MILTON, JESSICA. "A girl of eighteen, dark, fine-featured, with bright eyes, and a rich swift colour under her warm, tinted skin." Tired of living in an atmosphere of continual antagonism with her step-mother she runs away with Bechamel, who promises to help her to earn her own living by writing. *Wheels of Chance.*

MILTON, MRS. HETTY. Jessica's step-mother, "a successful little authoress and a still more successful widow." She writes under the pseudonym of "Thomas Plantagenet"; her only novel mentioned is "A Soul Untrammelled," a "witty and daring" book. When Jessica disappears she sets out in pursuit of her, accompanied by three of her greatest Men Friends, Dangle, Phipps, and Widgery. Finally, after sundry misadventures, she comes upon her step-daughter at Stoney Cross. *Wheels of Chance.*

377. MIND OF A MODERN STATE, THE. 12th chapter in *Future in America.* Emphasises the American need for constructive and co-operative intelligence. Wells visits three American universities—Columbia, Harvard, Chicago—and discusses the influence of the constructive spirit of the universities upon the nation as a whole.

378. MIND OF THE RACE, THE. A novel sketched out by George Boon; the first chapter, with conversations concerning it, fills the first half of *Boon.* The story is first suggested by Bliss, but Boon takes it over and entirely remodels it. It opens with an introduction about the "profound decadence of letters at the opening of the Twentieth Century." Certain British critics visit a villa by the sea (that described in W. H. Mallock's "New Republic"), proposing to hold there a summer congress to investigate the state of modern literature. An old caretaker sheds new light upon Mallock's characters. Other people arrive, among them Hallery. George Moore and Henry James wander away from the others and talk. (Here the story is dropped for a time while Boon talks about, and reads a tale, *The Spoils of Mr. Blandish,* "rather in the manner of," Henry James). A great congress is held at some central place somewhere on the Continent, and a vivid account is given of a Special Train to Basle, the carriages of which are occupied by the more prominent of modern British writers, who are journeying to the congress. After some discussion and the notes of a paper read before one section of the congress. Hallery is elected president and reads an address. Here the story, as written, comes to an end, save for a short disconnected fragment (not printed) which describes the murder of Dr. Tomlinson Keyhole, an eminent literary critic, by Hallery.

MINTER, MR. Husband of. Richard Remington's maternal aunt, a Five Towns pottery manufacturer, a "big and buoyant" man, but hard, acquisitive, with a contempt for education and no thought for his workers. He is gross, self-centred, rather stupid, "about as much civilized, about as much tamed to the ideas of collective action and mutual consideration as a Central African negro." After Mrs. Remington's death he has charge of her affairs, and Richard comes to stay with him during the holidays; at his house Richard first meets Margaret. Mrs. Minter is a "little woman with a scared look;" there are two quite objectionable daughters, Gertrude and Sybil. *New Machiavelli.*

379. MISS WINCHELSEA'S HEART. Queen, Oct., 1898; see Bib. II, 1900; 12th tale in *Twelve Stories;* 24th in *Country of the Blind.* Miss Winchelsea, a school-teacher of really excessive refinement, meets a very pleasant young man while on a visit to Rome. He asks her to marry him, but though she loves him she cannot face the prospect of becoming Mrs. Snooks. Finally he marries her friend Fannie, much to Miss Winchelsea's annoyance; at the same time he changes his name to Senoks and so by degrees to Sevenoaks. Two years after the marriage she visits them, to find that he is growing stout and becoming quite unrefined.

380. MR. BRISHER'S TREASURE. Strand Magazine, Apr., 1899; 11th tale in *Twelve Stories.* Mr. Brisher, while making a rockery in the garden of his prospective father-in-law, comes upon a buried treasure, a box full of half-crowns. He attempts to carry it away but is prevented by the older man's watchfulness. Some time later he is overjoyed to hear that the father has been arrested and imprisoned for issuing counterfeit half-crowns.

381. MR. BRITLING SEES IT THROUGH. See Bib. No. 60. In June, 1914, Mr. Direck, an American, brings an invitation to Mr. Britling, the famous writer, to lecture to a society in the United States. Arriving at Dower House, in Matching's Easy, Essex, he is introduced to the author's household—to Edith, Mr. Britling's second wife, to their two small sons, to Hugh Britling, Mrs. Britling's step-son, to Teddy and Letty, Cicely Corner, Aunt Wilshire and Herr Heinrich. A slight motor accident occurs and Mr. Direck's visit is prolonged until the middle of July, when he leaves for the Continent, now in love with Cicely. Mr. Britling is temporarily entangled with a young widow, Mrs. Harrowdean, with whom, however, he severs all connection upon the outbreak of war. On August 2nd Herr Heinrich receives his papers recalling him to Germany, and on the next day, amid the noise and happiness of Bank Holiday, comes the news of the invasion of Belgium. There follows a vivid account of the doubts and fears and enthusiasms of the early days of the war. Teddy and Hugh both join the army, the first as an officer, the other as a private. Mr. Britling enrolls as a special constable. Mr. Direck returns from Germany, bringing grim stories of Belgium's fate. Matching's Easy receives its share of refugees and soldiers in training. Aunt Wilshire, staying at a coast-town, is injured in a Zeppelin raid and dies within a few hours. In June, 1915, Teddy

leaves for France and two months later is reported missing; Hugh, who follows him to the front in July, gives in his letters graphic descriptions of life in the training-camps and in the trenches. Late in October comes the news of his death. The next day Mr. Direck, now a soldier in the Canadian army, journeys down from London to bring Letty word of her husband's death. She goes out into the fields, where Mr. Britling finds her lying beneath a hedge, weeping uncontrollably. They talk together, he telling her of his wonderful plans for the ending of all war through the establishment of the World State, and of his new idea of God as a person, finite and human. Presently she returns home to find Teddy waiting for her there, he having been a prisoner but escaping. Some weeks later Mr. Britling hears the news of the death of Herr Heinrich while a prisoner in Russia. That night he writes a letter of sympathy to the boy's Pomeranian parents. As he writes on his letter becomes more and more a dissertation upon the waste and folly of war and national antagonisms, upon the sorrow of the world and upon religion. Until, reaching the climax of his thoughts in the pearly light of the winter dawn, he comes to a realisation of God, " the only King."

382. MR. LEDBETTER'S VACATION. Strand Magazine, Oct., 1898 ; 9th tale in *Twelve Stories*. Mr. Ledbetter, a schoolmaster in orders, is spending his summer vacation by the sea. One night, inspired by whisky and the spirit of adventure, he enters a house, intending to do no more than carry away a small trophy of his adventure. The tenant of the house, Bingham, an

embezzling bank-manager, finds him there. He is leaving the country that night and makes Ledbetter pack up and carry his luggage down to the yacht which is waiting for him. The schoolmaster is forced on board and after a cruise of three weeks is landed on an island in the Grenadines. Eventually he gets to Jamaica, where he meets the narrator, who believes his story and assists him to get back to England in time to resume his scholastic duties.

383. MR. MARSHALL'S DOPPELGANGER. Gentlewoman, Aug. 21st, 1897 ; Cassell's Winter Annual, 1920. An incident related by a member of the Society for the Rehabilitation of Abnormal Phenomena. On Christmas Eve, 1895, the vicar and curate of the village of Sussexville see what they believe to be the drunken figure of Marshall, one of the villagers. Evidence is produced to prove that Marshall was elsewhere at the time, and the vicar believes that it must have been a doppelganger or phantasm of Marshall that they saw. But the sceptical curate finds the true solution of the mystery.

384. MR. SKELMERSDALE IN FAIRYLAND. Strand Magazine, 1901 or 1902 ; 5th tale in *Twelve Stories*. A young man, the village grocer, falls asleep one night upon Aldington Knoll and wakes to find himself in Fairyland. A Fairy Lady asks him to stay with her, but he, not realising his love for her till too late, insists that he must go, and finds himself upon the Knoll again. He returns to the village to find that he has been absent for three weeks. His engagement to a village girl is broken off and he spends night after

night wandering about the Knoll, calling to the Fairy Lady, hoping to see her again, but never realising his hope.

385. Mr. Wells Explains Himself (To Russian Readers in Particular). T.P.'s Magazine, Dec., 1911. Written in 1909 as a general introduction to certain Russian translations of the works of Wells, this article is mainly autobiographical. It gives an account of the circumstances of Wells's life and of the various types of books he has written.

386. Mr. Wells Hits Back. Sunday Express, Dec. 12th, 1920. A reply to Winston Churchill's article, "Mr. Wells and Bolshevism" (a criticism of the *Russia in the Shadows* articles). Analyses the mind of Mr. Churchill, with special reference to Bolshevism in general and Russia in particular.

387. Misunderstood Artist, A. Pall Mall Gazette, in Nov., 1894; the 1st of the "two other reminiscences" included in *Select Conversations*. A poet and an "artist in cookery" discuss art in a railway carriage.

388. Mode in Monuments, The. Pall Mall Gazette, Mar. 6th, 1894; 38th essay in *Personal Matters*. "Stray thoughts in Highgate Cemetery;" a protest against the ugliness of modern cemeteries and the stereotyped style of the monuments.

389. Modern Education, A. See Bib. II, 1918. Wells outlines his conception of a modern education, and of the parts played in it by the classics and by science; he protests

against the over-emphasising of the importance of classical studies.

390. Modern Government: Parliament and Real Electoral Reform. See *Preservation of the Party System*. 18th article in *Year of Prophesying*. A reform of the electoral system is "imminent." Proportional Representation is the only method which will kill the Party system; therefore it will be opposed to the end by the Party politicians.

391. Modern Ideas of Sin and Damnation. 6th chapter of *God the Invisible King*. "Sin is not the same thing as damnation," Wells writes; "damnation is a state, but sin is an incident." Life is a system of disharmonies both of body and spirit; salvation only lies in the escape through God from these individual disharmonies. Damnation is in satisfaction with existing things, in "failure and disinclination to make that escape." A lunatic is one who cannot control this or that part of himself; each man must strive to control that part of himself which will not serve God. He who believes and repents cannot be damned.

392. Modern Reviewing. Adelphi, July, 1923 (Contributors' Club). A note upon the omissions of modern reviewers.

Modern Socialism and the Family. Independent Review, Nov., 1906; reprinted as the 2nd paper in *Socialism and the Family* (q.v.).

393. Modern Utopia, A. See Bib. No. 25. This mingling of fiction and sociology gives a picture of life on a planet " like our planet, the same continents, the same oceans and seas," the inhabitants of which have attained to Utopian conditions. While mountain-climbing in Northern Italy two tourists, the Owner of the Voice (who is the narrator) and the botanist, are suddenly transferred " by an act of the imagination" to the world of Utopia. They come down from the Lucendro Pass, scarcely comprehending the change, to find the world strange and new and wonderful. They spend a night at an inn and next morning walk on along the Zermatt Valley, where they are overtaken by the Apostle of Nature. At Wassen there is difficulty with the authorities, who cannot identify these two visitors, but they are given temporary work and presently sent to London to meet their Utopian selves. The narrator has an interview with his Utopian double, and learns much of the world and government of Utopia. The spell is broken at last by the botanist, and the two find themselves once more in the London of this world. The chapter-titles are : 1, *Topographical*;   2, *Concerning Freedoms*;   3, *Utopian Economics*; 4, *The Voice of Nature*;   5, *Failure in a Modern Utopia*;   6, *Women in a Modern Utopia*;   7, *A Few Utopian Impressions*;   8, *My Utopian Self*; 9, *The Samurai*;   10, *Race in Utopia*;   11, *The Bubble Bursts*. There is a prefatory *Note to the Reader* and as Appendix, *Scepticism of the Instrument*.

MOGGERIDGE, LORD. Lord Chancellor of England, a " fluent Hegelian " and a lecturer on religion and æsthetics. He goes for a disastrous week-end to Shonts. *Bealby*.

MOGGERIDGE, REV. MR. An old, poverty-stricken, out-of-work curate who lives with his wife in Matilda Good's second floor front. " They had old-fashioned ideas about draughts, and there was a peculiar aged flavour about them ; they were, to be plain, a very dirty old couple indeed." He gives Harry Smith a bible stolen from a waiting-room. Both he and his wife die, within a few hours of one another, from influenza. *Dream*.

MONTGOMERY. Moreau's assistant, once a London medical student, now outlawed " because I lost my head for ten minutes on a foggy night." He is " a youngish man with flaxen hair, a bristly straw-coloured moustache, and a dropping nether lip." After Moreau's death he has a " damned good bank-holiday," gets drunk and is killed by the Sayer of the Law. *Dr. Moreau*.

MOONCALVES. The only animals seen by Bedford in the moon. They are beasts of enormous size, 200 feet in length and 80 in girth, with almost brainless heads, fat-encumbered necks, and faces with little nostrils, tight-shut eyes and slobbering mouths. The Selenites keep them in underground caverns during the night, drive them out each day to pasture, and kill them for food. *First Men in the Moon*.

MOONLIGHT FABLE, A. Collier's Weekly, Easter No., April, 1909 ; 5th tale in *Door in the Wall*; printed in *Country of the Blind* as *The Beautiful Suit* (q.v.).

MORAL OF THE MAURETANIA RACE, THE. Daily Mail, Dec. 20th, 1910 ; reprinted as *Off the Chain* (q.v.).

MORE, RACHEL. Stephen Stratton first meets her when she is seventeen, just after his return from South Africa. Some time later he meets her again in Germany and they are married, she knowing of his love for Lady Mary Justin. She loves her husband deeply and his intimacy with Lady Mary causes her pain. They have three children, Stephen, Rachel, and Margaret. *Passionate Friends.*

MOREAU, DR. A "prominent and masterful physiologist" who, ten years before the wreck of the "Lady Vain," is "howled out" of England for the wanton cruelty of his experiments. He comes to a Pacific island and continues his attempt to "find the extreme limit of plasticity in a living shape." He is killed by a puma which breaks loose while he is at work upon it. *Dr. Moreau.*

MORLOCKS, THE. Masters of the world of A.D. 802,701, descendants of the old labour classes forced underground ; from habit they live beneath the earth's surface, only coming out at night to capture and kill the Eloi for their food. They are ape-like, etiolated, with "chinless faces and great lidless pinkish-grey eyes." Their underworld is a vague place filled with throbbings and "great shapes like machines" and "flickering pillars." *Time Machine.*

MORRIS, AMANDA. Benham meets her while on his lonely walking tour through Sussex ; he thinks her the "freest, finest, bravest spirit" he has ever met and soon asks her to marry him. They travel together

but after the birth of their son he goes abroad alone ; she falls in love with Sir Philip Easton ; when Benham discovers their relations she begs him not to divorce her, but later changes her mind—he is on his way home to see her about this when he is killed. She is completely unable to appreciate Benham's ideas and motives, and cannot see why they should stand in the way of a "career." "Ideas are a brightness, the good looks of the mind. One talks ideas, but *the thing that is, is the thing that is.*" *Research Magnificent.*

*395. MOST NECESSARY MEASURES IN THE WORLD, THE. (Looking Ahead.) Daily Chronicle, Aug. 20th, 1914 ; 5th chapter of *War that Will End War.* Advocates the abolition of all private armament manufacture, and the "neutralisation of the sea" as two measures necessary to the peace of the world.

396. MOST SPLENDID FIGHTING IN THE WORLD, THE. (Looking Ahead.) Daily Chronicle, Sept. 9th, 1914. Prophesies that to a great extent this war will be fought in the air. The French and British must make up their aerial deficiencies, and blind the enemy artillery by driving the Germans from the sky ; the airmen will be the "aristocracy of the air." "One talks and reads of the heroic age and how the world has degenerated. But indeed this is the heroic age, suddenly come again."

397. MOTH—GENUS NOVO, A. Pall Mall Gazette, Mar. 28th, 1895 ; 14th tale in *Stolen Bacillus ;* 9th (as *The Moth*) in *Country of the*

* The number 394 omitted in error.

Blind; also Pearson's Magazine, Dec., 1904. An account of the great Hapley-Pawkins feud and of the events following Professor Pawkins's death. Hapley, staying in a quiet Kentish village, is haunted by thoughts of his late enemy. These thoughts at last materialise as a moth " singularly suggestive of Pawkins." He breaks his leg when pursuing the moth, and while he is confined to his bed, unable to move, it torments him to insanity.

398. MOUNTAIN WAR, THE. 2nd chapter of *The War in Italy.* Describes the Italian mountain fighting.

399. MUDDLEHEADEDNESS AND RUSSIA : With Some Mention of Mr. Shaw. Daily Chronicle, Dec. 31st, 1914. Letter to the editor, replying to G. B. Shaw's criticism of *The Future of the North of Europe.* Wells comments on the " irresponsible, muddle-headed, anti-Russian talk " of Shaw, and gives a frank statement of his opinion of Shaw and his mentality.

MUNDAY, MRS. A Whortley shopkeeper ; Lewisham lodges with her. She tells him that she would " rather have a good sensible actin' stummick than a full head, any day." *Mr. Lewisham.*

MURGATROYD, MISS. Proprietor and head-mistress of the School of St. George and the Venerable Bede a " sturdy, rufous lady with a resentful manner. . . . Her place was in the van. She did not mind very much where the van was going so long as she was in it." She has the " temperament of a sensational editor " and each term starts a new boom in the school. *Joan and Peter.*

MUSH, FREDDY. Catskill's secretary, a " short, thick-set, middle-aged young man . . . the natural hostility of whose appearance was greatly enhanced by an eye-glass." He is " awfully clever at finding out young poets and all that sort of literary thing." He dislikes Utopia because it has no swallows. *Men Like Gods.*

MUTIMER. The butler, " unquestionably Early Georgian," at Samphire House. He knows the secret of the hidden treasure, and when Mr. Blandish at last approaches it he finds it gone and Mutimer lying dead, " or at least helpless," on the cellar floor. Three sketches show Mutimer at different stages of the story. He has a wife who can " cook well," but " no children, no thought or possibility of children." *Spoils of Mr. Blandish.*

MWRES, ELIZABETH. Daughter of a Wind Vane and Waterfall Trust official, a girl of eighteen when she runs away with Denton rather than marry her father's friend Bindon. *Story of the Days to Come.*

400. MY ABOMINABLE COLD. Pall Mall Gazette, June 12th, 1894.

401. MY FIRST AEROPLANE. Strand Magazine, Jan., 1910. Short story.

402. MY FIRST FLIGHT. Daily Mail, Aug. 5th, 1912 ; 2nd essay in *An Englishman.* Account of Wells's first air-flight, made at Eastbourne in a Farman waterplane piloted by Grahame White. He comes down with the feeling that flying is a thing assured, and suggests that the development of the waterplane is a great step in the popularisation of flying.

MY LAST BOOK. Pall Mall Gazette, Feb. 14th, 1895 ; probably the essay reprinted as *The Book of Essays Dedicatory*.

403. MY LUCKY MOMENT. View, Apr. 29th, 1911. Autobiographical article.

404. MY SOCIALISM. Contemporary Review, Aug., 1908 ; reprinted in *First and Last Things*, Book 3, sections 3-11. Statement of Wells's conception of Socialism. See *Of General Conduct*.

405. MYSTERY OF THE PERENNIAL PARAGRAPH, THE. English Review, Oct., 1922. Gives the feelings of the " old worn author " towards his press-cuttings, and protests against the circulation of certain dull and quite fictitious stories which are printed over and over again in various periodicals. He gives three personal instances and contradicts the statements made.

406. MY UTOPIAN SELF. 8th chapter in *Modern Utopia*. The Owner of the Voice meets his Utopian self, one of the Samurai. He returns to the botanist to find him occupied with thoughts of the woman he had loved upon earth, and whose Utopian double he has just seen.

N

NARRATOR, THE. Of *The War of the Worlds*. A writer of speculative philosophy. His brother, a medical student, takes part in the Exodus from London. The Narrator's wife plays a very small part in the story.

407. NATIONALISATION AND A NEW MAGNA CHARTA. Daily News, Nov. 6th, 1920.

408. NATIONALISM AND NATIONALITY. (Some Liberal Ideals, 2). Daily Chronicle, Sept. 25th, 1916. See *Some Liberal Ideals*.

409. NATIONAL PLAN, A. (The Labour Unrest, 3). Daily Mail,, May 18th, 1912 ; see *The Labour Unrest*.

410. NATIONS IN LIQUIDATION. Cassell's Magazine, Feb., 1916 ; reprinted as 3rd chapter in *What is Coming?* Deals with certain war questions of political economy and forecasts the bankruptcy of western civilisation after the war.

" NATURAL HISTORY OF GREATNESS, WITH ESPECIAL REFERENCE TO LITERARY REPUTATIONS, THE." A paper read before section S (devoted to " Poiometry ") of the conference in *The Mind of the Race*. Notes on it are printed in Chapter 5, section 4 of *Boon*.

NATURE OF LOVE, THE. Independent Magazine, Aug. 13th, 1908 ; reprinted as section 2 of *Some Personal Things* (q.v.).

411. NATURE OF MAN, THE. Speaker, in Oct., 1903. Review of Metchnikoff's book, " The Nature of Man."

412. NATURE OF THE EFFORT DEMANDED FROM MANKIND, THE. (Probable Future of Mankind, 2). Review of Reviews, Nov., 1920 ; reprinted as section 2 of *Probable Future of Mankind* (q.v.). The League of Nations in its present form is manifestly inadequate ; its

creators have been afraid to carry their efforts for world unity too far. The task of bringing the world state into being is not a political but an educational one ; " the idea of a world commonweal has . . . to dominate education everywhere in the world. When that end is achieved, then the world state will be achieved, and it can be achieved in no other way."

413. NECESSARY POWERS OF THE LEAGUE, THE. 3rd chapter of *Fourth Year ;* 3rd chapter of *Anticipations of a World Peace.* The League of Nations must settle all international disputes, control all armaments, be the guardian of Egypt, India, Africa. " The plain truth is that the League . . . must do no less than supersede Empire."

414. NEED FOR STRENGTH AND CLEARNESS AT HOME, THE. Nation Sept. 5th, 1914. Discussion of what England must prepare for and face both during and after the war, urging the need for clearness of purpose.

415. NEED OF A NEW MAP OF EUROPE NOW, THE. (Looking Ahead). Daily Chronicle, Aug. 15th, 1914 ; 6th chapter in *War that will End War.* Insists that the British people must redraw the map of Europe now according to the dictates of reason and justice. They must " propagate the idea of it, and make it our national purpose." Gives an outline of the most obvious changes.

416. NEW ACCELERATOR, THE. Strand, Dec., 1901 ; 8th tale in *Twelve Stories ;* 27th in *Country of the Blind.* Professor Gibberne discovers a drug which stimulates

body and brain " heaven knows how many thousand times." He and the narrator take a dose and go for a remarkable walk upon the Folkestone Leas.

417. NEW ARMS FOR OLD ONES. (The Western Front, 2). Daily Chronicle, Dec. 4th and 5th, 1916 ; 4th chapter of *The Western War* (q.v.).

NEWBERRY, RICHARD. Chief shareholder and director of the firm of Crane and Newberry, of Thunderstone House, "a good-looking youngish man, with rather handsome regular features and a sort of bang of brown hair over his forehead." Fanny Smith runs away with him, to be his mistress ; he wishes to marry her, but his wife refuses to divorce him. After the war he and Harry Smith come into daily contact ; Fanny's name is never mentioned by one to the other. *Dream.*

NEW BIBLE, THE. (Salvaging of Civilisation, 4). Sunday Times, Apr. 17th, and 24th, and May 1st, 1921 ; reprinted as *The Bible of Civilisation* (q.v.).

418. NEW EDUCATION, THE. See *The New Englishman, etc.* 7th chapter in *What is Coming ?* Calls attention to the sudden break in the educational process of the universities, as a result of war demands ; an opportunity presents itself to start them afresh on more profitable lines. Outlines the educational necessities of a modern community.

NEW ENGLISHMAN AND THE NEW EDUCATION, THE. Daily News, Feb. 1st, 1916 ; reprinted as *The New Education* (q.v.). See also letter in reply to critics, Feb. 8th, 1916.

NEW EPOCH, THE. Daily Mail, May 23rd, 1910 ; reprinted as the second half of *The New Reign* (q.v.).

419. NEW IMPOSSIBILITY OF WAR, THE. (Probable Future of Mankind, 1). Review of Reviews, Oct., 1920 ; reprinted as Section 1 of *Probable Future of Mankind* (q.v.). War, becoming by the aid of science more destructive and less conclusive, must if it continues ultimately destroy civilisation. Unless man can eliminate war, he may retrogress to a level of enfeebled barbarism, or even be exterminated.

420. NEWLY DISCOVERED ELEMENT, THE. Saturday Review, Feb. 9th, 1895. Unsigned. Article on argon.

421. NEW MACHIAVELLI, THE. See Bib. No. 40. Richard Remington, the narrator, is the only son of a Bromstead (Kent) science teacher. To the age of twelve he is educated at a small preparatory school in Bromstead ; then he wins a scholarship and goes to the City Merchants School in London. Soon after this his father has an accident and dies, and the widow and her son move further into London to Penge. At fifteen he has a new experience, the " first clear intimation of a new motif in life, the sex motif," when he speaks to a young girl and her sister in the street. He is very friendly with a school-fellow named Britten ; the two plan a revival of the school magazine, but the project is taken out of their hands by the other boys. He goes to Cambridge, takes the Mental and Moral Science Tri-

pos, and three years later is given a lectureship in political science. During his years at Trinity he comes under the influences of both Kiplingism and Socialism, while all the time there grows in him a " dominating idea, the statesman's idea, that idea of sound service which is the protagonist of my story." At twenty-two he goes abroad for the first time, walking through Northern Italy with Willersley ; at Locarno he has a passing affair with a married woman named Milly. Presently he abandons his fellowship and comes to London, and during the next five years publishes two books, does a large amount of political journalism, and meets Evesham (the Prime Minister) and the Baileys. At the Baileys' house he renews his friendship with Margaret, an acquaintance of his Staffordshire cousins with whom he stayed in earlier years. They marry, and after a honeymoon in Venice, return to Westminster to live. Remington is elected Liberal member for the Kinghampstead division, during the election meeting for the first time Isabel Rivers, one of his keenest supporters. He comes into contact with Britten again, to find his friend a relentless critic of the Liberal Party. Gradually, during his three years in Parliament, Remington abandons " the pretensions and habits of party Liberalism," moving towards Conservatism and the idea of aristocracy. In 1909 he secedes to the Tories, a movement which results in an estrangement between himself and his wife, who is still staunchly Liberal. He resigns his seat and with certain friends of the New Tory Party starts " The Blue Weekly." In 1913 he contests

Handitch, and returns to the House with the Public Endowment of Motherhood as part of his programme. During these later years Isabel has been coming more and more into his life, taking part in his intellectual development and working with him on " The Blue Weekly." They realise that they are passionately in love. He goes to America, but returns immediately to spend a week with her. Scandal becomes general and they agree to part, it being arranged that she shall marry Arnold Shoesmith. But their parting becomes an impossibility, and they leave England to live together on the Ligurian coast. There Remington, comparing himself to the exiled Machiavelli, writes the story of his life.

422. NEW MAP OF EUROPE, THE. Cassell's Magazine, Apr., 1916 ; 9th chapter in *What is Coming ?* Speculates upon the map of Europe after the war.

423. NEW REPUBLIC, THE. 1st chapter in *Mankind.* Discusses the object of the chapters which follow : " To put in order, to reduce to principle, what is at present in countless instances a mass of inconsistent proceedings, to frame a general theory in accordance with modern conditions of social and political activity." It emphasises the fundamental nature ot life as " a tissue and succession of births " and presents the point of view of the New Republican.

424. NEW TEACHING OF HISTORY, THE. See Bib. No. 73. Comments upon the defects of the general method of teaching history ; mentions certain errors and deficiencies in *The Outline of History* ; replies

to a pamphlet " Mr. Wells as Historian," by A. W. Gomme, and also to two Catholic critics, Richard Downey and Hilaire Belloc. Wells considers the question of a Catholic Outline of History and concludes with some hopes for a " better teaching of history."

425. NEW WORLDS FOR OLD. See Bib. No. 34. An exposition of modern Socialism by one who is " by no means a fanatical or uncritical adherent." Wells defines the word Socialism and indicates the lines upon which the modern Socialist would carry out the reconstruction of society. He takes as his first principle a certain force " that struggles and tends to make and do," a Good Will in man, in the collective mind of the race. The first five chapters of this book are concerned with the fundamental ideas and principles of modern Socialism ; four more consider and dispose of certain common arguments against Socialism ; the remaining six give a broad outline of the development of Socialist thought from its beginnings to the present day, concluding with a picture of the life of the individual in the Socialist world. The chapter-titles are : 1, *The Good Will in Man ;* 2, *The Fundamental Idea of Socialism ;* 3, *The First Main Generalization of Socialism ;* 4, *The Second Main Generalization of Socialism ;* 5, *The Spirit of Gain and the Spirit of Service ;* 6, *Would Socialism Destroy the Home ? ;* 7, *Would Modern Socialism Abolish all Property ? ;* 8, *The Middle-Class Man, the Business Man, and Socialism ;* 9, *Some Common Objections to Socialism ;* 10, *Socialism a Developing Doctrine ;* 11, *Revolutionary Socialism ;* 12, *Administrative Social-*

ism ; 13, *Constructive Socialism ;*
14, *Some Arguments Ad Hominem ;*
15, *The Advancement of Socialism.*

426. NEW WORLD SPIRIT, THE.
Daily Express, Dec. 13th, 1921 ;
26th chapter in Washington. Deals
with the subject of, and certain
speeches on, the four-power Pacific
treaty, and with M. Viviani's appeal
for forbearance with France. It
pleads for an Afro-European treaty
worthy to set beside the Pacific
Treaty.

427. NEXT STAGE IN HISTORY·
THE. Daily News, Sept. 2nd, 1920·

NOLAN. A rich young man with
whom Mrs. Benham (see Lady
Marayne) runs away ; he dies
three days after her husband has
divorced her, leaving two-thirds
of his fortune to her son, William
Porphry Benham, " whom he
deemed himself to have injured."
Research Magnificent.

428. NO MORE SECRET TREATIES.
Daily News, Nov. 8th, 1918.

NORMANDY, BEATRICE. One of
" the innumerable cousins of Lady
Drew," at whose house, Bladesover,
she and George Ponderevo meet as
children. After his fight with
Archie Garvell, her step-brother,
they do not see one another till the
days of the Tono-Bungay boom.
They find that they still love one
another and once, though un-
willingly, she agrees to marry him.
When he returns from France after
his uncle's death he finds that she
is living with Lord Carnaby. *Tono-
Bungay.*

429. NORTH SEA, THE. Henley
House Magazine, Dec., 1889. Signed
H.G.W. Brief article.

430. NOSE, THE. Ludgate Monthly Magazine, Apr., 1896. Illustrated article.

431. NOTE TO THE READER, A.
Prefatory note to *A Modern Utopia.*
Explains the object of the book
and Wells's choice of the particular
form.

NUNEZ. A mountaineer of Ecuador. While attempting the ascent
of " the Matterhorn of the Andes "
with a party of Englishmen, he
falls a thousand feet or more into
a bank of snow, recovering consciousness to find himself in the
Country of the Blind. The natives
of the valley call him Bogota from
his constant references to that
city. *Country of the Blind.*

O

OBJECTIONS TO SOCIAL MUSIC.
Pall Mall Gazette, Pall Mall Budget,
in 1894 ; reprinted as *On Social
Music* (q.v.).

432. OBLITERATED MAN, THE.
See *The Sad Story of a Dramatic
Critic.* 14th tale in *Country of the
Blind.* The narrator, a shy, nervous,
colourless man, is made dramatic
critic for a London paper. He is
affected by the gestures and general
" emotional symbolism " of the
stage, and begins, unconsciously,
to imitate the actors. His manner
becomes so strange that the girl
he is to marry refuses to see him
again. He associates with actors
and gets worse and worse until his
whole personality is lost beneath a
cloak of dramatic gesture and
theatrical speech.

433. OF A BOOK UNWRITTEN. See *The Man of the Year Million*. 23rd essay in *Personal Matters;* also printed in the English Illustrated Magazine, Jan., 1902. Describes by means of extracts from an unwritten book by Professor Holzkopf, " the necessary character of the man of the remote future deduced from the existing stream of tendency."

OF A CROSS CHANNEL PASSAGE. Daily Mail, July 27th, 1909 ; reprinted as *The Coming of Bleriot* (q.v.).

434. OF A NEIGHBOUR AND A GARDEN. Pall Mall Gazette, Aug. 19th, 1895.

435. OF BELIEFS. Book 2 of *First and Last Things*. A statement of Wells's essential beliefs. His fundamental act of faith is " a declaration of the ultimate rightness and significance of things." He believes in predestination and in free will, but predestination " at the utmost . . . is an interesting theory like the theory that there is a fourth dimension " ; the belief in free will is the important belief— " I consider myself a free responsible person among free responsible persons." Next he analyses personal motives, and declares a synthetic, a simplifying belief essential. He believes in the ultimate oneness of the family of mankind, a oneness in which the individual is only an incident. He calls attention to the mystic element in life, and gives this as the " form of my belief." " It seems to me that the whole living creation may be regarded as walking in its sleep, as walking in the sleep of instinct and individualised illusion, and that now out of it all rises man, beginning to perceive his larger self, his universal brotherhood and a collective synthetic purpose to increase Power and realise Beauty." He has no belief in personal immortality ; the book concludes with a criticism of Christianity and other religions. In the 1917 edition, section 15, originally without a title, is replaced by a much longer one, *The Captain of Mankind*, in which Wells states his realisation that the spirit which leads mankind " is, in truth, what the vast majority of truly religious men have called God."

436. OF BLADES AND BLADERY. 12th essay in *Personal Matters*. Gives a few hints and words of advice to the would-be Blade.

437. OF CLEVERNESS. National Observer, March 9th, 1895 ; 13th essay in *Personal Matters*. Doubts the permanent attraction of cleverness, as typified in an acquaintance named Crichton ; it is more probable that there will be a return to dullness and so to peace.

438. OF CONVERSATION. Pall Mall Gazette, Oct. 11th, 1894 ; 5th essay in *Personal Matters*. A protest against " the social law of gabble." Why should one not visit a friend and instead of talking " look at your man until you have seen him enough, and then go ? "

439. OF CONVERSATION AND THE ANATOMY OF FASHION. Pall Mall Gazette, 1893 or 1894 ; 1st of the *Select Conversations*.

440. OFF THE CHAIN. See *The Moral of the Mauretania*. 3rd essay in *An Englishman*. With the modern development of cheap swift locomotion a growing section of the people will become migratory, moving from place to place as the seasons or general conditions change. Here is a new problem for politicians and statesmen to solve, that of the adaptation of this floating population to the public service.

441. OF G.B. AND PEASANTS AND CUCKOOS. Adelphi, Oct., 1923 (Contributors' Club). A brief note.

442. OF GENERAL CONDUCT. Book 3 of *First and Last Things*. Wells, holding that " conduct follows necessarily from belief," shows how he frames his " principles of conduct " upon the metaphysical basis and the beliefs stated in the two previous books of this volume. He considers the question of What is Good ?, discusses Socialism as a step towards the synthesis of the human purpose, criticises certain forms of Socialism, and discusses the primary social duties. In touching upon the question of organised brotherhoods of persons of similar ideas, he quotes the case of the Samurai in *A Modern Utopia*. Other problems are considered--of new religions and the Church, of secession from the Church, of military service and of modern war, he urging that in the evolving of the collective mind lies the only safeguard against war and poverty. He returns to more intimate personal matters. Even when a man has found the truth he is in danger of losing it again. He considers a man's attitude to his fellow-men, to aristocracy and democracy, to debts of honour, to the idea of justice. Half the people in this

world are " under age," inexperienced and easily misled. Any collective enterprise must be judged " as a whole and completely, as it conduces more or less to wholesome and hopeful births." There must be a freer intercourse between people and a better understanding of personal things. Wells deals with problems of sex and marriage, and concludes that conduct must be judged " in relation to the thing that is," the transgressor by " spirit and purpose " rather than by deed. In the 1917 edition the 11th section of this book has a short addition in which Wells discusses his " Prig Series " of novels : *The New Machiavelli, The Passionate Friends, Marriage,* and *The Research Magnificent.*

443. OF HORSES. Pall Mall Gazette, Dec. 10th, 1894.

444. OF READERS IN GENERAL. Saturday Review, March 30th,1895. Unsigned.

445. OF THE DIFFICULTIES OF REVIEWING. Pall Mall Budget, May 9th, 1895.

446. OF THE NEW REIGN. See *And Now* and *The New Epoch.* 4th essay in *An Englishman*. Writing just after the coronation of King George V., Wells wonders whether there is any justification for the general feeling that England is " waking up " at last. He considers the Navy, the Army, and education, and finds it hard to anticipate that " the New Epoch is likely to be a blindingly brilliant time for our Empire or our race."

447. OLIVE BRANCHES OF STEEL : SHOULD THE ANGELS OF PEACE CARRY BOMBS ? Westminster Gazette, Apr. 5th, 1924 ; 30th article in *Year of Prophesying*. Considers the air-warfare of the future and the useless armaments of Great Britain and other nations. Advocates disarmament : " The will for peace is futile without the courage to disarm."

OLIVER. An " extraordinarily dull " government official, " faithful and tender and true," who offers Mrs. Harrowdean " honourable marriage." When war breaks out Mr. Britling decides that " Oliver must have her," but apparently Oliver does not. *Mr. Britling.*

448. ON A TRICYCLE. Pall Mall Gazette, 1893 or 1894 ; 9th of the *Select Conversations*. The uncle compares tricycles and bicycles to the detriment of the latter.

449. ON ELEMENTARY SCIENCE TEACHING. Educational Times, Feb., 1896.

450. ON EXTINCTION. Chambers' Journal, Sept. 20th, 1893.

451. ON MORALS AND CIVILISATION. Fortnightly Review, Feb., 1897. Maintains that our civilisation depends upon the existence of " a rational code of morality to meet the complex requirements of modern life," and the organisation of the " forces of moral suggestion to render them operative." There is needed " the discipline of a common ideal," but " a definite stress of effort to determine the development of public ideals is wanting."

452. ON SCHOOLING AND THE PHASES OF MR. SANDSOME. New Budget, Apr., 11th, 1895 ; 7th essay in *Personal Matters*. Describes the small private school which the narrator attended as a boy, with particular reference to the changing moods of Mr. Sandsome, the master.

453. ON SOCIAL MUSIC. See *Objections to Social Music*. 6th of the *Select Conversations*.

454. ON STEPHEN CRANE. North American Review, Aug., 1900. Written soon after the death of Stephen Crane, this article deals with his work from an English standpoint.

ON SWEARING. Pall Mall Gazette, June 9th, 1894 ; reprinted as *The Book of Curses* (q.v.).

455. ON THE ART OF STAYING AT THE SEASIDE. Pall Mall Gazette, in June, 1893 ; 1st essay in *Personal Matters*. Holds that while " thousands of people think they have stayed at the seaside," in reality they " have only frequented a watering-place for a time." The art of staying at the seaside lies in a capacity for " classical simplicity, an ability to sit upon the beach in perfect mental and physical acquiescence."

456. ON THE CHOICE OF A WIFE. Pall Mall Gazette, in 1894 ; 3rd essay in *Personal Matters*. Gives advice to " the young fellow of eight or nine and twenty " concerning the wise choice of a wife.

457. ON THE NOVELS OF GEORGE GISSING. Contemporary Review, Aug., 1897. Analysis of the ten-

dencies and development of Gissing's work.

458. ON THE VISIBILITY OF CHANGE IN THE MOON. Knowledge, Oct. 1st, 1895. " Altogether there is plentiful *a priori* ground for denying that the moon is indeed an immutable dead world beyond any further indignities of change," though it is improbable that any change on the moon's surface could be easily observed. Changes that may take place will be discovered by " the systematic measurement and comparison of photographic charts extending over a considerable period of years."

459. OPEN LETTER TO ANATOLE FRANCE ON HIS EIGHTIETH BIRTH-DAY, AN. Westminster Gazette, April 19, 1924 ; 32nd article in *Year of Prophesying.* Deals mainly with France's appeal to and influence on readers of the English translations.

460. OPPORTUNITY OF LIBERAL-ISM, THE. Nation, Aug. 15th, 1914, 7th chapter in *War that will End War.* Reviews the European situation, urging the Liberals to do " fundamental things that will otherwise not get done for hundreds of years "—to insist upon a world-conference at the end of the war, to refuse partial settlements, to set up a Peace League, to end the private armament industry, and to " set going methods and machinery that will put the feeding and housing of the population and the administration of the land out of the reach of private greed and selfishness for ever."

461. ORGANISATION OF A COMMON CONSCIOUSNESS IN MAN, THE. (Prob-able Future of Mankind, 3). Review of Reviews, Dec., 1920 ; reprinted as Section 3 of *The Probable Future of Mankind* (q.v.). Among the mass of mankind there is a " manifest absence " of sufficient will to make possible the " political reorganisation of the world as a unity." There must be, through education, a world-wide " organisa-tion of a common consciousness in man." Established ideas will have to be overthrown ; there will be resistence, but this resistence must be crushed. The recent tour of the Prince of Wales is commented upon as " a propaganda of inanity unparalleled in the world's his-tory."

462. ORGANISATION OF FORE-SIGHT IN GREAT BRITAIN, THE. (Looking Ahead). Daily Chronicle, Jan. 19th, 1915.

463. ORGANISATION OF THE HIGHER EDUCATION, THE. 9th chapter in *Mankind.* Considers the education of the individual from the age of fifteen or so to adult citizenship, criticises the modern university and suggests sweeping reforms, and discusses the educa-tional value of books and the need for an organised Publishers' As-sociation.

OSTROG. The Boss. He is, be-fore Graham's awakening, head of the Wind Vanes Control. Secretly arming and organising the Labour Companies, he wakens Graham by means of injected stimulants and raises the people in revolt against the White Council, hoping so to win power for himself. *Sleeper Wakes.*

464. OTHER SIDE IN FRANCE, THE. See *H. G. Wells on the Other*

Side in France. 10th article in *Year of Prophesying* (misdated 17-11-23 : see *The Last of the Victorians*). Criticism of the French policy, illustrated by the case of M. Caillaux and with some reference to M. Philippe Millet.

465. OTHER WORLDS' INHABITANTS. Daily Mail, Nov. 4th, 1903.

466. OUR IGNORANCE OF THE U.S.A. Daily Mail, Feb. 26th, 1918.

467. OUR LITTLE NEIGHBOUR. New Budget, Apr. 4th, 1895.

OUT BANSTEAD WAY. Pall Mall Gazette, Nov. 25th, 1893 ; reprinted as *The Amateur Nature Lover.*

468. OUTLINE OF HISTORY, THE. See Bib. No. 70. An attempt to give the history of this world from the earliest times to the present day.

469. OUTLOOK FOR THE GERMANS, THE. Cassell's Magazine, May, 1916 ; 12th chapter in *What is Coming ?* Wells says that this is a war " not of races but of ideas," that there is no real hatred between Germany and Britain, and suggests the possibility of a revolution and the establishment of a democracy in Germany. The last sections insists that " the primary business of the Allies is not reconciliation with Germany," but the organisation of a world peace league. For many years there must be a certain " barrier of dislike " about Germany, but ultimate reconciliation is inevitable and necessary.

OWNER OF THE VOICE, THE. The narrator in *A Modern Utopia,*

" a whitish plump man, a little under the middle size and age, with such blue eyes as many Irishmen have, and agile in his movements and with a slight tonsorial baldness of the crown. His front is convex." His Utopian self is one of the Samurai, " a little taller than I, younger looking and sounder looking . . . he has made himself a better face than mine."

P

470. PAINS OF AN IMAGINATION, THE. Pall Mall Gazette, Sept. 20th, 1894.

471. PAINS OF MARRIAGE, THE. Pall Mall Gazette, in 1894 ; 12th and last of the *Select Conversations.* The Uncle, on the eve of his marriage to Mrs. Harborough, protests against certain wedding customs.

PALSWORTHY, LADY. The leader of Morningside Park society, widow of a knight who " had won his spurs in the wholesale coal-trade." Ann Veronica meets Manning at her house. *Ann Veronica.*

PARCHESTER, MR. Rector of a West End church, a " handsome, earnest, modern preacher," with the face of a saint rendered " generally acceptable " by the growth of side whiskers ; he preaches against anything which is unpopular. *Story of the Last Trump.*

PARKER. A maid, " still fallaciously young " but with " an inflexible air of correctness," engaged by Mrs. Bunting for the Sea Lady. She contrives several devices for her strange mistress's comfort. *Sea Lady.*

472. PARKES MUSEUM, THE. Pall Mall Gazette, Mar. 24th, 1894; 26th essay in *Personal Matters*. Account of a visit made by Euphemia and the narrator to a " museum of sanitary science."

PARKSON. The Friends of Progress hold their meetings in his rooms, he being a Whitworth Scholar at the Normal School of Science and the only member opulent enough to have a sitting-room. He is a Ruskinite and a Quaker, and " one of those exponents of virtue for whom the discussion of sexual matters has an irresistible attraction." He tells Lewisham about a girl, " a Paragon of Purity," with whom he is in love; Lewisham calls him a fool. *Mr. Lewisham.*

PARLIAMENTARY TRIANGLE, THE. 17th article in *Year of Prophesying;* see *How We Muddle Through the Years of Destiny.*

PARLOAD. Leadford's friend, a " tall, flaxen-haired, gawky youth . . . capable of vast enthusiasms," a sceptic and a Socialist. He is preoccupied, at the beginning of the story, with the wonder of the stars. After the Change he becomes " a great figure in a great time." *Days of the Comet.*

PARSONS. An apprentice at the Port Burdock Drapery Bazaar, Mr. Polly's closest friend, and the leading spirit among the " three P's." He is a cheerful, rather boisterous young man, with a very genuine love of books, to the delights of which he introduces Polly. He is dismissed for displaying too much originality in window-dressing and for assaulting his

employer. He goes to London and Mr. Polly loses sight of him. *Mr. Polly.*

473. PASSING OF THE EFFIGY, THE. Cassell's Magazine, Dec., 1916; 1st section of *War and the Future.* Written after Wells's return from the Western and Italian fronts (Aug. and Sept.), it explains why these visits were made and his attitude towards the war. Remarks upon its failure to produce any one great leader, and sees in this the " passing of the effigy," the spectacular hero, the Cæsar or Napoleon, of earlier wars. Describes meetings with Joffre, Pellé, Castelnau, and King Victor Emmanuel III.

474. PASSIONATE FRIENDS, THE. See Bib. No. 49. The autobiography of Stephen Stratton, only son of the rector of Burnmore. From boyhood he is the intimate friend of the Christian boys and their sister, Lady Mary, who live at Burnmore House. Before he is twenty he and Lady Mary are in love, but she is unable to face the prospect of comparative poverty with its crampings, its indignities, its loss of freedoms. At twenty-one she marries Justin, a wealthy financier, thus attaining the luxury which she deems so necessary. Stratton goes to South Africa and serves through the Boer War, not returning to England for more than four years. His father is now living in comfortable retirement at Guildford, a neighbour of the Justins. Stratton and Mary meet again, become lovers in deed, are discovered by Justin. He takes her away to Ireland, and a divorce is only averted by the lovers agreeing to the husband's terms. Mary

is now to become his wife in more than name, and Stratton is to leave the country for three years. He goes to Paris, Switzerland, and Italy, and then on an eastward-bound boat meets Gidding, an American. After some time in India, Burma, China, Japan and other Eastern countries he returns to Europe, in Germany becoming friendly with Rachel More, a young English girl who loves him and whom later he marries. He goes to America and renews his friendship with Gidding, who presently joins him in Europe. Together they set up a great printing and publishing business which has as its objects the issuing of " propaganda of all science, all knowledge, all philosophical and political ideas, round about the habitable globe," and the " systematic organisation of free publishing, exhaustive discussion, intellectual stimulation." Stratton is married at the end of 1906. In 1909 he hears from Mary and for the next two and a half years they correspond. In the summer of 1911 they meet, purely by chance, at a small hotel in Switzerland, where she is staying with her companion, Miss Satchel. They spend the day together, and Justin, hearing of this, again threatens divorce. But Mary, rather than that she or Stratton should face the disgrace and ruin of publicity, kills herself, leaving Stratton with the meagre consolations of wife, and family, and work.

PAST AND THE GREAT STATE, THE. See Bib. No. 44, note to collation.

475. PEACE OF THE WORLD, THE. See Bib. No. 55. A " discussion of the way in which peace may be organised and established out of the settlement of this war." Despite certain opposition, a World Council must be established upon which every country will be represented ; the end-of-the-war conference must not be confined to belligerents and it must discuss such matters as disarmament and control of armament manufacture. Suggests that a proposal for such a conference may come from the Tsar of Russia, from the Hague, or from America. In the meantime it is the duty of everyone to spread anti-war propaganda and to insist upon such a conference, thus building up public opinion in support of it.

475a. PEARL OF LOVE, THE. Short story written Jan., 1925 ; 18th tale in Vol. 10 of *The Atlantic Edition*.

476. PECULIAR DANGER OF NEW YEAR'S EVE, THE. Pall Mall Gazette, late Dec., 1893.

477. PECULIARITIES OF PSYCHICAL RESEARCH. Nature, Dec. 6th, 1894. Review of " Apparitions and Thought Transference," by F. Podmore. A letter in reply to a criticism of this review, Jan. 17th, 1895.

PEEVE, MR. Editor of "The Liberal." A man of " unvarying pessimism " who holds that " the brightest hope which remained to Liberalism was for a good Day of Judgment soon." *Men Like Gods*.

PENK. Cecil Burleigh's chauffeur. He is killed on Quarantine Crag. *Men Like Gods*.

PENTSTEMON, UNCLE. A relative of Mr. Polly, a man " aged rather than venerable . . . a fragment from the ruder agricultural past of our race," ; he takes a rather gloomy view of life, based upon considerable experience. He comes to both the funeral of Polly's father and Polly's wedding, and each time expresses his special dislike for Annie Larkins ; " a gad-about grinny she is, if ever was. A gad-about grinny. Mucked up my mushroom bed to rights, she did, and I 'aven't forgot it." *Mr. Polly*.

478. PERFECT GENTLEMAN ON WHEELS, A. Woman at Home, Apr., 1897 ; see Bib. II, 1897.

479. PERVERSION OF GERMANY, THE. Daily Chronicle, March 25th, 1915. Review of " When Blood is their Argument," by Ford M. Hueffer.

PETCHWORTH, LADY. Mrs. Pope's oldest friend, a " plump and blonde" widow, " one of those brighter influences which save our English countryside from lassitude." Her enthusiasms change quickly and often, but they are always for " something progressive and beneficial." She tries to make Summerhay a model village and to revive the old village life and customs. Magnet proposes to Marjorie at one of her garden parties. *Marriage*.

PETER FLIES. An excerpt from *Joan and Peter* printed in the Daily News sometime in 1918.

PETER, K.B.O. Air Pie, 1919. Reprint of a few paragraphs from *Joan and Peter*, Chap. 13, section 24.

480. PETERSBURG IN COLLAPSE. See *Russia in the Shadow*. 1st chapter of *Russia*. Account of general conditions in Petersburg under Soviet rule. Wells does not believe that the Bolshevik Government is responsible for these conditions.

481. PETERSBURG SOVIET, THE. 5th chapter of *Russia*. Brief account of Wells's visit to the Soviet on Oct. 7th, 1920. When the business was over he addressed the meeting, after which a film of the Baku Conference (described in The Quintessence of Bolshevism) was shown. He comments upon the lack of " organization, structure, and working efficiency " possessed by the Soviet.

PHILIPS, MADELEINE. An actress engaged to Captain Alan Douglas, and one of the party of caravaners which Bealby joins after his flight from Shonts. She is a slender and (to Bealby) beautiful young woman whose " fair hair a little tinged with red poured back from her forehead . . . she had the sweetest eyes in the world " ; " she knew clearly that she was made for love, for she had made herself for love, and she went through life like its empress with all mankind and numerous women at her feet." *Bealby*.

482. PHILOSOPHER'S PUBLIC LIBRARY, THE. Daily Mail, Apr. 28th, 1904 ; 10th essay in *An Englishman*. A brief description of the " sort of public libraries " a rich philosopher might found.

PHILOSOPHERS THAT MATTER, THE. See *The Ten Most Important Books in the World*.

PHI-OO. One of the two Selenites sent by the Grand Lunar to guard and study Cavor. He is one of the administrative class, and has a "tremendously hypertrophied brain . . . with the rest of his organism both relatively and absolutely dwarfed." He serves as interpreter during Cavor's talk with the Grand Lunar. *Men in the Moon.*

PHIPPS. The youngest member of the Rescue Party, "a callow youth of few words, faultless collars, and fervent devotion" to Mrs. Milton. *Wheels of Chance.*

PIDDINGQUIRK, WILLIAM. Second porter at a drapery store, a teetotaller and non-smoker, and of "eminent respectability." By paying attention to points of "policy" (such as attending his employer's chapel) he rises to be a shop-assistant, whereupon he jilts the servant-girl to whom he is engaged and marries a milliner. *Jilting of Jane.*

PLAICE, MR. An "Oxford gentleman" and publisher's reader who has the ground-floor at Matilda Good's house. He is stooping and tall "with a cadaverous face that was mostly profile," and he disapproves of Harry Smith's educational plans. *Dream.*

483. PLAIN NECESSITY FOR A LEAGUE, THE. 8th chapter of *Fourth Year;* 7th of *Anticipations of a World Peace.* Points out certain things — mechanical progress, increasing destructiveness of modern war—which make a united League of Free Nations a "plain necessity."

PLATT. An apprentice at the Port Burdock Drapery Bazaar, and one of the "three P's." He is

"white-faced and dark, and disposed to undertones and mystery and a curiosity about society and the demi-monde." After the dismissal of Parsons he becomes merely a "tiresome companion." *Mr. Polly.*

PLATTNER, GOTTFRIED. Modern Languages master at the Sussexville Proprietary School, where he also teaches Chemistry, Commercial Geography, Book-keeping, Shorthand, Drawing and other subjects. A pupil brings him a strange green powder and while experimenting with it he is blown into another world. Upon his return after nine days it is found that the right and left sides of his body have been transposed. *Plattner Story.*

484. PLATTNER STORY, THE. New Review, Apr., 1896 ; 1st tale in *Plattner Story ;* 15th in *Country of the Blind.* While experimenting with a green powder, Plattner causes an explosion and disappears instantaneously. When he reappears nine days later in an unexpected and inexplicable manner, he tells a strange story of his experiences in an Other-World, where he has spent the whole period of his absence, amid the curious phantom-like Watchers of the Living. During the day of this world the Other-World is shadowy and dim, while Sussexville is plainly visible ; during the night a green sun illuminates the strange world and Sussexville fades from view. Upon the ninth day Plattner is watching a deathbed scene in the village, and sees the Hand of Death outstretched towards the bed. He turns to run, stumbles, there is an explosion, and he finds himself once more actually in Sussexville.

485. PLATTNER STORY AND OTHERS, THE. See Bib. No. 10.

486. PLEASURES OF QUARRELLING, THE. 35th essay in *Personal Matters*. Describes the joys of quarrelling, to the author " the vinegar and pepper of existence."

PLESSINGTON, HUBERT. Husband of Aunt Plessington, " just a little reminiscent of the small attached husbands one finds among the lower crustacea ; . . . if he had been left to himself he would probably have been comfortably fat in his quiet little way. But Aunt Plessington . . . said he had a great gift for practical things, and made him see after everything in that line while she did the lecturing." Before his marriage he was an Oxford don. *Marriage.*

PLESSINGTON, MRS. The vigorous earnest sister of Mrs. Pope, " a tall, lean woman, with firm features, a high colour and a bright eye, who wore hats to show she despised them, and carefully dishevelled hair. . . . Her voice was the true governing-class voice, a strangulated contralto, abundant and authoritative ; it made everything she said clear and important . . . and she had over her large front teeth lips that closed quietly and with a slight effort after her speeches, as if the words she spoke tasted well and left a peaceful, secure sensation in the mouth." She thinks only of " getting on " and making herself generally known; she has a movement of her own, " a progressive movement of the utmost scope and benevolence which aimed at extensive interferences with the food and domestic intimacies of the more defenceless lower classes." Marjorie Pope is her favourite niece, and it is largely through her persuasion that Marjorie accepts Magnet's proposal of marriage. Trafford finds her " intolerable " ; she reminds him of " some larger sort of hen—which cackles because it must." *Marriage.*

487. POET AND THE EMPORIUM, THE. New Budget, June 6th, 1895 ; 8th essay in *Personal Matters*. A Poet narrates his furniture-purchasing experiences to his friend Bellows.

488. POLITICAL AND SOCIAL INFLUENCES. 7th chapter in *Mankind*. Discussion of the administration of the modern state, and a criticism of the British and American systems of government, concluding with a sketch of a possible " scheme of honour and privilege " and of an " approximation towards the socialisation of property."

489. POLITICS AS A PUBLIC NUISANCE. Westminster Gazette, Dec. 1st, 1923 ; 12th article in *Year of Prophesying*. The modern general election is " a monstrous foolery " ; Proportional Representation is the " only civilised method of democracy."

490. POLLOCK AND THE PORROH MAN. New Budget, May 23rd, 1895 ; 8th tale in *Plattner Story*. Pollock, assistant to a Sierra Leone trader, quarrels with a local witch-doctor who tries to kill him. He hires a Mendi rough to murder the witch-doctor, and the native soon brings him the head of his enemy. A few days later he leaves the country, but the head follows him in a most uncanny way, and even

when he has got rid of it appears to him in his dreams and then when he is awake. He kills himself to escape the head.

POLLY, ALFRED. The dyspeptic draper whose biography is related in *The History of Mr. Polly.* He is " an artless child of nature, far more untrained, undisciplined and spontaneous than an ordinary savage." He has an abiding love of literature (Shakespeare, Boccaccio, Rabelais), and a fondness for curious phrases and for words which he cannot and does not attempt to pronounce correctly. His temperament prevents him from being a commercial success, for he judges life by the " rare veins of unbusinesslike joy " which he encounters occasionally ; he travels the roads seeking romance (one flash of which, indeed, is granted him), seeking adventure, longing for the old days of Chaucer and the Canterbury Tales. His mother dies when he is seven ; his father keeps a music and bicycle shop for some years, eventually retiring upon an annuity to the Johnsons' Easewood house.

PONDEREVO, EDWARD Uncle of George Ponderevo, and the inventor of Tono-Bungay. When he appears first in the story he is a young Wimblehurst chemist, a " restless, fretful, garrulous " buzzing man, who clamours for " Scope " and is filled with ideas of the Romance of Commerce. With the passing of years and the coming of prosperity he becomes plump and inclined to dyspepsia and flabbiness. He is influenced by " this Overman idea, Nietzsche," and by the Napoleonic legend, particularly with regard to women. His earliest dreams are piratically inclined, and he is at no

time painfully honest, though more from want of imagination than from any essential immorality. *Tono-Bungay.*

PONDEREVO, GEORGE. The narrator of *Tono-Bungay* (q.v.).

PONDEREVO, MRS. George's mother, housekeeper at Bladesover House. She is a hard woman who knows " with inflexible decision her place and the place of everyone in the world." She dies soon after George is apprenticed to his uncle Edward. Her husband, whom she never mentions, left her and went to one of the colonies.

PONDEREVO, SUSAN. The wife of Edward Ponderevo, a delightful, loving, lovable, witty, faithful woman. She has a keen sense of humour and a " disposition to connubial badinage, to a sort of gentle skylarking." After her husband's financial success she takes up the study of sociology and physiology.

POPE, DAPHNE. The eldest of the five Pope children, a large red-haired girl. When Marjorie elopes with Trafford she " gets " Magnet " on the rebound " and he marries her instead. *Marriage.*

POPE, MARJORIE. The second of the Pope children and the " clever " girl of the family. She is delicately pretty, with copper-red hair and clear grey-blue eyes. Aunt Plessington wishes her to follow in her steps as a public speaker, and sends her each of the novels of Mrs. Humphrey Ward as it appears ; she is an exceptionally good speaker. Her parents send her to Bennett College, Oxbridge, where she makes many friends and gets into debt with the local tradesmen. It is partly because of the worry of these debts that she consents to marry Will Magnet. She and Trafford have four children, Margharita, Godwin, Richard and Edward. *Marriage.*

POPE, MRS. Marjorie's mother, a " fine-featured, anxious-looking little woman," who has " clipped the wings of her own mind . . . so successfully that all her conclusions had become evasions, all her decisions compromises. Her profoundest working conviction was a belief that nothing in the world was of value but ' tact,' and that the art of living was ' to tide things over.' " She finds comfort and peace of mind in the study of Christian Science. *Marriage.*

POPE, PHILIP. Marjorie's father, an intolerable egotist who suffers continually " from indigestion and extreme irritability " ; he is " an irascible atheist with a respect for usage and Good Taste, and has an abject fear of the disapproval of other gentlemen of his class." Inheriting the family coach-building business, he makes a " stand " against modern types of vehicles and against motor-cars, and finally sells the business and retires rather than bring it up-to-date. During his ownership of the works he organises the East Purblow Experiment, an illegal attempt at social reform which provides him with a subject to talk and write about for the rest of his life. He becomes a busy publicist, writing letters, making speeches, taking chairs, hoping that some day he may be invited " to contest a constituency in the interests of reaction and the sounder elements in the Liberal party." To his family he is irritable, spiteful and grumbling. He is friendly with Magnet and detests Trafford. *Marriage.* He appears briefly in *Sir Isaac Harman* as " one of those odd people who are called publicists because one must call them something, and who take chairs and political sides and are vice-presidents of everything and organise philanthropies, write letters to the papers, and cannot let the occasion pass without saying a few words and generally prevent the institutions of this country from falling out of human attention."

POPE, ROMOLA. The younger of the " pseudo-twins," the fourth of the Pope children. *Marriage.*

POPE, SYDNEY. The elder of the " pseudo - twins " (as she and Romola are called " because of a strong tendency to be twins in spite of the year between them ") ; the third daughter of Mr. and Mrs. Pope. *Marriage.*

POPE, THEODORE. The only son and youngest child of Mr. and Mrs. Pope. In honour of his birthday Mr. Magnet gives the picnic at which he proposes to and is accepted by Marjorie. *Marriage.*

491. POPULARISING SCIENCE. Nature, July 26th, 1894. Scientific knowledge must be made more general. This cannot be done by writing or lecturing down to the public, nor will the " facetious adornment of popular scientific statements " assist. After commenting upon the lack of construction in scientific books and papers, proposes the lines that the " genuine populariser of science " should follow.

PORNICK, ANN. Daughter of a New Romney haberdasher. As a girl she is Kipps's first love, and when he meets her again in Folkestone, where she is a servant, he breaks off his engagement to Helen Walshingham to run away with her and marry her. *Kipps.*

PORNICK, SIDNEY. Ann's brother and Kipps's boyhood friend. He becomes a bicycle repairer and sets up a shop in Hammersmith ; as a Socialist he does not " 'old with wealth." His wife is mentioned, once as Fanny and again as Bessie. They have one child, Walt Whitman Pornick.

492. PORTUGAL AND PROSPERITY: THE BLESSEDNESS OF BEING A LITTLE NATION. Westminster Gazette, March 1st, 1924 ; 25th article in *Year of Prophesying.* Written during a visit to Portugal. "National sovereignty lies at the root of all Portugal's present troubles " ; suggests a combine of Latin states.

493. POSE NOVEL, THE. Pall Mall Gazette, May 21st, 1894 ; 14th essay in *Personal Matters.* Discusses the " pose novel " which every " tadpole author " writes.

494. POSSIBLE BREAKDOWN OF CIVILISATION, THE. New York World, Nov. 27th, 1921 (not printed in England owing to dispute with Daily Mail) ; 15th chapter in *Washington.* Wells surveys the " condition of Europe to-day." He cannot see that the Washington Conference is considering this problem at all.

495. POSSIBLE COLLAPSE OF CIVILISATION, THE. New York World, in Jan., 1909 ; 23rd essay in

An Englishman. Considers the instability of the modern currency and financial systems, and the overdevelopment of war ; suggests that the twentieth century may quite possibly see a set-back in the progress of civilsation, even a worldwide collapse.

496. POSSIBLE INDIVIDUALITY OF ATOMS, THE. Saturday Review, Sept. 5th, 1896. Unsigned. Scientific article.

POTWELL INN, THE. The peaceful riverside inn where Mr. Polly finds his final happiness. *Mr. Polly.* Also mentioned in *Marriage.*

PRACTICAL PROBLEM, THE. Westminster Gazette, Mar. 8th, 1924 ; reprinted as *Reconstruction of the League of Nations.* (q.v.).

497. PREFACE to " L'Angleterre, Sa Politique Intérieure." See Bib. III, 1917.

498. PREFACE to " Catalogue of Paintings of Aircraft." See Bib. III, 1917.

499. PREFACE to *First and Last Things.* (1917 revised edition). Dated July 1st, 1917. Wells states the changes which have taken place in his general religious views since 1908.

500. PREFACE to " The Gay-Dombeys." See Bib. III, 1919.

501. PREFACE to *God the Invisible King.* Dated May, 1917. Traces briefly the main line of the beliefs set forth in the following chapters, and defines the subsequent meaning of certain disputable terms.

502. PREFACE to *In the Fourth Year*. Dated May, 1918. Discusses propaganda for the League of Free Nations.

503. PREFACE to *Mankind in the Making*. Dated July, 1903. Discusses the "aim and scope" of the book.

504. PREFACE to *Mankind in the Making*. (1914 edition). Criticises the book, saying that this new edition is justified mainly by one chapter, *The Problem of the Birth Supply*.

505. PREFACE to "The Peculiar Major." See Bib. III, 1919.

506. PREFACE to *The Sleeper Awakes*. Tells the circumstances under which the original version of this book, *When the Sleeper Wakes*, was written and published, and states the main alterations which have been made.

507. PREFACE to "Underground Man." See Bib. III, 1905.

508. PREFACE to *When the Sleeper Wakes*. (1921 edition). Wells confesses his doubts that the prophecies of this story could ever come true, and his disillusionment concerning the intelligence of capitalists. "'Ostrog'... gave way to reality when I drew 'Uncle Ponderevo.'"

509. PREFACE to "Youth in the Universities." See Bib. III, 1922.

PRELIMINARY SOCIAL DUTY, THE. Independent Magazine, July 30th, 1908; reprinted as section 6 of *Of General Conduct* (q.v.).

PRENDICK, EDWARD. Narrator of *The Island of Doctor Moreau*, a young man who has "taken to natural history as a relief from the dulness of my comfortable independence," and who has spent some years under Huxley at the Royal College of Science. The preface to this book is signed by Charles Edward Prendick his nephew.

510. PRESENCE BY THE FIRE, THE. Penny Illustrated Paper, Aug. 14th, 1897; Cassell's Magazine, late 1915.

PRESERVATION OF THE PARTY SYSTEM. Westminster Gazette, Jan. 12th, 1924; reprinted as *Modern Government: Parliament and Real Electoral Reform*. (q.v.).

511. PRESIDENT AT ARLINGTON, THE. Daily Mail, Nov. 14th, 1921; reprinted as the 5th chapter of *Washington*. Account of the burial of America's Unknown Soldier at Arlington National Cemetery on Armistice Day, 1921. Particular mention is made of the personality and the speech of President Harding.

PRINCHESTER, THE BISHOP OF. See Edward Scrope.

512. PROBABLE DIFFUSION OF GREAT CITIES, THE. 2nd chapter in *Anticipations*. Discusses the effect of improved means of transport upon the great cities of the future, and the "coming phases in that extraordinary expansion, shifting and internal distribution of population that has been so conspicuous during the last hundred years."

513. PROBABLE FUTURE OF MANKIND, THE. Series of 4 essays, Re-

view of Reviews, Oct., Nov., Dec., 1920,; Jan., 1921 ; printed under the titles : 1, *1he New Impossibility of War ;* 2, *The Nature of the Effort Demanded from Mankind ;* 3, *The Organization of a Common Consciousness in Man ;* 4, *The Awakening of Passion for the World State* (see under these titles) ; reprinted as the first chapter of *Salvaging of Civilisation.* Attempts to answer the questions, " What else has to go if war is to go out of human life ? " and " What has to be done if it is to be banished for ever from the future experiences of our race ? "

514. PROBLEM OF THE BIRTH SUPPLY, THE. 2nd chapter in *Mankind.* An examination of the claims of a " so-called science, the science of Eugenics, to direct our lives in certain important particulars."

515. PROBLEMS OF POLITICAL ADAPTATION. Times, July 29th, 1916 ; 4th chapter of *Elements of Reconstruction.* Considers the legislative and administrative changes necessary for the effective carrying out of the schemes proposed in the preceding chapters. Wells mentions the absence of and need for clear thinking, and goes on to criticise the Machine of Government, with particular application to the question of local reference and to the Party System, advocating Proportional Representation as a solution of difficulties.

516. PROJECT OF A WORLD STATE, THE. See *Why a World State is Necessary.* 3rd chapter of *Salvaging of Civilisation.* Man's political ideas have not progressed as rapidly as have his scientific knowledge and physical activities. Europe is not only tied, politically and com-

mercially, by international complications, but is in constant danger of an outbreak of war. The British Empire is in no way exempt. Only a World State will suffice to save civilisation.

PROPAGANDA OF THE LEAGUE, THE. 8th and last chapter of *Anticipations of a World Peace,* reprinted from the last two paragraphs of *1he Study and Propaganda of Democracy* (q.v.).

517. PROPHETIC HABIT OF MIND, THE. 1st chapter in *Future in America.* Wells discusses the " prophetic habit " in himself, and his intentions in visiting America.

518. PROPORTIONAL REPRESENTATION. Westminster Gazette, May 31st, 1924 ; reprinted as a pamphlet *The P.R. Parliament* (q.v.) and also as *The Extinction of Party Government* (q.v.). A review of the methods and advantages of Proportional Representation, with some comments on the attitude of the party politicians to the system.

P.R. PARLIAMENT, THE. See Bib No. 87.

519. PROTEAN GAS, THE. Saturday Review, May 4th, 1895. Unsigned. Scientific article.

PROTHERO, WILLIAM. Benham's friend at school and college, " a sturdy sort of boy, generously wanting in good looks," and a professed coward. He " stimulates " Benham and for years they are inseparables. He stays on at Cambridge and becomes a Fellow of Trinity. Together they visit Russia and, later, China, where Prothero is killed in a gambling den. *Research Magnificent.*

520. PROTYLIAN VAPOURINGS.
Science Schools Journal, Feb., 1887.
30 lines of light verse celebrating a
fellow-student's essay on the pro-
tyle. Signed H. G. W.

521. PROVINCE OF PAIN, THE.
Science and Art, date not traced.

PUNT, MRS. MAY. A "small
woman dressed in the borrowed
mourning of a large woman." She
comes, with her "sharp-nosed, observant" son to the funeral and
the wedding. *Mr. Polly.*

522. PURE AND NATURAL MAN,
THE. Pall Mall Gazette, Oct. 16th,
1893.

523. PURPLE PILEUS, THE. Black
and White, Xmas No. 1896 ; 11th
tale in *Plattner Story ;* 17th in
Country of the Blind. Mr. Coombes,
a struggling shopkeeper, bullied by
his wife, and her noisy friends,
leaves the house one Sunday afternoon filled with a great weariness
with life. Careless, half hoping
it may contain some deadly poison,
he eats a purple fungus which he
finds in a country lane. He becomes intoxicated and returns to
the house for a "jolly evening."
He scares his wife into submission
and her friends out of the house.
Five years later he is quite prosperous, "a master now," with three
assistants in his shop.

PURSUIT OF WISDOM, THE. See
What Everyone Should Read.

524. "PUT NOT YOUR TRUST
IN DREADNOUGHTS." Daily Mail,
Apr. 8th, 1913 ; 2nd article in
War and Common Sense (q.v.). The
British naval policy is wrong, Wells
holds ; he prophecies the main

events of the next naval war. Destroyers, submarines and water-
planes will be the real weapons ; the
Dreadnought is becoming obsolete.
Most essential of all is research,
the systematic "anticipation and
preparation of our future war
invention."

PYBUS, MRS. A "small, white-
faced, anxious woman . . . wearing
amiability as one wears a Sabbath
garment." Upon her husband's
death she is left in some want, and
this leads her sister, Unwin (q.v.)
to suggest to Lady Charlotte Sydenham that Joan might be put in her
charge. As a consequence Joan
and Peter are kidnapped. *Joan
and Peter.*

Q

QUESTION IN THE FOREGROUND,
THE. Daily Mail, Nov. 16th, 1921 ;
reprinted as *What is Japan ?* (q.v.).

525. QUESTION OF SCIENTIFIC
ADMINISTRATIVE AREAS IN RELA-
TION TO MUNICIPAL UNDERTAKINGS,
THE. Printed without title as Appendix I in *Mankind* (see Bib. No.
22). Wells's test of administration
is "efficiency ; " he criticises the
present administrative areas as
based on a past order of things.
Cheap swift locomotion has produced a large shifting delocalized
population which has neither time
for, nor inclination to, follow local
politics. Under modern conditions,
too, such things as roads, water and
electrical supply, poor law, education, etc., need "wide views, wide
minds and wide areas." To leave
these things in the hands of the
"localized men" is to "sin against
efficiency and the light." If the
existing areas are to remain, "then,

on the whole, my vote is against municipal trading." He suggests that the main water-sheds should be taken as the boundaries of modern administrative areas.

526. QUICK WAY TO ESSEN, THE. Daily Express, June 23rd, 1915.

527. QUINTESSENCE OF BOLSHE-VISM, THE. See *Blundering Bolshe-vism.* 3rd chapter of *Russia.* Ex-plains what the Bolshevik Govern-ment is and how it came into being despite the numerical inferiority of the Party. The Bolsheviks are Marxist Socialists ; they are finding to-day that their hopes are not being realised. Western Europe fails them and they turn to the East. Wells mentions his meetings with Zenovieff and Zorin, gives his opinion of Marx and Marxism, and describes a film of the Baku Con-ference which he sees in Petersburg.

R

528. RACE CONFLICT : IS IT AVOIDABLE ? THE. Westminster Gazette, July 19th, 1924 ; 46th article in *Year of Prophesying.* Urges education as the only way of avoiding irritating race-conflicts (as between America and Japan) and consequent war.

529. RACE IN UTOPIA. 10th chapter in *Modern Utopia.* The "imaginative grasp" of the majority of men is quite inadequate for the task of thinking in terms of the World-State. From this inade-quacy comes the idea of national and racial superiority, the prejudice against so-called inferior races. In a modern Utopia all races would be treated alike, given the same edu-cation, the same laws and the same opportunities. The narrator con-siders alternatives to a world-state.

530. RACE-PREJUDICE. Daily Chronicle, Nov. 21st, 1906 ; In-dependent Magazine, Feb. 14th, 1907. A review of "Race-Pre-judice," by Jean Finot, and "White Capital and Coloured Labour," by Sydney Olivier.

531. RAJAH'S TREASURE, THE. 16th tale in *Thirty Strange Stories.* A slight tale of a rajah who possesses a mysterious treasure, for which he is murdered by his heir and some of his officials. The treasure turns out to be a store of whisky.

531a. RATE OF CHANGE IN SPECIES, THE. Saturday Review, Dec. 15th, 1894. Unsigned. Points out the superior survival capacity of species which breed numerously and with brief generations.

RAMAGE. A stockbroker and proprietor of a financial newspaper, and a neighbour of the Stanleys at Morningside Park. Ann Veronica goes to him for advice after her flight to London. He lends her £40 and tries to make love to her. His wife is an invalid. *Ann Veronica.*

RAMBOAT, MARION. George Pon-derevo's wife. He sees her first in the South Kensington Art Museum, and speaks to her in a 'bus. After the preliminary success of Tono-Bungay they are married, and for a time are happy together. Quarrels become frequent, and she divorces him after his week with Effie Rink at Cromer. With the allowance he gives her she takes a small farm in Sussex, and when that fails goes into partnership with her friend, Smithie. Eventually she marries a Mr. Wachorn and passes out of George's life altogether. *Tono-Bungay.*

532. REAL SOURCE OF THE LABOUR TROUBLE, THE. Daily Mail, Oct. 10th, 1910.

533. REAL THREAT TO CIVILISATION, THE. Daily Mail, Nov. 26th, 1921 ; 14th chapter in *Washington*. Insists upon the fact of the breakdown of civilisation from after-effects of the war. If civilisation is to be saved, the burden of debts must be lifted, and a stable economic system restored.

534. REASONABLE MAN'S PEACE, A. See Bib. No. 64. Wells blames the Allies' statesmen for the prolongation of the war due to lack of any clear statement of their war-aims.

535. RECENT STRUGGLE FOR PROPORTIONAL REPRESENTATION IN GREAT BRITAIN, THE. 10th chapter in *Fourth Year*. Summary of some of the arguments used in a House of Commons debate upon Proportional Representation. Several members of Parliament are quoted and criticised.

536. RECKONING FOR THE WAR, THE. London Magazine, Dec., 1914.

537. RECONCILIATION, THE. See *The Bulla*. 11th tale in *Thirty Strange Stories*. Two men meet after years of enmity caused by a woman and attempt a reconciliation. They get drunk, quarrel again, and Temple attacks and kills Findlater with a whale's bulla (ear-bone).

538. RECONSTRUCTION OF THE FABIAN SOCIETY. See Bib. No. 31.

539. RECONSTRUCTION OF THE LEAGUE OF NATIONS : THE PRACTI-CAL PROBLEM. See *The Practical Problem*. 26th article in *Year of Prophesying*. The League of Nations must be denationalised and reconstructed upon a cosmopolitan basis.

REDCAR, LORD. The greatest of the Four Towns' coal-owners and landlord of most of the district. He is a handsome young man who refuses to be dictated to by a " lot of bally miners " and comes down to the Bantock Burden pit to defy the strikers. Edward Verral is his friend. *Days of the Comet*.

540. REDISCOVERY OF THE UNIQUE, THE. Fortnightly Review, July, 1891. Wells's first important printed essay, and his " first quarrel with the accepted logic." In it he propounds a theory that everything is unique, that " nothing is strictly like anything else," dwelling upon the " fallacy of the common noun " which has led to the disregard of this uniqueness. He applies his theory to number, and to the destruction of the atomic theory and of logic. Finally he applies it to morality : " beings are unique, circumstances are unique, and therefore we cannot think of regulating our conduct by wholesale dicta."

541. RED ROOM, THE. Idler, Mar., 1896, Chapbook (Chicago), in 1896 ; 9th tale in *Plattner Story ;* 16th in *Country of the Blind;* see also Bib. No. 8. The narrator comes to spend a night in the haunted Red Room of Lorraine Castle. He lights the room with several candles and settles down. Presently the candles begin to wink out faster than he can relight them. As the last flame dies he turns to the fire, only to see that sink and go out. Terror seizes him and he rushes to the door, falling down the steps

outside. When he recovers consciousness it is daylight; he tells the three old housekeepers that the room is haunted by Fear.

REDWOOD, PROFESSOR. " One of those scientific men who are addicted to tracings and curves." He, with Mr. Bensington, is the first maker of Herakleophorbia, and the father of the first of the Giant Children. Upon the revolt of the Giants he is arrested and kept in custody for two days; then he is sent to Chislehurst with Caterham's peace terms. Edward Monson Redwood, his son, the first of the Children, is brought up with the three Cossars; he and the Princess of Weser Dreiburg meet and love one another, and when the revolt begins he takes her to the fort at Chislehurst. *Food of the Gods.*

542. RE-EMERGENCE OF MR. LLOYD GEORGE, THE. Westminster Gazette, Dec. 8th, 1923; 13th article in *Year of Prophesying.* An analysis of the mentality of Mr. Lloyd George.

REEVES, ANNA. After the Change she comes to Mrs. Leadford " to daughter her—after our new custom." After Mrs. Leadford's death Anna and William Leadford marry. *Days of the Comet.*

REINHART, HETTY. Peter Stubland's chief girl friend, a beautiful young woman who has a studio in London. Joan detests her and calls her " a dirty little cocotte." Peter is staying with her in Italy when war breaks out. After his marriage to Joan she is mentioned no more. *Joan and Peter.*

RELIGION IS NOT ALTRUISM. See *From a Study Fireside.*

RELEASE OF MAN, THE. John o' London's Weekly, Feb. 28th, Mar. 7th, 14th, 1925, American Magazine, Mar., 1925; reprinted as *The Ten Great Discoveries* (q.v.).

543. RELIGION OF ATHEISTS, THE. 4th chapter of *God the Invisible King.* " It is a curious thing that while most organised religions seem to drape about and conceal and smother the statement of the true God, the honest atheist, with his passionate impulse to strip the truth bare, is constantly and unwittingly reproducing the divine likeness." In support of this opening statement Wells discusses the ideas of, and quotes extensively from works by, Metchnikoff, McCabe, Chalmers Mitchell, Gilbert Murray and Sir Harry Johnston. These writers all advocate devotion to the Service of Man rather than to the Service of God; but without the unifying presence of the True God, the Service of Man seems to Wells " no better than a hobby or a sentimentality."

544. RELIGIOUS REVIVAL, THE. (How People Think About the War, 3). Daily News, Dec. 22nd, 1916; 3rd chapter of *How People Think about the War* (q.v.).

545. REMARKABLE CASE OF DAVIDSON'S EYES, THE. Pall Mall Budget, Mar. 28th, 1895; 11th tale in *Stolen Bacillus;* 7th in *Country of the Blind.* Davidson, stooping between the poles of an electromagnet during a thunderstorm, has " some extraordinary twist given to his retinal elements through the sudden change in the field of force due to the lightning." For three weeks he is blind to the world about

him, but sees an island beach and the sea and a ship which stands off-shore. As he moves about London so he seems to move about the island, which is later identified as a small rock south of Antipodes Island. His vision of the immediate world returns slowly, that of the island fading correspondingly until his sight is normal again.

546. REMINDER ABOUT WAR, A. See *Two Possibilities*. 21st chapter in *Washington*. A word-picture of the next war (between France and England, or America and Japan) which must come if the world will not organise for peace. Deals particularly with the effect of aerial attack upon civilians and upon civilisation.

REMINGTON, ARTHUR. Richard Remington's father, a science master at the Bromstead Institute, a lank-limbed, shabby, untidy man, naturally incompetent but abounding in practical enterprise and possessing a " thoroughly sanguine temperament." He has considerable sympathy with his son, but falls while pruning a grape-vine and breaks his neck when Richard is thirteen years old. *New Machiavelli*.

REMINGTON, MRS. Richard Remington's mother, an intensely religious-minded woman, with fixed and perfectly definite Low-Church ideas, quite unable to understand or tolerate her husband's scepticism. She dies from appendicitis two or three years after her husband's death. *New Machiavelli*.

REMINGTON, MARGARET. Richard Remington's wife, a hard-working, studious girl, slender and graceful, who first meets Remington when

she is twenty. Five years later they meet again at the Baileys' house, and soon after this are married. She is a staunch Liberal and his secession from the Party causes an estrangement. When she learns the full truth of his friendship for Isabel Rivers she is terribly distressed, but almost as much for his pain as for her own. When he leaves her and goes away with Isabel she feels that nothing can console her. *New Machiavelli*.

REMINGTON RICHARD. Whose autobiography is set down in *The New Machiavelli* (q.v.).

547. REMINISCENCE, A. Pall Mall Gazette, Mar. 11th, 1894 ; possibly reprinted as *How I Died* (q.v.).

548. REPORT OF THE SPECIAL COMMITTEE APPOINTED IN FEBRUARY, 1906, TO CONSIDER MEASURES FOR INCREASING THE SCOPE, INFLUENCE, INCOME, AND ACTIVITY OF THE FABIAN SOCIETY. See Bib. II, 1906.

549. RESEARCH MAGNIFICENT, THE. See Bib. No. 58. The story of " a man who was led into an adventure by an idea." William Porphyry Benham is the only child of a Seagate schoolmaster. His mother runs away with Nolan, who dies and leaves a large part of his fortune to her son, whom he feels himself to have wronged. She, divorced, marries Sir Godfrey Marayne, a surgeon. During boyhood, Benham sees his mother only rarely ; while at Cambridge, quite frequently. He is still at school when his idea comes to him, " an almost innate persuasion that he had to live life nobly and thoroughly." While still at school, too, he encounters the first limitation which holds man

P

back from the aristocratic life—
fear. A physical coward, he has to
fight hard all his life to overcome
this limitation. From Cambridge
he comes to London and receives
control of his money. He has
vague ideas of a political career.
Involved in an intrigue with a
widow, Mrs. Skelmersdale, he comes
to a realisation of the second limitation, at first termed Sex, though
later he substitutes the more general
term Indulgence. Awaking suddenly
to the fact of his entanglement, he
goes for a walking tour alone in
Surrey and Sussex. After some
deliberation he comes to the conclusion that he must, before he can
embark upon any career, work out
for himself " a theory of his work
and duty in the world." He decides
to begin by making a tour of the
world. In Sussex he meets Amanda
Morris and falls in love with her.
He returns to London, quarrels with
his mother about his future, sees
Mrs. Skelmersdale for the last time,
and gets ready for his journey. He
sees Amanda to say good-bye and
asks her to marry him. Their
honeymoon, in accordance with his
plans, takes them through Switzerland, the Austrian Tyrol, Northern
Italy, and down the coast to Monte-
negro and Albania. She shows a
complete lack of understanding of
his ideas. He is taken ill and they
return home. For a time he lives in
England, but he knows that he
cannot thus fulfil what he believes
to be his part in life. He visits an
old school and college friend, Prothero, and finds him lost in a pre-
occupation with Sex. Together
they travel through Berlin to War-
saw and Moscow, Benham following
his own lines of thought, Prothero
still deep in his. In Moscow Prothero meets a Russian prostitute,

Anna Alexievna, and then leaves
Benham to return home. The
latter goes on to Kieff, then returns
too to England, where he finds his
wife is very friendly with Sir Philip
Easton ; this brings him to the
third limitation—jealousy. He goes
again to Moscow, where he wit-
nesses a revolution (Jan., 1906),
then travels on south through
Astrakhan, Turkistan and Afghan-
istan to India. There he hears that
Amanda has borne him a son, and
again he comes back to her. She
wishes him to stay with her, but he
will not. Back in the East he
notices a change in the tone of her
letters to him, realises that she has
been unfaithful, and feels that the
woman he loved is dead. He fights
against his jealousy as something
unworthy of an aristocrat, but visits
England without warning and sur-
prises Amanda and her lover Easton.
She pleads successfully against a
divorce and makes one last attempt
to win back her husband, but fails
in this. From then until his death
in 1913 he travels about the world.
During a visit to China, Prothero is
murdered in a gambling den because
Benham (after having sent money
twice previously) refuses to pay his
friend's debts. In his travels he is
brought constantly against the
fourth and greatest limitation—
prejudice. At last Amanda writes
to ask if he will let her divorce him.
He is on his way home to see her
when he meets White, an old school-
friend, in Johannesburg, during the
strike riots of 1913. They talk
together and Benham tells him of
his research magnificent, of his idea
for the government of the world
by a natural aristocracy, and of the
book he is writing. Benham is
killed in an attempt to prevent
soldiers firing on a crowd.

549a. REVIEWERS AGAIN, THE. Adelphi, Aug., 1923 (Contributors' Club). Continuation of *Modern Reviewing*.

REVIEWS. Wells reviewed scientific and educational books fairly regularly for The Saturday Review from Dec., 1894, till Apr., 1897, and fiction almost weekly from Mar., 1895, till 1897. The majority of these criticisms are unsigned ; a few of the more important bear the signature, H. G. Wells. Since 1897 he has contributed occasional reviews to a variety of periodicals ; there may be mentioned as of some special interest one of James Joyce's " Portrait of the Artist as a Young Man " (Nation, Feb. 24th, 1917) ; see also in this Dictionary Nos. 26, 52, 60, 68, 114, 168, 178, 221, 223, 252, 304, 411, 477, 479, 530, 574, 601, 670, 672, 713.

REVIVAL OF THE OLD LEARNING, THE. Westminster Gazette, Feb. 2nd, 1924 ; reprinted as *The Mandarins at the Gate* (q.v.).

550. REVOLUTIONARY SOCIALISM. 11th chapter in *New Worlds*. Considers the Socialism of Karl Marx and his followers, the evil of the " unreasonable fatalism " of the Marxist, and that nobler Anarchism which is the " ultimate ideal of human intercourse."

551. RIDDLE OF THE BRITISH, THE. (How People Think about the War, 4). Daily News, Jan. 5th, 1917 ; reprinted as 4th chapter of *How People Think about the War* (q.v.).

RIDLEY. Lord Barralonga's " small, almost jockey-like chauffeur." He is killed on Quaratine Crag. *Men Like Gods*.

552. RIGHT METHODS IN ELECTIONS, THE. Daily News, Apr. 12th, 1917.

RINK, EFFIE. A typist at the Tono-Bungay offices in Raggett Street. She and George Ponderevo fall passionately in love with one another and spend a week together at Cromer. After Marion has divorced him, George lives with Effie at Orpington for some time. Finally she starts a typewriting bureau, which she runs with " brisk vigour and considerable success." She marries a young poet " because he needed nursing " and George sees her no more. *Tono-Bungay*.

RIVERS, ISABEL. Although only a schoolgirl at the time of the Kinghampstead election, she is one of Remington's keenest workers and has read all his books and other writings. After the election they keep up their friendship, and when she leaves college she comes to London to help with the editing of the " Blue Weekly." They find suddenly that they are in love, and though they make several efforts to break away from one another, end by running away together to Italy. At the time that Remington writes his life-story they have one child. *New Machiavelli*.

RIVERTON. A Young Cambridge graduate, now an officer in the army, who loves Eleanor Scrope. He has to leave suddenly for France and she meets him secretly in Kensington Gardens where, quite by chance, her father comes upon them. *Soul of a Bishop*.

ROYAL SOCIETY FOR THE DISCOURAGEMENT OF LITERATURE, THE.

Which visits and finally swamps the conference on the Mind of the Race. The aim of the Society is " to stop all this thinking." *Boon.*

553. RUINS. (The Western War, 1). Daily Chronicle, Nov. 13th, 1916 ; reprinted as Chapter 1 of *The Western War* (q.v.).

RUMBOLD. The Fishbourne china-dealer and Mr. Polly's neighbour. During the great fire Polly rescues Rumbold's deaf mother-in-law, and the china-dealer breaks the silence of nearly fifteen years to come and thank him. *Mr. Polly.*

RUSPER. The Fishbourne iron-monger, a nervous man with a defect of the palate which " caused a peculiar clinking sound, as though he had something between a giggle and a gas-meter at work in his neck ; " his head is peculiarly egg-shaped. He takes a certain interest in books, and his friendship with Mr. Polly is based on this fact. But their " literary admirations " are quite different, Rusper being full of " large windy ideas " on Modern Thought and the Welfare of the Race. Their friendship ceases altogether after Rusper's marriage and a quarrel which ends in a summons and cross-summons. *Mr. Polly.*

554. RUSSIA AND ENGLAND : A STUDY IN CONTRASTS. Daily News, Feb. 1st, 1914. Written just after Wells's first visit to Russia.

RUSSIA IN COLLAPSE. (Russia in the Shadows, 2). Sunday Express, Nov. 7th, 1920 ; reprinted as *Drift and Salvage* (q.v.).

RUSSIA IN THE SHADOW. (Russia in the Shadows, 1). Sunday Ex-

press, Oct. 31st, 1920 ; reprinted as *Petersburg in Collapse* (q.v.).

RUSSIA IN THE SHADOWS. A series of five articles printed in the Sunday Express weekly from Oct. 31st to Nov. 28th, 1920, and reprinted, mostly under new titles, as the bulk of the volume *Russia in the Shadows.* The titles of the articles are : 1, *Russia in the Shadow* ; 2, *Russia in Collapse ;* 3, *Blundering Bolshevism ;* 4, *Toilers in the Wreckage ;* 5, *The Dreamer in the Kremlin.* See also *Mr. Wells Hits Back.*

555. RUSSIA IN THE SHADOWS. See Bib. No. 71. An account of a fifteen-day visit to Petersburg and Moscow made by H. G. Wells and his elder son in September and October, 1920. The general con-ditions of life in Petersburg, the position of artists and scientists under Bolshevik rule, the character of the Bolshevik Government, its reconstructive efforts, the Peters-burg Soviet—all these are discussed at some length. An interview with Lenin is recorded, also conversations with other Bolshevik leaders. The book is illustrated by thirteen photographs. The chapter-titles are : 1, *Petersburg in Collapse ;* 2, *Drift and Salvage ;* 3, *The Quint-essence of Bolshevism ;* 4, *The Crea-tive Effort in Russia ;* 5, *The Peters-burg Soviet ;* 6, *The Dreamer in the Kremlin ;* 7, *The Envoy.*

S

SAD STORY OF A DRAMATIC CRITIC, THE. New Budget, Aug. 15th, 1895 ; 16th tale in *Plattner Story.* Reprinted as *The Obliterated Man* (q.v.).

SALVAGING OF CIVILISATION, THE.
A series of 7 articles printed in the
Sunday Times, Mar. 27th to May
22nd, 1921 ; reprinted, some under
new titles, as the bulk of the
volume, *The Salvaging of Civilisation.* The original titles are : 1,
Why a World State is Necessary ;
2, *The Enlargement of Patriotism ;*
3, *The World State—An Outline
Sketch ;* 4, *The New Bible ;* 5,
Schooling and the World ; 6, *The
Ideal School ;* 7, *Adult Education.*

555a. SALVAGING OF CIVILISA-
TION, THE. See Bib. No. 72.
Advocates the foundation of a
single world state as the only
effective way of preventing future
wars and the breakdown of civilisation ; suggests a " Bible of Civilisation " to teach common ideas and
ideals to the people of the whole
world, and concludes with an
attempt to solve certain modern
educational difficulties. The chapter-titles are : 1, *The Probable
Future of Mankind ;* 2, *The Project
of a World State ;* 3, *The Enlargement of Patriotism to a World State ;*
4, *The Bible of Civilisation : Part
One ;* 5, *The Bible of Civilisation :
Part Two ;* 6, *The Schooling of the
World ;* 7, *College, Newspaper and
Book ;* 8, *The Envoy. Index.*

556. SAMURAI, THE. 9th chapter
in *Modern Utopia.* The Owner of
the Voice and his Utopian self
discuss the history, constitution,
duties and religion of the order of
the Samurai, the " voluntary nobility " who rule Utopia.

SARGON KING OF KINGS. Collier's
Weekly, Feb. 21st—May, 1925.
Reprinted as *Christina Alberta's
Father* (q.v.).

SARNAC. A physiologist of two
thousand years hence, the friend and

lover of Sunray. He dreams and
then relates to his friends the life
of Harry Mortimer Smith. See
The Dream.

SATCHEL, STELLA SUMMERSLEY.
Companion to Lady Mary Justin,
her " secretary in title," her " moral
guarantor in fact." Her report of
Lady Mary's meeting with Stratton
in Switzerland determines Justin
upon a divorce. *Passionate Friends.*
Later she becomes Lady Harman's
secretary. *Sir Isaac Harman.*

557. SCEPTICISM OF THE INSTRU-
MENT. Mind, July, 1904 ; reprinted with some alterations and
omissions as an appendix to *A
Modern Utopia ;* several passages
are quoted in Book 1 of *First and
Last Things.* Was originally read
to the Oxford Philosophical Society,
Nov. 8th, 1903. Wells outlines
briefly the " particular metaphysical
and philosophical system in which
I do my thinking, and . . . one or
two points in which I seem
myself to differ most widely from
current accepted philosophy."

558. SCHOOLING. 6th chapter in
Mankind. After discussing the
curriculum of the modern school,
it sets forth an improved scheme of
school-work which takes as its
base the statement that the " pressing business of school-work is to
widen the range of intercourse."

559. SCHOOLING OF THE WORLD,
THE. Sunday Times, May 8th,
1921 ; reprinted, with *The Ideal
School* (q.v.) as the 6th chapter of
Salvaging of Civilisation. The world
is under-educated ; Wells outlines
an ideal education for the average
youth, and goes on to consider the
question of the lack of educational
facilities and in particular the
lack of " really inspired and in-

spiring teachers." This last difficulty must be overcome by the "machining of education," the stereotyping of courses. School equipment must be improved and supplemented with libraries of lesson notes, maps, pictures, diagrams, and so on, and cinematograph and gramophone. This standardization of lessons should be accomplished, and the schools of the world run, by some central international organization which could work "cheaply, abundantly, on a big scale."

560. SCHOOLMASTER AND THE EMPIRE, THE. Westminster Gazette, Oct. 21st, 1905 ; 16th essay in *An Englishman*. A criticism of the average master in the upper-class British school. Wells charges him with dullness and lack of originality, vigour or inspiration, and with clinging to out-worn tradition. It is not the schools which are wrong, but the schoolmasters.

561. SCHOOLS OF A NEW AGE : A FORECAST, THE. Westminster Gazette, July 26th, 1924 ; 47th article in *Year of Prophesying*. Education is the world's prime necessity ; in the town of the future the school or university " will be the central architecural fact of the place, the group of buildings about which the homes will cluster."

562. SCIENCE IN EDUCATION AND INDUSTRY. Times, July 17th, 1916; 1st chapter in *Elements of Reconstruction*. Discusses the national neglect of science, taking the dye-question as one example. The British economic system is compared with those of America and Germany, and the necessity for scrapping the old-fashioned methods

of this country is insisted upon ; they must be replaced not by the German methods of twenty years ago, but by those of the future. Scientific research must combine with industry.

563. SCIENCE IN SCHOOL AND AFTER SCHOOL. Nature, Sept. 27th 1894. A criticism of current methods of science-teaching. Letter in reply to comments, Nov. 29th.

564. SCIENCE LIBRARY, SOUTH KENSINGTON, THE. Pall Mall Gazette, May 3rd, 1894.

565. SCIENTIFIC AGRICULTURE AND THE NATION'S FOOD. Times, July 19th, 1916 ; 2nd chapter in *Elements of Reconstruction*. Advocates state syndication without confiscation ; discusses the end of the Socialist movement with its idea of expropriation, and the growth of the idea of nationalisation by amalgamation, and the working of this latter scheme in the case of the food supply of the Empire.

566. SCIENTIFIC WAR. Windsor Magazine, Jan., 1915.

567. SCRAPPING THE GOLD STANDARD. Westminster Gazette, Jan. 19th, 1924 ; 19th article in *Year of Prophesying*. A review of "A Tract on Monetary Reform," by J. M. Keynes. Wells agrees that the gold standard has failed and will pass, but he believes (while Keynes still holds to " Private Capitalism ") that the " system of economics run on the motive of service " advocated by Keynes " is not individualism at all : it is Socialism."

SCROPE, EDWARD. Bishop of Princhester. The only son of a country rector, he is brought up in an atmosphere of faith, and goes straight into the Church from his university. After some years as curate, vicar, and bishop suffragan, he becomes Bishop of Princhester. Earlier in life he marries Lady Ella, they have five daughters, and his home-life is happy and settled. The story of his religious doubtings, his three visions, and his secession from the Church is told in *The Soul of a Bishop* (q.v.).

SCROPE, LADY ELLA. Wife of Edward Scrope, daughter of an earl, a pale-faced, dark-haired woman, grave and kind. Accustomed to help her husband in his public work, she finds she is unpopular in Princhester. Her husband's secession from the Church dismays her : " In one day there had come clamouring upon her, with an effect of revelation after revelation, the idea of drugs, of heresy and blasphemy, of an alien feminine influence, of the entire moral and material breakdown of the man who had been the centre of her life." In the end she acquiesces : " Wither thou goest I will go . . . thy people shall be my people and thy God my God." *Soul of a Bishop.*

SCROPE, ELEANOR. Eldest daughter of Edward Scrope and his wife, educated at Newnham. She finds no comfort in orthodox religion, and supports her father in his secession from the Church, finding that his religion " is after all just the same religion that I have been wanting." At Cambridge she meets Riverton, the brother of a college friend ; they fall in love with one another. Her four sisters are Clementina, Daphne,

Miriam and Phœbe. *Soul of a Bishop.*

SCRYMGEOUR, MRS. HELEN. A " plump, blond little woman " who writes novels. Edward Ponderevo has an " affair " with her after reading " Napoleon and the Fair Sex "—until Aunt Susan hears of it and puts an end to it at once. *Tono-Bungay.*

568. SEA LADY, THE. See Bib. No. 21. The Sea Lady, a mermaid, comes ashore at Sandgate ostensibly to gain a soul (for mermaids have no souls), but in reality to meet Harry Chatteris, with whom she has been in love since she first saw him in the South Seas. She pretends to be drowning and is rescued by the Buntings, who receive her as a guest. She attracts both Chatteris and Melville (another friend of the Buntings and second cousin to the narrator) for there is in her " the quality of the open sky, of deep tangled places, of the flight of birds . . . of the open sea." She tells them that their life is but a dream and that there are better dreams. Under her influence Chatteris neglects his political work and breaks his engagement to Adeline Glendower. Her attraction for him grows and grows until one beautiful moonlit night, " a night out of fairyland," he takes her in his arms out across the white beach, out into the waves, swimming out to sea and to his death.

SEA LADY, THE. A very beautiful mermaid, " born ages and ages ago in some dreadful miraculous way in some terrible place near Cyprus." She is an immortal, born of the elements, and soulless. While with the Buntings she adopts the name of Doris Thalassia Waters. *Sea Lady*.

569. SEA-RAIDERS, THE. Weekly Sun Literary Supplement, Dec. 6th, 1896 ; 7th tale in *Plattner Story;* 13th in *Country of the Blind*. A detailed account of a raid made upon the south coast of England by a species of deep-sea cephalopods.

570. SECOND MAIN GENERALISATION OF SOCIALISM, THE. Grand Magazine, Oct., 1907 ; 4th chapter in *New Worlds*. Argues against private ownership of any but the most personal property, and particularly against private control of the food and fuel supply, so coming to the second main generalisation : " The Socialist holds that the community as a whole should be inalienably the owner and administrator of the land, of raw materials, of values and resources accumulated from the past, and that private property must be of a terminable nature, reverting to the community and subject to the general welfare."

571. SECRET PLACES OF THE HEART, THE. See Bib. No. 76. Sir Richmond Hardy, striving to force his ideas for the world-control of fuel upon the Fuel Commission, is breaking down from overwork. He consults Dr. Martineau, a Harley Street specialist. There are three weeks before the Commission resumes its sittings after Whitsuntide, and the doctor suggests a motoring holiday in south-west England for that period. The two are to travel together and talk things over ; Hardy is to " take stock " of himself, to attempt to get into the " secret places " of his heart. They start from London

in one of Sir Richmond's two cars, but at Taplow he damages it in a fit of temper and they are held up at Maidenhead for two days until the second car is ready for use. Here Hardy relates his sexual history, the story of his married life, his infidelities, and his need for a feminine sexual element in all things. And of the brilliant young artist, Martin Leeds, who has been his mistress now for four years. He tells of his work on the Fuel Commission, and how he turns to women for rest and reassurance. The second car arrives and they go on to Silbury Hill and Avebury. Here their discourse becomes archæological, and they talk of the Mind of the Race in the days of the Heliolithic culture. Next day they reach Stonehenge, where Sir Richmond makes friends with V.V. Grammont, an American girl who is wandering about southern England on her way to meet her father at Falmouth in a few days time. V.V., too, is keenly interested in archæology. Hardy takes her and her companion, Belinda Seyffert, to Salisbury in the car. They dine and spend the evening together. Dr. Martineau does not approve of this new arrangement, and in the morning he leaves the other three to visit a friend in Bournemouth. Hardy and the two women return to Avebury, and for that day the " sustaining topic was this New Age Sir Richmond foreshadowed, this world under scientific control." Next day they go on to Glastonbury and Wells. Hardy and V.V. talk of their work, and she tells him the story of her life, of her love-affair with Caston, an artist, and her engagement to a man she does not love. The next night, in the moonlight at Tintern, they tell their love for one another. That night he lies awake, torn between his new-found love, his work on the Fuel Commission, and Martin Leeds. He decides that he must leave V.V. In the morning, motoring to Bath, V.V. tells him that they must part, that their work for the world must come before everything. They arrange to write to one another of their work. For the rest of the day they talk about the past of the race and of the New Age which is soon to dawn. At Exeter, on the following day, they part, she going to Falmouth, he to Ruan to see Martin. Dr. Martineau hears no more of Sir Richmond until late in the following October, when he appeals to the doctor to patch him up that he may complete his work upon the Commission. A few weeks later this work is done and he collapses with pneumonia. The Majority Report of the Commission is adopted, and three days later Sir Richmond dies in his sleep. Dr. Martineau gives considerable assistance to Lady Hardy, and receives Martin Leeds, who has asked to see her lover's body. She breaks down at the sight, to the doctor's embarrassment.

572. " SECURITY "—THE NEW AND BEAUTIFUL CATCHWORD. Daily Mail, Nov. 21st, 1921 ; 10th chapter in *Washington*. Wells derides the idea of militant security which is pursued by all the powers at the Washington Conference. " The only security for a modern state now is a binding and mutually satisfactory alliance with the power or powers that might otherwise attack."

573. SELECT CONVERSATIONS WITH AN UNCLE (NOW EXTINCT) AND TWO OTHER REMINISCENCES. See Bib. No. 3. A volume of short monologues or " disarticulated essays." The twelve gathered together under the general title of Select Conversations purport to give the opinions of the narrator's uncle, a wealthy, middle-aged Afrikander, upon certain conventions and fashions of the time. Two very slight sketches conclude the volume, and a Prefatory Note introduces the uncle. The Select Conversations are : 1, *Of Conversations and the Anatomy of Fashion ;* 2, *The Theory of the Perpetual Discomfort of Humanity ;* 3, *The Use of Ideals ;* 4, *The Art of Being Photographed ;* 5, *Bagshot's Mural Decorations ;* 6, *On Social Music ;* 7, *The Joys of Being Engaged ;* 8, *La Belle Dame Sans Merci ;* 9, *On a Tricycle ;* 10, *An Unsuspected Masterpiece ;* 11, *The Great Change ;* 12, *The Pains of Marriage.* The " two other reminiscences " are *A Misunderstood Artist* and *The Man With a Nose.*

SELENITES. The lunar inhabitants described in *Men in the Moon.* They are strange insect - like creatures of an average height of five feet, swathed about in garments of leather and a metallic substance. Like ants they have a great variety of forms, " differing in size, differing in the relative size of part to part, differing in power and appearance." They live in vast caverns and passages in the interior of the moon, only the moon-calf guards coming out during the day. Among those mentioned by name are the Grand Lunar, Phi-oo, and Tsi-puff.

574. SEQUENCE OF STUDIES, THE. Nature, Dec. 27th, 1894. Review of three books on physiology,

biology, and microscopy respectively.

**575. SERFDOM OF IGNORANCE :
THE RIGHT OF WOMEN TO KNOW-
LEDGE, THE.** Westminster Gazette,
June 7th, 1924 ; 40th article in
Year of Prophesying. Urges the
right of all women, poor as well
as rich, to a full knowledge of their
own bodies and of sexual hygiene.

**SEX ANTAGONISM : AN UN-
AVOIDABLE AND INCREASING FACTOR
IN MODERN LIFE.** 52nd article in
Year of Prophesying ; see *The An-
tagonism of Sex.*

SEYFFERT, BELINDA. A " sort
of companion " to V.V. Grammont.
She is a short, plump, unattractive
young woman from Philadelphia.
Dr. Martineau detests her. *Secret
Places.*

**576. SHABBY SCHOOLS OF THE
PIOUS : DRAINS AND THE ODOUR
OF SANCTITY, THE.** Westminster
Gazette, June 28th, 1924 ; 43rd
article in *Year of Prophesying.* A
criticism of the " denominational
schools " of England, many of
which are " in an advanced state
of decay."

577. SHADOW ON THE EARTH. A.
Daily Express, Dec. 12th, 1921 ;
25th chapter in *Washington.* Following a visit to the Washington Correspondence Club for negroes, Wells
considers the problem of the negro
race and the administration of
Central Africa. He advocates international control, the abandon-
ment of military training for negroes, and the development of
education.

SHALFORD, EDWIN. Proprietor
of the Folkestone Drapery Bazaar,
where Kipps is apprenticed. He is
an irascible little man with a great
belief in the efficacy of " Fishency "
and " System." *Kipps.*

SHARPSER, SUSAN. A lady novelist, a friend of Lady Beach-Mandarin, who takes her to call on
Lady Harman. She seems to be
continually " pecking observations
out of life as a hen pecks seeds
amidst scenery." *Sir Isaac Harman.* Also appears in *Mr. Britling* and *Soul of a Bishop.*

SHELDRICKS, THE. Neighbours
of the Stublands at Limpsfield. Mr.
Sheldrick is a " large, loose painter
man held together by a very hairy
tweed suit." Finally, his suit worn
out, he " goes to pieces altogether "
and dies. He has a " small facetious " wife who moves to London
after his death and writes reviews
and verse ; her house forms a centre
for a large circle of friends, among
whom are Joan and Peter. Three
daughters mentioned by name are
Antonia, Babs, who goes on the
stage, and Sydney. During the
war they all become pacifists. *Joan
and Peter.*

SHOESMITH, ARNOLD. One of
Remington's school friends ; they
meet in later life. Shoesmith,
knowing of Remington's relations
with Isabel Rivers, wishes to marry
her, and to prevent scandal it is
arranged that he shall do so. But
almost at the last moment Remington and Isabel run away together.
New Machiavelli.

578. SHOPMAN, THE. Pall Mall
Gazette, Nov. 23rd, 1894 ; 17th
essay in *Personal Matters.* The narrator, who finds shopping the
" most exasperating of all the
many trying duties of life," des-

cribes a typical visit to an out-
fitter to purchase a pair of gloves.
He ends with the query : " Is
killing a salesman murder, like
killing a human being ? "

579. SHORT HISTORY OF THE
WORLD, A. See Bib. No. 77. In
a brief preface Wells states that the
" especial end " of this book " is
to meet the needs of the busy
general reader, too driven to study
the maps and time charts of " *The
Outline of History* " in detail, who
wishes to refresh and repair his
faded or fragmentary conceptions
of the great adventure of mankind.
It is not an abstract or condensation of that former work."

580. SHOULD HISTORY BE
TAUGHT ON A NATIONAL OR INTER-
NATIONAL BASIS ? See Bib. II,
1923. Wells's affirmative answer
to this question repeats arguments
used in earlier discussions.

SINGAPORE ARSENAL, THE. 4th
article in *Year of Prophesying ;*
reprinted from *The Fifteen-Year-
Old Mr. Amery* (q.v.).

581. SIX GREATEST MEN IN HIS-
TORY, THE. Strand Mag., Sept.
Oct., Nov., 1920. This discussion,
contributed to by Zangwill, Lodge,
Walkley, Hewlett, Shaw, Hall Caine,
Clodd, Lord Riddell, and Chester-
ton, was started by an interview
with Wells by Bruce Barton in the
Sept. No., and continued in the
two following months. Wells's only
written contribution was a half-
page note at the very end, *H. G.
Wells Sums Up.* The men chosen
by Wells were Gautama Buddha,
Christ, Aristotle, Asoka, Roger
Bacon, Lincoln.

SKELMERSDALE, MILLY.   A
" pretty little widow " who meets
Benham in London. She talks
to him, takes him to concerts,
and is sympathetic. Almost sur-
prisingly he realises one day how
intimate they are, that she is
his mistress. At last, during his
walk through Sussex, he decides to
see her no more. *Research Magnificent.*

SKINNER, MR. AND MRS. ALFRED
NEWTON. The " extremely dirty "
couple engaged by Mr. Bensington
to manage the Experimental Farm
at Hickleybrow. He is a large-
faced man " with a lisp and a
squint . . . slashed slippers . . . and
a manifest shortness of buttons."
She is " a very little old woman,
with . . . a face which was . . .
almost exclusively nose." There is
a mystery and a considerable doubt
about Mr. Skinner's death ; Mrs.
Skinner leaves the Farm and goes
to live with her daughter (a Mrs.
Caddles) at Cheasing Eyebright,
taking with her a tin of Herakleophorbia. *Food of the Gods.*

582. SLEEPER AWAKES, THE. See
Bib. No. 15a.

583. SLIP UNDER THE MICRO-
SCOPE, A. Yellow Book ; 17th
tale in *Plattner Story ;* 18th in
Country of the Blind. Hill, a
cobbler's son and a scholarship
student at the College of Science,
is in love with Miss Haysman, a
paying student. In the first examination he heads the list with
Wedderburn, another paying student and his rival for the favour of
Miss Haysman. During the second
examination Hill moves a slip
purely by accident, and so identi-
fies an object. It has been most

strictly ordered that the slip must not be touched, so, knowing that he has not been observed, he says nothing. He comes out head of his class. Later he tells everything to a professor, is disqualified and has to leave the college. The last sentences of the story make it clear that Wedderburn too has moved the slip and that perhaps Miss Haysman cared more for Hill than he had suspected.

SMALLWAYS, ALBERT PETER. The hero of *The War in the Air* (q.v.), a " progressive Smallways " and one of Wells's typical Cockney characters. His elder brother, Tom, is a Bun Hill greengrocer.

SMITH, ERNEST. The eldest of the Smith children ; he works at a London garage, driving hired cars. *Dream.*

SMITH, FANNY. The elder of the Smith girls, and Harry's favourite sister. She is " a very pretty girl, with a white face from which her brown hair went back in graceful, natural waves and curls, and she had very dark blue eyes." She is a " voracious reader of novels " and tries to make Harry speak correctly. Her employer, a pork butcher, wants to marry her. She runs away with Newberry, who gives her the education and the luxury she longs for ; they are very happy together. It is through her influence that Harry finds work at Thunderstone House, and after their re-union she helps him with his education. Later she assists him to get Hetty away from Sumner. *Dream.*

SMITH, HENRY MORTIMER. The " I " of Sarnac's dream, the young-

est of the four Smith children. See *The Dream.*

SMITH, MRS. MARTHA. Harry's mother, a miserable, narrow-minded woman, the product of her environment. She never forgives Fanny for her " sin " nor understands Harry's desire for education. *Dream.*

SMITH, MORTIMER. Harry's father, a Cherry Gardens greengrocer, who adds to his income by selling produce stolen from Lord Bramble's garden by John Julip. He is a weak, unenterprising, uneducated man with a certain faith in an incomprehensible Providence. (" Providence is as deep as E is I, and you can't get be'ind 'im ") ; when things go wrong he takes to drink, and is eventually knocked down by a motor-car and killed. *Dream.*

SMITH, Prudence. Harry's younger sister, a vague but unpleasant personality. She remains in the mind chiefly as a sneak and petty thief. *Dream.*

SMITHERS. A student with Lewisham at the Normal School of Science. He is sceptical of the genuineness of spiritualistic manifestations and has many arguments with Lagune (q.v.), who invites him to take part in a séance. At this séance Smithers, with Lewisham's assistance, exposes Chaffery as a fraud. *Mr. Lewisham.*

SMITHIE. Marion Ramboat's greatest friend, " a thin, bright-eyed, hawk-nosed girl of thirty-odd." She runs a gown-shop, and after the Ponderevos' divorce Marion goes into partnership with her. *Tono-Bungay.*

SNOOKS, E. K. A very polite young schoolmaster who travels to Rome in the same party as Miss Winchelsea and her friends. He helps them with their luggage and meets them several times in Rome. When he asks Miss Winchelsea to marry him she refuses because of his name. A little later he marries her friend Fanny and changes his name to Sevenoaks. *Miss Winchelsea's Heart.*

584. SO-CALLED SCIENCE FO SOCIOLOGY, THE. Independent Review, May, 1906 ; Littell's Living Age, July, 1906 ; 14th essay in *An Englishman;* see also Bib. II, 1907. Originally read before The Sociological Society on Feb. 28th, 1906. Denies that sociology is a science at all, and criticises the work of those "modern idols," Comte and Spencer. " The uniqueness of individuals is the objective truth." " Sociology must be neither art simply, nor science in the narrow meaning of the word at all, but knowledge rendered imaginatively and with an element of personality, that is to say, in the highest sense of the term, literature." There are two literary forms through which valid sociological work may be carried on ; first, the social side of history, and second, smaller in bulk and " altogether under-rated and neglected," the creation and criticism of Utopias.

585. SOCIAL CHANGES IN PROGRESS, THE. (How People Think about the War, 5). Daily News, Jan. 12th, 1917 ; reprinted with *Labour After the War,* as chapter 5 of *How People Think About the War* (q.v.).

SOCIAL CONDITIONS AND THE SOCIAL FUTURE IN THE UNITED STATES OF AMERICA. First printed in " Harmsworth's Popular Educator " about 1909 ; reprinted as *The American Population* (q.v.).

SOCIAL FORCES IN ENGLAND AND AMERICA. Title of the American edition of *An Englishman* (see Bib. No. 50).

586. SOCIALISM A DEVELOPING DOCTRINE. 10th chapter in *New Worlds.* Traces the growth of Socialism from its beginnings through the early pre-Marxian period.

587. SOCIALISM AND FREE LOVE. THE RELATIONS OF THE STATE AND THE CHILD. Manchester Guardian, Oct. 10th, 1906.

588. SOCIALISM AND POLITICS. Socialist Review, June, 1908.

SOCIALISM AND THE BUSINESS WORLD. Letter to Magazine of Commerce, Aug., 1907 ; reprinted in *The Middle-Class Man, the Business Man, and Socialism* (q.v.).

589. SOCIALISM AND THE FAMILY. See Bib. No. 30. The first of these two papers defines and discusses the relationship between Socialism and the Socialist movement and the middle classes, " three distinct things," with special reference to the present position of the Family as the unit of contemporary civilisation. The second and shorter paper refutes " the charge that Socialism tends to Free Love." Together they state " pretty completely the attitude of Modern Socialism to family life."

SOCIALISM AND THE GREAT STATE.
See Bib. No. 44, note to collation.

SOCIALISM AND THE MIDDLE
CLASSES. Fortnightly Review,
Nov., 1906 ; 1st paper in *Socialism
and the Family* (q.v.). Originally
read to the Fabian Society in
Oct., 1906.

590. SOCIALISM AND THE SCIEN-
TIFIC MOTIVE. See Bib. No. 81.
A survey of some main political
questions, concluding : The Labour
Party " recognises the need of an
educated community led by its
teachers. It sees in such men, and
not in the wealth gatherers, the
aristocracy of the new world."

591. SOCIAL PANACEAS. See *The
Craving for One Simple Cheap
Remedy.* Part of the 6th essay,
The Labour Unrest, in *An Englishman.* To-day there is a great
outcry for simple panaceas, for
some easy solution of national
difficulties. People wish for an
oligarchy, an autocracy ; Wells
protests against these foolish hopes.
Everyman, he says, is the only
saviour of the state. He protests
also against the idea that education
has failed. There are no easy
social panaceas ; the people must
save themselves by thinking for
themselves, by clarifying their ideas,
until they can bring the Great State
into being of themselves.

592. SOLDIERS' MESSAGE, THE.
Daily Mail, Jan. 4th, 1918.

SOLOMONSON, SIR RUPERT. A
friend of Trafford, and owner of the
aeroplane which crashes on the
Buryhamstreet Vicarage lawn. He
is a " square-rigged Jew, with not
so much a bullet-head as a round-

shot, cropped close." A rich financier, his definition of business is
" keeping something from some-
body else, and making him pay
for it." He persuades Trafford
to let him market his synthetic
rubber, thus enriching both of them.
Lady Solomonson, whom Trafford
and Marjorie meet at Vevey, is
" an extremely expensive-looking
fair lady with an affectation of
cynicism, . . . and a queer effect
of thinking of something else all
the time she was talking." *Marriage.*

593. SOME ARGUMENTS *Ad
Hominem.* See *Every Day Life in
a Socialist State.* 14th chapter in
New Worlds. A brief description
of life as it would be in a Socialist
State, taking particularly the cases
of the teacher, the business man,
the farmer, the medical man, the
artist, the servant, the average man,
the now wealthy man, and concluding with a note upon patriotism
in the World State.

594. SOME ASPECTS OF AMERICAN
WEALTH. 5th chapter in *Future
in America.* Discusses the American millionaire both as " spender "
and philanthropist, and, while admitting a certain truth in some
cases, refutes the " preposterous accusations " sometimes made
against them.

595. SOME COMMON OBJECTIONS
TO SOCIALISM. Grand Magazine,
Mar., 1908 ; 9th chapter in *New
Worlds.* Considers and answers,
briefly, the more common objections
to Socialism—that it abolishes property and the family, that it is
contrary to Christianity, that it
destroys individual freedom and
crushes Art, Invention, and Literature.

596. SOME FINE WORDS AND BAD PASSPORTS. Westminster Gazette, Dec. 29th, 1923; reprinted as *Cosmopolitan and International* (q.v.) Protests against the present nationalist organization of the world, taking as one illustration of its effect the thousand inconveniences (of passports, change of money, customs, etc.), which the world-traveller, the "cosmopolitan," has to suffer.

597. SOME LIBERAL IDEALS. General title of three articles printed in Daily Chronicle, Sept. 18th, 25th, and Oct. 2nd, 1916. The particular titles are: 1, *Free Trade is Peace: Tariffs are War;* 2, *Nationalism and Nationality;* 3, *The Idea of Allied Combines.*

598. SOME PERSONAL THINGS. Book 4 of *First and Last Things.* Wells sees personal love as a synthetic thing, the "individualised correlative of Salvation." In writing of Love and Death he recalls certain friends who have died—R. A. M. Stevenson, W. E. Henley, York Powell. He concludes with the words: "In the last resort I do not care whether I am seated on a throne or drunk and dying in a gutter. I follow my leading. In the ultimate I know, though I cannot prove my knowledge in any way whatever, that everything is right and all things mine."

599. SOME POSSIBLE DISCOVERIES. 25th essay in *An Englishman.* Wells believes that for many years there will be few if any sensational discoveries in mechanical science. He suggests that the astonishing achievements will come rather in the sphere of medical research, in the enhancing of the individual

effectiveness of the human body and mind. The suggestions of Dr. Metchnikoff are mentioned. Wells prophecies man's increasing control over himself, and a development of philosophical and scientific method.

600. SOME STIFLED VOICES. See *Intruders at Washington.* 22nd chapter in *Washington.* Considers certain side issues at the Conference, the presence of unofficial delegates from Corea, India, Syria, China, and deals generally with the question of the political suppression of persons and peoples. These things Wells regards as incidental to the present world system. Establish world-peace, and the "black sins against civilisation" will vanish. He advocates the complete freedom of China from foreign intervention.

601. SOMETHING GOOD FROM BIRMINGHAM. Science Schools Journal, Apr., 1889. A review of "Comus," a contemporary Birmingham magazine of art and literature. 200 words. Signed H.G.W.

602. SOUL OF A BISHOP, THE. See Bib. No. 65. Edward Scrope is Bishop of Princhester, a diocese in the heart of industrial England. From childhood, at school and university, as curate, vicar, bishop suffragan and bishop, he lives in an atmosphere of faith and never thinks of doubting his religion. In 1911 and the following years he is worried by industrial troubles. 1913 brings suffragette violence and three ecclesiastical scandals in his diocese. Doctrinal doubts begin to worry him, and despite the use of drugs he suffers from insomnia. With the outbreak of war in 1914

he recovers for a time, but the feeling of futility returns. After a sleepless night following a theological argument, he goes to London to consult his physician, Dr. Brighton-Pomfrey. But the doctor has been called away to France, his place being taken for the time being by Dr. Dale, a young man with modern ideas. He gives the Bishop a tonic under the influence of which Scrope has the first and second visions, in which he sees God and talks with the Angel of God. After the First Vision he calls on Lady Sunderbund, an American widow, and tells her something of his new ideas and beliefs. She comes to Princhester to try and help him, thereby arousing the jealousy of Lady Ella, the Bishop's wife. With a second dose of the tonic he experiences the Second Vision, in which the Angel of God shows him the world awakening to a realisation of God. His wife finds him in a trance and throws the rest of the liquid away. That day he preaches at a confirmation service in Princhester Cathedral; a vision of the imminence of God comes to him. He comes down from the pulpit with the realisation that he can never minister in the Church again, and after a short holiday with Eleanor, his eldest daughter, he leaves the Church. Some months later he tries to find Dr. Dale again, only to learn that he is dead and that the secret of the tonic died with him. The Scrope family comes to live at Notting Hill. Lady Sunderbund wishes to build an ornate temple from which Scrope may proclaim his new faith, but he finds her schemes impossible, much to the relief of Lady Ella. He goes for a walk one day in Kensington Gardens; there he sees Eleanor who has come down from Cambridge to meet Riverton, a young officer with whom she is in love. After a talk they leave him and as he sits there the Third Vision comes to him, strengthening his faith. Returning home he tells his family why he left the Church, and they tell him that they know that he has done what is right. Yet he feels that they are not really thinking for themselves but only following him as the head of the family.

603. SPAIN AND ITALY WHISPER TOGETHER. Westminster Gazette, Dec. 15th, 1923; 14th article in *Year of Prophesying*. The " Black French Policy " is bringing Latin Europe together in a protective alliance. Wells speculates upon the future effects of this alliance.

SPECIAL TRAIN TO BALE, THE. In *The Mind of the Race* (q.v.). Travellers by this train mentioned (in most cases with some characteristic comment) are : Mary Austin, Barrie, Clutton Brock, Rupert Brooke, R. S. Bourne, Maurice Baring, Belloc, A. C. Benson, Marie Corelli, G. K. and Cecil Chesterton, F. S. Flint, Philip Guedalla, Denis Garstin, Cunninghame Graham, Ford Madox Hueffer, Hardy, Hewlett, James Joyce, R. W. Kauffman, D. H. Lawrence, Robert Lynd, Leonard Merrick, Viola Meynell, Rose Macaulay, James Milne, Compton Mackenzie, Katherine Mansfield, Marmaduke Pickthall, G. B. and Mrs. Shaw, St. John Ervine, James Stephens, Dixon Scott, Clement Shorter, Upton Sinclair, H. M. Tomlinson, Hugh Walpole, and Geoffrey Young.

604. SPECTACLE OF PLEASURE, THE. (The Labour Unrest, 3).

Daily Mail, May 15th, 1912 ; see *The Labour Unrest.*

SPEECHES. The speeches of H. G. Wells have been comparatively very infrequent. The most important, apart from those included in the Dictionary under Nos. 98, 124, 179, 557, 584, 589, 593, and 646, will be found in Bib. II. (see *Shakespeare Day,* 1917 ; *Report 1916 to 1918, &c.* 1919 ; and *The University of London,* 1922). Reference may be made to a very full report of a speech made at the Milton Hall, Manchester, on Nov. 7th, 1922 (*Why Mr. Wells is a Labour Man,* Manchester Guardian, Nov. 8th, 1922) : to a speech made before the Petersburg Soviet on Oct. 7th, 1920, and printed verbatim (in Russian) in the next issue of Pravda : and to another speech, *Teachers, Labour, and the Commonweal,* reported at length in the Labour Magazine, Dec., 1923.

605. SPIRIT OF FASCISM : IS THERE ANY GOOD IN IT AT ALL ? THE. Westminster Gazette, July 12th, 1924 ; 45th article in *Year of Prophesying.* Commenting on the murder of Signor Matteotti, Wells states his conviction that in Education lies the only remedy for the destructive, terrorist spirit of Facism—and of Communism too. " Only as that develops will the vehement self-righteous and malignant ass abate his mischiefs in the world."

606. SPIRIT OF GAIN AND THE SPIRIT OF SERVICE, THE. Grand Magazine, Nov., 1907 ; 5th chapter in *New Worlds.* Wells refutes the charge that the spirit of gain is the strongest trait in human nature, but shows that under present circumstances a man is forced to consider the motive of gain in the greater proportion of his actions. The Socialist does not wish to abolish all competition, but only certain forms of it, the eradication of which will leave men free to compete for fame, love and honour.

607. SPOILS OF MR. BLANDISH, THE. See *The Mind of the Race.* A novel " rather in the manner of Henry James " sketched out by George Boon and told to his friends. Mr. Blandish, who is " the very soul of Henry James," buys Samphire House and settles down in it. An atmosphere of mystery hangs over the place : his friends, his " Early Georgian " butler, and his gardener all behave in an unaccountable way. At last Mr. Blandish discovers the secret, a hoard of 1813 brandy, bricked up in an unused cellar. He makes arrangements for selling it and then approaches the cellar, only to find the last drop gone, and Mutimer, the butler, lying " dead, or at least helpless," upon the floor.

STANLEY, ANN VERONICA. The fifth and youngest child of Mr. Peter Stanley, and the heroine of *Ann Veronica.* She is a good-looking girl, fine-featured, with an " acute sense of form and unusual mental lucidity " . . . " vehemently impatient . . . to do, to be, to experience." Her sisters, Alice and Gwendolen, are both married ; her brothers, Jim and Roddy, do not live at home. Ann Veronica is mentioned in *Marriage* as Mrs. Godwin Capes, " a dark-eyed, quiet-mannered . . . woman of impulsive speech and long silences, who had subsided from an early romance

Q

(Capes had been divorced for her while she was still a mere girl) into a markedly correct and exclusive mother of daughters."

STANLEY, MOLLIE. Peter Stanley's sister, who comes to Morningside Park as his housekeeper after the death of Ann Veronica's mother. She carries herself with a "certain aristocratic dignity . . . acquired through her long engagement to a curate of family." *Ann Veronica.*

STANLEY, PETER. Ann Veronica's father, a London solicitor; he is "a lean, trustworthy, worried-looking, neuralgic, clean-shaven man of fifty-three," a worthy Englishman of a rather stupid type, with strict and jealous ideas concerning the freedoms of daughters.

608. S T A R, T H E. Graphic Christmas No., 1897 ; 2nd story in *Tales of Space ;* 20th in *Country of the Blind ;* 2nd in *Door in the Wall ;* see also Bib. No. 16a. Describes the invasion of this solar system, early in the 20th Century, by a strange star from the deeps of space. This star collides with Neptune, and the two bodies, locked in one flaming mass, fall sunward. Their course is deflected by Jupiter, and earth and star come so close together that they swing about one another before the star continues its sunward flight. Fire, earthquake, tempest, flood, death and destruction unimaginable shake the earth, and after the passing of the star the men who survive find that the earth is hotter, the sun larger, the moon smaller. The story ends with a note upon the occurrence by a Martian astronomer.

609. STATE BABIES. (Utopianisms, 3). Daily Mail, Apr. 20th, 1905.

610. STATE - BLINDNESS. 9th chapter in *Future in America.* Discussing the "mental quality of America," Wells comments upon the average American's lack of any "sense of the state." He illustrates his point by extensive quotations from and comments on a book by J. Morgan Richards. Concludes with an account of a visit to Oneida.

STELLA, LADY. A "very great lady of the modern type," one of the party which enters Utopia in Catskill's car. She survives the catastrophe at Quarantine Crag. *Men Like Gods.*

611. STINKS. Daily Mail, Dec. 28th, 1897.

612. STOLEN BACILLUS, THE. Pall Mall Budget, June 21st, 1894 ; 1st tale in *Stolen Bacillus ;* 3rd in *Country of the Blind ;* also in Pearson's Magazine, June, 1905. A bacteriologist, wishing to impress a visitor, shows him a sealed glass tube and tells him that it contains living cholera bacteria. The visitor, who is an anarchist, steals the tube. He is pursued by the bacteriologist, the latter by his wife, she bringing the shoes, hat and so on which he has forgotten in his haste. An exciting cab-chase follows. It is brought to an end by the accidental smashing of the tube ; the anarchist swallows its contents, defies his pursuer, and walks away. The bacteriologist explains to his wife that the tube contained a cultivation of a new species of bacterium which causes the blue patches on certain monkeys.

613. STOLEN BACILLUS AND OTHER INCIDENTS, THE. See Bib. No. 6.

614. STOLEN BODY, THE. Strand Magazine, Nov., 1898; 10th tale in *Twelve Stories*. Mr. Bessel, an elderly business man, conducts a series of experiments with a friend to test the possibility of " projecting an apparition of oneself by force of will through space." After several attempts he succeeds in leaving his body and wanders across London through a strange spirit world to appear before his friend, Mr. Vincey. He returns to his body to find that an evil spirit has taken possession of it in his absence. For some hours this evil spirit rages up and down the London streets, smashing and destroying, at last to fall into a deserted shaft, breaking several ribs and limbs. Mr. Bessel is able to send a message to his friend through a medium, and then to re-enter his body, vacated by the evil spirit after the fall. He is rescued by his friends.

615. STORY OF A GREAT SCHOOL-MASTER, THE. See Bib. No. 85. This brief biography of the late F. W. Sanderson gives, in eight chapters, an impression of his personality and a summary of his life-work, to tell which " is to reflect upon all the main educational ideas of the last half-century." The first chapter is mainly personal; the second and third deal with his early years at Oundle and the gradual changes effected by his conception of group work rather than competition as an incentive to learning. The growth of his ideas is traced in quotations from sermons and addresses, and chapter six discusses the way in which the war turned him " from a successful schoolmaster into an amateur statesman," vitally concerned with education as a solution of the world's difficulties. The seventh chapter deals with his unfinished House of Vision, while the last quotes his final lecture practically in full and relates the circumstances of his tragic death.

616. STORY OF THE DAYS TO COME, A. Pall Mall Magazine, about 1897; 4th story in *Tales of Space*. Elizabeth Mwres, the only daughter of a prosperous business man of the 22nd century, is in love with Denton, a flying-stage attendant. Her father, wishing her to marry his friend Bindon, puts difficulties in her way, but she leaves home and with Denton runs away into the country. In all England now there are but four cities; for the rest—lonely countrysides visited only by the servants of the Food Company. In a very few days they return to London, where they live in comfort for the next few years on her money. Their resources fail and he has to find work, but so unsuccessfully that they are forced to accept the degradation of the Labour Company's uniform. There follow unhappiness, discomfort, sorrow; they are forced into surroundings which disgust them, and their little daughter dies. They give up all hope; it even seems that they must be parted. Then Bindon dies, leaving all his wealth to Elizabeth, thereby restoring the couple to happiness. London, the life of the people, the civilisation generally, are similar to those described in *When the Sleeper Wakes*.

617. STORY OF THE INEXPERI-ENCED GHOST, THE. Strand Magazine, Mar., 1902.; 6th tale in *Twelve Stories*. Clayton, sleeping at an old inn, meets the ghost of a London schoolmaster, who, after making himself visible that he may " haunt," has forgotten the passes by which he may return to the ghost-world. At last, with Clayton's help, he remembers and vanishes. The following evening Clayton relates his experience to a circle of sceptical friends, and repeats the gestures used by the ghost. For a moment he stands with outflung arms, then his face changes and he falls forward dead. See also Bib. II, 1902.

618. STORY OF THE LAST TRUMP, THE. See *Boon.* A little child, playing in an attic in Heaven, finds the trumpet of Judgment Day and drops it over the battlements on to the earth. Eventually it turns up in a small second-hand shop. Two young men, attempting to sound it as the result of a bet, attach it to a powerful foot blow-pipe. . . . There is a sudden sound cut short, a flash, and a hand and arm of fire smites down to seize the trumpet ; for an instant all over the world God and his angels are seen in the sky. Mr. Parchester, a West End rector, is struck with a sudden realisation of the presence of God, and rushes out into the street, telling people that the Kingdom of Heaven is at hand. No one pays any attention to him, and his Bishop advises him to see a doctor. At last he returns home, his vision gone, his realisation lost.

619. STORY OF THE LATE MR. ELVESHAM, THE. Idler, May, 1896 ; 3rd tale in *Plattner Story ;* 11th in *Country of the Blind.* Elvesham, a great philosopher and a rich man, tells Eden, a London medical student, that he wants to make him his heir. He assures himself of the young man's perfect health, and then at a dinner of celebration gives him a powder in a glass of wine. After a confused night Eden wakes to find himself in Elvesham's bed—in Elvesham's body ! The aged philosopher, knowing that death cannot be very far away, has found a means by which he may change bodies with Eden, transferring all his personality and knowledge to that of the younger man. When Eden tells what has happened, he is deemed to be insane, and in desperation commits suicide. As it happens, Elvesham is already dead, having been knocked down and killed at a crowded crossing.

620. STORY OF THE STAMPS, THE. Pall Mall Gazette, Aug. 24th, 1894.

621. STORY OF THE STONE AGE, A. Idler, May-Sept., 1897 ; 3rd story in *Tales of Space.* Ugh-lomi and Eudena, flying from their tribe and the persecution of the chief, Uya, make their home together on a cliff. Ugh-lomi returns and kills his enemy, bringing back to Eudena the necklace of the chief's wife. They are attacked by a cave bear, which they kill by rolling a stone down a cliff upon him. Later Ugh-lomi gets astride a horse, which gallops away and throws him off near the home of the Sons of Uya, who call to him that their dead chief has returned to them in the form of a lion. Again he returns to Eudena, but a few days later she is carried off by the tribe as a sacrifice to the lion. Ugh-lomi follows and is terribly injured in the killing of the great beast. For many days he lies unable to move, fed by the faithful Eudena. They are discovered by the tribe but rout their attackers, Ugh-lomi thus making himself chief in succession to Uya.

STRATTON, STEPHEN. Whose autobiography forms the matter of *The Passionate Friends*. It is to his son Stephen that the book is addressed, that the boy as he grows up may have some understanding of his father and of the things in life which he will have to face.

622. STRAY THOUGHTS IN AN OMNIBUS. Black and White, Aug. 4th, 1894.

STUART, NETTIE. Elder daughter of Mrs. Verral's head gardener, vaguely related to the Leadfords. She and William Leadford " had kissed and become sweethearts before we were eighteen years old." When she runs away with Edward Verral, Leadford follows them to Shaphambury, meaning to kill them both. See *In the Days of the Comet*.

STUBLAND, ARTHUR. Peter's father, a good-looking young man with a fine profile, though Oswald Sydenham remembers him as " a blonde sort of ass with a tenor voice who punched copper "--that, with book-binding and poster-collecting, being his chief occupation. He and his wife Dolly make wills appointing Oswald sole guardian of both Peter and Joan, but later Arthur alters his secretly to make his two sisters and Lady Charlotte Sydenham guardians with him. He is unfaithful to his wife; she discovers

this, but they are reconciled and go to Italy together, where they are drowned. *Joan and Peter*.

STUBLAND, DOLLY. Arthur's wife, daughter of George Sydenham, vicar of Long Downport. Soon after her discovery of her husband's unfaithfulness, her cousin, Oswald Sydenham, asks her to run away to Africa with him, but she refuses and goes to Italy with Arthur. *Joan and Peter*.

STUBLAND, PETER. The only child of Arthur and Dolly, born in the summer of 1893. The novel, *Joan and Peter*, is very largely the story of his life.

STUBLAND, PHŒBE AND PHYLLIS. Arthur's two sisters who have practically full control of Peter and Joan for several years after the death of his parents. They are both ardent femininists and educationists, and participate in " the Stubland break back to colour," dressing in pre-Raphaelite styles. Phœbe is author of several volumes of essays and poems; she also edits a monthly paper and is a militant suffragette. *Joan and Peter*.

623. STUDY AND PROPAGANDA OF DEMOCRACY, THE. 11th and last chapter of *Fourth Year;* last two paragraphs reprinted as *The Propaganda of the League* (q.v.). Wells holds that the study and propaganda of democracy and of the League of Free Nations is the " duty of every school-teacher, every tutor, every religious teacher, every writer, every lecturer, every parent, every trusted friend throughout the world."

624. STUDY OF SIX, A. See Bib. II, 1907. The " six " are Burns,

Keir Hardie, Shaw, Webb, Hyndman, and " Me."

625. SUBTLE EXAMINEE, THE. University Correspondent, Apr. 15th, 1891.

626. SUGGESTION FOR PENALISING GERMANY'S COMMERCE, A. (Looking Ahead). Daily Chronicle, Feb. 1st, 1915. With the coming of peace and the resumption of trade, the devastated industrial areas of France, Belgium and Poland will be unable to compete with the undamaged industrial areas of Germany. Wells suggests that Great Britain should form a customs alliance with her allies, and " set up a tariff against German goods in Great Britain, in all our Empire, and in the Empires of our Allies." Such an alliance would not only protect the Allies at the end of the war ; it would decrease Germany's borrowing power and thus bring nearer the day of her defeat.

SUMNER, FRED. A soldier who seduces Hetty, Harry Smith's first wife ; the one child born to her is his. After she has been divorced he marries her, gambles away all his and her money, and joins a racing gang which blackmails bookmakers ; he is constantly drunk and Hetty finds him unendurable. When she leaves him he first threatens, and then shoots and kills, Harry Smith. *Dream*.

627. SUMS. Daily Mail, Dec. 24th, 1897.

SUNDERBUND, LADY AGATHA. An American widow who is " enormously rich " with a " disposition to profess wild intellectual passions." Meeting the Bishop of Princhester at a week-end party, she talks with him about " 'iligion " (she speaks with " a pretty little weakness of the r's "). After the first vision he calls upon her in London and tells her something of his doubts and new beliefs. She follows him to Princhester, settles down there and becomes an active worker in the Church. When he secedes she asks to be allowed to help him in the spreading of his new religion, desiring to build him a " Temple of the One T'ue God." He realises that she will never understand him, and therefore refuses her offer. *Soul of a Bishop*.

SUNRAY. The friend and lover of Sarnac ; she is " very like " Hetty Marcus. Other men and women of the future mentioned in *The Dream* are Radiant and Starlight (a brother and sister, " dark, handsome people of southern origin "), and Willow and Firefly (" two fair women " who are " very much attached " to them). These five form the audience for Sarnac's story, with the later addition of the master of the guest-house where it is continued and completed. They are quick-minded, healthy men and women, with " bare strong bodies," very like the Utopians of *Men Like Gods*.

627a. SWORD OF PEACE, THE. Daily Chronicle, Aug. 7th, 1914 ; 2nd chapter in *War that will End War*. Written Aug. 3rd, 1914. Wells prophecies that while Russia holds Germany to the east and Britain keeps the seas, France, with our aid, should be over the Rhine within a few months. When German Imperialism has been smashed (" within the next two or three months ") the Western Powers will be able to organise to bring about a lasting world-peace. "Every sword that is drawn against Germany is a sword drawn for peace."

SYDENHAM, LADY CHARLOTTE. An aunt of Oswald Sydenham, " one of those large, ignorant, ruthless, low-church, wealthy, and well-born ladies who did so much to make England what it was in the days before the Great War." She has " a pale blond fuss of hair . . . a large, pale, freckled, square-featured face with two hard blue eyes . . . a harsh voice, slow, loud, and pitched in that note of arrogance which was the method of the ruling class in those days." When her husband dies he makes Oswald his heir and Lady Charlotte's trustee. Arthur Stubland sees her once and is rather impressed by her, and as a consequence makes her one of the four joint-guardians of Peter and Joan. Her only act for some years is to have them secretly christened, but in 1903 she realises her responsibilities and has them kidnapped; they are rescued by Oswald, of whom she is in deadly fear. About 1912 she takes to politics, and is an opponent of the Insurance Act and of women's suffrage. In 1914 she subscribes beyond her means to the Ulster rebellion funds, and after the outbreak of war gives herself wholeheartedly to the persecution of all Germans not related to royalty. The food-shortage and the air-raids drive her to live in Ulster. *Joan and Peter.*

SYDENHAM, DOLLY. See Dolly Stubland.

SYDENHAM, OSWALD. A cousin of Dolly Sydenham. He enters the Navy as a midshipman, and at the age of twenty wins the V.C. by throwing a live shell overboard during the bombardment of Alexandria. It bursts in the air and shatters the right side of his face; his eyesight is damaged and he has to leave the Navy. For a time he studies under Huxley at the Normal School of Science. In 1885 he goes to Africa and remains there for three years under Harry Johnston. Returning to England, he falls in love with Dolly, goes back to Africa in an official position, and when next he sees her she is married to Arthur Stubland, and Peter has come into the world. Once he asks Dolly to run away with him, but she refuses; he never sees her again. Under Arthur's will he is one of the four guardians; Dolly's will gives him sole control. In 1903 he settles down to fulfil his duties as their guardian. He is irritated by the ignorance and narrow outlook of the majority of people in England, and comes to believe that education is the most important thing in the world. For several years he devotes himself to the study of education, anxious to give his wards the best possible chances. With the outbreak of war in 1914, he tries to enlist, and at last goes to France as an officer in an African labour corps. He is wounded by a bomb and sent home before the end of 1916. The children always call him Nobby from his resemblance to Peter's doll. *Joan and Peter.*

SYDENHAM, WILL. Dolly Sydenham's brother and the father of Joan Debenham. He is " a gross, white-faced literary man" who takes to " scornful, reactionary journalism, dramatic criticism, musical comedy lyrics, parody, and drink." *Joan and Peter.*

SYMPOSIUMS. Although Wells's reply to one editor, " I never sympose" (John o' London's Weekly, Apr. 14th, 1920), neither was nor is entirely accurate, his contributions in this direction have been comparatively few. Among them may be mentioned those on *The Fiction of the Future* (Ludgate Magazine, Sept., 1896) ; *The Decay of the Novel* (Young Man, Jan., 1903) ; *The English House of the Future* (Strand Magazine, Dec., 1903) ; *Authors at Work* (Bookman, Nov., 1908) ; *What Will England be Like in 1930* ? (Strand Magazine, Aug., 1917) ; *Why I Go to the Pictures* (Daily Herald, May 10th, 1919) ; *Courage in the Writing of Fiction* (Bookman, Oct., 1923) ; *How Our Novelists Write Their Books* (Strand Magazine, Oct., 1924).

628. SYNDICALISM OR CITIZENSHIP. Daily Mail, June 7th, 1912 ; see *What the Worker Wants*, Bib. II, 1912. Syndicalism, Wells believes, is an impossible social fragmentation, and can only lead to social conflict. He denies that this is an age of specialisation. Puts forward the idea of national labour conscription, and insists that all possible irksome work must be done by labour-saving machinery in order to reduce the necessary hours of toil. " Not a Labour State do we want, nor a Servile State, but a powerful Leisure State of free men."

T

629. TALE OF THE TWENTIETH CENTURY, A. Science Schools Journal, May, 1887. An absurd, high-spirited story of the application, with disastrous results, of a perpetual motion invention to the London underground railways. 1600 words. Signed S.B. (i.e., Septimus Browne).

630. TALES OF LIFE AND ADVENTURE. A cheap edition published in 1923 by W. Collins Sons & Co., Ltd., London, of 21 short stories by Wells, selected by J. D Beresford. The second of three uniform volumes. The stories are : 1, *The Argonauts of the Air ;* 2, *In the Modern Vein ;* 3, *A Catastrophe ;* 4, *The Lost Inheritance ;* 5, *A Deal in Ostriches ;* 6, *Through a Window ;* 7, *The Flying Man ;* 8, *The Diamond Maker ;* 9, *The Hammerpond Park Burglary ;* 10, *The Jilting of Jane ;* 11, *The Cone ;* 12, *The Stolen Bacillus ;* 13, *The Lord of the Dynamos ;* 14, *The Treasure in the Forest ;* 15, *The Obliterated Man ;* 16, *A Slip Under the Microscope ;* 17, *Jimmy Goggles the God ;* 18, *Miss Winchelsea's Heart ;* 19, *Filmer ;* 20, *Mr. Ledbetter's Vacation ;* 21, *Mr. Brisher's Treasure.*

631. TALES OF SPACE AND TIME. See Bib. No. 16.

632. TALES OF THE UNEXPECTED A cheap edition published in 1922 by W. Collins Sons & Co. Ltd., London, of 15 short stories by Wells, selected by J. D. Beresford. The first of three uniform volumes. The stories are : 1, *The Remarkable Case of Davidson's Eyes ;* 2, *The Moth ;* 3, *The Story of the Late Mr. Elvesham ;* 4, *Under the Knife ;* 5, *The Plattner Story ;* 6, *The Crystal Egg ;* 7, *The Man who could Work Miracles ;* 8, *A Dream of Armageddon ;* 9, *The New Accelerator ;* 10, *The Door in the Wall ;* 11, *The Apple ;* 12, *The Temptation of Harringay ;*

13, (Mr.) *Skelmersdale in Fairyland;*
14, (The Story of) *The Inexperienced
Ghost*; 15, *The Stolen Body.*

633. TALES OF WONDER. A cheap
edition published in 1923 by W.
Collins Sons & Co. Ltd., London, of
17 short stories by Wells, selected
by J. D. Beresford. The third of
three uniform volumes. The stories
are : 1, *In the Abyss;* 2, *Pollock
and the Porroh Man;* 3, *The Tri-
umphs of a Taxidermist;* 4, *In the
Avu Observatory;* 5, *The Flowering
of the Strange Orchid;* 6, *Æpyornis
Island;* 7, *The Sea Raiders;* 8,
The Red Room; 9, *The Purple
Pileus;* 10, *The Star;* 11, *A Vision
of Judgment;* 12, *The Valley of
Spiders;* 13, *The Truth about
Pyecraft;* 14, *The Magic Shop;* 15,
The Empire of the Ants; 16, *The
Country of the Blind;* 17, *The
Beautiful Suit.*

634. TALK WITH GRYLLOTALPA,
A. Science Schools Journal, Feb.,
1887. In this discussion, arising
from a picture, Wells holds that
" your duty to aid in the developing
of humanity is a vast thing, doubtless, but nearer, and every day
before you, is your duty to serve
your neighbour." 700 words.
Signed Septimus Browne.

635. TANKS. Daily Chronicle,
Dec. 18th, 1916 ; 5th chapter of
The Western War (q.v.).

TARVRILLE, LORD. A cousin of
Lady Mary Christian who tries to
act as peace-maker between her
brothers and husband and Stephen
Stratton, his sympathies being entirely with the latter and Mary.
Passionate Friends. One of his
dinners which becomes " a marvel
and a memory " is mentioned in

New Machiavelli. Lady Tarvrille
appears in the latter book and again
in *Sir Isaac Harman.*

636. TEACHER AS STATESMAN,
THE. Torchbearer, July, 1924.

TEDDY. Mr. Britling's secretary,
" a pleasant young man with a lot
of dark hair and fine blue eyes."
He lives in a small cottage near the
Dower House, with his wife, their
baby, and his sister-in-law, Cicely
Corner. When war breaks out he
joins the army as an officer. In the
summer of 1915 he is reported
missing and then killed, though
actually he has been taken prisoner,
escapes, and presently returns to
Matching's Easy. His wife Letty,
a " pretty young woman," takes
his place as secretary when he joins
the army. *Mr. Britling.*

637. TEMPTATION OF HARRINGAY,
THE. St. James's Gazette, Feb. 9th,
1895 ; 7th tale in *Stolen Bacillus.*
Harringay, an artist, paints a man's
head. It becomes increasingly
unsatisfactory, finally waking to
life and wiping the paint from its
devil's face. It criticises his work
and offers him five masterpieces in
exchange for his soul. Harringay
steadfastly refuses, and after a
struggle paints out the face with
green enamel.

637a. TEN GREAT DISCOVERIES,
THE. See *The Release of Man.* 5th
essay in Vol. 27 of *The Atlantic Edition.* Wells, discriminating between
Discovery and Invention, maps out
" man's history into ten great
phases of discovery." They may
be recorded briefly : 1, Implements;
2, Tabu; 3, Speech; 4, Fire; 5,
Domestication of Animals; 6, Agriculture, etc. ; 7, Subjugation of
Water; 8, Writing; 9, Finance;
10, Oneness of the World. He sug-

gests Scientific World Economics and World Education as the next two discoveries.

638. TEN MOST IMPORTANT BOOKS IN THE WORLD, THE. John o' London's Weekly, Mar. 21st, Apr. 7th & 14th, 1923 (the last instalment under the title *The Philosophers that Matter*). In making his selection Wells stresses the word " important " and thinks most " not of delights but powers." In each case he gives reasons for his choice, and dismisses reluctantly certain deserving claimants. He concludes : " The ten most important books does not mean necessarily the ten most important books to read." His choice includes the following : 1, The Book of Isaiah ; 2, Gospel of St. Mark ; 3, " The Great Learning " ; 4, The Koran ; 5, Plato's " Republic " ; 6, Aristotle's " History of Animals " ; 7, Marco Polo's " Travels " ; 8, Copernicus's " Revolutions of the Heavens " ; 9, Bacon's " New Atlantis " ; 10, Darwin's " Origin of Species."

639. TESTIMONIAL TO BOOKS, A. Daily News, Nov. 22nd, 1915.

640. TEXT-BOOK OF BIOLOGY. See Bib. No. 1.

TEXT-BOOK OF ZOOLOGY. See Bib. No. 1, note.

641. " THAT PROBLEM ! " Henley House Magazine, Aug., 1891. Signed H. G. Wells.

642. THEORY OF QUOTATION, THE. Pall Mall Gazette, Mar. 22nd, 1894 ; 28th essay in *Personal Matters*. An argument against quotation, or, where it may be necessary, against acknowledged quotation. " The only honest method of quotation is plagiary."

643. THEORY OF THE PERPETUAL DISCOMFORT OF HUMANITY, THE. Pall Mall Gazette, in 1893 ; 2nd of *Select Conversations*. The Uncle expounds a theory that humanity is doomed to perpetual discomfort through the non-fulfilment of reform until after the passing of the generation which each reform would have satisfied.

THERE IS NO PEOPLE. Daily Mail, Apr. 9th, 1904 ; reprinted as *Is There a People* (q.v.).

644. THINGS THAT LIVE ON MARS, THE. London Magazine, Mar., 1908, and Cosmopolitan Magazine, Mar., 1908.

645. THIRTY STRANGE STORIES. See Bib. No. 13. The tales in this volume are : 1, *The Flowering of the Strange Orchid ;* 2, *Æpyornis Island ;* 3, *The Plattner Story ;* 4, *The Argonauts of the Air ;* 5, *The Story of the Late Mr. Elvesham ;* 6, *The Stolen Bacillus ;* 7, *The Red Room ;* 8, *A Moth (Genus Novo) ;* 9, *In the Abyss ;* 10, *Under the Knife ;* 11, *The Reconciliation ;* 12, *A Slip under the Microscope ;* 13, *In the Avu Observatory ;* 14, *The Triumphs of a Taxidermist ;* 15, *A Deal in Ostriches ;* 16, *The Rajah's Treasure ;* 17, *The Story of Davidson's Eyes ;* 18, *The Cone ;* 19, *The Purple Pileus ;* 20, *A Catastrophe ;* 21, *Le Mari Terrible ;* 22, *The Apple ;* 23, *The Sad Story of a Dramatic Critic ;* 24, *The Jilting of Jane ;* 25, *The Lost Inheritance ;* 26, *Pollock and the Porroh Man ;* 27, *The Sea Raiders ;* 28, *In the Modern Vein ;* 29, *The Lord of the Dynamos ;* 30, *The Treasure in the Forest.*

646. THIS MISERY OF BOOTS. See Bib. No. 32. The pain caused by ill-made, ill-fitting, badly-repaired

boots is taken as one example of the foolish (because unnecessary) suffering brought about by the present system of private ownership of property. Wells finds a remedy for this suffering in Socialism, which seems to him neither impossible nor against human nature, though he warns his reader that it will mean a revolution, a complete change, in the " everyday texture of life." (The substance of the third section is reprinted in Chapter 4 of *New Worlds*.)

THOMAS. A footman at Shonts. He torments Bealby until the latter attacks him with a toasting fork and flies above-stairs from his pursuit. After Bealby's disappearance he is sympathetic and distressed. *Bealby*.

647. THOUGHT IN THE MODERN STATE. 10th chapter in *Mankind*. " Literature is a vitally necessary function of the modern state." Wells suggests a scheme for the state endowment of general literature—a scheme which, however, he repudiates in the *Preface* to the 1914 edition.

648. THOUGHTS FROM H. G. WELLS. Selected by Elsie E. Morton. See Bib. II, 1913.

THOUGHTS ON A BALD HEAD. Pall Mall Gazette, Mar. 1st, 1895 ; reprinted as *Incidental Thoughts on a Bald Head* (q.v.).

649. THOUGHTS ON CHEAPNESS AND MY AUNT CHARLOTTE. New Budget, May 17th, 1895 ; 1st essay in *Personal Matters*. Protests against the handing down from one generation to another of ancient household goods so valuable that one lives in daily terror of breaking or damaging them. " For my part I love cheap things, trashy things . . . things as vulgar as primroses, and as transitory as a morning's frost."

650. THREATENED UNIVERSITY, THE. Saturday Review, Dec. 14th, 1895. A page letter to the editor.

THREE VITAL QUESTIONS. 5th chapter of *Anticipations of a World Peace ;* reprinted from section 2 of *Getting the League Idea Clear in Relation to Imperialism* (q.v.).

651. THROUGH A MICROSCOPE. Pall Mall Gazette, Dec. 31st, 1894 ; 34th essay in *Personal Matters*. An account of the minute but curious living creatures which may be found in a single drop of water, touching in semi-humorous fashion upon their manner of existence.

652. THROUGH A WINDOW. See *At a Window*. 6th tale in *Stolen Bacillus*. During his convalescence, Bailey's chief amusement is to watch through his bedroom window the boats and people which pass up and down the river outside. The culmination of his interest comes when a Malay runs amuck and is pursued. The chase passes from side to side of his limited view, ending in his room with the killing of the madman.

653. THUS FAR. Daily Mail, Nov. 23rd, 1921 ; 12th chapter in *Washington*. Summary of the first ten days of the Conference. It must become a " Recurrent World Conference " or all its effect and purpose will be lost and forgotten.

654. TIDSTANKAR. See Bib. No. 54.

655. TIDYING UP THE LANGUAGE QUESTION. With Particular Reference to Russian. Daily Chronicle, June 6th, 1916.

656. TIME MACHINE, THE. See Bib. No. 4. This brief novel opens at the Time Traveller's Richmond home with the Traveller expounding

a theory of Time as the Fourth Dimension. He shows his small circle of friends first a working-model of, and then the actual, Time Machine. A week later the narrator goes again to Richmond, and this time the Traveller tells them of his first and only flight into time. On the saddle of the machine he had flung himself far into futurity, stopping at the year 802701 A.D. He finds the Thames valley a magnificent garden ; London has disappeared save for gigantic but crumbling palaces of granite and marble and aluminium. Mankind has differentiated into two races, the Eloi and the Morlocks. The Eloi are fragile, childlike people and, with the exception of Weena, a girl he saves from drowning, take little interest in him or in his machine. The latter is mysteriously stolen, and it is only then that he realises the existence of the Morlocks, a bestial people who live in caverns and passages beneath the surface of the earth, allowing the Eloi to possess the earth on sufferance, feeding and clothing them from long habit, and preying upon them for their meat. After several adventures with the Morlocks, during one of which Weena is killed, he recovers the Machine and travels once more into the future, until more than thirty millions of years have passed and the earth has at last come to rest with one face to the dull red sun, now so near as to obscure one tenth of the sky. Then he comes back, stopping his machine at eight o'clock on the evening of the day of his departure. Most of his guests incline to the belief that his tale is " a gaudy lie " and a few days later he sets out again with camera and knapsack to secure proof of the reality of his time-travelling. From the instant of his departure he is never seen again.

TIME TRAVELLER, THE. A scientific inventor and writer upon physical optics, " one of those men who are too clever to be believed." His story of his adventures in the far distant future form the greater part of *The Time Machine*.

TOILERS IN THE WRECKAGE. (Russia in the Shadows, 4). Sunday Express, Nov. 21st, 1920 ; reprinted as *The Creative Effort in Russia* (q.v.).

657. TONO-BUNGAY. See Bib. No. 37. This novel is the autobiography of George Ponderevo, only son of the housekeeper at Bladesover House, where he spends his holidays. Here he plays with the young cousins of Lady Drew—Beatrice Normandy, whom he loves, and her step-brother, Archie Garvell. He fights with Garvell and is sent away, finally being apprenticed to his uncle, Edward Ponderevo, a Wimblehurst chemist. The uncle, owing to an unlucky speculation, has to sell his shop. George stays on with his successor until, winning a scholarship, he goes to London as a student at the South Kensington Technical School. He meets Ewart, an old school friend, and Marion Ramboat, with whom he falls in love. Edward Ponderevo, using some trust money he is holding for George, markets a new patent medicine, " Tono-Bungay," pushing its sale by extensive advertising. George joins him as general organiser. The business is a great financial success and George is able to marry. He and Marion do not get on together, and

she divorces him after some trouble over Effie Rink, a typist. Edward, unable to restrain himself, enters upon fresh enterprises, each of which seems to pay well ; he goes on and on, floating new companies and amalgamating old ones and revivifying them. His old style of living fails to satisfy him, and he wanders from Camden Town, via Redgauntlet Mansions, Beckenham and Chislehurst, to his last home, Lady Grove. Even this last is not enough, and he commences but never completes the building of an immense mansion at Crest Hill. He strives to acquire " Style and Savoir Faire," to become a member of Society ; the possibility of buying a title attracts him. George, meanwhile, takes up the study of aerial navigation at Lady Grove, and after experiments with gliders builds his first navigable balloon, Lord Roberts' Alpha. It meets with disaster, but he sets about the making of its successor. Beatrice Normandy comes into his life again, and he finds that he still loves her. She consents to marry him, but evades any definite arrangement and then withdraws her promise. A financial crisis arises, Edward is threatened with disaster, and George sails for West Africa to steal a boatload of quap, a rare and valuable mineral deposit of which they have heard. Up to a certain point the expedition is successful ; the ship is loaded with its precious cargo and evades the guarding gunboat only to sink at sea some distance north of Cape Verde. The crew are picked up by a homeward-bound liner, and George arrives in England to find his uncle's bankruptcy placarded all over the country. He sees Edward, and then goes to his Aunt Susan at Lady Grove. Here

he is followed by his harassed and weary uncle, bankrupt and forger, driven from London by the continual questioning of his creditors. George, hoping to save him from the law, flies with him to France in the Lord Roberts B. They reach an inn in Luzon Gare, and there Edward, after a few days' illness, succumbs to a fever and dies. George returns to England and attempts to straighten out his uncle's involved affairs. He meets Beatrice, now Lord Carnaby's mistress, but though she loves George she will not marry him. For a few days they meet, lovers frankly and openly, and then she leaves him for ever. He turns again to engineering and becomes a builder of destroyers. The last chapter describes the trial run of X2, " my latest and best," down the Thames from above Hammersmith Bridge past Westminster, the Embankment, St. Paul's, London Bridge, the Tower, and so " dreaming into the night out upon the wide North Sea."

" TONO-BUNGAY." The patent medicine, " slightly injurious rubbish," which forms the first foundation of Edward Ponderevo's fortune, and gives a title to George Ponderevo's autobiography. It is made in various forms and strengths, but essentially it is " mischievous trash, slightly stimulating, aromatic and attractive, likely to become a bad habit and train people in the habitual use of stronger tonics." *Tono-Bungay.*

TOOMER, HORACE. A friend of George Brumley. The " spirit of scurrility incarnate," yet doing his best to be an English gentleman, he finds " relief in attacking with a merciless energy all that was new, all that was critical, all those fresh and nobler tentatives that admit of unsavoury interpretations." *Sir Isaac Harman.* Mentioned in *Ann Veronica* and *New Machiavelli* as one of the " giant leaders " of the Fabian Society.

658. TOPOGRAPHICAL. 1st chapter of *Modern Utopia.* Only a planet similar to this earth will suffice for the creation of a modern Utopia. The Owner of the Voice and the botanist, transferred from this world to that of Utopia " by an act of the imagination," descend from the Lucendro Pass into strange new surroundings. The language of Utopia is discussed.

659. TRAFFIC AND REBUILDING. Eye Witness, June 22nd, 1911 ; 13th essay in *An Englishman.* Considers the London traffic problem and the idea of a railway clearing house. He asks : " Do we want London rebuilt ? " and if so, need it necessarily be rebuilt upon its present site ?

TRAFFORD, MRS. The mother of Richard Trafford, and widow of a brilliant pathologist who died before he was thirty. She devotes herself, from the day of her husband's death, to educating their only child to follow in his steps. She helps him in his work and encourages him to talk to her of everything which interests him. When he marries Marjorie she refuses to live with them, and when he tells her of his decision to go to Labrador she persuades him to take his wife with him. *Marriage.*

TRAFFORD, RICHARD ANDREW GODWIN. " One of those rare scientific men who really ought to be engaged in scientific research,"

a man with a mind like " some insatiable corrosive," " extraordinary fertile in exasperating alternative hypotheses." When the story begins he is twenty-six years old, a tall, fair, blue-eyed, good-looking man, Professor of Physics at the Romeike College and a Doctor of Science ; later he becomes an F.R.S. He and Marjorie have four children, Margharita, Godwin, Richard and Edward. See *Marriage.*

660. TRAGEDY OF COLOUR, THE. 11th chapter of *Future in America.* Wells, despite the general American prejudice against the negro, finds something very likeable in these gentle, simple-mannered, dark-skinned people. Particularly does he admire the " steadfast effort " of hundreds among the black population to keep a hold upon civilisation and to gain refinement and learning. He quotes part of a conversation with Booker T. Washington.

661. TRAIL OF VERSAILLES, THE. Daily Mail, Nov. 10th, 1921 ; 3rd chapter in *Washington.* Traces certain parallels between the conference at Versailles and that at Washington ; Wells considers the absence of Germany and Russia a grave omission.

662. TRANSFIGURATION OF POR-CHUCK, THE. Pall Mall Gazette, May 25th, 1894.

663. TRANSIT OF MERCURY, THE. Saturday Review, Nov. 24th, 1894. Unsigned. Discusses the recent transit.

664. TREASURE IN THE FOREST, THE. Pall Mall Budget, about 1894 ; last tale in *Stolen Bacillus;*

10th in *Country of the Blind.* Two British wastrels somewhere in the East murder a Chinaman to gain possession of a treasure chart. They seek for and find the store of gold, only to be killed by the poisoned thorns which guard the treasure.

665. TRIUMPH OF FRANCE, THE. See *H. G. Wells on the Ruhr Triumph*, 3rd article in *Year of Prophesying.* Writing on the occasion of a French victory in the Ruhr, Wells comments on " the centuries old policy of French predominance in the European world." He protests against France's aggressive militarism.

666. TRIUMPHS OF A TAXIDERMIST, THE. Pall Mall Gazette, about 1894 ; 4th tale in *Stolen Bacillus.* Some professional reminiscences of a Taxidermist.

667. TRIVIALITY OF DEMOCRACY AND THE FEMININE INFLUENCE IN POLITICS, THE. Westminster Gazette, Aug. 23rd, 1924 ; 51st article in *Year of Prophesying.* A conversation with an un-named friend who holds that a democracy as a whole can only understand and be serious about very trivial things. The " big things of human life " are going to be " managed in some other fashion " than through Parliament. " Thus my friend and I found it very difficult to gainsay him."

668. TROUBLE OF LIFE, THE. Pall Mall Gazette, Aug. 2nd, 1894 ; 2nd essay in *Personal Matters.* A protest against the Bothers of Life— washing, shaving, answering letters, talking to people. Euphemia is mentioned as the " Bother Commander-in-Chief."

669. TRUE FORTUNE TELLING. Daily Mail, June 7th, 1906.

670. TRUTH ABOUT GISSING, THE. Rhythm, Dec., 1912 (Lit. Sup.). A criticism of two books about Gissing ; a critical study by Frank Swinnerton, and " The Private Life of Henry Maitland," by Morley Roberts.

671. TRUTH ABOUT PYECRAFT, THE. Strand Magazine, Apr., 1903 ; 4th tale in *Twelve Stories ;* 28th in *Country of the Blind.* Pyecraft, the " fattest clubman in London," takes an Eastern medicine in order to " lose weight." Almost instantaneously, without any other change, he becomes so light that he floats up against the ceiling of his room. His friend overcomes the difficulty by suggesting underclothing sewn with discs of lead.

672. TRUTH AND THE TEETOTALER. Morning Post, Nov. 21st, 1901. Review of " Alcoholism," by Archdall Reid.

TSI-PUFF. One of the two Selenites sent by the Grand Lunar to guard and study Cavor. He is one of the erudite class and has a pear-shaped head. *Men in the Moon.*

673. TWELVE STORIES AND A DREAM. See Bib. No. 23.

TWELVE TRUSTEES, THE. Originally a body of men chosen by Warming to hold Graham's wealth, their successors become as the White Council, through the acquisition of property, the rulers of the earth. Fearing to lose their power when Graham wakens they decide to poison him, but are prevented and finally overthrown by Ostrog. *Sleeper Wakes.*

674. TWENTY-FOUR PORTRAITS. See Bib. II, 1920.

675. TWO CHIEF DANGERS, THE. New York World, in Feb., 1908.

TWO POSSIBILITIES. Daily Express, Dec. 6th, 1921 ; reprinted as *A Reminder about War* (q.v.).

676. TWO STUDIES IN DISAPPOINTMENT. 10th chapter of *Future in America*. A discussion of a certain " quality of harshness " which seems to appear and disappear amid the general kindliness and hospitality of America. Wells gives point to his remarks by quoting the cases of MacQueen and Gorki.

677. TWO WAYS, THE. Nation, Sept. 12th, 1914 ; reprinted only in translation (see *Tidstankar*). Considers the conditions " under which a pacifist civilisation may hope to destroy its antagonist without complete loss of its own character in the process." Wells finds a way in the organisation of pacifist states to " control and watch the manufacture of explosives and weapons " all over the world. He advocates a period of state service for every citizen and the financial control of the Press to render it unbribeable. Reply to a criticism by John Bailey, Oct. 3rd.

TWO WAYS OF WOMEN, THE. Daily News, May 20th, 1916 ; reprinted as *What the War is doing for Women* (q.v.).

U

678. UBIQUITOUS GOLD. Saturday Review, June 22nd, 1895.

Unsigned. Gold, in one form or another, exists practically everywhere. When the present sources of supply run out, science will be able to extract it from " fields and rocks and gardens."

UGH-LOMI. The hero of *A Story of the Stone Age*. One of the Sons of Uya, he is driven away from the tribe because of his love for Eudena ; finally he kills Uya and becomes chief.

UGLIEST THING IN LONDON, THE. Pall Mall Gazette and Pall Mall Budget, April 12th, 1894 ; reprinted as *The Man with a Nose* (q.v.).

UNCLE, AN. A middle-aged bachelor, the author's paternal uncle, who having attained wealth and distinction in South Africa comes to London, where he is a constant companion of his nephew. He is talkative with an " irresponsible gaiety," and has a low opinion of many of the fashions and conventions of the period which he expresses in *Select Conversations* Eventually he marries Mrs. Harborough and his conversations come to an end.

679. UNDER THE KNIFE. New Review, Jan., 1896 ; 6th tale in *Plattner Story ;* 12th in *Country oj the Blind*. The narrator, while undergoing an operation, has a dream in which he dies. His spirit hangs motionless, unfeeling, in space, while the earth, bearing his deserted body spins away from him ; his mind moves more and more slowly, until a thousand years pass in what seems no more than a second. The earth, the planets, the stars, fall away from him until the universe of matter is no more than a vanishing point of

light. Then across the gulf of blackness appears a shadowy hand holding a rod ; a face is seen above the hand and a great voice sounds ! He wakes to find that the operation has been successful.

680. UNDYING FIRE, THE. See Bib. No. 68. A modern adaptation of the Book of Job ; there is a Prologue in Heaven, the scene of the rest of the story is a lodging house at Sundering-on-Sea. Satan wagers with God that Man, beset by trouble, will not " even remember God." God tells Satan to " try Man to the uttermost. See if he is indeed no more than a little stir amid the slime, a fuss in the mud that signifies nothing." Job Huss, borne down by pain and trouble, is staying in the dingy apartments of Mrs. Croome at Sea View. Until lately the well-known and successful headmaster of Woldingstanton, a great and modern public-school in Norfolk, misfortune has attacked him on every side. Two boys die at the school during an epidemic, two more are burnt to death in a school fire ; an assistant master is killed in a laboratory explosion. Huss's savings are lost by his solicitor's speculations, and he and his wife receive the news of their only son's death in France. Huss, suffering from an internal pain, visits a Dr. Barrack who diagnoses his trouble as cancer and advises an immediate operation. Mrs. Huss makes things worse by blaming him for all that has happened. Upon the morning of the operation he is visited by Sir Eliphaz Burrows, William Dad (governors of the school), and Joseph Farr, head of the technical section. The two governors are anxious that Farr should take Huss's place as head-master. The greater part of the book is a record of the conversation between Huss and his visitors ; knowing that the operation may be fatal he speaks to them as fully and sincerely as possible. He discusses the task of the teacher, reviews his life-work, and shows how it would all be nullified and frustrated by the appointment of Farr as his successor. Together they bring under discussion religion, theology, the beauty and cruelty of Nature, the apparent indifference of God, immortality, and spiritualism. Dr. Elihu Barrack, who has come in to prepare his patient, joins in the argument and states his idea of a Process beyond the comprehension of and indifferent to Man. Huss tells them that, in spite of their varying ideas, the four of them are alike in that they submit to things as they are ; he alone does not submit, rebelling by the spirit of God within him. God, not all-powerful, struggles through Man to attain the organised unity of the world that, competition, hatred, rivalry thrown aside, the race may sweep forward to ever new triumphs. The conversation is interrupted at last by the arrival of Sir Alpheus Mengo, the specialist who is to perform the operation. While under chloroform Mr. Huss has a dream in which he is Job, sitting for ever outside the ancient city of Uz, arguing with Eliphaz, Bildad, Zophar and Elihu. And there he —Man—talks with Satan and with God. God tells him that if only he has courage there lies within him the power to rule all things. He wakes from his dream. Three weeks pass. The operation has been successful and with the removal of the morbid growth his full strength returns. In France victory seems

R

at hand. A distant cousin has died and left him a considerable fortune. The other governors and old boys of the school—led by Kenneth Burrows, the nephew of Sir Eliphaz —protest against the attempt to put Farr in his place. And finally there comes news that his son, though a prisoner, is alive.

681. United States, France, Britain, and Russia, The. (Looking Ahead.) Daily Chronicle, Apr. 15th, 1916 ; reprinted, with *World Languages* (q.v.), as the 10th chapter in *What is Coming?* Speculates upon the future development of these four countries "whose destinies are likely to become more closely interwoven than their past histories have been." The three prime necessities for the propagation of understanding and intercourse between these countries are (1) a lingua-franca, (2) a knowledge of one another, and (3) a more accessible English language. Suggests the founding of a national publishing house to provide an abundant supply of English and French and Russian books in both Russian and Latin type.

University of London Election Addresses. See Nos. 146, 147, 148 & 745. See also No. 314.

682. Unknown Soldier of the Great War, The. Daily Mail, Nov. 12th, 1921 ; 4th chapter in *Washington.* Dated Nov. 11th. Referring to the burial of Unknown Soldiers in many countries, Wells attempts a portrait of the Unknown Soldier of all the countries which fought in the late war.

683. Unsuspected Masterpiece, An. See *Upon an Egg.* 10th of the *Select Conversations.* The uncle

discourses (for his nephew's benefit) upon a stale egg.

Unwin. The "abject confidential maid" of Lady Charlotte Sydenham. She, anxious to help her sister, Mrs. Pybus, suggests the kidnapping of Joan and Peter to her mistress. *Joan and Peter.*

Upon an Egg. Pall Mall Gazette and Pall Mall Budget, June 7th, 1894 ; reprinted as *An Unsuspected Masterpiece* (q.v.).

684. Use of Ideals, The. Pall Mall Gazette, about 1893 ; 3rd of the *Select Conversations.* The ideal must be kept a refreshing contrast to reality ; it must never be allowed to become an inconvenience.

685. Utopian Economics. 3rd chapter in *Modern Utopia.* A study of money, local administration, economics, personal property and machinery in a modern Utopia. The Owner of the Voice and the botanist breakfast at the inn, and leave it to wander along the Urseren Valley.

686. Utopianisms. A series of 5 articles printed in the Daily Mail, March to June, 1905. The special titles are : 1, *Garden Cities ;* 2, *A Cottage in a Garden ;* 3, *State Babies ;* 4, *Joint Households ;* 5, *A Woman's Day in Utopia.*

V

687. Vain Man and his Monument, The. Pall Mall Gazette, Jan. 3rd, 1895.

688. Valley of Spiders, The. Pearson's Magazine, March, 1903 ; 3rd tale in *Twelve Stories ;* 26th in *Country of the Blind.* Three men, riding in pursuit of a girl, come into a valley where they are attacked by great spiders which drift down the wind in webs like balls of thistle-down, letting down clinging stream-ers and attacking their prey from above. Two men escape, leaving the third to his fate. There is only one horse left, so the leader kills the second man and rides back, abandoning the chase.

VERRAL, EDWARD. The wealthy son of a deceased Four Towns land-owner. He elopes with Nettie Stuart, the daughter of his mother's head gardener ; after the Change he marries her. *Days of the Comet.*

689. VERY FINE ART OF MICRO-TOMY, THE. Pall Mall Gazette, Jan. 24th, 1894.

690. VETERAN CRICKETER, THE. Pall Mall Gazette, Apr. 5th. 1894 ; 15th essay in *Personal Matters.* A character sketch of an old cricketer, once a famous professional, now reduced by old age and sciatica to umpiring in local matches. He is contemptuous of modern cricket and abounds in reminiscences of the old days of his own glory.

VICAR OF CHEASING EYEBRIGHT, THE. " One of the least innovating of vicars, a most worthy, plump, ripe, and conservative-minded little man." He plays a considerable part in the life of young Caddles. *Food of the Gods.*

691. VISION OF JUDGMENT, A. Butterfly, Sept., 1899, signed D.O. ; 22nd story in *Country of the Blind.* The whole population of the earth stand before God on the Day of Judgment. Ahab, the Tyrannous Man, is placed upon the palm of God's hand, a figure of

dignity " daring no lies, daring no pleas, but telling the truth of my iniquities before all mankind." Then the Recording Angel reads from his book not only the king's greater sins but his smaller misdeeds, until Ahab weeps with outraged vanity and is driven to seek refuge in God's sleeve. Next comes a Saint, boasting of his " holy discomforts." Again the Angel reads, and the Saint joins Ahab in the sleeve. Where pre-sently comes all mankind, into " the shadow of the robe of God's charity."

VISION OF THE WORLD OF THE FUTURE, A. Daily Express, Dec. 19th, 1921 ; reprinted as the 1st half of *What a Stably Organised World Peace Means for Mankind* (q.v.).

VOICE OF AMERICA, THE. Sun-day Express, Dec. 11th, 1921 ; reprinted as *America's Rôle in World Peace* (q.v.).

692. VOICE OF NATURE, THE. 4th chapter in *Modern Utopia.* The visitors meet a talkative man, an " apostle of Nature." He criticises Utopia, and refuses to believe that a still more unsatisfactory world can exist.

VOULES, MR. Uncle to Miriam Larkins, whom he " gives away " at Mr. Polly's wedding. He is a licensed victualler and makes the social arrangements. A fat, deter-mined, genial man. *Mr. Polly.*

W

WADDY. Arthur Kipps's paternal grandfather ; he leaves Kipps £26,000 when he dies. His son, Kipps's father, died in Australia " years and years " before. *Kipps.*

693. WALCOTE. Science Schools Journal, Dec., 1888 and Jan., 1889. A tale of an 18th century Chritsmas Eve. Edwin, his cousin Claude, and Vitzelley, a friend, discuss the mysterious disappearance, just one year before, of Edwin's elder brother, Sir Harry. As the clock strikes twelve, a parrot in the room cries out words which accuse Edwin of Harry's murder. Edwin confesses, kills the parrot, and commits suicide.

WALK ALONG THE THAMES EMBANKMENT, A. See Bib. No. 34a.

WALLACE, LIONEL. A brilliant politician whose life is haunted by memories of a garden which once, as a child, he entered through a door in a wall. He tells the story of his experiences to an old school friend, Redmond. See *The Door in the Wall*.

WALSHINGHAM, HELEN. Daughter of a Folkestone solicitor, member of a "county family. Related to the Earl of Beaupres." She is a dark, slender girl, "as beautiful as most beautiful people." Kipps worships her from a distance for a long while, and after inheriting his fortune is engaged to her for some time. After his marriage to Ann Pornick, she elopes with a married man. *Kipps*.

WALSHINGHAM, YOUNG. Helen's brother, a slender, dark young man with "fluctuating resemblances to the young Napoleon." He reads Nietzsche and thinks "that in all probability he was the Non-Moral Overman referred to by that writer. He wore fairly large-sized hats." When Kipps puts his money in his charge he speculates with it, loses it all, and "takes 'is 'ook." *Kipps*.

WAMPACH, BISHOP. The Rev. Mr. Parchester tells him of the sound and the vision he has heard and seen. The Bishop, who has long been jealous of the rector, advises him to see a doctor and take a long rest. *Story of the Last Trump*.

694. WANTED, A STATESMAN OF IMPERIAL POLICY. Daily Chronicle, June 14th, 1917 ; 1st section of *Getting the League Idea Clear in Relation to Imperialism*. Originally sent to The Times, it was rejected as "being altogether too revolutionary." It points out that the British Empire as it exists to-day is a "provisional thing" which "must give place ultimately to the higher synthesis of a world league."

WAR-AIMS CONTROVERSY, THE. 6th chapter of *Anticipations of a World Peace ;* a reprint of Section 3 of *Getting the League Idea Clear in Relation to Imperialism*, and *The War Aims of the Allies Compactly Stated*.

694a. WAR AIMS OF THE ALLIES COMPACTLY STATED, THE. 6th chapter in *Fourth Year*. A "plain statement of the essential cause and process of the war." World peace must be established by unity, which is only obtainable by means of a league of free nations, or by the absolute dominance of one state.

695. WAR AND COMMON SENSE. See Bib. No. 47. The three articles reprinted in this pamphlet are: 1, *The Common Sense of Conscription.;* 2, "*Put Not Your Trust in Dreadnoughts.*" ; 3, *The Balance of Present and Future*. See each of these titles.

WAR AND SOCIALISM, THE. See Bib. No. 53a.

696. WAR AND THE FUTURE. See Bib. No. 62. An account of a short tour made by Wells on the French and Italian fronts in the late summer of 1916. First he visits Italy, seeing the fighting upon the Isonzo and among the mountains ; he meets the King of Italy. Returning to France (where, on his way to Italy, he had previously met General Joffre) he visits the ruins of Fricourt, Dompierre, Arras and Soissons. From the base at Amiens he goes right up to the front line trenches. Near Paris he visits a large shell factory, and upon his return to England is permitted to see the newly-invented Tanks. The last section of the book is devoted to a consideration of contemparary thought upon questions raised by the war. Here the writer gives his first clear statement of the conception of God as the King of a world-system of republican states. The titles of the four sections of this book are : 1, *The Passing of the Effigy* ; 2, *The War in Italy* ; 3, *The Western War* ; 4, *How People Think about the War.*

697. WAR AND THE WORKERS, THE. See Bib. II, 1918.

698. WAR ECONOMICS. An Open Letter. Daily Chronicle, May 2nd, 1916. " The following letter by Mr. H. G. Wells addressed to Sir Hedley le Bas was called forth by an invitation to the novelist to write in support of the National War Savings Committee, the official organisation formed to promote economy in private expenditure during the war." Editor's note.

699. WAR IN ITALY, THE. (August, 1916). 2nd part of *War and the Future.* In three chapters : 1, *The Isonzo Front* ; 2, *The Mountain War* ; 3, *Behind the Front.* See each of these titles.

700. WAR IN THE AIR, THE. See Bib. No. 35. Bert Smallways, partner in the insolvent firm of Grubb and Smallways, bicycle agents and general repairers, is the one progressive member of an unprogressive family. His elder brother, Tom, is content to stay at home and dig his garden, but Bert goes rushing about the country first on a racing- and later on a motor- cycle. The latter, his last asset, meets with disaster one Whit-Monday, while, Bert all unwitting, the war-clouds gather about the world. Bert and Grubb give up the shop and decide to tour the South Coast as masked minstrels, " young men of family doing it for a lark." They begin at Dymchurch, but their first performance is interrupted by the arrival of a balloon belonging to Butteridge, the famous inventor of a flying-machine. Bert is accidentally carried away, alone in the basket, by the balloon, which drifts eastward over the North Sea to be shot down in an immense German aeronautic park in Franconia. The Germans believe him to be Butteridge, and in a dazed condition he is hurried on board the " Vaterland," flagship of a great air-fleet which is just starting for America, the first move in a German bid for world-supremacy. His identity is discovered too late ; he is made to hand over the plans of the Butteridge machine (found in the balloon basket) but not before he has made rough copies of them. From the " Vaterland " he sees the Battle of the North Atlantic and the terrible air-bombardment of New York. Disabled in a battle with American aeroplanes, the German flagship, caught in a storm, drifts to Labrador, whence the crew are rescued, after some days, by the "Graf Zeppelin." Meanwhile the whole world has risen in war. With the news of the launching of the German air-fleet, the Asiatic ships take to the air east and west, appearing simultaneously over America and India, where the natives rise in revolt against the British. All Europe is plunged into a chaos of aerial battles and bombardments. At the Battle of Niagara (which Bert, left behind in the emergency, watches from the ground) the German fleet is disbanded by the Asiatics. He takes refuge on Goat Island, where he is made a prisoner by the smashing of the bridge. The German flag-ship, the "Hohenzollern," is brought down on the island, and Prince Karl Albert, the German commander, and an officer, become fellow prisoners. They quarrel, and Bert shoots the Prince; the officer is drowned in attempting to escape across the broken bridge. Bert escapes on an Asiatic flying-machine and comes down near an American village. He reveals the fact that he has copies of the Butteridge plans and is at once rushed off to the President. But now the whole world is in chaos, the fabric of civilisation is dropping to pieces, the earth is devastated by the Purple Death, and people drop back into a state of semi-savagery. Bert succeeds in crossing the Atlantic, lands at Cardiff, and tramps to London. There he finds Edna Bunthorne, "his Edna," and marries her after shooting a local bully

and making himself leader of the dead man's band. There is a brief Epilogue in which Tom Smallways, meeting the latest of his nephews (Bert's sons) reviews the war and the period since the war.

701. WAR IN THE TWENTIETH CENTURY. 6th chapter in *Anticipations*. A forecast of the conditions of warfare during the next hundred years, emphasising the necessity for the efficient training of the individual not only in the Army and Navy, but also in the civil population of the country.

702. WAR LANDSCAPE, THE. (The Western Front, 1). Daily Chronicle, Nov. 27th, 1916; reprinted as 3rd chapter of *The Western War* (q.v.).

WARMING, E. A cousin of Graham, the Sleeper. He is the first to see the possibility of using Eadhamite as a road substance, and the organiser of the "enormous network of public ways that speedily covered the world"; in this way he makes a tremendous fortune all of which he leaves to Graham, appointing a council of twelve trustees. *Sleeper Wakes;* mentioned in *Story of the Days to Come*.

703. WAR OF MATERIAL, THE. Daily Chronicle, Oct. 15th, 1914. "This is a war not only of men but of things." Without material modern war is impossible; the workshops at home are as essential as the soldiers at the front, and the men in those workshops must labour to ensure a supply of material for the soldiers. The vital target of the Western War must be Westphalia, not Berlin. Essen must be smashed for ever.

704. War of the Mind, The. Nation, Aug. 29th, 1914 ; 11th and last chapter in *War that will End War.* Urges that the " ultimate purpose of this war is propaganda, the destruction of certain beliefs and the creation of others." Writers and speakers must combine to " gather together the wills and understanding of men for the tremendous necessities and opportunities of this time."

705. War of the Worlds, The See Bib. No. 14. During an opposition a huge outbreak of incandescent gas is observed on the planet Mars. It occurs toward midnight and lasts but a few seconds. A similar outbreak is observed upon each of the following nine nights. Some days later, on a Friday, about midnight, a great green star falls to earth on Horsell Common, near London, burying itself deep into the ground. It proves to be a gigantic cylinder, thirty yards in diameter, the first of ten such shot through space from Mars. All that day the end of the cylinder unscrews, and at sunset falls out. Signs of life are observed within, and a Deputation of responsible men advances under cover of a white flag with the intention of communicating with the Martians, only to be ruthlessly wiped out by the Heat-Ray. Many spectators are killed by the same means. That night a second cylinder falls in the pinewoods to the north of Woking. Soldiers are brought up against the Martians (repulsive inhuman creatures) on Horsell Common ; the pinewoods are shelled. The narrator's house, on Maybury Hill, is within range of the Heat-Ray ; he secures a dog cart and drives

his wife to a cousin's house at Leatherhead. He returns to Maybury Hill, reaching there just as the third cylinder falls at Pyrford, a few seconds after midnight ; the horse bolts, he is thrown from the cart, and as he lies on the ground he sees the first two Martian Fighting Machines go striding past toward Pyrford. He reaches his house, and there is joined by an Artillery Man, the only one of his battery to survive, who tells him the events of the day. The narrator is so impressed that he decides to rejoin his wife at once and to leave the country. To avoid the Martians at Pyrford he has to make a detour through Epsom, and he and the Artillery Man journey together as far as Weybridge. Everywhere soldiers are coming up to oppose the Martians, and refugees are flying Londonward. At Shepperton Lock four Fighting Machines attack the terrified people ; one is struck by a shell and the others retreat with the wreckage. British artillery is concentrated about Kingston and Richmond. The narrator, separated from his companion, travels alone along the river to Walton, where he meets a curate. They rest for two days in a house at Halliford. Meanwhile great excitement has prevailed in London ; on the Monday morning comes the news that the Kingston and Richmond defences have been smothered by the Black Smoke and that the Martians are advancing on London. At once an exodus begins, for the most part to the north, though thousands make for the sea, hoping to escape to the Continent. This is the course followed by the narrator's younger brother. At High Barnet he rescues two ladies from the attack of three men, and accompanies them in their pony-chaise. On Wednesday they reach the sea near Tillingham and get on board a small steamer. Three Fighting Machines approach the shipping; they venture into the water and two are destroyed by the torpedo-ram " Thunder Child." On Monday morning the narrator and the curate journey to Sheen, there entering another house in search of food. The fifth cylinder falls just outside, burying the house under tons of earth, so that the only exit is across the pit, now guarded by the Martians. For nine days the two men creep silently about the kitchen and scullery, watching the Martians through a crack in the wall. The curate goes mad, and the narrator, to save himself, is forced to kill him. On the fifteenth day he escapes from the house and wanders into London, finding the city an almost deserted ruin, strangely tinted by the luxuriant growth of the Red Weed. On Putney Hill he meets the Artillery Man again, but leaves him after two days. In South Kensington he hears the mournful wailing of the Martians, and next morning, coming over the crest of Primrose Hill, he finds the Martians dead in an enormous redoubt, killed by the disease germs of this planet, and already half-eaten by dogs and crows. The news is flashed about the world, the return to London commences immediately, and food-ships sail to the relief of the starving people. The story ends with the reunion of the narrator and his wife, each of whom had given up all hope of seeing the other alive again.

706. WAR OF THE WORLDS, THE. Strand Magazine, Feb., 1920. A condensation of the above; see Bib. No. 14, note. It is prefaced with an introduction by Wells, *An Experiment in Illustration* (q.v.).

707. WAR THAT WILL END WAR, THE. Daily News, Aug. 14th, 1914.

708. WAR THAT WILL END WAR, THE. See Bib. No. 53. The titles of the 11 articles in this volume are : 1, *Why Britain Went to War ;* 2, *The Sword of Peace ;* 3, *Hands Off the People's Food ;* 4, *Concerning Mr. Maximilian Craft ;* 5, *The Most Necessary Measures in the World ;* 6, *The Need of a New Map of Europe ;* 7, *The Opportunity of Liberalism ;* 8, *The Liberal Fear of Russia ;* 9, *An Appeal to the American People ;* 10, *Common Sense and the Balkan States ;* 11, *The War of the Mind.*

709. WASHINGTON AND THE HOPE OF PEACE. See Bib. No. 74. The titles of the 29 articles in this volume are : 1, *The Immensity of the Issue and Triviality of Men ;* 2, *Armaments : the Futility of Mere Limitation ;* 3, *The Trail of Versailles ;* 4, *The Unknown Soldier of the Great War ;* 5, *The President at Arlington ;* 6, *The First Meeting ;* 7, *What is Japan ? ;* 8, *China in the Background ;* 9, *The Future of Japan ;* 10, " *Security* "—*the New and Beautiful Catchword ;* 11, *France in the Limelight ;* 12, *Thus Far ;* 13, *The Larger Question Behind the Conference ;* 14, *The Real Threat to Civilisation ;* 15, *The Possible Breakdown of Civilisation ;* 16, *What of America ? ;* 17, *Ebb Tide at Washington ;* 18, *America and Entangling Alliances ;* 19, *An Association of Nations ;* 20, *France and England—the Plain Facts of the Case ;* 21, *A Reminder About War ;*

22, *Some Stifled Voices ;* 23, *India's Place in the World ;* 24, *America's Rôle in World Peace ;* 25, *A Shadow on the Earth ;* 26, *The New World Spirit ;* 27, *Load of War Debt ;* 28, *Brotherhood of Peoples ;* 29, *What a Stably Organised World Peace Means for Mankind.* An Appendix gives the text of speeches by M. Briand and Mr. Hughes. The 3 articles not printed in Great Britain were Nos. 11, 15 and 16. Of the rest, the majority appeared in the newspapers under the titles used in the volume, but with the following exceptions : 7, *The Question in the Foreground ;* 13, *From Washington to Europe ;* 18, *Dogmas that are Dying ;* 19, *America's Living Project ;* 20, *Future of the Entente ;* 21, *Two Possibilities ;* 22, *Intruders at Washington ;* 24, *The Voice of America ;* 29, *A Vision of the World of the Future and the Great World at Peace.*

WATERS, DORIS THALASSIA. See *The Sea Lady.*

710. WAY TO A LEAGUE OF NATIONS, THE. See Bib. II, 1919.

711. WAY TO CONCRETE REALISATION, THE. 1st chapter of *Fourth Year ;* 1st of *Anticipations of a World Peace* (100 words omitted). Discussion of the constitution of the League of Nations, Wells suggesting that the League may grow, almost imperceptibly, out of the Peace Conference.

712. WE, AT THE BASE. (Looking Ahead). Daily Chronicle, Sept. 3rd, 1914. A criticism of official methods, with particular reference to the recruiting campaign and the ways of the " Maffick family." Wells advocates the organization

and classification of the whole manhood of the nation between the ages of 15 and 60, and the use of women to fill certain posts for the duration of the war. " The country is neither apathetic nor unwilling, but it has been baffled, and it is still baffled. It is perplexed by blethering people."

WEENA. The only one of the Eloi (q.v.) mentioned by name. The Time Traveller saves her from drowning and she becomes his friend, following him everywhere. She is killed during the fight in the wood, her body being burned in the subsequent fire. *Time Machine.*

713. WELL AT THE WORLD'S END, THE. Saturday Review, Nov. 27th, 1896. A review of Morris's book with Wells's reminiscences of the author.

714. WELLS, ESQ., B.Sc., H. G. Royal College of Science Magazine, Apr., 1903. Autobiographical article.

715. WELLS CALENDAR, THE H. G. See Bib. II, 1911.

WELLS EXPLAINS HIMSELF, MR. See *Mr. Wells, &c.*

WELLS HITS BACK, MR. See *Mr. Wells, &c.*

715a. WELLS ON THE BEAUTY OF FLYING, H. G. Westminster Gazette, Sept. 29th, 1923 ; reprinted as *The Beauty of Flying* (q.v.). Recalls aeroplane journeys made by Wells himself in 1923, and regrets the way in which international complications retard the development of long-distance flying.

WELLS ON THE LEAGUE OF
NATIONS, H. G. Westminster Gazette, Oct. 20th, 1923; reprinted
as *The League of Nations Again*
(q.v.).

WELLS ON THE OTHER SIDE IN
FRANCE, H. G. Westminster Gazette, Nov. 24th, 1923; reprinted
as *The Other Side in France* (q.v.).

WELLS ON THE RUHR TRIUMPH,
H. G. Westminster Gazette, Oct.
6th, 1924; reprinted as *The
Triumph of France* (q.v.).

WELLS REPLIES TO WINSTON
CHURCHILL, H. G. Westminster
Gazette, Nov. 10th, 1923; reprinted
as *Winston* (q.v.).

WELLS'S VIEWS OF FREE TRADE,
H. G. Westminster Gazette, Nov.
17th, 1923; reprinted as *The Last
of the Victorians* (q.v.).

716. WEMBLEY EMPIRE: AN EX-
HIBITION OF LOST OPPORTUNITIES,
THE. Westminster Gazette, May
24th, 1924; 38th article in *Year
of Prophesying*. Criticises the Wembley exhibition as an imperialist
affair, ungenerously conceived.

WENDIGEE, JULIUS. A Dutch
electrician, who, while experimenting with inter-planetary wireless
communication, receives a message
from Cavor. He invites Bedford
to stay with him at his observatory
upon the St. Gothard. *Men in the
Moon.*

WESER DREIBURG, THE PRINCESS
OF. Whose family is noted for its
lack of stature. Dr. Winkles, a
remote connection, feeds her with
Herakleophorbia, not anticipating

such a terrific result. Like the other
Children of the Food, she grows to
nearly forty feet in height. When
she grows to womanhood she is
kept in seclusion and ignorance of
the existence of the other giants,
until one morning she meets Young
Redwood in the park by the palace.
They fall in love, and at the beginning of the revolt she goes with
him to the Cossars' pit at Chislehurst. *Food of the Gods.*

WESTERN FRONT, THE. Under
this general heading appeared the
two articles *The War Landscape* and
New Arms for Old Ones, reprinted as
chapters of *The Western War;* two
more articles, *Ruins*, and *The
Grades of War*, reprinted as chapters
of *The Western War*, appeared
under the general title of *The
Western War.*

717. WESTERN WAR, THE. (September, 1916). 3rd part of *War
and the Future;* in 5 chapters, all
reprinted from the Daily Chronicle,
Nov. and Dec., 1916: 1, *Ruins;* 2,
The Grades of War; 3, *The War
Landscape;* 4, *New Arms for Old
Ones;* 5, *Tanks*. Wells visits the
ruined towns and villages behind
the front. Discusses the theory
and development of modern war,
the part played by the aerial
forces and by camouflage, the
place of infantry and artillery, and
the importance of economic organisation in a country to increase
its fighting efficiency. Describes
a journey to the front-line trenches
and a visit to a French shell factory
and ammunition dump. After his
return from France he sees the
Tanks, and prophecies their development into " land-ironclads "
of enormous proportions.

718. WHAT ARE THE LIBERALS TO DO ? Daily Mail, June 19th, 1913.

719. WHAT A STABLY ORGANISED WORLD PEACE MEANS FOR MANKIND. See *A Vision of the World of the Future* and *The Great World at Peace*. 29th chapter in *Washington*. In this, the last paper written from Washington, Wells draws a picture of the world as it might be were international complications and the fear of war swept aside, were each country free to develop along its own lines in perfect security, and were the energy now devoted to preparation for war devoted instead to education and invention. It is with this vision before him (he writes) that he must " needs go about this present world of disorder and darkness like an exile doing such feeble things as I can towards the world of my desire, now hopefully, now bitterly, as the mood may happen, until I die."

720. WHAT EVERYONE SHOULD LEARN AT SCHOOL. John o' London's Weekly. Oct. 6th, 13th, 20th and 27th, 1923. Begins by condemning the existing schools of Great Britain and America, shabby, poverty-stricken places utterly different from the splendid buildings the schools of the future will be, "more important by far than the local bank or the chief local stores." Then comes to the more particular question of the subjects to be taught ; Oundle School under Sanderson is cited as a modern example of the ideal school. " His or her place in space and in time and in the adventure of life, is what everyone should learn at school." School-

ing should continue till the age of sixteen at least, with a partial continuation for three years longer. The finished scholar should have a good knowledge of the English language, and some of Latin and Greek and two modern foreign languages, a knowledge of general history, of science, and of how " to use hand, brain, and body nimbly and effectively."

721. WHAT EVERYONE SHOULD READ. John o' London's Weekly, May 5th, 19th and 26th, 1923 (the 2nd and 3rd parts were entitled *The Pursuit of Wisdom* and *Art Exists for Joy* respectively, but a note printed subsequently stated that Wells was not responsible for any but the original title, the article being written as one). Everyone, Wells believes, should have some knowledge of the world's history, of the universe, of contemporary events, of the Gospels and of Plato's " Republic," and " for the rest, steady and intensive reading of biography, of discussion, of the sincerer sorts of fiction, along the line of the individual reader's interests and curiosities."

WHAT H. G. WELLS THINKS ABOUT *The Mind in the Making*. See Bib. No. 75.

722. WHAT IS COMING ? See Bib. No. 59. An attempt to portray general conditions both during and after the war. Wells writes of the establishment of a world peace, of the conditions and end of the war, of national bankruptcy, of the need for reconstruction and increased efficiency, of nationalisation of labour, of administration and the part of the Press, of women and the War, of the map of Europe

after the War and the future of certain nations, of the administration of the colonies and of the future of Germany. Six chapters originally appeared in Cassell's Magazine under the general title, *What is Coming?* The titles of the 12 chapters are : 1, *Forecasting the Future ;* 2, *The End of the War ;* 3, *Nations in Liquidation ;* 4, *Braintree, Bocking, and the Future of the World ;* 5, *How Far will Europe Go Toward Socialism ? ;* 6, *Lawyer and Press ;* 7, *The New Education ;* 8, *What the War is Doing for Women ;* 9, *The New Map of Europe ;* 10, *The United States, France, Britain, and Russia ;* 11, *The " White Man's Burthen " ;* 12, *The Outlook for the Germans.*

723. WHAT IS CRAM ? University Correspondent, Mar. 18th, 1893.

724. WHAT IS JAPAN ? See *The Question in the Foreground:* 7th chapter in *Washington.* Considers the effects of Japanese militarism upon world peace, emphasising the differences between Eastern and Western modes of thought and education.

725. WHAT IS SOCIALISM ? See Bib. II, 1924.

726. WHAT IS SUCCESS ? T.P.'s and Cassell's Weekly, Nov. 24th, Dec. 1st, and 8th, 1923. Commenting on Lord Beaverbrook's book, " Success," Wells cites Lord Northcliffe and Lloyd George as examples of " tremendous failures " who " have done nothing but sprawl across the attention of mankind." The rest of the essay is mainly an account of Wells's relations with Northcliffe and his impressions of

him. Concludes that " the only true measure of success is the ratio between what we might have been . . . on the one hand, and the thing we have made of ourselves on the other."

727. WHAT MAY BE DONE. (The Labour Unrest, 4). Daily Mail, May 16th, 1912 ; see *The Labour Unrest.*

728. WHAT MUST BE DONE NOW. (The Labour Unrest, 6). Daily Mail, May 20th, 1912 ; see *The Labour Unrest.*

729. WHAT OF AMERICA ? New York World and Chicago Tribune, Nov. 28th, 1921 ; 16th chapter in *Washington.* Considers the effect of a European and West Asian collapse upon life in America. The effect would not be really marked for many years, but Wells does not believe that America, for other than materialist reasons, will allow the civilisation of Europe and Asia to break down.

730. WHAT THE WAR IS DOING FOR WOMEN. Ladies Home Journal, early May, 1916 ; see *The Two Ways of Women.* 8th chapter in *What is Coming?* Wells recalls the main points of the pre-war women's movement, and remarks how women have " made good and proved their right to the vote." The war, he says, " is bringing us rapidly to a state of affairs in which women will be much more definitely independent of their sexual status, much less hampered in their self-development, and much more nearly equal to men than has ever been known before in the whole history of mankind."

WHEELER, BABS. A "minute swaggering person, much akimbo, with a little round, blue-eyed innocent face that shone with delight at the lark of living." She works at Sir Isaac Harman's International Bread and Cake Stores, and is an enthusiastic member of the National Union of Waitresses and a principal cause of trouble at the International Hostels. *Sir Isaac Harman.*

731. WHEELS OF CHANCE, THE. See Bib. No. 9. Mr. Hoopdriver, a Putney draper's assistant, has just learnt to cycle and decides to spend his summer holiday in a tour along the South Coast. One Wednesday morning he starts out from the shop, riding through Kingston and Surbiton, where he meets the Young Lady in Grey for the first time. Between Esher and Cobham he passes a cyclist dressed in a brown suit similar to his own, and beyond Cobham the Young Lady mistakes him for the "other cyclist in brown" for whom she is waiting. The next day he comes upon them together on the road to Haslemere; she is crying, and Mr. Hoopdriver comes to the conclusion that something must be wrong. Ultimately it is revealed that the man, Bechamel, is helping the girl, Jessica Milton, to escape from her stepmother and to Live her Own Life, his real object being her seduction. Their route coincides with that of Mr. Hoopdriver, and Bechamel, believing him to be a detective employed by Mrs. Bechamel, attempts to bribe him. Hoopdriver decides to follow them. At Bognor Bechamel makes a nearly successful attempt to compromise Jessica. Mr. Hoopdriver offers his assistance; she accepts and runs away with

him, he in his haste taking Bechamel's cycle. They ride together back through Winchester and westward to Salisbury, turning south again to Ringwood, where she hopes to hear from her old schoolmistress, Miss Mergle. They stay at hotels as brother and sister, and for a time Mr. Hoopdriver does his best to maintain a story that he is a colonial, a retired ostrich-farmer; at last he breaks down and confesses his true position. Meanwhile Mrs. Milton, the stepmother, has set out in pursuit of Jessica, aided by three friends and admirers, Phipps, Widgery and Dangle. They trace her to Botley, but she disappears again, and it is not until the Rescue Party is reinforced by Miss Mergle, that they come up with her at Stony Cross, six days after her first meeting with Hoopdriver. He is in love with her now, and determines to undertake his own education that he may be more worthy of her friendship, though he doubts his capabilities and the lasting power of his determination. Jessica returns home, promising to write to him and to send him books. He spends the rest of his short holiday riding slowly back to the shop.

732. WHEN THE SLEEPER WAKES. See Bib. No. 15. Graham, a politician of to-day, a young man of thirty or so, falls into a trance after a long period of insomnia induced by overwork. Large sums of money are left to him by relations and others, and these accumulating through the years of his long sleep he wakes at last to find himself, because of his vast wealth, nominal Master of the World of A.D. 2100. The real power is held by the White Council, a small circle of men who

have charge of his interests and rule the world in his name. The Council fears the loss of its power, and decides to kill Graham, but he is rescued by the agents of Ostrog, a political rival of the Council. Ostrog arms and raises in revolt the Labour Companies, and in the name of Graham strikes to seize world-power for himself. The Council turns out the city lights, and in the confusion Graham is separated from his friends and wanders alone through the mob-filled streets of London, at last making his way to the wind-vane offices in Westminster where Ostrog has established his headquarters. The White Council is overthrown and Graham acclaimed Master. For some days he is content to leave the administration of affairs in the hands of Ostrog, spending his time studying the life of this strange London and in learning to fly. But he is brought to action by Helen Wotton, Ostrog's niece, who tells him of the oppression of the people, and determines to take control himself. The people of the Labour Companies refuse to disarm, and Ostrog secretly arranges for negro police to be brought to London. Graham forbids this, whereupon Ostrog unsuccessfully attempts to imprison him. Fighting commences again, this time between the people and the soldiers of Ostrog, the struggles centring round the flying stages which are defended by the Ostrogites that the aeroplanes bringing the black police may be able to land safely. The aeroplanes from Africa approach, and Graham goes up in an aeropile to hold them back until the last stages are captured. He routes the first fleet and pursues the flying Ostrog.

The last two stages are blown up and, caught in the air-waves of the explosions, Graham's machine is overturned and crashes him to his death.

WHITE. " The journalist and novelist," a member of the Rationalist Press Association. He is at school and college with Benham; they meet again in Johannesburg, and Benham dies in his arms. Before he dies he makes White promise to " see to that book of mine " ; White goes through Benham's papers and publishes a " laborious uncertain account of Benham's life and thought." *Research Magnificent.*

WHITE COUNCIL, THE. See *The Twelve Trustees.*

733. " WHITE MAN'S BURTHEN," THE. Cassell's Magazine, June, 1916 ; 11th chapter in *What is Coming?* A consideration of the future administration of the African and Eastern colonies of European countries, suggesting the possibility of an Arabic renascence, and that on the whole " the path of safety lies in the direction of pooling them and of declaring a common policy of progressive development leading to equality." Suggests the establishment of some great " permanent over-riding body " to deal with things in a broader manner than is possible to any " nationalism " or " patriotic imperialism."

WHY A WORLD STATE IS NECESSARY. (Salvaging of Civilisation, 1). Sunday Times, Mar. 27th, 1921 ; reprinted as *The Project of a World State* (q.v.).

734. WHY BRITAIN WENT TO WAR. War Illustrated, Aug. 22nd, 1914 ; 1st chapter of *War that will End War.* A " clear exposition

of what we are fighting for." The cause of Britain's participation in this war was the invasion of Belgium ; the object is the smashing of Prussian Imperialism, thus to ensure a world peace, to " exorcise a world madness and to end an age."

735. WHY SOCIALISTS SHOULD VOTE FOR MR. CHURCHILL.. An Open Letter to an Elector in N.W. Manchester. Daily News, Apr. 21st, 1908.

735a. WHY THE WAR WILL BE OVER BY NEXT JUNE. Sunday Pictorial, Sept. 17th, 1916. Written just after Wells's visit to the Western and Italian fronts : "affirms his convictions" that the Germans will offer peace before November and that it "will come before next June."

WICKSTEAD, MR. Lord Burdock's steward. He pursues Griffin, cornering him between a drift of nettles and a gravel pit. Unable to escape, Griffin murders him with an iron bar. *Invisible Man.*

WIDGERY. " One of those big fat men who feel deeply." He hears of Jessica Milton at Midhurst, hurries to tell Mrs. Milton, and so launches the Rescue Party, of which he forms a member. *Wheels of Chance.*

WIDGETTS, THE. Neighbours of the Stanleys at Morningside Park, a " cheerful, irresponsible, shamelessly hard-up family." Mr. Widgett is a journalist and art critic, and his red-headed daughters, Hetty and Constance (who are art-students), are Ann Veronica's chief friends ; they assist her in her revolt and flight to London. Teddy Widgett, the only son, a blond young man, has a great admiration for Ann Veronica and offers to marry her, " just a formal marriage," in order to free her from parental control. He carries her bag to the station when she runs away to London. *Ann Veronica.*

736. WIFE OF SIR ISAAC HARMAN, THE. See Bib. No. 52. Lady Harman, Visiting Black Strand with an " order to view," meets George Brumley, a well-known author and owner of the house. He shows her the drawing-room and garden, and she has tea with him. A week later her husband, Sir Isaac Harman, comes to view the house and incidentally meets Lady Beach-Mandarin, who shortly afterwards calls on Lady Harman and invites her to lunch. Sir Isaac, who hates Lady Beach-Mandarin, forbids his wife to return the call. They have been married now for eight years, he being nearly fifty, she about twenty-six ; they have four children. He is proprietor of the International Bread and Cake Stores, and has purchased his title by contributing to party funds. About this time, Lady Harman begins to be troubled by new ideas, instilled into her by her sister Georgina, an enthusiastic suffragette, and by Susan Burnet. Sir Isaac has an old-fashioned conception of marriage and objects strongly to her " idees." She goes out to lunch with Lady Beach-Mandarin, visits Hampton Court with Mr. Brumley, and is late in getting home. As a consequence Sir Isaac buys Black Strand immediately and takes her there, keeping her a prisoner for nearly a fortnight by refusing to give her money. Lady Beach-Mandarin and Mr. Brumley make unsuccessful attempts to rescue her. At last she pawns a ring, with Susan Burnet's assistance, and travels to London. There she smashes a post-office window and

goes to prison for a month. Upon her release she returns to her husband, who gives way to her upon certain points. He commences the building of Hostels for his employees, and Lady Harman is promised considerable control in their management. Three years pass in moderate comfort. Lady Harman spends much time with Mr. Brumley (who is in love with her), planning out details of the working of the Hostels, in which, for all their care, there is considerable trouble and friction. Sir Isaac becomes jealous and tells her that she must choose between her friend and the Hostels ; he has her followed when she goes out. Then he has an attack of ill-health and they go abroad. At Santa Margherita he dies very suddenly and unexpectedly. Lady Harman returns to England determined that, having once regained her freedom, she will never again risk it in marriage. Sir Isaac, too, has provided in his will that, in the event of her marrying again, the control of the Hostels shall pass into the hands of a committee. She asks the disappointed Mr. Brumley to continue to help her, to be still her friend.

737. WILD ASSES OF THE DEVIL, THE. See *Boon, &c.* This tale, only a portion of which is written, is suggested to Boon by Wilkins's assertion that modern thought is more disconnected than ever. An author, living on the South Coast, goes for a walk one stormy day and meets a devil, a weak irresolute individual, who has been turned out of Hell to seek for and recapture certain Wild Asses of the Devil which he allowed to escape in the excitement following Gladstone's arrival. These Asses have assumed

human shape, but revert to their true form at midnight on Walpurgis Night. The author helps the devil in his quest. After many adventures they track down a prominent politician and follow him to the House of Commons on Walpurgis Night. At midnight he changes to a Wild Ass. They attempt his capture and are thrown out of the building by the attendants, who have not seen the change.

WILKINS, EDGAR. A novelist, first mentioned in *Ann Veronica* as one of the Fabian Society leaders. In *The New Machiavelli* he is present at Lord Tarvrille's famous dinner. Lady Harman (in *Sir Isaac Harman*) meets him, a " flushed man with untidy hair," at a dinner given by Lady Tarvrille ; he tells her, while talking of authors and morals, that his own life will not bear examination. She hopes to meet him again but he is involved in some scandal and disappears from London society. In *Boon* he is one of that author's circle of intimate friends, " a man of a peculiar mental constitution ; he alternates between a brooding sentimental egotism and a brutal realism. . . . Wilkins still spends large portions of his time thinking solemnly about some ancient trouble in which he was treated unjustly." He attacks Boon's idea of a collective Mind of the Race. After the outbreak of war he takes a hopeful view of things, in contrast to Boon's pessimism. He is referred to in *Mr. Britling.*

WILLERSLEY. An Oxford man with whom Remington goes for his first holiday abroad, a walking tour in northern Italy ; a rather solemn man with an enthusiasm for " social service." He disapproves strongly of Remington's intrigue with the woman at Locarno. Remington writes of him as doing " vast masses of useful, undistinguished, fertilizing work." *New Machiavelli.*

738. WILL GERMANY BREAK INTO PIECES ? Westminster Gazette, Nov. 3rd, 1923 ; 7th article in *Year of Prophesying.* Discusses the future of Germany, and Wells's belief that " she will rise again out of her present darkness . . . the central and leading Power . . . of a reconstructed Europe."

WILLIAM. A " deaf and clumsy man of uncertain age and a vast sharp nosiness." He drives the horse caravan with which Bealby travels for two days ; he is inside the caravan stealing chocolates when it runs away down-hill. *Bealby.*

WILL LATIN-AMERICA LEAVE THE LEAGUE ? Westminster Gazette, Dec. 22nd, 1923 ; reprinted as *Latin America and the League* (q.v.).

WILL SOCIALISM DESTROY THE HOME ? See Bib. No. 33 ; also *Would Socialism Destroy the Home ?*

739. WILL THE EMPIRE LIVE ? See *Cement of Empire.* 5th essay in *An Englishman.* The British Empire has neither common economic interests nor a common enemy ; it has, in fact, no unity. Only one thing can hold it together, a unity of outlook and language ; the English language must be taught in all parts of the Empire, the best of English literature must be made available to everybody in the Empire. But Wells has no hope of any such things being done ; the Empire is an accident—as it came so it may go.

740. WILL THE WAR CHANGE ENGLAND ? War Illustrated, Feb. 20th and 27th, 1915 ; Daily Mail, Feb. 27th, 1915. Wells believes that " England has come back to reality at last," and that the " Englishman of the future will be a keener, abler, better educated, and more reasonable type than the Englishman of the immediate past."

WILMINGTON. A very serious boy who is at school with Peter and later falls in love with Joan. After the outbreak of war he writes long serious letters to her. He is killed in 1916. *Joan and Peter.*

WILSHIRE, JANE. A distant cousin of Mr. Britling, who addresses her as " Aunt." She is " a large irrelevant middle-aged lady in black, with a gold chain and a large nose," the latter (she asserts) a relic of the Duke of Wellington's friendship with Mr. Britling's greatgrandmother. She spends her time visiting friends and relations. In 1915 she is wounded in a Zeppelin raid and dies. *Mr. Britling.*

WINCHELSEA, MISS. A High School mistress whose romance is told in *Miss Winchelsea's Heart.* She is a young woman of incredible refinement, with great literary and historical enthusiasms.

WINKLES, STEPHEN, F.R.S., M.D., F.R.C.P., D.Sc., J.P., D.L., &c. One of Redwood's pupils, " the sort of doctor that is in manners, in morals, in methods and appearance, most succinctly and finally expressed by the word ' rising.' " He takes a keen and inquisitive interest in Herakleophorbia from the first, and has " such a convincing air of proprietorship " that Bensington is "disposed to regard him as the original inventor of the whole affair." He is continually putting himself forward as one intimately connected with it, making statements in public, etc., and administers it to at least one of his patients (the Princess of Weser Dreiburg) in complete ignorance of its probable effect. He also gives it to his own youngest son, but without effect. *Food of the Gods*.

741. WINSTON. See *H. G. Wells Replies to Winston Churchill*. 9th article in *Year of Prophesying*. A reply to Churchill's criticism of Wells's essay, *The Future of the British Empire* (q.v.).

WINTERBAUM, PHILIP. With Joan and Peter at the School of St. George and the Venerable Bede, a dark-eyed, fuzzy-haired, sheepfaced, self-satisfied boy ; he has a lively imagination and is always the hero of his imaginings. He is for ever comparing things, "grading them, making them competitive and irritating. There was no getting ahead of him." When he meets Joan at Cambridge he falls in love with her, and takes her out to theatres and night-clubs. When the war breaks out he enlists in the cavalry and is killed at Loos. *Joan and Peter*.

WINTERSLOAN, MR. An artist who illustrates Magnet's work. Magnet brings him to Buryhamstreet, where he annoys Mr. Pope by winning a game (" The Great Departed ") by very doubtful methods. *Marriage*.

742. WOMAN'S DAY IN UTOPIA, A. (Utopianisms, 5). Daily Mail, June 7th, 1905.

743. WOMEN IN A MODERN UTOPIA. 6th chapter on *Modern Utopia*. A study of the position of women in a modern Utopia, of the problems of motherhood and marriage and divorce, of the endowment of motherhood, and of the equality of the sexes. Plato's "Multiple Marriage" is discussed.

744. WONDERFUL VISIT, THE. See Bib. No. 5. The Rev. Mr. Hilyer, vicar of Siddermorton, shoots at and brings down what he believes to be a bird, only to find that he has wounded an angel " of Italian art, polychromatic and gay . . . from the land of beautiful dreams." He invites the Angel to his house. The visitor knows nothing of the things of this world, of Pain, Birth, Death, Hunger or the social system, and his host's explanations are somewhat ineffectual. The neighbours—Dr. Crump, Lady Hammergallow, the Mendhams, Sir John Gotch—refuse to believe the Angel's story and, for various reasons, demand that he shall leave the village at once. After a terrible afternoon at Hammergallow House, and some trouble with Gotch, the protests against his presence rise to such a height that the vicar sadly prepares for his visitor's departure. The Angel meets Gotch and thrashes him for putting up barbed wire ; he returns to the Vicarage to find it in flames. Delia Hardy, the vicar's little maid, who loves the Angel, has rushed into the house to save his violin, and he goes to her rescue. The roof falls in on them and as the flames shoot upward a little girl has a "pretty fancy of two figures with wings that flashed up and vanished among the flames." The vicar dies within a year.

745. WORLD, ITS DEBTS AND THE RICH MEN, THE. See Bib. No. 79. Wells expresses his " conviction of this progressive break-up of the civilised organisation that is going on," spreading westward from Russia. Europe is weighed down by debts, and " the old political parties " are " just doing nothing at all about it." He explains the Labour Party's " Capital Levy " proposal and goes on to speak of the attitude of the Labour Party to property in general.

WORLD LANGUAGES. (Looking Ahead). Daily Chronicle, May 13th, 1916 ; reprinted as section 2 of *The United States, France, Britain and Russia*.

746. WORLD SET FREE, THE. See Bib. No. 51. This somewhat disconnected romance of the Twentieth Century is in five chapters, with a Prelude. The Prelude gives a brief generalised account of man's " attainment of external power " from earliest times to the present day. The first chapter begins in 1933 with the solving of the problem of inducing radio-activity and utilising atomic energy The consequences—the new atomic engines and their uses, the industrial revolution and the labour unrest, the development of flying—are all described, largely by quotations from " Frederick Barnet's Wander Jahre," an autobiographical novel published in 1970. From the same work is taken an account of the war between the Central Powers of Europe and Russia, France and England which breaks out in 1958. This, the " last war," becomes world-wide, and Paris, Berlin, East London, Chicago and other great cities are made uninhabitable by the dropping of atomic bombs ; terrible damage is done all over the world. A truce is declared and a conference of ninety-three kings, statesmen and thinkers is held at Brissago, in Italy, with the ex-King Egbert of Italy as president. This Assembly becomes the new world-government. Only one ruler withholds, and he, the King of the Balkans, is killed in a vain attempt to win world-power through treachery. Chapter 4 describes the world after the war, the reconstruction of social and commercial life, the establishment of a world-language, and other developments of the new civilisation. The final chapter tells of the last days of Marcus Karenin, a prominent member of the world education committee. In a surgical station in the Himalayas, where he is to undergo a serious operation, he talks with a few companions of the dark days of the world before the war, of sex, of science, of the common mind of the race, and of the future to which mankind, united and at peace, may now progress.

WORLD STATE—AN OUTLINE SKETCH, THE. (Salvaging of Civilisation, 3). Sunday Times, Apr. 10th, 1921 ; reprinted as the second half of *The Enlargement of Patriotism to a World State* (q.v.).

WOTTON, HELEN. Ostrog's niece, " one of the most serious persons alive." She tells Graham that the great majority of the people are enslaved and unhappy, and that Ostrog will do nothing to help them ; she appeals to him to use his power. It is largely her influence which makes him quarrel with Ostrog and risk his life in the defence of London. *Sleeper Wakes.*

747. WOULD MODERN SOCIALISM ABOLISH ALL PROPERTY ? Grand Magazine, Jan., 1908 ; 7th chapter in *New Worlds.* A discussion of the " current theory of property," and of the attitude of the modern Socialist towards that theory and towards personal property, small savings, and expropriation.

748. WOULD SOCIALISM DESTROY THE HOME ? Grand Magazine, Dec., 1907 ; 6th chapter of *New Worlds ;* also printed as a pamphlet, *Will Socialism Destroy the Home ?* (q.v.). An answer to the widespread misconception that Socialism must necessarily destroy the Home. The attitude of the Socialist to Marriage and Religion is also discussed.

749. WRITING OF ESSAYS, THE. Pall Mall Gazette, Feb. 2nd, 1894 ; 25th essay in *Personal Matters.* Discusses the influence of writing materials upon the style of essay produced, and concludes with a few words on the art of the essay.

Y

YACOB. A " kindly man when not annoyed," the father of Medina-saroté and master of Nunez. *Country of the Blind.*

750. YEAR OF PROPHESYING, A. See Bib. No. 88. The titles of the fifty-five articles in this volume are : 1, *The League of Nations and the Federation of Mankind ;* 2, *The Beauty of Flying ;* 3, *The Triumph of France ;* 4, *The Singapore Arsenal ;* 5, *The League of Nations Again ;* 6, *The Aviation of the Half-Civilised ;* 7, *Will Germany Break Into Pieces ? ;* 8, *The Future of the British Empire ;* 9, *Winston ;* 10, *The Other Side in France ;* 11, *The Last of the Victorians ;* 12, *Politics as a Public Nuisance ;* 13, *The Re-emergence of Mr. Lloyd George ;* 14, *Spain and Italy Whisper Together ;* 15, *Latin America and the League ;* 16, *Cosmopolitan and International ;* 17, *The Parliamentary Triangle ;* 18, *Modern Government : Parliament and Real Electoral Reform ;* 19, *Scrapping the Gold Standard ;* 20, *The Hub of Europe : Czecho-Slovakia and France ;* 21, *The Mandarins at the Gate : The Revival of the Old Learning ;* 22, *Lenin : Private Capitalism against Communism ;* 23, *The Fantasies of Mr. Belloc and the Future of the World ;* 24, *A Creative Educational Scheme for Britain : a Tentative Forecast ;* 25, *Portugal and Prosperity : The Blessedness of being a Little Nation ;* 26, *Reconstruction of the League of Nations ; the Practical Problem ;* 27, *The Labour Party on Trial : The Folly of the Five Cruisers ;* 28, *Dictators or Politicians ? The Dilemma of Civilisation ;* 29, *Youth and the Vote : The Rejuvenescence of the World ;* 30, *Olive Branches of Steel : Should the Angels of Peace Carry Bombs ? ;* 31, *The Case of Unamuno : The Feeble Republic of Letters ;* 32, *An Open Letter to Anatole France on his Eightieth Birthday ;* 33, *The European Kaleidoscope : The German Will in Default ;* 34, *China : The Land out of the Limelight ;* 35, *Air Armament : The Supremacy of Quality ;* 36, *Labour Politicians : The Evaporation of the Intelligentzia ;* 37, *Constructive Ideas and their Relation to Current Politics ;* 38, *The Wembley Empire : An Exhibition of Lost Opportunities ;* 39, *The Extinction of Party Government ;* 40, *The Serfdom of Ignorance : The Right of Women to Knowledge ;* 41,

Blinkers for Free Youth : Young America asks to Hear and See ; 42, The Lawlessness of America and the Way to Order ; 43, The Shabby Schools of the Pious : Drains and the Odour of Sanctity ; 44, The Incompatibility of India : Divorce or Legal Separation ; 45, The Spirit of Fascism : Is there any Good in it at all ? ; 46, The Race Conflict : Is it Unavoidable ? ; 47, The Schools of a New Age : A Forecast ; 48, The Impudence of Flags : Our Power Resources and My Elephants, Whales, and Gorillas ; 49, Has Communism a Future ? The Possibility of a Socialist Renascence ; 50, The Little House : as it was, is now, and apparently ever will be ; 51, The Triviality of Democracy and the Feminine Influence in Politics ; 52, Sex Antagonism : An Unavoidable and Increasing Factor in Modern Life ; 53, Living Through : The Truth about an Interview ; 54, The Creative Passion ; 55, After a Year

of Journalism : An Outbreak of Auto-Obituary.

751. YIELDING PACIFIST AND THE CONSCIENTIOUS OBJECTOR, THE. (How People Think about the War, 2.) Daily News, Dec. 18th, 1916. See *How People Think about the War.*

752. YOUTH AND THE VOTE : THE REJUVENESCENCE OF THE WORLD. Westminster Gazette, March 29th, 1924 ; 29th chapter of *Year of Prophesying.* Advocates better education to the age of eighteen, and universal enfranchisement at eighteen, as the " path to a real civilisation."

Z

753. ZOOLOGICAL RETROGRESSION. Gentleman's Magazine, Nov. 7th, 1891.

THE SUBJECT INDEX

The numbers in this index refer to those prefixed to final titles in the Dictionary, not to pages.

A

255

I

Ireland, 267, 468.
 Effects of the war in, 516,
 in 1914, 309.
Islam, 468. 579.
 Future of, 733.
Isonzo front, The, 303, 699.
Italy, 371, 421, 468, 579.
 Army organisation in, 303.
 Behind the front in, 48.
 German economic enterprise in, 48.
 King Victor Emmanuel III. of, 473.
 Mountain war in, 398, 699.
 The war in, 48, 303, 398, 699.
 after the war, 516.
 and alliance with Spain, 603.
 and her attitude to allies and enemies,
 699.

J

James Henry, 17, 38, 61, 161, 258,
 378, 468, 517, 594.
 Story in the style of, 607.
James, William, 28, 61, 217, 225, 244,
 377.
Japan, 64, 78, 208, 468, 579, 600, 724,
 729.
 Adaptability of, 64.
 Birth control necessary in, 208.
 China and, 78, 208.
 Education in, 724.
 Future of, 208.
 Government of, militaristic, 208,
 724.
 Korea and, 600.
 Population problem in, 208.
 and war with America, 546, 724.
Jealousy, The natural aristocrat and,
 549.
Jerome, J. K., 17, 348.
Jesus Christ. See Christ.
Joffre, Marshal, 473.
Johnston, Sir H. H., 309, 319, 468,
 500, 543, 602.
Joint households, 310.
Joyce, James, 378. See also Reviews
 (in Dictionary).
Judgment Day, Story of, 691.
Jury system, The, 488.
Justice, 442.
 American contempt for abstract, 328,
 676.
 Love and, 442.

K

Kamenev, 480.
Kant, Emmanuel, 638.
Keeling, Frederick, 286.
Kenna, Alderman (of Chicago), 100.

Keun, Odette, 60.
Keynes, J.M., and the failure of the
 gold standard, 567.
Kinetic type of man in a modern
 Utopia, 556.
Kingdom of God on earth the only
 hope for lasting peace, 151.
Kipling, Rudyard, 421, 435, 442, 468,
 657.
Komensky. See Comenius.
Koran, The, 579, 638.
Korea, 468, 600.
 Japanese suppression in, 600.
Kriegspiel, 348.

L

Labour, 127, 317, 318, 319, 330, 354,
 409, 468, 532, 585, 591, 604, 628,
 727, 728.
 Long view of, 354.
 Modern, 318.
 National organisation of, in war, 242.
 after the war, 585.
 and Capital, The problem of, 274.
 and Central Africa, 319.
 and nationalisation, 354.
 conscription, 225, 317, 318, 628, 727.
 distrust of governing classes, 127.
 in America, 141.
 in the Great State, 225.
 in the past and to-day, 127.
 revolt, 317.
 trouble, Source of the, 532.
 unrest, 49, 318, 727.
 unrest and the spectacle of pleasure,
 604.
Labrador, 371, 468.
Lamias, Women as, 320.
Land-ironclads, 321, 635, 717.
Labour Government, The first, 245.
 The Intelligentsia and, 316.
 and armaments, 315.
 and the housing problem, 346.
Labour Party, The,
 and the Capital Levy, 745.
 and education, 590.
 and private enterprise, 590.
 and property, 745.
Landlords, 2.
Lang, Andrew, 72.
Langley, Professor, 38, 192, 402, 468.
Language,
 Beginnings of, 47.
 English, 47, 95.
 A world-, 681.
 of flowers, 322.
 of the future, 95.
 of a modern Utopia, 658.
 question, Tidying up the, 655.

T